Created and Directed by Hans Höfer

INSIGHT GUIDES
SRI Lanka

Based on a Manuscript by Herbert Keuneman
Updated by Abbas Esufally
Edited and Produced by John Gottberg Anderson

Editor in Colombo: Ravindralal Anthonis

HOUGHTON MIFFLIN COMPANY

APA PUBLICATIONS

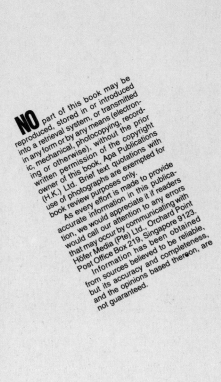
SRI Lanka

Sixth Editions (2nd Reprint)
© **1993 APA PUBLICATIONS (HK) LTD**
All Rights Reserved
Printed in Singapore by Höfer Press Pte Ltd

Distributed in the United States by:	Distributed in Canada by:	Distributed in the UK & Ireland by:	Worldwide distribution enquiries:
Houghton Mifflin Company	**Thomas Allen & Son**	**GeoCenter International UK Ltd**	**Höfer Communications Pte Ltd**
2 Park Street	390 Steelcase Road East	The Viables Center, Harrow Way	38 Joo Koon Road
Boston, Massachusetts 02108	Markham, Ontario L3R 1G2	Basingstoke, Hampshire RG22 4BJ	Singapore 2262
ISBN: 0-395-66310-5	ISBN: 0-395-66310-5	ISBN: 9-62421-014-4	ISBN: 9-62421-014-4

ABOUT THIS BOOK

Paradise was a word used to describe Sri Lanka by its many visitors: a lush green tropical island surrounded by glorious sand beaches and deep, crystal-clean blue water. Now, paradise is torn by violence and political conflict that few insiders or outsiders can understand.

This is the supreme challenge to a publisher of travel literature like Apa Publications. But it is the kind of challenge that Apa has anticipated by adopting a sound, clear journalistic style of reporting with a rich background of history and fine photographs.

The Apa concept was enunciated by its founder, Hans Höfer, a native of West Germany, when he published his first edition *Insight Guide: Bali* in 1970. That prize-winning book and succeeding guides reflected Höfer's training in the Bauhaus tradition. To ensure that *Insight Guide: Sri Lanka* conformed to the Apa tradition, Höfer named a team of experienced editors to gather the best available local writers and photographers.

The original manuscript for *Insight Guide: Sri Lanka* was a labor of love by the late **Herbert Keuneman**, a lifelong resident of the country who had been a journalist, college instructor and Anglican priest. After Keuneman's death, the manuscript was taken over by **K.V.J. de Silva**, a leading book dealer and collector in Colombo who collaborated in the production of this book.

The chore of preparing the manuscript fell to **John Gottberg Anderson**, Apa's former managing editor for Asia. He and editorial researcher **Linda Carlock** spent several months in Sri Lanka shaping the book into its final form. Together with Colombo-based editor-writer photographer **Ravindralal Anthonis**, they logged thousands of miles of travel on an island only 140 by 270 miles in dimension.

Anderson, a native of America's Pacific Northwest, joined Apa in 1981 upon completion of the prestigious Gannett Fellowship program in Asian studies at the University of Hawaii. A one-time newspaper reporter in Honolulu and editor in Seattle, he had previously traveled for several years in the Pacific, Asia and Europe. Anderson was the chief editor of Insight Guides to Nepal and Burma.

Carlock, who researched much of the material in this book and developed the Travel Tips, has been with Apa since 1980. Formerly the manager of Apa's Hawaii office, Carlock is a graduate of Western Washington University.

Anthonis is by profession a tea broker and manager of a family trading business. Fifteen years of jungle excursions have taken Anthonis to every corner of his island home, and he has taken advantage of his domestic travels to pen numerous articles for newspapers and magazines in Colombo and overseas.

Dr. Kingsley M. de Silva is Sri Lanka's leading resident historian. His book, *A History of Sri Lanka*, had a great impact in Asian history circles throughout the world. De Silva holds the Chair of Sri Lanka History at the University of Peradeniya.

Mallika Wanigasundra, a professional journalist for 25 years, was a graduate of Ceylon University. She was formerly a reporter, feature writer and editor for the *Associated Newspapers of Ceylon*, the *Ceylon Observer* and the *Ceylon Daily News*. She now serves as a correspondent to *Depth News Asia*, and contributes to *Asia 2000* magazine and *Earthscan*.

Roland Silva, our expert on archaeology and the classical arts, is the director general

Keuneman

Anderson

Carlock

Anthonis

Weeramunda

of the UNESCO-Sri Lanka Project of the Cultural Triangle aimed at excavating and restoring major monuments in central Sri Lanka, as well as Sri Lanka's deputy commissioner of archaeology. Silva is a London-trained architect by profession.

Dr. Ediriwira Sarachchandra, professor emeritus of Sinhalese literature at the University of Peradeniya, is considered Sri Lanka's leading expert on traditional dance and theater. The author of numerous plays, novels, short-story collections and essays of literary criticism, Sarachchandra is credited with having revived traditional Sinhalese theater in the 1950s by experimenting with folk drama in a modern context.

Dr. Anthony Joseph Weeramunda, chairman of the Sociology Department at the University of Colombo, was a PhD anthropology graduate of the University of Washington in Seattle. Weeramunda taught at San Diego State University before returning to his native land in 1977. He has contributed to several scholarly journals and his work has been featured in two books: *Religion and Social Conflict in South Asia* and *Mother Worship: Themes and Variations*.

Naturalist **Rodney Jonklaas** is Sri Lanka's premier underwater explorer. Born in Kandy, he studied botany, zoology and geography at Ceylon University. Jonklaas is director of a sports shop, an explorer of foliage plants, a consultant and conservationist for Sri Lanka's National Aquatic Resources Agency. He is the author of the book, *Collecting Marine Tropicals*, and had been published in numerous magazines, including *Skin Diver* and *Serendib*, the AirLanka inflight magazine.

R. Ian Lloyd, who is represented in this volume by more than 100 photographs, grew up in Midlands, Ontario, Canada. He studied at the Rochester (New York) Institute of Technology and the Brooks Institute of Photography in Santa Barbara, California, and later produced audiovisuals in North America, Australia and Europe.

Tom Tidball, a resident of Sri Lanka since 1973, took up a photographic career in the late '70s, and has since been featured in *Serendib* and *Pacific* magazines, UNICEF publications, and various local journals.

Sriyani Tidball, Tom's wife, is a graduate of the University of Nebraska. She manages her husband's photographic business and writes articles to magazines and newspapers.

Purandara Sri Bhadra Marapana, a descendant of Kandya royalty, is the founder of the Ratnapura Gem Bureau and Museum in Ratnapura and Colombo. He operates a training center and gallery for painters, metal workers, and gem and jewelry designers.

The plethora of fine photographs included in this book represents the work of an international team of cameramen. Many were taken by **Roland Ammon**, a Bangkok-based Swiss photographer who specializes in shooting festivals. Ammon is a regular contributor to the German magazine *Stern*. Other photos were taken by Scotsman **Marcus Brooke**, Englishman **Philip Little**, German **Manfred Gottschalk**, and Americans **Jan Whiting** and **Eric Oey**. Other contributions were by **Thomas Schoellhammer**, **Alain Evrard**, **K.A. Tillekeratne**, **Nihal Fernando**, **Rohan Weeresinghe**, **Henry Sofeico** and **Louise Renkema**.

Thanks go to Dr. P.R. Anthonis; the family of former prime ministers D.S. and Dudley Senanayake; Asiaweek magazine; and to Leo Haks and dozens of others who helped in the production of this book.

K.M. de Silva

Lloyd

Jonklaas

S. Tidball

Silva

CONTENTS

History

People

Sights

—edited by John Anderson

Features

Maps

TRAVEL TIPS

A Voyage To Serendipity

"Sri Lanka." The name rolls off the tongue like a waterfall tumbling from lush mountain slopes. It has the rhythm of a primitive drumbeat and the refinement of a cup of fine tea, the sparkle of a sapphire and the spice of a savory curry. Like the land itself, the name is as colorful as a market bazaar, as mysterious as a Buddhist chant, as awesome as a skewered fire-walker.

Here is a nation where the full gamut of history can be surveyed in a single day's journey. Primeval jungles teem with wild leopards and elephants. Wondrous ruins testify to great civilizations of ages past. Vast rural stretches reveal a diverse race of people whose dedication to the land is exceeded only by their devotion to their varied religions. In the urban center, Colombo, Western progress and technology are superimposed on the frenzy of traditional Asian metropolis. Modern beach resorts, meanwhile, offer visitors unspoiled sands and 20th Century Luxury.

Few places on earth, if any, have packed the variety of experiences available in Sri Lanka into such a small area. This fascinating land is only 270 miles long and 140 miles across at its widest point – smaller than Ireland and only slightly larger than the American state of West Virginia. It is this compactness that makes this island, once known as Ceylon, an ideal travel destination. A road and rail network connects all corners of the country, and a variety of accommodations will suit all tastes and pocketbooks. Add to this the unbridled hospitality of the Sri Lankan people, and the country truly becomes a traveler's paradise, a "serendipitous" pleasure.

Long ago, this island was called Serendib. An 18th Century English writer had Sri Lanka in mind when he coined the word "serendipity" – the faculty of making happy and unexpected discoveries by accident.

But Sri Lanka is no accident. It is an experience. Discover it for yourself.

Preceding pages: father-and-son net fishermen on South Coast; the Gal Vihara of Polonnaruwa, the replica of the reclining statue (extreme right) has been transferred to the museum; frescoes at Sigiriya; the Ruwanweli Seya at Anuradhapura. **Left**, lush countryside.

The ancient mariners of Greece could not say "Tambapanni," as she was then called. So they called her "Taprobane." The seafarers of old Arabia called her "Serendib," a word that has since evolved into the soothing state of mind known as serendipity. Latter-day adventurers came up with the nickname, "Pearl of the Orient."

But perhaps the romantics best summed up the shape and substance of this unique island when they called it "The Teardrop of India." For if the face of the great Indian subcontinent had ever shed a tear of joy, one which froze in mid-air as it fell from her chin, that teardrop would undoubtedly have become the island of Sri Lanka.

Sri Lanka shimmers in the blue expanse of the Indian Ocean, sharing the same continental shelf as India. In fact, it is a mere 30 miles (48 kms) from the subcontinent to Sri Lanka's northernmost extremity, Point Pedro. The island occupies a spot on the world's maps that stretches roughly from 6° to 10° North Latitude and from 80° to 82° East Longitude. It measures 270 miles in length and 140 miles in width at its broadest point (435 by 225 kms), a total land are of 25,332 sq miles (65,610 sq kms). Dambulla, famous for its ancient cave temple, marks the geographical center of the island. The old port town of Dondra occupies the island's southern tip. Beyond the lighthouse at Dondra Head, there's not another speck of land before the icy wastes of Antarctica.

Geological Foundations: Geologists believe the entire island of Sri Lanka once lay beneath the seas. It first poked out of the water in the late Mesozoic Era, but began sinking again during the middle Tertiary Period. The bones and fossils of sea creatures metamorphosed into thick Miocene limestone, giving new substance to the island as it reemerged. Since then, its shape has remained unaltered, but for the ravages of erosion – some of which has been accelerated in modern times by men who illegally harvest limestone and reef coral for the manufacture of lime for cement and a cheap kind of paint.

Meanwhile, long centuries of geological up-heavals have produced the hills, mountains and escarpments that distinguish parts of the landscape. The island bulges to 8,281 feet (2,524 meters) at its highest point, Pidurutalagala, overlooking the town of Nuwara Eliya. As in most of Sri Lanka, the land here curves up softly above its surroundings, the result of centuries of bubbling up, then settling back down again into as earthen depression geologists call a peneplain. Yet the traveler will find the going steep between the peneplains.

Beneath the carpet of grass, brush and forest that covers Sri Lanka is a rock floor of gneisses and schists topped with a layer of graphite, crystalline limestone and quartzites. Various granites and pegmatites like charnockite and pink tongila occasionally intrude upon this brittle but beautiful stone carpet.

Sri Lanka's climate is tropical. There are extremely hot areas on the northwest coast, where temperatures occasionally climb above 100°F (38°C). Inland towns and cities tend to be humid – sometimes as much as 85 percent – producing oppressive conditions.

But the humidity is lower in the countryside, breezes brush most coastal areas, and the mercury often drops in the mountains to the 50s and 60s Fahrenheit. No snow has ever been recorded in Sri Lanka, but frost has enveloped its high peaks at times. The four seasons don't exist in Sri Lanka.

Only a subtle evening drop in temperature in the hot, dry zone reminds islanders that the months of October, November and December have arrived. A meteorological effect known to local weathermen as "a depression in the Bay of Bengal" brings gloomy, rainy days to the island. These wet and windy conditions move in unexpectedly, linger for a few days, then dissolve just as suddenly into sunshine and warmth.

The clouds and rains rumble in more regularly and seriously at the two times of year that come close to being seasons – the monsoons. The southwest monsoon pours from April to June, while the northeast monsoon visits the island from mid-October until mid-February.

Monsoons are actually seasonal winds that carry rain with them. These "trade winds" were identified in the 1st century A.D. by a Greek

Left, jade-eye leopard.

seaman named Hippalaus, who realized they could be used for sailing. These were the same winds that had brought ancient traders from Greece, India, China, Arabia and Rome to the old port of Mahatittha, presently called Mantai (near modern Mannar), making it one of the great emporiums of the East. The profits that flowed in through the port may have financed the glorious architectural achievements of ancient Anuradhapura, Sri Lanka's first capital.

The southwest monsoon enters Sri Lanka in an area between the cities of Chilaw, north of Colombo, and Hambantota in the south. Rain averages 60 to 80 inches along the coast; as much as 120 inches soaks hill towns like Maskeliya and Watawala. But the northeast

The northeast monsoon makes its way into Sri Lanka on a broad front that extends from Pulmoddai on the northeast coast to Arugam Bay in the southeast. It dumps its rains all over the island. The foothills of the eastern sector around Mahiyangana can be drenched by more than 130 inches.

In recent years, rapid deforestation has been blamed for upsetting the normal monsoon patterns, creating ecological and environmental problems for agriculture and other facets of life in Sri Lanka. Development projects, the slash-and-burn techniques of *chena* cultivation, farming and illicit logging have severely ravaged the island's forests.

Recent survey maps put Sri Lanka's veil of

coast remains relatively dry.

An interesting feature of the southwest monsoon is the *kachchan* wind. This part of the trade wind has lost its moisture and brings a furnace blast of hot air similar to the *khamsin* of Egypt or the *sirocco* of North Africa. It often begins about mid-morning as a mild zephyr after a chilly dawn in the North Central Province. It gradually increases in warmth and intensity until mid-day when it can reach gale force. The *kachchan* blows across the open plain, withering and wilting all vegetation in its path and sucking up stagnant spots of water. Then it dies in the early evening, leaving the nights still and warm.

forest at 25 percent, little enough to cause the unstable weather conditions that have produced long droughts. Large reservoirs, once shiny sheets of water, have deteriorated into cracked, bone-dry beds during some of these spells, curtailing growing activities. Hydroelectric production slowed. Even the bones of animals of national park wildlife are found bleaching in the burning sun.

Despite the devastation of the forests, Sri Lanka remains a fairyland of rolling hills, verdant valleys, rainforests hung with orchids, slopes carpeted with ferns, and eerie wind-swept plains. In fact, all that spectacular scenery can be seen in the course of a three-hour drive from Colombo.

Lures of the land: The sights are most abundant in the hill country. All the highest mountains are found here: besides the Pidurutalagala, there are the 7,850-foot Kirigalpotta, the 7,741-foot Totupola, and the Sri Pada, better known as Adam's Peak, measuring 7,360 feet (2,243 meters). Ranges include the Namunukula, Rakwana and aptly named Knuckles.

From these lovely mountains flow the many rivers of Sri Lanka. The longest by far is the Mahaweli. It starts its 207-mile (333-km) journey near Adam's Peak and winds its way into the Indian Ocean at Koddiyar Bay near Trincomalee. The Aruvi Aru in the Northern Province is the second longest at 104 miles

(167 kms). Other major rivers include the 90-mile-long Kelani, the Maduru Oya, Walawe and the Kalu. The only major river that does not begin in the highlands is the 97-mile-long Kala Oya. Its source is the gigantic Kalawewa reservoir, built in the 5th Century.

Most rivers are navigable for most of their length by boats that have a shallow draft. The Mahaweli can be traveled to its mouth from north of Mahiyangana. Sri Lankans often take

Left, the huge tank called Parakrama Samudra dominates the landscape of Polonnaruwa. **Above,** a rubber tapper slices a latex-rich tree, at a Kalutara plantation.

refreshing baths in their streams, since none are infested with dangerous water worms. They also provide a rich source of food; sport fishermen are tempted by the tenacious fish known as the *mahseer.*

Where there are hills and rivers, there are also waterfalls. Sri Lanka has more than its share of beauties. The tallest is the Diyaluma or the "Koslanda Bridal Veil." It drops 694 feet (212 meters) in shimmering splendor, making it one of the highest falls on earth. Other falls include Kurundu Oya (620 feet), Ratna Ella (365 feet), Ramboda (329 feet), Devon (281 feet), Dunhinda (190 feet), and the small but lovely St. Clair.

Unfortunately, some of Sri Lanka's most scenic waterfalls have given way to progress. The once thunderous roar of the awesome 377-foot Laksapana Falls has been muted by the construction of the Canyon Dam across the Maskeli Oya. Only a trickle now squirts across its mighty rock face.

Man-made wonders: Yet man has tampered with the nature of the island of Sri Lanka almost as long as he has lived here. The philosophy of the ancient monarchs was expressed by the 12th Century King Parakramabahu I when he said: "Let not one drop of water reach the sea without first serving man."

The legacy of those ancient rulers are thousands of man-made tanks – reservoirs that dot the lowlands and foothills of the island. The natural clay beds of the dry zone would be able to hold tons of water after monsoon rains, but under scorching sun and a warm breeze these lakes quickly evaporate.

The water table in these regions can drop down as much as 100 feet (30 meters) below the surface. So Parakra-mabahu I and the kings who ruled before and after him built irrigation tanks, called *wewa,* to provide a steady source of water for agriculture, no matter what the weather conditions. So thorough was their work that, according to Surveyor General R.L. Brohier, a 1904 count disclosed that there were 11,200 *wewa* in the Anuradhapura and Northern provinces alone.

The tanks range in size from that of a football field to giants covering many square miles. Even today, their construction would involve stupendous feats of engineering. From each *wewa* the ancient engineers wove webs of irrigation canals. Indeed, no contemporary civilization in any part of the then-known world had such a superior system. When combined with the magnificent *dagobas* of Anuradhapura and the palace ruins atop Sigiriya, these ancient tanks and irrigation systems stand as mute testimony to a bygone era of an amazingly advanced degree of technological know-how.

The *wewa* still help feed the people of Sri Lanka today. Most are stocked with good eating fish like the gourami and tellapia. Norwegian assistance is currently helping to restock the tanks with a fast-breeding, hardy strain of carp. More important is the role of the tanks in providing irrigation for agriculture. Beyond the urban alleys of Colombo, agricultural plots checker the landscape. Two of the oldest systems practised are paddy and *chena* cultivation.

Paddy is utilized both in the lowlands and the Hill country. When the rains begin, seeds are sown in nursery fields. After germination, the tiny seedlings are replanted in the main fields where they grow until harvest time. Sri Lanka has two major paddy crops annually. Rice for the *maha* crop is sown in August and September for harvest in February and March. The *yala* crop is sown after the advent of the southwest monsoon as a supplementary crop. The style of paddy cultivation has remained almost unchanged over the centuries, but for the replacement of the water buffalo by tractors in some areas.

Chena cultivation is an older system found in the low country and the foothills. Its survival remains an enigma in light of the fact that the planter's risks and long months of hard labor far outweigh the economic return.

In *chena* cultivation the farmer first sets fire to an area of forest during the dry season, when the tinder is parched. During the northeast monsoon, he plants various types of seeds. The grower must stand close guard against hundreds of birds who initially attack the seeds and later return for the buds and grains. At night, rodents and animals like elephants and wild boar pose a severe threat to the crop. As a defense, the farmer erects huts on stilts around his field where he and his laborers pull sentry duty each evening. They shout, use fire-crackers and occasionally fire old muzzle-loading guns to frighten the scavengers away. The latter practice can have disastrous results – especially if an elephant is wounded. The agonized animal will often become a rogue, terrorizing villages in his path.

Crops produced from a *chena* field might include cucumber, okra, bitter gourd, *brinjal* (long eggplant), watermelon, pumpkin, tomato, climbing bean, green gram (mung bean) and *loofah* (dishcloth gourd). Grains include Indian corn and sesame. Chilies are a supplementary crop. The most serious aftermath of *chena* cultivation is its effect on the land. When the harvest is over, the cultivator moves to another area to repeat the process. He leaves behind a burnt patch of irreplaceable jungle, its topsoil turned into useless silt.

Probably the only positive contribution that *chena* cultivation has made to the island is to its musical culture. It started off as a deterrent against sleep – to stay awake and alert all night, the cultivator and his companions sing to themselves. Their songs have taken on a musical form that has come to be known as *pel kavi* – songs of the huts. The mellow, lilting ballads are beautiful to hear.

'Granary of the East': The most important export crops in Sri Lanka are tea, rubber, coconut and sugar cane. Tea is found almost exclusively in the hill country and foothills, while rubber thrives on the lower-elevation slopes, and coconut is often found on the coastal plains. Sugar cane is a dry-zone crop. The island has four sugar factories located at Kantalai, Galoya, Sevanagala and Pelwatte.

Other common crops include citronella, cinnamon, cocoa, coffee, cardamom, areca nut and cloves in the wet zone; and tobacco in the arid regions. The entire tobacco crop goes straight into the factory of the Ceylon Tobacco Company, which holds a monopoly on the manufacture of cigarettes in Sri Lanka.

It may take several more generations before destructive practices like *chena* cultivation and the harvesting of limestone can be totally curtailed. These age-old practices are integral in the lives of many islanders and in some cases, the sole livelihood of entire villages.

Nevertheless the government's increasing concern has finally been transformed into action with various plans for reforestation, desilting, restoration of irrigation works, and the acceleration of major new irrigation projects on the Mahaweli Ganga and Maduru Oya. More and more farmers are receiving state assistance, including training in proper cultivation techniques. Sri Lankans may soon see the day when their teardrop of an island again is known as the "granary of the east."

Natural beauty is an integral part of the Sri Lankan experience. The morning mist in the hills around Kandy whets one's appetite.

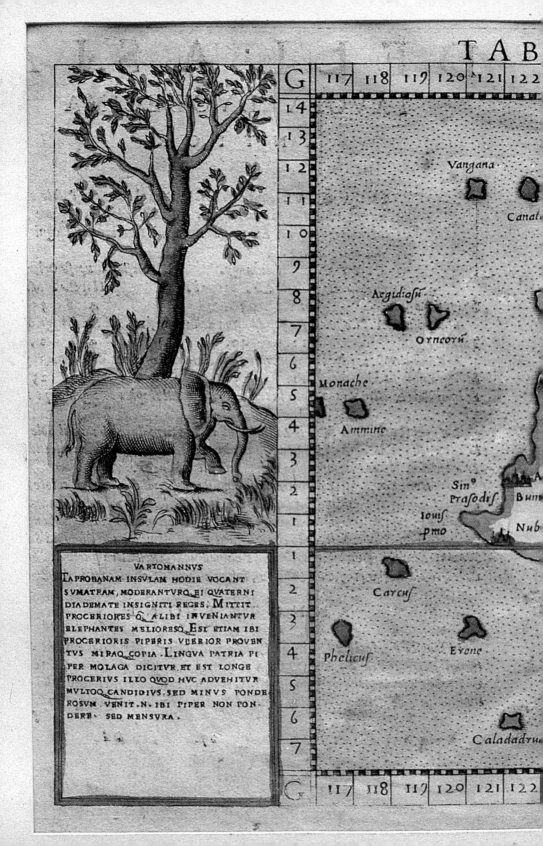

| G | 117 | 118 | 119 | 120 | 121 | 122 |

Vangana

Canat

Aegidiosū

Oyncorū

Monache

Ammine

Sin⁹
Prasodis

Iouis
pmo

Carchs

Phelicus

Eyone

Caladadru

VARTOMANNVS

TAPROBANAM INSVLAM HODIE VOCANT
SVMATRAM, MODERANTVRQ EI QVATERNI
DIADEMATE INSIGNITI REGES. MITTIT
PROCERIORES Q. ALIBI INVENIANTVR
ELEPHANTES MELIORESQ. EST ETIAM IBI
PROCERIORIS PIPERIS VBERIOR PROVEN
TVS MIRAQ COPIA. LINGVA PATRIA PI
PER MOLAGA DICITVR, ET EST LONGE
PROCERIVS ILLO QVOD HVC ADVEHITVR
MVLTOQ CANDIDIVS, SED MINVS PONDE
ROSVM VENIT. N. IBI PIPER NON PON-
DERE. SED MENSVRA.

| G | 117 | 118 | 119 | 120 | 121 | 122 |

124 125 126 127 128 129 130 131 132 133 134 135 | G

INDIAE PARS

14
13
12
11
10
9
8
7
6
5
4
3
2
1

Boreum pino

Susuara

Talacori
Galidi

Modutti

Margana
Iogana

Anubingara

MARE INDICVM

Anurogrammum
regia

Nagadiba
Maagram
mum

Nagadiba

Soani

Galibi montes

Gangeſ ſt.

Oxia
pmo

Procuri

Semni

Adiſamū

TAPROBANA

ſoliſ por

zibala

quę ante ſe
Poduce Habet inſulaſ
1378

Malea mons

Abaratha
Tarachi

Bocana

Bocani

Baracuſ fl.

Paſcua

Elepťantum

Æquinoctialis

Vliſpada
Rhogadani

Nacaduna

Nanigiri
Bachi oppidum

zaba

1

Hodoca

Anium
prom

Dagana

Corcobara

Gumara

2
3

Arana

4

Alaba

5

Baſſa

Balaca

6
7

"The Prince named Vijaya, the valiant, landed in Lanka, in the region called Tambapanni, on the day that the Tathagata (Buddha) lay down, between the two twin-like sala trees to pass into *nibbana*."

Those words, full of the mystery and intrigue that befit any prose about Sri Lanka, herald the beginning of the island's recorded history. They come from a magnificent literary achievement known as the *Mahavamsa*. In combination with its sequel, the *Culavamsa*, the *Mahavamsa* constitutes the primary source of the rich his-

British colonial servant who discovered the long-fabled Commentary at an obscure cave temple at Mulgirigala in the southern part of the island. The *Mahavamsa* treats the founding of Sri Lanka with an inventive interpretation of the coming of the Sinhalese, the island's predominant race. Experts believe the Sinhalese were people of Indo-Aryan origin who first came to the island from North India about 500 B.C. The *Mahavamsa* equates their coming with the arrival of Vijaya, the legendary founding father of the Sinhalese.

torical tradition of Sri Lanka. It is a history so colorful and complete that German Indologist Wilhelm Geiger wrote in 1932: "It is a well-known fact that for hardly any part of the continent of India is there such an uninterrupted historical tradition as for the island of Ceylon (Sri Lanka)."

The *Mahavamsa* and *Culavamsa* were complied beginning in as far back as the 6th Century A.D. by Buddhist monks (*bhikkus*). They consisted primarily of what at first seemed to be fabulous tales of mythical beings and miracles. But though these great literary works were rooted firmly in fact, their true value was not ascertained until the year 1826, when a

Vijaya and his followers arrived on the island at the time of the *parinibbana*, the passing away of the Buddha, according to the *Mahavamsa*. The proximity of the two events emphasizes Sri Lanka's historical role as the bulwark of Buddhist civilization. The foundations were laid in this passage from the *Mahavamsa*:

'When the Guide of the World, having accomplished the salvation of the whole world and reached the utmost stage of

Preceding pages: a reproduction of Ptolemy's 2nd Century A.D. map of "Taprobanam." <u>Above</u>, 19th Century tribal Veddhas near Mahiyangana.

32

blissful rest, was lying on the bed of his *nibbana*, in the midst of the great assembly of the gods, he the great Sage, the greatest of those who have speech, spoke to Sakka who stood near him: "Vijaya, son of King Sinhabahu, is come to Lanka from the country of Lala with 700 followers. In Lanka, O Lord of gods, will my religion be established, therefore carefully protect him and his followers and Lanka."'

The other component of the multi-ethnic society that has flourished in Sri Lanka for more than 2,000 years, the Tamils, are also dealt with in the *Mahavamsa*. Of Dravidian origin, the Tamils established substantial urban and trading centers in South India in the 3rd Century B.C. Although there is no firm evidence of the date of their arrival in Sri Lanka, the mercantile patterns indicate that Tamils first came to the island as traders about 300 B.C. They also came in a second wave as invaders.

Despite the influx and influence of Tamil culture, the North Indian character of the Sri Lankan society has always persisted. Neither conflict nor ethnic considerations could keep the two races apart, however. The early Sri Lanka was multi-ethnic, certainly, not an island divided by concerns for maintaining ethnic "purity."

A prehistoric spirit world: One major area in which the *Mahavamsa* comes up short is in its description of the indigenous population and cultures that existed before the Indo-Aryan colonization. That chronicle refers only to the tribes of *yaksas* and *nagas* who owe their existence more to the illustrative imaginations of the island's ancient literati than to factual beings and events of the island's prehistory. In fact, Fa Hsien, a Chinese traveler who spent time in Sri Lanka, wrote in the 5th Century A.D. that the island "had originally no human inhabitants, but was occupied only by spirits and *nagas* with which merchants of various countries carried on trade."

Judging from existing information about prehistoric times on the Indian subcontinent, *homo sapiens* probably first appeared in Sri Lanka about 500,000 B.C. A few objects have been discovered on the island that date back to the subsequent paleolithic culture of the second Stone Age period.

Stone cultures emerged in the region about 10,000 B.C. in two distinct phases – pre-pottery and pottery. As in India, the first phases probably endured until about 1,000 B.C. The second phases may have ended in some parts of Sri Lanka with the introduction of metal three or four centuries later.

The only surviving traces of the presence of mesolithic man, modern man's last link to the Stone Age, are a few stone and bone implements. These tools were produced using abrasion and the solid-core drill, techniques that were introduced during the island's second pottery phase.

The groups that practised stone-working technologies are called the Balangoda cultures. They first made an impact on island life about 5,000 B.C. and eventually spread throughout Sri Lanka. Balangoda man survived until at least 500 B.C. when he began to wane under the advance of sophisticated cultures brought by early settlers from India. Pockets of Balangoda peoples may have continued living until much later periods in the rain forests of Sabaragamuwa. Immigrants did not penetrate those remote woodlands until well into the 10th Century. A Stone Age tribe called the Veddhas still inhabits parts of the interior and may be descended from legendary *yaksas* and *nagas* of the *Mahavamsa*.

Continuing archaeological excavations and discoveries are expected to further clarify the changing picture of the prehistoric Sri Lanka. A shell cave which was uncovered at Kitulgala in the foothills east of Colombo has yielded a wealth of artifacts now being studied and documented by archaeologists. There is even new evidence that suggests the domestication of certain plants in Sri Lanka and the rest of the region may have occurred as early as 15,000 to 10,000 B.C.

Some experts now contend that Southeast Asia was the cradle of human civilization. Their theories are based on striking evidence that a Hoabinhian culture of Southeast Asian origin had been practising agriculture, making pottery, and fashioning stone tools thousands of years earlier than the people of West Asia, India or China. The Hoabinhian influence reached the Philippine and Indonesian archipelagos, Burma, Thailand, Malaysia and many other countries in the region. However no positive evidence has been actually produced linking the Hoabinhians with Sri Lanka's prehistoric cultures. Yet the island's very location – on sea routes probably traveled by the dugout canoes of the Hoabinhians – suggests a possible connection.

The ancient civilizations of Sri Lanka emerged and flourished in the island's dry zone – the extensive northern plain region and the smaller plain in the southeast that together encompass more than two-thirds of the island. Early settlements sprang up on river banks in this region. The pioneers' subsisted on rice, a crop that depended on the vagaries of the monsoons.

Settlements quickly spread across the plains, prompting an urgent need for a means of coping with the geological and geographical peculiarities of the dry zone and its frequent droughts. Thus, Sri Lanka became one of the greatest irrigation civilizations of the ancient world.

Geniuses of irrigation: Large-scale irrigation networks began crisscrossing the parched landscapes which started as early as the 1st Century A.D. Sri Lanka's engineers utilized the waters of the Mahaweli Ganga and other rivers that flowed down to the plains from the mountains of the wet zone. The construction of their canals and channels exhibited an amazing in-depth knowledge of trigonometry; and the design of their reservoirs or *wewas* revealed a thorough grasp of hydraulic principles. Their dams had broad bases able to withstand very heavy pressures. Outlets for the discharge of water were installed at suitable points in the embankment. The method of regulating the flow of water from these "tanks," as the artificial lake reservoirs are called today, was ingenious. By the 3rd Century B.C., Sri Lankan engineers had invented the *bisokotuwa* (valve pit), the prototype of sluices regulating the flow of water from contemporary reservoirs.

The increasing sophistication of irrigation technologies enabled Sri Lanka's early settlers to extend the water networks throughout the dry zone by the 6th Century A.D. Engineering milestones included the Kantalai tank built by King Mahasena (274-302). It covered 4,560 acres, was fed by a canal 25 miles long, and was contained by a dam 50 feet high. Even more superior in technology was the Kalawewa constructed by King Dhatusena (460-478). It encompassed seven square miles and had a dam 3½ miles long and 36 to 58 feet high with a spill

The Sacred Tooth Relic came to Sri Lanka in the 4th Century A.D. in the hair of a princess. A Kelaniya Temple mural recalls the event.

of hammered granite. A canal 54 miles long and 40 feet wide linked it to the city of Anuradhapura and played an integral role in the development of that ancient capital. The first 17 miles of this canal, known as the Yoda Ela or Giant's Canal, had a gradient of only six inches' slope per mile!

Subsequent centuries saw even more remarkable developments in the irrigation of Sri Lanka. By the end of the 8th Century, irrigation systems enabled the islanders to open extensive tracts of land to cultivation.

Cores of civilization: Against this backdrop of technological and agricultural growth, two important cores of Sinhalese civilization rose in the irrigated plains of the dry zone. Anuradhapura, in the center of the northern plain, and Polonnaruwa, further to the southeast near the Mahaweli Ganga, in time and in succession became the capital cities of the whole Sinhalese kingdom.

Polonnaruwa boasted one of the largest and most spectacular of Sri Lanka's ancient tanks, the Parakrama Samudra, the sea of Parakrama. It was built by Parakramabahu I (1153-1186), one of the greatest of the Sinhalese rulers. The bund of the Parakrama Samudra was nearly nine miles long and rose to an average height of 40 feet. Nothing of this scale was built again until Sri Lanka regained her independence from the British in 1948.

The third core of Sinhalese civilization, Ruhuna, was located near modern Magampattu, in the far southeast of the dry zone where the climate is even more severe, and rainfall less reliable, than in the kingdoms to the north. The region was settled by the ancient Sinhalese almost as early as Anuradhapura and a well-developed irrigation system was established there at least 2,000 years ago. Ruhuna periodically asserted its independence from the other two centers of Sinhalese power and served as a refuge for their defeated kings or rival claimants to those thrones. However, it was frequently controlled from Anuradhapura, and more effectively from Polonnaruwa, and seems never to have rivaled those cities in economic power or population resources.

Buddhism: bedrock of culture: Another significant facet of life in ancient Sri Lanka was Buddhism. It had an impact on the island and its people as important in social and political affairs as was the development of irrigation technology in the field of economic activity.

Buddhism, which probably reached Sri Lanka earlier, was formally received in the 3rd Century B.C. during the reign of Devanampiyatissa, a contemporary of the last great emperor of India's Maurya dynasty, Asoka. Tradition has it that Asoka sent the first Buddhist missionaries to Sri Lanka.

In time, Buddhism became the state religion and the bedrock of the culture and civilization of the Sinhalese. The intimate connection between the Sinhalesē and Buddhism foreshadowed the fusion of religion and national identity that now has such a profound influence on the country. The Sinhalese believe theirs is a divine mission, that they are a "chosen people" destined to protect and preserve the Buddhist faith within their island home.

Sri Lanka's irrigation network formed the basis for a thriving economy with a large agricultural surplus that sustained a vibrant civilization. Buddhism gave that civilization dignity and elegance. It inspired the architectural and sculptural splendors of ancient Sri Lanka. Anuradhapura and Polonnaruwa were transformed into bejeweled testaments to the wealth and refinement of Sri Lanka's Buddhist rulers of old.

Anuradhapura awed visitors with its magnificent stupas. The stupa or *dagoba*, an architectural innovation imported from northern India, usually enshrined relics of the Buddha and other celebrated illuminati of early Buddhism. That makes them objects of veneration even today. These solid hemispherical domes provide a subdued but effective expression of the quintessence of Buddhism. They blend simplicity and serenity. The imposing size of the stupas of Anuradhapura exemplified the state's commitment to Buddhism and demonstrated the wealth it had at its command. The Abhayagiri, enlarged in the 2nd Cent-ury A.D. to more than 280 feet, and the Jetavanarama, at more than 400 feet, were both taller than Egypt's third pyramid at Giza. In fact, the Jetavanarama may be the largest monument in the Buddhist world and one of the largest of all religious structures. It towers above the St. Paul's Cathedral in London and nearly matches the height of St. Peter's in the Vatican.

The wealth gleaned from the agriculturally sound economy and the inspirations of the Buddha combined to make ancient Anuradhapura a sprawling city, one of the greatest of

its day. Polonnaruwa, which became the center of Sinhalese civilization in the 11th Century, remained compact. But it contained all the magnificent tanks, *dagobas*, palaces, parks and sculptural embellishments characteristic of a capital city of ancient Sri Lanka.

Kings and castes: Great irrigation civilizations of the ancient world, like those of China and the Middle East's Fertile Crescent, had typically authoritarian, bureaucratic and centralized political structures. Although some scholars believe Sri Lanka's political system also fit that mold, there is evidence that the island's rulers demonstrated a greater tolerance of local autonomy. Rarely was the entire island controlled by a single ruler.

In theory, Sri Lanka's king exercised absolute rule. But custom and tradition put formidable constraints on his absolutism. He used part of his agricultural surplus to "pay" his officials and gave many of them grants of land from which they earned additional revenue. Buddhist monasteries also received land grants and eventually came to control extensive landholdings. The ruler maintained some rights over all lands in his kingdom, but private individuals – mainly among the nobility, merchants and institutions like monasteries – were permitted to "buy" and "alienate" land. Land and rights to it, as well as the accompanying power, came to be shared by large numbers of individuals and institutions. It was held under a variety of tenurial obligations.

Thus ancient Sri Lanka became more a feudal kingdom than an authoritarian state. The military aspects of feudalism were absent, as were contractual relationships between lord and vassal. But the two main attributes of feudal polity existed – the comparative weakness of central authority and the importance of land as a determinant of social and economic relationships. Like European feudalism, there was also an obligation of service as a condition of holding land. Relations between some agricultural workers and landholders could be judged feudal. The vital difference was that the nature of that obligation was affected by a

person's caste.

Caste considerations eventually formed the basis for social stratification of Sri Lankan society. This practice was another transplant from India, but the caste system in Sri Lanka took on its own characteristics. As in India, the service or occupational role of an individual was the primary distinguishing function of caste. But the Sinhalese system, in contrast to India's, provided no religious justification for

Left, courtly passions like those of old Anuradhapura are recalled in a Ratnapura painting. Above, a modern Sigiriya warrior greets tourists near Kasyapa's 5th Century fortress.

caste. The Buddha himself had condemned the system as iniquitous. So Sri Lanka's religious difference considerably softened the impact of the caste system.

The rise of Anuradhapura: The flourishing civilization of Sri Lanka's northern plain proved a tempting target, highly vulnerable to invasion from South India. As early as 237 B.C., two Tamil adventurers had usurped the Sinhalese throne and ruled the plain for 22 years. Not long after, a Chola general from South India, named Elara, ruled Anuradhapura for 44 years. He had a reputation for running and maintaining a just and impartial administration.

Sinhalese rule returned to the island after a successful 15-year campaign against Elara waged by Dutugemunu, a prince from Ruhuna. Dutugemunu killed Elara in a climactic battle in 161 B.C. and truimphantly recaptured Anuradhapura, thereby unifying Sri Lanka under a single monarch for the very first time. His capital became the island's administrative center and remained so for nearly nine centuries.

The *Mahavamsa* dramatises Dutugemunu's war against Elara was dramatised as a major confrontation between the Sinhalese and Tamils. But evidence suggest that Elara commanded much support among the Sinhalese and that Dutugemunu had to actually battle resistance within his own ranks. Thus his victory over Elara was not so much a triumph of self-conscious Sinhalese protonationalism over a Dravidian usurper. In fact it was a victory for centralization of government. In the words of the *Mahavamsa*, after his triumph over "92 Damila (Tamil) rulers, Dutugemunu ruled over the island in a single sovereignty."

Yet, the Sinhalese persisted in using Tamil assistance to settle disputed successions and dynastic squabbles, which contributed to their kingdom's political problems. An important illustration of such a situation occurred during the rule of King Kasyapa (473-491 A.D.).

Kasyapa had violently seized the throne by killing his father, Dhatusena who was the builder of the great Kalawewa irrigation tank. In order to protect himself from the rage of his brother Mugallan, the rightful heir to the throne, Kasyapa fled from Anuradhapura to the security of the rock fortress called Sigiriya. In his hands, a barren and forbidding granite outcrop soon became a royal residence of exquisite taste, a palace perched on top of the rock with ornamental gardens at the base and large areas of the rock covered with frescoes. But Mugallan had mustered an army of Indian and Sinhalese mercenaries, and he defeated his brother on the vast plain at the foot of the rock.

The role of South Indian auxiliaries thus became an increasingly important element in the armies of Sinhalese rulers. Leaders like Mugallan, who literally owed their position to the support of the Indians, showered these mercenaries with favors. In effect, these Tamils went from being mere soldiers to king-makers. At the same time, they became a volatile and unpredictable group, a turbulent element which was often the greatest threat to the stability of the realm.

The Indian peril: The 5th and 6th centuries marked the introduction of a related threat to Sri Lanka – the rise of three powerful Hindu states in South India, the Pandyas, Pallavas and Cholas. These Dravidian states were militantly Hindu and swept every trace of Buddhism from South India. The Tamils of Sri Lanka consequently became more conscious of their own ethnicity. They began to assert their identity in terms of culture, language and religion – Dravidian, Tamil and Hindu. And Sri Lanka's Tamil settlements also became bases of support for would-be South Indian invaders.

Two Sinhalese dynasties ruled Sri Lanka from Anuradhapura during these transitionary times. India's Mauryas had usurped the throne from the first Lambakanna dynasty in 455. They persevered until the reign of Sanghatissa II in 614 when he gave way to Mugallan III and the second Lambakanna dynasty.

Subsequently, the Sinhalese became drawn into the fluctuating fortunes of the three South Indian kingdoms. The weaker Sinhalese kingdoms occasionally came under the complete influence, if not control, of one or the other of the Indian kingdoms. They managed to maintain their identity by playing the Pandyas, Pallavas and Cholas against each other. This foreign policy proved successful through both the 7th and 8th centuries when Anuradhapura managed to bask in the glories of its truly magnificent *dagobas* and *wewas* in comparative tranquility.

But Sri Lankan involvement in the affairs of South India became infinitely more entangled when the Pandyans invaded the island in the 9th Century. The Pandyans sacked Anuradhapura and imposed a substantial indemnity as the price of their withdrawal. Shortly after the Pandyans left, the Sinhalese turned the tables and invaded Pandya in support of a rebel

Pandyan prince. They sacked the city of Madurai in the process, reducing it to ruins. In combination with harassment from the Pallavas in the north, the power of the Pandyans became substantially weakened.

Anuradhapura falls, Polonnaruwa emerges: Meanwhile, the Cholas began emerging as a monumental threat to all powers in the region. In a desperate attempt to cripple them, the Sinhalese made an ill-fated alliance with Pandya in the 10th Century and attacked the powerful Chola empire. The Pandyans lost. Their leader fled to Sri Lanka bearing the Pandya insignia. The Sinhalese faced retribution from the mighty Cholas who wanted to add the Pandya insignia to their trophy room and avenge the involve-

ment of the Sinhalese in the failed attack.

Mahinda V ascended to the throne of Anuradhapura in 982. He was the last Sinhalese leader to rule Sri Lanka from that glorious city. During the reign of Rajaraja the Great (985-1018), the Cholas conquered all of South India, then set their sights on Sri Lanka. The strong Chola army swept quickly into the island, overrunning Anuradhapura in all triumph.

They ravaged the city and mutilated its majestic Buddhist monuments. The Cholas also captured the Sri Lankan ruler and imprisoned in South India, where he died in captivity.

For the next 75 years, the Cholas ruled Sri Lanka as a province of South India – the only instance of direct Indian control in the island's history. Under the reign of Rajaraja's son Rajendra (1018-35), Chola power even extended beyond the South Asian mainland, posing a serious threat to the Sri Vijaya empire of Malaya and Sumatra.

One major change that occurred under the Chola rule was the abandonment of Anuradhapura as a capital city. The Cholas shifted the island's power base to Polonnaruwa which was nearer to the Mahaweli River on the eastern side of the dry zone. They made the switch largely for security reasons. The river itself afforded some protection. The city also commanded a strategic location from which to guard against an invasion from Ruhuna, the nationalistic drive of Sri Lanka's indigenous people. Vijayabahu I mounted a long offensive riot against Polonnaruwa. The Cholas surrendered in 1070 and left the island for good.

Although Vijayabahu had recaptured the deteriorating city of Anuradhapura early in his campaign, he never considered restoring its former glory as the center of Sinhalese civilization. He remembered how it had been sacked again and again in the past and knew that it was dangerously exposed to future invasion from India. Polonnaruwa had the virtue of greater protection from the Indian peril.

Polonnaruwa had its own share of fabulous Buddhist architecture and an irrigation network that had been built up over the centuries

refuge of any potential Sinhalese liberation force – since it lay near the main crossing on the Mahaweli which an advancing army from Ruhuna must ford. Last but not least, Polonnaruwa was less vulnerable to the swarms of malarial mosquitoes that often plagued Anuradhapura and its population.

Still, the Cholas – like many of the occupation armies of history – were ultimately unsuccessful in defending themselves against the

British colonial artists could only guess at Ceylon's former greatness. Left, 1864 views of the Thuparama at Anuradhapura. Above, the Alahana Pirivena at Polonnaruwa.

by earlier Sinhalese leaders like Mahasena, who had constructed its famous Minneriya tanks in the 3rd Century A.D. Vijayabahu concentrated his efforts on repairing the heavy damage Polonnaruwa had incurred under Chola rule.

Indian summer of Sinhalese kings: Vijayabahu ruled for 40 years. Inexplicably, the authors of the *Culavamsa* did not give him any credit that he deserved for his skilful liberation campaign over the Cholas and for his achievements in the more prosaic fields of administrative recovery and economic regeneration. Vijayabahu even restored Buddhism to prominence. The faith had been buried by the fiercely Shaivite Hinduism of the Cholas. Yet the *Culavamsa* reserves its kudos for Parakramabahu I, who ruled the island from Polonnaruwa between 1153 and 1186.

Parakramabahu emerges as the hero of the *Culavamsa* much as Dutugemunu dominates the *Mahavamsa*. He succeeded in unifying all of Sri Lanka under his control and also built a remarkable series of irrigation works that included the massive 5,940-acre Parakrama Samudra. He also added public and religious monuments. All helped to make the city of Polonnaruwa as impressive as Anuradhapura had once been though on a smaller scale.

Nevertheless, the reign of Parakramabahu, with all its achievements in reviving the ancient grandeur of the kingdom, proved only to be the Indian summer of Sinhalese greatness. Indeed, the king's vigorous rule, particularly his ambitious foreign policy, may have contributed to the suddenness and completeness of the collapse which followed so soon after his death.

A brief period of order and stability under the reign Nissanka Malla (1187-96), during which Polonnaruwa reached the zenith of its development. Nissanka added splendid architectural features that rivaled those of ancient Anuradhapura. They included the *vatadage*, the Angkor Wat-style Satmahal Prasada, and the colossal Buddha statues of the Gal Vihara.

However, Nissanka Malla's death touched off renewed dynastic disputes among the Sinhalese that hastened the downfall of the kingdom. The island became vulnerable when some of the Sinhalese claimants to the throne invited aid from South India and other countries in the attempts to establish their claims. The ensuing political instability prompted new invasions by Chola and Pandya adventurers. Eventually those culminated in a devastating campaign of pillage when a pirate named Magha, who came from the South Indian State of Kalinga, conquered Polonnaruwa and exerted many years of ruthless control over the island.

A Tamil State, A Kandyan Kingdom: The death and devastation wrought upon Sri Lanka by the South Indian invaders have become the stuff of folklore and mythology. Inevitably, the stories have magnified the horror of those turbulent times and have created the persistent image that the Tamils are the implacable historical enemy of the Sri Lankan nation and the Sinhalese people. The Tamils are blamed for the collapse of Sri Lanka's irrigation civilization in the 13th Century. But the political instability inherent within the Sinhalese kingdom during that period played an equally important part.

Polonnaruwa, Ruhuna and the rest of the ancient Sri Lankan cities were virtually abandoned after the death of Magha in 1255. The Sinhalese people retreated deeper and deeper into the hills of the island's wet zone in search of greater security and a new economic base. Temporary capitals were set up at Dambadeniya, Kurunegala, Panduvas Nuwara, Yapahuwa, Gampola, Dedigama and Sitawaka for short periods of time. Trading soon became an important adjunct to agriculture as the Sinhalese gathered cinnamon found in the forest for export through ports on the southwest coast.

Internal Disorders Pose a Greater Threat: In fact, a geographical separation developed between the Sinhalese and the Tamils. Until the beginning of the 20th Century, there was a vast forest belt laying between the Tamil kingdom, that was mostly concentrated in the Jaffna peninsula at the extreme northern tip of the island, and the Sinhalese in the southwest region.

Sri Lanka remained in a state of flux during the 14th and 15th centuries. Yet a third political entity began developing in the heart of the island. That occurred during the lengthy reign of Parakramabahu VI (1411-67), the last Sinhalese king who managed to reestablish rule, albeit somewhat tenuously, over the whole island. His power base was Kotte, near modern Colombo. In the last years of his reign, his control over the mountainous nucleus of the island around Gampola was challenged. So he appointed a prince of the Gampola royal house as its administrator, a move that signaled the first hint of a claim on the region from the house of Kandy.

After the death of Parakramabahu, the island again reverted to divisive struggles. Jaffna reasserted itself as an independent Tamil kingdom under Pararajasekaram (1479-1519) and the Kandyans asserted their independence from Kotte. These internal disorders may have distracted Sri Lankans from an even greater threat from a distant land – the territorial appetite of the European colonialists.

The kings of Kandy were not known for being merciful. Among their punishments was execution by elephant.

European ambitions arrived with the Portuguese during the early 16th Century. The newcomers sought to establish a trading settlement in the growing port city of Colombo on the southwest coast. By then, the Sinhalese kingdom of Kotte had completely collapsed into petty partitions among three separate rulers.

The Portuguese were more interested in controlling the island's commerce than in absorbing its territory. In the process, they began to intrude in the affairs of the coastal regions. By the year 1600, after converting some of the

to sour after Portuguese incursions into the Kandyan ports of Batticaloa and Trincomalee. Senarath's son, Rajasinha II, conducted a vigorous campaign against Portugal, forming an alliance with the Dutch.

The primary interest of the Dutch, as in the East Indies and parts of Southeast Asia, was spices. They received a promise of a monopoly over the island's spice trade in return for help in driving out the Portuguese. But the Kandyan compact with the Dutch proved as ill-fated as the earlier alliance with the Portuguese.

Sinhalese royalty to Catholicism and breaking a strong bid for dominance by the rulers of the rebel state of Sitawaka, the Portuguese had effectively controlled the southwest coastal region and managed to snuff out the last Tamil kingdom ever to rule Jaffna as an independent state.

It was the attempt to bring the Kandyan kingdom under control that proved more troublesome, and eventually led to the demise of Portugal's power in *Ceilao*, as they knew the country. Senarath (1604-1635) reestablished the kingdom of Kandy following a short-lived conquest by Sitawaka. He entered into a treaty with the Portuguese in 1617 but relations began

The Dutch recaptured the eastern ports for the Kandyans. But when they regained Galle and Negombo in 1641, they decided to keep these ports for themselves. The Hollanders also seized the Portuguese fort of Colombo in 1656 and drove the last of the Iberians from *Ceylan*, as it was now known, in the year 1658 with the capture of Jaffna. In defiance of their pact with the Kandyan rulers, the Dutch held onto most of this captured territory. Sri Lanka had merely exchanged the rule of one European power for another. Through it all, the Kandyan kingdom stubbornly maintained its independence. In the course of time, Kandy's survival as an independent Sinhalese kingdom led to the emergence of a dichotomy among the Sinhalese themselves – a distinction between the low-country coastal people and the Kandyans of the interior.

The Impact of Foreign Rule: Moreover, it was under the Portuguese and Dutch that Sri Lanka's Muslim community emerged as an identifiable ethnic influence. The Moors had achieved a dominant commercial position in the island soon after they arrived as traders in the 8th and 9th centuries. But they had remained unobtrusive. The Portuguese, by their uncompromising hostility to the Muslims, and the Dutch, by their penchant for implementing separate legal codes for each ethnic group under their administration, emphasized the distinctive identity of

privileged status. The impact of the Portuguese and Dutch on the island's economy was equally significant. Both monopolized the export trade in cinnamon. Profits from this valuable commodity became the mainstay of European revenues in Ceylon, marking the beginning of a fundamental change in Sri Lanka's revenue system – dominance of the export sector over the traditional sources of state revenue.

Finally, there was the European impact on the islanders themselves. Though the Portuguese ruled Sri Lanka's maritime regions for a much shorter period of time than the Dutch, they had a more powerful and lasting influence on the people. Conversions to Roman Catholicism stood the test of harassment under the

the Moors within Sri Lankan society.

A fresh element of pluralism came to the island with the introduction of Christianity in all its sectarian manifestations. The Portuguese brought Roman Catholicism, the Dutch Calvinism, and the English would introduce Anglicanism. Each religion enjoyed a special relationship with the ruling powers. Converts to the version of Christianity in vogue, especially under the Portuguese and Dutch, enjoyed a

Reminders of former European dominance abound in Galle. Left, a handful of Portuguese and Dutch coins. Above, an 18th Century gravestone in the Groote Kerk.

Dutch. Since the second quarter of the 19th Century, Roman Catholics have constituted 90 percent of the island's Christian community. On the other hand, Calvinism disappeared without much trace almost as soon as Dutch rule of the coast gave way to the British.

The local languages have absorbed some Portuguese and Dutch words. Portuguese was spoken in the island and used in the schools until well into the 19th Century. In fact, a Portuguese dialect still survives in some parts of the island. Many Sinhalese of the low country have adopted and retained Portuguese names like de Silva, de Soysa, Fernando, Peiris, Perera, and de Mel – even where they have long since abandoned the Roman Catholicism that went with such names.

Taking Kandy From Its Kings: While Portugal and The Netherlands left their marks on Sri Lanka, their influence pales when stacked up against that of the strongest European power which exercised the greatest control over the island – Great Britain. The first phase of the British conquest of Sri Lanka took place during 1795 and 1796. Those years were all it took for the mighty British Navy to drive the Dutch from the island they called Ceylon. They seized the strategic ports of the coast for themselves.

Meanwhile, the Kandyans' grip on their own empire was weakening. A South Indian dynasty of the Nayakkars had managed to assume

exploded into the "Great Rebellion" of 1817-1818, the most formidable insurrection of the whole British colonial period. Only a long ruthless campaign enabled the British to break the resistance of the Kandyans once and for all. For the first time since the rule of Parakramabahu I and Nissanka Malla, the entire island came under the control of a single power. The humiliating difference was that the rulers were British.

Under the Union Jack: The British maintained separate administrative systems for the Kandyan kingdom and their Dutch acquisitions until the year 1832. The way to consolidation of the island's rule under a single administration was paved by Governor Sir Edward Barnes. He had

power in Kandy in 1739 through a series of marriage alliances with the Sinhalese rulers, who had run out of male heirs. This actually proved a temporary boon to the kingdom as the Nayakkars staged a Buddhist revival and became more Kandyan than many Kandyans. But their intrigues with the Portuguese and Dutch characterized them as a possible thorn in the hide of British colonial aspirations.

The Kandyans managed to beat back a first British attack force in 1803. But the dynastic divisions that arose in the kingdom in ensuing years led to the cession of Kandy to the British in 1815. The elimination of the Kandyan monarchy fanned new flames of resistance that

constructed a road system that opened the Kandyan provinces to the rest of the island and placed their military control firmly in British hands. One of the secrets of Kandy's long survival over the previous two centuries of military pressures applied by Western powers was the fact that most of its country was wilderness suited to the guerrilla warfare techniques mastered by the Kandyans. The road system effectively eliminated the potential of guerrilla-type activities.

The consolidation of British rule ushered in an attempt to establish in Ceylon the superstructure of a *laissez-faire* state. The British appointed a Commission of Eastern Inquiry known as the Colebrooke-Cameron Commission. The reforms proposed by the group were similar to those being introduced in British India, but their impact was more far-reaching here. The Commission recommended changes in Ceylon aimed at eliminating mercantilism, state monopolies, discriminatory administrative regulations and interference in the state economy. The reforms marked the first successful attempt to break away from the Dutch pattern of colonial administration and to install a more enlightened government.

British rule brought with it a remarkable transformation of Ceylon's economy in the middle of the 19th Century. The key feature was the introduction of coffee as a plantation

traordinary resilience over the next three decades. The pattern established still prevails. The three major crops – tea, rubber and coconuts – formed the foundations of the economy.

The British dominated the tea trade and had great concern in rubber from the 1880s until some time after independence. They were somewhat less involved in the coconut trade. British commercial interests also controlled shipping, banks, insurance and the import-export trade.

Life on the Plantations: The indigenous population participated in every level of plantation agriculture. Local capitalists, smallholders and peasants controlled more than a third of the coffee acreage. Their share of the tea industry was modest but they were influential in

crop in the mid-1830s. That move proved so successful that coffee soon replaced cinnamon as the staple of the island's export trade. The number of plantations multiplied. Eventually by 1870, coffee was king. However, a virulent leaf disease had developed which put an end to that, all but wiping out the crop and the trade during that same decade.

Nevertheless, the plantation agriculture fashioned by the British demonstrated an ex-

The history of Ceylon according to the Dutch: left, the 17th Century landing at Mannar and defeat of the Portuguese; and right, "The Murder of Mr. Kofter by the Cingalese."

rubber and predominant in coconut.

The South Indian immigrants usually provided the labor on the coffee plantations, then return home after the harvests. A significant change in the pattern of immigration occurred when tea and rubber replaced coffee as the dominant plantation crops. Those commodities required year-round attention. South India again provided the labor, this time as permanent or semi-permanent residents. The immigrant laborers also worked in the building of roads, railways and harbors and in various types of tedious and unpleasant jobs. Eventually, they formed the core of a plantation and urban proletariat that was cut off from the local population and culture. They wound up living in rural plantations or city slums, a new element of plurality in the island's multi-racial society. Even until today, there is a sharp distinction between the so-called "India Tamils" and the long-established "Jaffna Tamils."

A New Social Class Appears: At the other end of the changing social spectrum was the appearance of a new class of elite Ceylonese. This group used the wealth they accumulated through capitalist enterprise as their ticket to social status.

Initially, members of ancient Sri Lanka's aristocracy were absorbed into this new elite class. But they soon found themselves falling behind in two important areas of social mobility – the acquisition of a Western education and participation in capitalist enterprise. The traditional position of the aristocracy at the pinnacle of Sri Lanka's social hierarchy thus came under challenge by the new capitalist class. These fledgling members of the new elite consisted mainly of low-country Sinhalese, with a sprinkling of Tamils and other minorities, who had a penchant for an anglicized lifestyle. This development later had profound consequences on the political evolution of the country.

One of the adverse effects of the rise of the plantations was the lopsided development of the economy. Traditional agriculture fell into neglect. Governor Sir Henry Ward (1855-1860) initiated an effort to rehabilitate the island's deteriorating irrigation systems in an effort to revive cultivation in the dry zone. But those efforts proved half-hearted and ultimately misguided, and did not result in any significant upgrading of peasant agriculture. In fact, famine, poverty, destitution and starvation plagued the dry zone of Sri Lanka around the turn of the 20th Century. Although the British had brought peace and a measure of stability to the island, they had failed to allay the economic hardships of the Sinhalese peasant.

Catering to Colonialism: The reform movement ignited by the Colebrooke-Cameron reforms spilled over into every sphere – political, economic and social – during the 1830s and 1840s. But the last quarter of the 19th century saw a marked change in policy. Only in plantation enterprise was the old zest and energy maintained. In other areas, the British administration became much more sympathetic to the conservative forces in Sri Lankan society.

The first notable reversal of attitudes occurred in the religious arena. In the early days

of British colonial rule, men like Governor Stewart Mackenzie (1837-1841) believed in the urgency of converting the local "heathens" to Christianity. The ties between Buddhism and the state were formally severed by colonial decrees in the 1840s, to the dismay of the Kandyans. But in the latter part of the 19th Century, under the administrations of Sir William H. Gregory (1872-1877) and The Honorable Sir Arthur H. Gordon (1883-1890), policy abruptly changed. Spurred on by a Buddhist revival among the populace, Gregory cultivated an active interest in Buddhism and a realization of its importance in society. He emphasized the government's neutrality in religious affairs. Gordon expanded on that theme

by emphasizing the government's special obligations to Buddhism.

These two governors also differed sharply from their colonial predecessors on the question of caste and aristocracy. They turned back the clock to earlier times, when caste divisions were more distinct, by throwing their support to the traditional members of the island's aristocracy. Gregory even admitted members of the Kandyan nobility to a kind of junior partnership in the administration of the country. By the 1880s, the Kandyans no longer tried to stir up resistance to the British. Instead, they settled into roles as associates of the British rulers.

Gregory's administration was notable for

one other development in administrative policy – a reversal of the earlier policy of using changes in provincial boundaries to break up the unity of the Kandyan provinces. Between 1873 and 1889, three Kandyan provinces – the North Central, Uva and Sabaragamuwa – were carved out, giving expression to the fact that the Kandyan problem, in the sense of a "traditional" nationalism guided by an aristocratic leadership, had ceased to be a serious threat to the continued stability of British rule.

By the last quarter of the 19th Century, the long history of Kandyan resistance to the British ended. A capitalist economy developed on the foundation of plantation agriculture and trade. One of the most far-reaching effects was

the growth of a new elite who were largely an indigenous class. The wealth they accumulated through capitalist enterprise became a very effective channel of social mobility.

Apart from investment in plantation agriculture, the most significant avenues of profit-making were the control of graphite mining and export and the transportation of coffee. Most profitable and productive of all was the liquor industry. The new capitalist class used

Left, Kandyan King Rajasinha II as portrayed by a Dutch artist. Right, Englishman Robert Knox, who lived in Ceylon in that ruler's captivity between 1660 and 1680.

the wealth it accumulated to send its children to British and European universities, thus bolstering the elite status won through success in commercial ventures.

Andrew Carnegie, the American industrialist and philanthropist, visited Ceylon in 1879 and immediately noted the effects of Gregory's reforms. He wrote:

"The new blood of home rule in local affairs has aroused local patriotism and established numerous bodies throughout the country, each a centre from which good influences radiate, organizations into which good impulses flow, to crystallize into works of public utility, while at the same time an *esprit de corps* is created which must tell more and more ... If that people cannot develop under self-government, they deserve to fall away and give place to a better race; but they will not fail."

The Emergence of Nationalism: Partly as a reaction to the British legitimization of the old aristocracy, the last three decades of the 19th Century saw the first phase in the emergence of nationalism in modern Sri Lanka. Incipient nationalist sentiment assumed religious undertones, asserting the need for the primacy of Buddhist values and warning that Buddhism was in danger. Adherents to this ideology appealed to Ceylon citizens to look to the glories of the past and to compare those days with the contemporary reality of foreign domination.

The rise of a temperance movement in the early part of the 20th Century added momentum to the increase in nationalist sentiment. The distillation of liquors like *arrack* and toddy, which ran contrary to Buddhist tenets, was controlled by Sinhalese capitalists, many of whom had been converted to Christianity by British associations. The temperance movement gained grass-roots support for nationalism among the common man, who had gained little from British rule. However, there was no attempt being made to channel the mass emotions into a sustained and organized political movement.

Even among the nationalists, faith in the permanence of British control over Ceylon remained largely unshaken. Nobody in political life at the turn of the 20th Century would have believed that the island would regain her independence within 50 years.

The Riots of 1915: Britain's rigid political rule over Ceylon underwent little change during the 19th Century. The stagnant administration continued into the first two decades of the 20th

Century. Colonial authorities resisted pressure from sectors of the elite for a share in the administration of the country. Even the First World War did not change their position.

Neither did Britain's handling of the Sinhalese riots of 1915. A surge of nationalistic and ethnic pride among the Sinhalese, brought on by the centennial of the fall of the Kandyan kingdom, evolved into attacks against a Muslim community of Coast Moors, disliked for their insensitivity to traditional rites of Buddhism and their controversial sales practices. The British, fearing the clashes could escalate into attacks against the colonial administration, came down hard on the Sinhalese and Buddhists involved. They jailed members of the temperance movement and leaders of a youthful political organization.

The British approach proved successful, putting a damper on radical political movements. The keynotes of Sri Lanka's reform movement continued to be restraint and moderate. The formation in 1919 of the Ceylon National Congress, a political party hampered by conservative domination, was evidence of the continuing strength of moderate attitudes.

Winning the Vote: In sharp contrast, the 1920s were characterized by bolder initiatives in politics. Working-class activity and trade unionism increased, particularly in Colombo and its suburbs. A leading proponent of this approach was A.E. Goonesinha. At the same time, there was a breakdown of the comparative harmony in interests and outlook which had exemplified relations between Sinhalese and Tamil politicians in the first two decades of the 20th Century. Led by the Tamils, minority groups – anxious to protect their interests – became increasingly concerned about the possible transfer of a substantial measure of political power to the Sinhalese leadership.

At the urging of Governor Sir Hugh Clifford (1925-1927), Britain appointed a special commission on constitutional reform, chaired by the Earl of Donoughmore. News of the commission exacerbated the communal and political tensions in the island. Each group was eager to voice its opinions and proposals to the Donoughmore Commission. Eventually, the commission recommended the institution of "a semi-responsible government" system composed of local politicians. The constitutional reforms introduced in 1931 on the basis of that recommendation amounted to the first step towards self-government.

Even more far-reaching in its impact on the country was the simultaneous introduction of universal suffrage. All Ceylonese men and women over the age of 21 received the right to vote, a major departure in Britain's administration of a crown colony. Ceylon thus became the first British colony in the world to enjoy universal suffrage, apart from white settlement colonies that had developed into dominions. In fact, it had taken Britons themselves nearly a century of agitation to win universal suffrage. The first universal vote in British history occurred in the general election of 1929, just two years before Ceylon's first election.

In Britain, the extension of the franchise followed the expansion of educational opportunities and the development of a political consciousness. In Ceylon, that process was reversed. The vote served as a means of emancipating the people from ignorance; it inculcated in them an awareness of their political rights and obligations.

Rise of the Welfare State: The establishment of an electorate based on universal suffrage was a major factor in the reemergence of a Buddhist nationalism. This appealed to the democratic electorate, but its potentially divisive effects in such a plural society dissuaded the constitutional leadership from sanctioning it. The vote also played a role in strengthening working-class movements. A Marxist leadership superseded the Goonesinha group and made inroads in politics. But the massive rural vote swamped the labor vote. Immigrant Indian plantation workers, the larger segment of the working class, followed their own leadership. The labor movement wound up being divided into two separate, sharply divided and mutually suspicious segments, to the advantage of more moderate leaders.

On a different level, the introduction of universal suffrage made progress in the area of social welfare, especially the years between 1936 and 1947. The achievements of that period included a comprehensive program of restoring the irrigation works of the dry zone, and the resettlement to that zone of peasant "colonists" from other parts of the country. The dynamism and vision of the Minister of Agriculture and Lands, Don Stephen Senanayake, inspired this return to the heartland of the

Preceding pages: Kandyan chiefs in ceremonial costume. Right, the Colombo-to-Kandy railway on the Kadugannawa Incline.

irrigation civilizations. Inspired by values of welfarism inherited from their colonial administrators, the new government embarked on a wide-ranging program of free education, free health services, and food subsidisation, in a move that formed the basis of Ceylon's welfare state. Sri Lanka would later reap the rewards of free education when it achieved the highest rate of literacy among its Southeast Asian counterparts, and now ranks among the highest in the developing world. Additionally, the government instituted education, health and food subsidies in a move that formed the basis of Ceylon's mini-welfare state.

The final phase in the transfer of power from British to Sri Lankan hands began under

MR. G. C. S. COREA Ceylon's Ambassador in Washington, looks on while Mr. Hume Wrong, Canadian Ambassador to the United States, presents the Order of the British Empire and the Distinguished Flying Cross to Group Captain L. J. Birchall (right) of the Royal Canadian Air Force at Washington on April 29.

Senanayake's leadership. The former Minister conceived of a gradual transition to independence in which Ceylon, would initially win Dominion status. His critics in the Ceylon National Congress saw no need for such a transitionary phase in the country's constitutional evolution. But Senanayake displayed a concern for the role the country's minorities would play in an independent Ceylon, and feared that an immediate break with the British would fuel hostility toward a leadership that was essentially Sinhalese and Buddhist.

The Second World War: A turning point in world history briefly sidetracked Sri Lanka's political aspirations – World War II. Unlike the

neighboring India, Ceylon's leaders pledged full support to Great Britain and the Allies when hostilities engulfed the globe in the year 1939. Ceylon's major ports at Colombo and Trincomalee subsequently became important links between Europe and the war's Asian theater. The local politicians who continued agitating for action on the issue of independence were temporarily silenced when Governor Sir Andrew Caldecott issued detention orders against them in 1940, under wartime emergency legislation.

Well aware of the strategic position of Ceylon, Japan attacked its ports in April 1942. In little more than a week, more than 1,000 Allied troops and Sri Lankan civilians died defending the island. The respected British historian Sir Arthur Bryant said that a Japanese naval victory in Ceylon would have given Japan total control of the Indian Ocean and brought down the Churchill government. Churchill himself was said to have considered the Japanese attack on Ceylon the most dangerous moment of the entire war. But the British defense proved triumphant in what some analysts consider a crucial defeat for the Japanese.

A Free Nation: With the dismissal of yet another foreign threat to Sri Lanka, Senanayake submitted a proposed constitution in 1944 that underscored the importance of maintaining the state's religious neutrality. In response, Britain appointed a commission that year led by Lord Soulbury. He recommended that a constitution be drawn up similar to the one proposed by Senanayake's group. It provided for internal self-government in the island while retaining some imperial safe-guards in matters of defense and foreign policy.

The unsatisfied Sri Lankans pressed for the removal of the latter provisions. Britain conceded. Ceylon celebrated the return of its independence from foreign domination on February 4, 1948. In contrast to the turbulence that tore apart the Indian sub-continent and Burma during similar independence initiatives, the transfer of power proved to be smooth and peaceful in Ceylon. The underlying frustration and resentment of the long years under a colonial administration did not burst violently to the surface until nearly a decade later.

Above, World War Two hero Captain L.J. Birchall was still news in Colombo in 1949. **Right**, the first prime minister of independent Ceylon, D.S. Senanayake.

D.S. Senanayake's mature statecraft provided an impressive start for Ceylon in the difficult process of nation-building and national regeneration. Despite the 70 percent majority of Sinhalese and 67 percent majority of Buddhists (1948 figures), the country's first prime minister continued his policy of diffusing Sinhalese-Buddhist dominance and refused to mix state power and politics with religion.

The prime minister's moderate policies enabled his United National Party (UNP) to stabilize its position in the country and strengthen its hold in Parliament after independence. The main opposition continued to come from the Marxist left, but they were too divided by ideological disputes and personality conflicts to mount an effective challenge to the UNP.

By 1950, Ceylon's economy regained some of the buoyancy it had lost during World War II. Importers began to pay premium prices for rubber and tea. That enabled the government to earn enough capital to finance the welfare measures which the population had come to expect. In an attempt to achieve self-sufficiency in rice and other foodstuffs, the government poured more money into the redevelopment of the dry zone. The massive Gal Oya irrigation project was financed from budget surpluses. The Senanayake Samudra tank, constructed near the East Coast at Inginiyagala as part of this scheme, was four times larger than the Parakrama Samudra.

Yet, the failure of Senanayake's government to emphasize basic changes in the economic structure inherited from the British would prove fateful. In economics as in politics, he put too much faith in maintaining the status quo.

Upon Senanayake's death in 1952, the momentum of his party's early achievements managed to sweep his son, Dudley, into the prime minister's chair. But the economy began to falter soon afterwards. An attempt to reduce food subsidies ignited violent opposition in August 1953, at the instigation of left-wing parties. More importantly, religious, cultural and linguistic issues gathered steam and rocketed into a force too powerful for the existing

Sri Lankan Prime Minister Dudley Senanayake and Indian Prime Minister Indira Ghandi at a conference in the late 1960s.

social and political structure to accommodate.

The first major challenge to the UNP government was organized By S.W.R.D. Bandaranaike, a senior Cabinet colleague of the senior Senanayake. He had defected to the opposition with a small group of supporters in 1951, then formed his Sri Lanka Freedom Party (SLFP) two months later. He fashioned that group into a centrist political force which appealed to all interest groups dissatisfied with the UNP, but opposed to Marxist solutions.

The SLFP aimed its program at rural areas where Marxists had failed to make much impact and where disillusionment with the UNP was growing. Neglected by the UNP and Marxists alike, the Buddhist leadership also threw its weight behind the SLFP.

In 1956, Bandaranaike and his SLFP, with the aid of smaller splinter parties, won a landslide victory in the general election.

The SLFP takes charge: The performance of the UNP in the 1952 election was so impressive, that, at the time it had appeared a monolithic party system might be in the offing for Ceylon. The election of Bandaranaike in 1956 changed all that. In the context of the British colonial experience in Asia and Africa, the change in power proved to be a rare example of the transfer of a system through a democratic and constitutional election from a legatee of the British to a thoroughly indigenous successor.

Sri Lanka holds the longest record of democratic elections in any former British colony in the world. It is a record of enviable impartiality in the conduct of such elections. The electorate turned a government out of office on six successive occasions prior to October 1982.

But Bandaranaike's victory also sanctioned the rejection of Senanayake's concept of a nationalism based on plurality. The SLFP's new brand of nationalism was democratic and populist, but it also proved divisive. Combined with the worldwide celebration of the 2,500th anniversary of the death of the Buddha that same year, the 1956 election became the catalyst for a decade of ethnic and linguistic tensions and religious strife which occasionally erupted into race riots.

Finally, the new government proved to be a major setback for the Marxists. Their cosmopolitan outlook and support for a multiethnic secular polity were unpopular concepts in this era of linguistic nationalism. They were compelled to compromise on these issues without any sort of substantial political benefits.

Bandaranaike's so-called "middle way" was essentially opportunistic and ideologically hazy. But it gave the common people of Ceylon a sense of dignity and self-respect. It promised social change and justice, economic independence from foreign powers, and complete political sovereignty.

However, Bandaranaike's administrative skills never matched his ambitions. He was unable to keep the warring factions of his cabinet together, let alone the deteriorating fabric of the society. His weaknesses culminated in his assassination in September 1959. His murder was engineered by a powerful *bhikku* who had been one of his strongest supporters in the election campaign in 1956. The order was carried out by yet another *bhikku*.

The assassination helped boost Dudley Senanayake and the UNP back into power in March 1960. But it also prompted the reorganization of the SLFP under the slain leader's powerful widow, Sirimavo Bandaranaike. The UNP found its position shaky and called for a new election only four months after its victory. Mrs. Bandaranaike rolled to victory. She came to dominate the politics of the island for nearly two decades.

A shift to socialism: Unlike her husband, Mrs. Bandaranaike was not reluctant to take on the two most explosive issues of the time. She immediately sought to pursue her husband's goal of uniting the country under a single national language, Sinhalese. She also tried to bring private schools under state control. Thus, she antagonized Roman Catholics as well as Tamils. Mrs. Bandaranaike viewed socialism as a means of redressing the balance in favor of Sinhalese-Buddhist nationals. To that end, she nationalized a wide variety of foreign and local economic enterprises in an attempt to wrest them from the foreign capitalists and minority groups which controlled them.

One notable achievement in her first term occurred in 1964 when Mrs. Bandaranaike joined with Indian Prime Minister Lal Bahadur Shastri to repatriate more than 500,000 Indian Tamils from Ceylon to their ancestral homes. In return, Ceylon agreed to absorb 300,000 Sri Lanka residents of India.

But the SLFP's continuing shift to the left precipitated its downfall. The SLFP formed a coalition with the Trotskyist Lanka Sama Samaja ("equal society") Party (LSSP) in an attempt to broaden its base. That move failed.

Besides, Mrs. Bandaranaike's first years in power were marred by ethnic and religious confrontations resulting in long periods of rule under emergency powers. She also narrowly escaped an abortive coup attempt by high-ranking police, military and naval officers. The SLFP lost the general elections of March 1965, with Dudley Senanayake returning to power.

Dudley Senanayake made the best of his term in office. Under his leadership, the UNP-dominated Parliament enjoyed five years of power. During those years, Senanayake succeeded in maximizing agricultural productiv-

ity by closing in on his goal of self-sufficiency in food production.

The UNP was unable, however, to stop rising unemployment among the educated. Senanayake also failed to transform his planned ethnic and religious reconciliation into legislation, because of divisions within the ranks of his party on those issues. In addition, a five-year experiment with the lunar calendar proved to be impractical.

Meanwhile, Bandaranaike put together a new coalition called the United Front. It included the LSSP and the pro-Moscow Communist Party. That combination won a decisive electoral victory in 1970. But they had even less success than the UNP in battling unemployment, rising prices, and scarcities of essential items of consumption. By early 1971, the United Front faced a deadly threat from an ultra-left organization called the Janata Vimukti Peramuna, which commanded the support of educated youths, the unemployed and the disadvantageously employed. With an odd assortment of home-made bombs and weapons, youths attempted to overthrow the government in April 1971 by trying to kidnap the Prime Minister and attacking police stations around the country. The government firmly put down the insurrection; some of the young leaders were killed and more than 10,000 were arrested.

Fall of the United Front: The insurgency failed,

but it had a marked effect on future developments in Ceylon. The credibility of the United Front as a genuinely socialist government had been challenged, with the result that Bandaranaike implemented a series of radical economic and social changes. State control over trade and industry was accelerated and expanded to the point where government dominated the economy. The Land Reform Law of 1972 marked the first phase in the nationalization of the plantations. By 1975, all

Prime Minister Sirimavo Bandaranaike (left) and President J.R. Jayawardene put party politics aside during this 1980 meeting.

private agricultural enterprises, including the vast tea estates, had been absorbed.

The government also adopted a new republican constitution in May 1972. If officially changed the country's name from "Ceylon" to "Sri Lanka," and vested state power in a unicameral legislature called the National State Assembly. It also extended the ruling coalition's term of office by two years to May 1977, a move which greatly antagonized opposition parties and brought the United Front into further disrepute. Other provisions in the constitution further alienated the Tamil minority. Their aspirations for a fair share in the political structure has now escalated into demands for a separate Tamil state called "Eelaam," independent from Sri Lanka. The most militant of the separatists are the educated unemployed, a substantial force in Tamil society.

The reputedly socialist measures of the Bandaranaike government did little to improve living standards for the country's poor. They did even less to stimulate economic growth. The serious balance-of-payments deficit inherited by the United Front government deteriorated into a crisis. Inevitably, support for the Bandaranaike government began to collapse along with the economy. Rifts appeared in the United Front coalition as the SLFP and LSSP factions wrestled over the question of how to halt the economic slide. The acrimony peaked in October 1975 with the expulsion of the LSSP from the government.

The political benefits of hosting the conference of Non-aligned Nations in Colombo in August 1976 was too little too late. The United Front government tried to cement its tenuous hold on Parliament by proposing an amendment to the constitution that would postpone the 1977 elections. That move backfired. Even a group of SLFP cabinet ministers opposed it.

The Bandaranaike government made a futile last-minute bid to reconcile itself with the Tamil United Liberation Front while its coalition slowly fell apart. Left-wing members of the SLFP left the party. The Communist Party soon followed.

By the end of February 1977, the United Front had dissolved. Only a dispirited and demoralized SLFP was left to face Sri Lanka's worse wave of strikes in 20 years. The strikes were engineered by its former coalition partners. For the first time since 1960, there was no serious opposition or electoral pact against the UNP in the general election of 1977.

When the first announcements of election results are unduly delayed in Sri Lanka, the populace, glued to radios, takes it as an unmistakable sign that the ruling party has been turned out of office.

Such was the case on July 21, 1977. When the avalanche of figures finally began rumbling across the air waves three hours later than expected, the green-shirted supporters of the United National Party were already pouring into the streets of the island's cities. They danced and dodged the fireworks that whizzed around them and rent the air. The belated election results confirmed what the highly politicized electorate of nearly seven million voters already suspected. A record 86.7 percent of the electorate had dropped ballots into the boxes ousting Sirimavo Bandaranaike from the Prime Minister's seat along with her crumbling Sri Lanka Freedom Party.

The victor in that fateful election was Junius Richard Jayewardene, leader of the UNP and a vigorous and perceptive political strategist. While his supporters celebrated into the early-morning hours of election night, the cool "J.R." reportedly retired for the evening. He had single-handedly engineered the UNP's biggest victory in the history of independent Sri Lanka, a remarkable resurrection of a party that had lost the previous election in 1970 by a landslide.

With its stubborn streak of independence and destiny, the island's electorate had opted for new leadership for the sixth time since Sri Lanka had achieved independence in 1948. It had vented its frustration and disillusionment with the outgoing party in no uncertain terms.

Jayewardene stepped into the Prime Minister's chair as his UNP assumed 140 of the 168 seats in the National State Assembly, having polled nearly 51 percent of the total vote. The shattered SLFP mustered a paltry eight seats, polling just under 30 percent. Not only had it lost the election, it was nudged out of the opportunity to assume the role of the loyal opposition. That job went to the Tamil United Liberation Front, which won 18 seats in the Assembly though it received only seven percent of the total vote. For the first time in

A young laborer takes a breather during construction of a building.

modern Sri Lanka, a Tamil, Appapillai Amirthalingam, became Leader of the Opposition.

Anatomy of a defeat: The common man's disenchantment with the SLFP grew out of the hardships that hit him increasingly harder through the 1970s. The most serious problems were economic. There was a severe shortage of rice, sugar, dairy products, bread, textiles, drugs and many other essentials. The decrease in life's necessities was combined with an increase in bureaucratic measures. The queue had become a way of life. Rations, curbs, controls, barriers, permits and red tape engulfed the average citizen, making the most mundane pursuits torturous exercises in futility.

The middle classes had also been squeezed beyond endurance by economic crises and the business and land-owning elite found their livelihoods threatened. They lamented the social legislation engineered by the United Front coalition of the SLFP, the leftist LSSP and the Communist Party. It had aimed for a radical redistribution of wealth in an attempt to reduce inequalities in income and the quality of life.

While serving as Finance Minister in 1948, Jayewardene had declared: "If the entire national income is distributed among the population, it would make beggars of us all."

When he rose to the top of his nation's political hierarchy in 1977, Jayewardene was quick to implement his ideology. He dismantled the rigid controls that the SLFP had leveled on Sri Lanka's economic sectors, liberalized trade and foreign-exchange laws, tackled inefficiency and stagnation in the public corporations, and eased state intervention in the affairs of private companies.

The liberalized economic policies were buttressed by new monetary and fiscal measures. The rupee, which had been precariously anchored to a two-tiered exchange rate, was devalued and permitted to float against a basket of trade-weighted currencies. Using the economic miracles accomplished by Singapore as its model, the UNP set about transforming Sri Lanka into South Asia's financial center. Prestigious foreign banks opened offices. Offshore banking was established and a small merchant banking sector began to flourish.

Return of the foreigners: The new stable political climate and attractive investment incentives have resulted in the return of foreign companies that had fled the island during the SLFP years. Jayewardene himself had once referred to multinational companies as "robber barons." But he was well aware of the positive impact they could have on his ailing economy. He saw foreign investment as playing a major role in development by supplying the capital, technology, training and employment – and in providing access to markets – necessary to lift Sri Lanka into the ranks of the world's developed nations.

Today, Sri Lanka's economy rests firmly on the foundation of foreign aid and investment. Leading development projects, such as the Mahaweli irrigation scheme, depend almost entirely on outside assistance. This situation of aid-dependence had been deplored and considered unhealthy even by the then-Finance Minister, Ronnie de Mel, to whom fell the unenviable duty of jetting around the world with a begging bowl. Minister de Mel was later removed from his post by former President J.R. Jayewardene in 1987. Nevertheless, the government did strive for independence, most notably in prioritizing self-sufficiency in food production.

Whereas Mrs. Bandaranaike's virulent anti-Western policies had distanced Sri Lanka from the economic favors provided by countries like the United States, Jayewardene took a decidedly pro-Western, pro-American approach. The UNP also maintained a lower profile in the international non-aligned movement, a radical departure from the activist policies of previous regimes. Relations were fostered with the Arab world. But Sri Lanka's bid for membership in the Association of South East Asian Nations (ASEAN) was rejected in 1982.

The Jayewardene regime ushered in a new era in Sri Lanka's politics, as well as in economics. The UNP-dominated Assembly quickly approved a new constitution that transformed the "Republic of Sri Lanka" into the "Democratic Socialist Republic of Sri Lanka" in 1978.

Although somewhat a misnomer for a country which has enthroned private enterprise as king, the Democratic Socialist Republic embraced a new political structure that was a sharp departure from the Westminister model of parliamentary government. In fact, the new government took on some of the features of the American and French presidential systems.

Under the new Constitution, the President, whose role had previously been limited to that of a ceremonial Head of State, was invested with an unprecedented concentration of power that makes him head of state, chief executive, and commander-in-chief of the armed forces. He also appoints the chief justice and the attorney general of the nation, and enjoys immunity from court action against official or private acts. Jayewardene exchanged the mantle of Prime Minister for that of President on February 4, 1978.

Another revolutionary move was the change in election procedures for the Parliament. Now voters cast ballots for a party or a group of independents rather than for an individual candidate. Ballots no longer contain the names of candidates, just the names of parties. The system is known as "proportional representation."

Each party that qualifies for election receives a proportionate share of the 196 Assembly seats, based on the number of votes it polls. A minimum of 12.5 percent of the total vote in each district is needed to win a seat.

The UNP claimed that the new system would better reflect the choices of the voters and reduce the huge majorities that have characterized the Assemblies of the past. By-election, once held to fill seats that became vacant during a term, have been eliminated in favor of replacements appointed by the party holding that seat. The new constitution thus gives the party hierarchy virtually unlimited power over its rank-and-file and can permit it to put unpopular members in Parliament. Members (MPs) can even be expelled if they fall out of favor with the party.

While Buddhism receives prominent mention in the preamble to the new constitution and Sinhalese is considered the official language of Sri Lanka, the Tamil minority has been accorded a place in the constitution with the upgrading of its tongue to the status of a national language. The status of English is that of a 'Link-Language.'

The '82 Election: The provisions of the 1978 constitution were put to the test sooner than expected. The country's eight million-plus voters went to the polls twice in the span of two months in 1982. In October, they voted in a presidential election for the first time. In December, they again cast ballots in a referendum that would extend the term of Parliament for six years – until 1989. But both instances marked a departure from the constitution and required amendments. A presidential election had not been expected until 16 months later. The early call solidify its position before any opposition parties could mount a respectable challenge, and before new economic problems could arise that might erode support for the UNP. The strategy worked.

The civic rights of Mrs. Bandaranaike had been revoked in 1980 for overstepping her constitutional powers as Prime Minister. That made her ineligible for election or even to canvas for candidates. This had tossed the SLFP into turmoil. It splintered into two factions bidding for leadership. The challenge to Bandaranaike came from an unexpected quarter – that of her party deputy, Maitripala Senanayake. The commissioner of elections eventually recognized Bandaranaike's faction as the official party.

sistent on an independent state of "Eelam," chose to sit out the election. A wave of terror and intimidation by the Liberation Tigers party further limited voter turnout.

A show of support: Jayewardene buried the opposition in the election, receiving nearly 53 percent of the 6.6 million votes cast. The SLFP, led by Hector Kobbekaduwa took 39 percent.

More significantly, Jayewardene carried 21 of the country's 22 districts. He lost only Jaffna, which went for a candidate fielded by the Tamil Congress Party.

A three-month state of emergency was declared following the presidential election, in a successful attempt to head off possible violence. Jayewardene capitalized on the five-

Meanwhile, the LSSP also split into factions divided over whether to join hands in a united opposition to the UNP. They failed to agree on a united front. Each group offered its own candidate. That virtually erased their chances of ousting Jayewardene. It was exactly what the president had expected.

The Tamil United Liberation Front, still in-

The Mahaweli Scheme is providing Sri Lanka's people with electricity and a vast amount of newly irrigated land. The Polgolla Dam is one of many.

sixths majority enjoyed by his government in Parliament to extend its term for a further six years and called a referendum to approve it. Although the referendum call stirred great controversy the UNP staunchly maintained that its policies had been endorsed by the presidential poll and argued that the extension was essential to provide the stability and time required to complete its ambitious program of development.

The referendum came down to a battle between the forces which favored the UNP's open-market economy and those which supported the welfare state. Although it was a heated contest, the ruling government prevailed, with 54.7 percent in favour of the extension.

The Jayewardene government's dual victory proved to be an unprecedented accomplishment in a country where electorates had acquired the habit of choosing a new leadership every time there was an election. President Jayewardene once vowed to "roll up the electoral map for 10 years." That's exactly what he did.

'Black July': But the Jayewardene government suffered a serious setback in mid summer 1983. An increase in terrorist acts by the Liberation Tigers climated in the ambush of a Sinhalese army patrol in Tamil-dominated Jaffna in July. Twelve soldiers and an officer perished. Sri Lanka's Sinhalese majority reacted with fierce reprisals against Tamils throughout the island.

In a week of terrifying rioting, now known as "Black July," racist mobs went on the rampage in an orgy of murder, looting and arson. Tamil-owned shops, factories and homes were burned to the ground and decimated. The Pettah wholesale market, largely operated by Tamil merchants, was reduced to a heap of ashes. In all, 387 persons died, and 90,000 others were herded into refugee camps. Some 20,000 were rendered homeless.

With the assistance of the armed forces and a strictly enforced curfew, the government restored law and order. The Rehabilitation of Property and Industries Authority (REPIA) was established to protect the ownership of all destroyed or abandoned properties, and to assist in their rehabilitation.

Within a few days after the rioting, a constitutional amendment outlawing all separatist movements have been passed by Parliament. It set heavy penalties against any public official or professional refusing to take an oath of allegiance to the "unitary state" of Sri Lanka. Sixteen MPs representing the TULF refused to take the oath and thus forfeited their seats in Parliament. The mantle of the Leader of the Opposition thus fell on the young shoulders of Anura Bandaranaike, son of the former SLFP prime ministers.

After many very bleak months, the tourism industry also showed signs of recovery, thanks in part to the annual convention of the Pacific Area Travel Association (PATA) in Colombo in April 1984.

Except for a few sporadic incidents of terrorism (credit taken by the Liberation Tigers and a few other splinter groups) every now and then, Sri Lanka had a quiet year after "Black July." However, the latter part of 1984 saw

terrorism escalating once more, this time with a more sinister and deadly face. Bombs placed in public places and a renewed drive to gain control of the north and east by the terrorists resulted in heavy casualties on the Sri Lanka armed and police forces.

According to experts, the terrorists were trying to create a situation similar to July 1983, a backlash by the Sinhala people so that they could achieve their end in the ensuing melee. Their goal was to achieve the State of Eelam by 14th January 1985, Thaipongal day. But due to quick measures taken by the State in imposing emergency regulations and strictly enforced curfews, the terrorists failed in their aim.

In Colombo, the All-Party Conference summoned by then-President J.R. Jayewardene, early that same year, with the participation of 10 mainstream political parties and religious groups, after months of discussions ended in a stalemate. Despite all this, happily for Sri Lanka, tourism went on as usual with hardly any ill-effects on the foreign visitors to the island.

Reshaping the rivers: One of the corner-stones of the Jayewardene government in its efforts to turn Sri Lanka into a developed country was the Accelerated Mahaweli Scheme.

Flowing down from the central hills, the Mahaweli River meanders through breathtakingly beautiful valleys and rugged mountain terrain, finally mating with the sea near Trincomalce. Its waters usually give succor to the land. But occasionally, swollen flood waters have turned the benign river into a raging torrent that wreaks havoc on man and beast. At other times it shrivels up, depriving farmers of its life-giving waters. Those devillish tantrums are now contained. The Mahaweli scheme has slowly tamed the mighty river – shaping it, diverting it, trapping it into reservoirs, guiding it through channels and powerhouses.

Although the scheme was launched in the mid Sixties, it received a shot-in-the-arm from the Jayewardene government. Original cost estimates soared from US$400 million to US$2 billion by 1982 and astronomically higher since.

Appropriately, Canadian engineers working on the site of a proposed dam in the thick jungles that border the Maduru Oya river accidentally excavated an ancient dam and sluice. The discovery has since been designated a significant archaeological discovery, a masterpiece of ancient island hydro-engineering.

Another facet of the scheme (under the direction of West Germany), saw the creation of the largest body of regulated water in Sir Lanka in the Rangdenigala region. This modern "tank" traps 800 million cubic meters of water behind a dam 485 meters long and 94 meters high.

The linchpin of the project is the 122-meter high, mile-long, double-curvature Victoria dam, in the picturesque Dumbara Valley, and which the British contractors completed two months ahead of schedule in 1984. That same year saw the completion of work on the Kotmale Oya, a tributary of the Mahaweli.

Yet another development project that accrued considerable political benefits for the Jayewardene government was the establishment of the Free Trade Zone at Katunayake on the outskirts of Colombo. The first garment

event of eventual local acquisition.

Putting on a new face: In the field of urban development, the UNP leadership has fashioned a plan for a major facelift for Colombo. They will restore the dignity of the Dutch and British-style architecture while adding glass and concrete high-rises to the skyline.

Parliament also got a facelift. The ceremonial opening was held in early 1984. A new multi-million dollar Parliament and governmental complex and administrative capital, known as Sri Jaywardhanapura (after the official name of the 15th Century Sinhalese capital at Kotte), was constructed in the reclaimed swamps of Kotte, just east of Colombo.

The crowning achievement of the new ad-

factory opened at this 160-square-mile zone in 1978. Now, more than 26,000 people, 85 percent of them young women in colorful skirts and blouses, trek to work at the FTZ each day.

Created to attract foreign investment, the zone has not lived up to expectations but has made a sizeable dent in the island's chronic unemployment problem. Foreign investors in the 47 operational industries receive 10-year tax holidays, tax exemptions, duty-free imports of raw materials, and compensation in the

Sri Lanka's new Parliament complex occupies a man-made island in Lake Diyawanna Oya in Kotte, a 15th Century Sinhalese capital.

ministrative capital is the parliamentary center (a gift from the government of Japan and built at a cost of US$43 million) which rises on a picturesque island in the middle of Lake Diyawanna Oya, a work of art designed by the country's foremost architect, Geoffrey Bawa. Its imposing oriental splendor incorporates the influences of generations of artists and sculptors and rivals some of the glorious structures of ancient Sir Lanka.

Sir Jayawardhanapura has three administrative complexes, residential zones, parks, gardens, a sports stadium, a museum, and other amenities of a planned city. But the lavish complex has sparked concern in some quarters.

As one political wit observed: "Do we really need a five-star parliament?"

Yet the needs of the common man were not ignored. High priority was given to the construction of public housing, which was directed by then-Prime Minister Ranasinghe Premadasa, and which saw the construction of more than 100,000 units throughout the island between 1977 and 1983. His vision was to build one million more by the end of the decade.

The Indo-Lanka Peace Accord of 1987: Since 1985 violence began to escalate once again in the northern and eastern regions of the country. The largest and best organised of the many terrorist groups was the Liberation Tigers of Tamil Eelam (LTTE), popularly known as the "Tigers", who spearheaded the campaign of violence and destruction. Many of the terrorist groups received considerable sympathy and support in the form of financial aid, weapons and training from international sympathisers.

The Sri Lanka government's campaign against the terrorists caused a steady exodus of refugees to Tamil Nadu, numbering 100,000 by 1987. Reports from fleeing refugees of death, destruction and starvation stirred up a heated campaign among the people of Tamil Nadu who brought pressure on the Indian central government to intervene in the conflict.

One result of these developments was the infamous "air-drop" incident in June 1987, when Indian Airforce planes entered Sri Lankan air-space dropping thousands of food parcels over the northern towns. The Indian move followed a similar exercise attempted by them by sea, a few days earlier, which had been repulsed by the Sri Lanka Navy.

The Indian action was condemned by the Sri Lanka government as a blatant and aggressive violation of the nation's sovereignty. India defended her actions on "humanitarian grounds", also claiming she had a right to intervene in the island's affairs if she felt her own security was threatened.

This unhappy confrontation, seen as a "David and Goliath" type situation, was finally resolved the following month. The July 1987 Peace-Accord signed in Colombo by then-Prime Minister of India, Rajiv Ghandi and former Sri Lankan President J.R. Jayewardene, was the result of intensive diplomatic activity following the Indian action, which had brought home to Sri Lankan policy-makers the geopolitical realities of the region, and impressed on the Indians the grave repercussions to their own country of encouraging terrorism across the waters. Under the terms of the Accord, a 45,000 strong Indian Peace-Keeping Force (IPKF) was dispatched to northern and eastern Sri Lanka, charged with the responsibility of disarming the terrorist groups and bringing peace to the strife-torn nation.

Sadly, however, Sri Lanka was to be plunged into a new reign of terror following the Accord. The Peace Accord had aroused the wrath of militant extremists who regarded it as a "sell-out" to the traditional enemy, India. The country was plunged into a ferocious and bloody campaign of terror aimed at toppling the democratically-elected government and abrogating the hated Accord.

The extremist campaign was organised and led by the militant and ruthless Janatha Vimukthi Peramuna (JVP or People's Front) which in 1971 had masterminded the failed coup attempt on Mrs. Bandaranike's government. The terror campaign was to grip this tiny island in a web of fear, leaving thousands dead in its wake. Over the next two years, the nation's economy was brought to a virtual standstill, with its once impressive growth rate plunging to less than two percent almost overnight. The tourist industry also plummetted with arrivals slowing to a trickle, especially in the southern coastal regions which was the JVP heartland.

Premadasa takes over: Sri Lanka went to the polls once again in December 1988 to elect a new President. The elections were conducted against the backdrop of violence and political assasinations by the JVP.

Former Prime Minister Ranasinghe Premadasa emerged victorious becoming Sri Lanka's new President and head of the new ruling UNP. The new President wasted no time in calling for the withdrawal of the IPKF whose presence on Sri Lankan soil had instigated the rebellion. This was achieved by April 1990, when the last of the 45,000 troops finally left the shores of Lanka, to the relief of many a Sri Lankan.

At the same time, a renewed counter-subversive drive to crush the JVP onslaught was launched. Through a campaign of intimidation and violence during the greater part of 1989, the JVP had virtually succeeded in bringing the government and economy to a standstill. The breakthrough came in early November that same year, when Sri Lanka's most wanted man, Rohana Wijeweera, the leader of the JVP, was shot dead along with his deputy, by Sri Lankan security forces. The stranglehold the group had over life in Sri Lanka was thus broken. Remaining pockets of resistance were rapidly wiped out thereafter, heralding a new dawn of relative peace once again on this tortured land.

Liberalisation reaps rewards: Undeterred by violence and rebellion in many parts of the island, the government of President Premadasa proceeded on a wide-ranging program to further the liberalisation drive begun by former President Jayewardene in 1979.

The restructuring of the economy includes a major deregulation drive to free a number of state-owned corporations to the private sector. Trade liberalisation has reduced tariffs on manufactured items and eased exchange con-

trols making them more market-orientated. Steps to encourage foreign investment have led to the lifting of restrictions on foreign equity participation, which includes the abolition of the 100 percent tax levied on transfers of Sri Lankan company shares to foreigners.

These measures have borne fruit with the passage of time. Sri Lanka's growth rate which averaged at 2 percent a year for the years of upheaval, 1987 to 1989, climbed back to a commendable 6.2 percent in 1990. Inflation

The Independence Memorial Hall in Colombo – a monument to Sri Lanka's struggle for independence.

which averaged 20 percent in 1990, was on the way down by the beginning of the new year.

Despite continued fighting between Tamil militant groups and government forces, foreign investors are flocking to the Sri Lanka stock market, driving share prices to dizzying heights. In 1990, the All Shares Index leaped more than 50 percent to record heights. Trading volume has also sky-rocketed from an average US$80,000 per day, to US$1.8 million per day.

The government's economic program has been two-fold. Along with economic measures to liberalise the economy and encourage investment, an equally important feature has been the Janasaviya poverty-alleviation program, launched on the personal initative of President Premadasa.

The Janasaviya Program is a response to a range of problems such as rural poverty, unemployment, landlessness, and income disparity. These problems have been identified as the major reasons for the southern rebellion, which received significant support from dissatisfied youth with high educational achievements but few job prospects in an economy battered by years of civil strife.

The Janasaviya Program aims to help the rural poor to raise their income by acquiring skills in productive employment. Carried over a period of two years, the program envisages offering a monthly allowance of Rs. 2,500 (about US$75) per family to the poorest section of the population – about 7 million. Part of the funds will be invested on behalf of the families and returned to them at the end of two years to be used to set up self-employment projects for which they would have received training. The program has received considerable funding from the World Bank, which now recognises the need for specifically targetted poverty-alleviation programs in developing countries.

The revival of the tourist industry by leaps and bounds since 1989, is indicative of the degree of normalcy which has returned to Sri Lanka. Tourists continue to pour in thereby aiding the island's economic miracle.

Even though the Separatist problem persists, and continues to bedevil the north and east, and despite bleak prospects for a quick resolution of the conflict, peace reigns elsewhere in Sri Lanka. Hopes abound in the hearts and minds of the Sri Lankans - optimists by nature - that they will once again be able to live in the peace and harmony of a united and democratic Sri Lanka.

SOCIETY AND RELIGION

At the sacred shrine of Kataragama on Sri Lanka's southeast frontier, and at the pinnacle of Adam's Peak on the brink of the wild Hill Country, thousands upon thousands of pilgrims gather to pay homage to their lords and gods. They are Sinhalese, Tamil, Moor and Burgher; Buddhist, Hindu, Muslim and Christian. Racial and religious distinctions play little or no part in their attendance, except in the nuances of individual worship.

This dramatic mingling of the isle's various groups, sharing a common physical space in worship, exemplifies the ethnic mix of Sri Lanka. Racially, it is a melting pot. Culturally, it is a mosaic. Each of the groups persists in a unique complex of belief, custom, rite and ritual that regulates individual life and social behavior.

Although an individual will readily identify himself as belonging to a specific group, this is primarily a proud statement of membership in a culture, not a claim to racial superiority.

There is no doubt that the names of members of the different ethnic groups signify some degree of racial uniqueness. Tamils, for example, are of Dravidian origin, while Moors have Arabian ancestry. Certain physiological features may further support claims to racial differences. Yet the overriding fact remains that in the course of the island's history, there has been such a high degree of intermixing and blending of physical characteristics that it is hardly possible to distinguish a member of one ethnic group from another purely by physical appearance.

Sir Lanka is not the only country which hosts a variety of socially and culturally distinct racial groups. Perhaps what is special in the Sri Lankan case is that so much cultural diversity is found within the confines of a geographically small nation.

Just as a wide variety of natural species compete and thrive in separate ecological niches in a piece of tropical jungle, so do the many social species in Sri Lanka coexist within a common socio-political habitat. Cultural traits and practices define the niche of each group. At the same time, other shared traits enable all the different groups to mix and mesh.

Tensions and conflicts are bound to occur when distinct ethnic groups, occupying a small and limited physical territory, compete for survival and dominance. Sites like Kataragama, with its sacred "theater," allow for the cathartic removal of some of these tensions. The religiously motivated dance of the *kavadi* and the walk across the sacred fire can suspend smoldering conflict.

The nature of ancestral identity and consciousness in Sir Lanka is extremely complex. Religious and ritual idioms are far more productive than political or constitutional mechanisms in promoting ethnic harmony. For ethnicity is not merely an ideological phenomenon in Sir Lanka: it is a deeply emotional one.

Preceding pages: muralist Donald Friend's impression of Sri Lanka's people. **Left**, a Hill Country man on *poya* day.

If legend is fact, then the Sinhalese people are descended from a lion (*sinha*) whose blood (*le*) still courses through their veins.

Mahavamsa chroniclers date the beginning of island history to the arrival of a North Indian prince named Vijaya, the grandson of an ancestral lion. (Tradition suggests that his father, a minor king named Sinhabahu, had been raised by a lioness.) Vijaya landed almost by accident in the area of modern-day Mannar and called the new-found territory "Tambapanni," after its copper-colored sand. The time of his arrival was, not coincidentally, said to be the precise moment that the Buddha took his last breath on earth at Kusirara in India and entered *parinibbana*.

According to the *Mahavamsa*, an enchantress named Kuveni, a member of a tribe called the *yaksas*, tempted Vijaya's followers into captivity. But the hero, protected by a charmed thread, could not be seduced, even when Kuveni appeared to him as a dark princess with long flowing hair. Vijaya seized Kuveni's tresses and threatened to cut off her head unless she released his bewitched companions.

The demoness agreed, and furthermore offered to help Vijaya slay and cast out her own kin on the condition that he made her his queen. Together, the odd couple achieved mastery over the land. But after a few years, Vijaya grew tired of his *yaksa* queen and banished her to the forest, where she was stoned to death by her surviving tribespeople.

Historical research confirms that the original Indo-Aryan settlers came from North India to the island of Sri Lanka, where they mingled with the indigenous races (*yaksas* and *nagas*) and introduced their Prakrit language, which over the course of several centuries evolved into Sinhala.

After his betrayal of Kuveni, Vijaya brought a new queen from Madura, thereby beginning a tradition of importing royal wives from India – as well as art, architecture, the caste system, and the Buddhist religion.

The Arrival of Buddhism: Buddhism of the Theravada school is still the primary influence in the lives of the overwhelming majority of the Sinhalese people. The Sinhalese race comprises 74 percent of the population of Sri Lanka, or about 11 million people; 69 percent of the population, more than 10 million persons, consider their faith to be Buddhism. In every part of the island except the Northern Province and the northeastern coast – comprising the least fertile sixth of the country – Sinhalese and Buddhists are predominant.

Though the terms are not necessarily synonymous (numerous Sinhalese have converted to Catholicism and Protestantism, and certain others have opted for Hinduism or Islam), Buddhist ethics and traditional lifestyles have left a lasting impression.

The timing of Vijaya's landing on "Tambapanni," coinciding as it did (according to the chronicles) with the Buddha's death, is said to have given special significance to Sri Lanka's historical role as a protector of the faith. During the Buddha's lifetime, in fact, he is said to have transported himself to Sri Lanka on at least three separate occasions to visit the holy places of Mahiyangana, Nagadipa and Kelaniya. Some say he left his footprint atop Sri Pada, Adam's Peak. But it was not until 236 years after Vijaya's landing, in 250 B.C., that Buddhism became entrenched in Sinhalese culture.

It was during the reign of King Devanampiyatissa at Anuradhapura that the great Indian Emperor Asoka, the champion of Buddhism, sent his own son Mahinda to Sri Lanka to convert the island and its ruler.

As the story goes, Devanampiyatissa was on a deer-hunting trip in the rugged hills of Mihintale, eight miles east of Anuradhapura, when he spotted a majestic *sambhur* browsing in a thicket. The king pursued the animal up a mountain – where, instead of the elk, he encountered a *thera*, a sage, who called him by name.

Mahinda introduced himself to the king with a riddle:

"What name does this tree bear, O King?

"This tree is called a mango."

"Is there yet another mango besides this?"

"There are many mango trees."

"And are there yet other trees besides this mango and the other mangoes?"

"There are many trees, sir; but those are trees that are not mangoes."

Left, a woman at work in a paddy field.

"And are there, besides the other mangoes and those trees which are not mangoes, yet other trees?"

"There is this mango tree, sir."

"Thou hast a shrewd wit, O King," assured Mahinda.

Thus satisfied, he preached the Buddhist Dharma to King Devanampiyatissa. He accompanied the king back to Anuradhapura, and remained in Sir Lanka for 48 years, during which time the Buddhist religion became thoroughly inculcated in Sinhalese thought.

"Buddha" is a title which means "Enlightened One." The historical Buddha, Siddhartha Gautama, lived in the 5th and 6th centuries B.C. in the area of what is today northern India

and southern Nepal. A minor prince, he abandoned the palace life at the age of 29 to search for an end to man's suffering. After five years as a wandering ascetic, he began to meditate under a ficus tree near Benares. It was here that he discovered the ancient "Middle Way," rejecting extemes of pleasure and pain, and became enlightened.

The Buddha's Doctrine: Gautama preached a doctrine based on the "Four Noble Truths" and the "Eightfold Path." We suffer, he said, because of our attachment to people and things in a world where nothing is permanent. We can rid ourselves of desire, and do away with suffering, by living with attention to wisdom (right

views and right intent), morality (right speech, conduct and livelihood) and mental discipline (right effort, mindfulness and meditation).

The Buddha disavowed the existence of a soul, pointing out that one's essence is forever changing. We are trapped in the endless, illusory cycle of *samsara*, or rebirth, by our *karma*, the chain of cause and effect equal to our good and evil deeds, he said. The way out is faithful adherence to the Dharma, the Buddhist doctrine. In this way, one can put an end to the effects of *karma*, thereby escaping *samsara* and achieving *nibbana*, which is essentially extinction of "self" and cessation of desire. It is not heaven, nor is it annihilation. It is a quality of existence.

In the centuries following the Buddha's life, many doctrinal disputes arose, leading to various schisms in the philosophy. Most important was the break between the Theravada school, which today predominates in Sir Lanka and Southeast Asia, and the Mahayana school, which spread north and east from India.

Theravada is a more orthodox form of Buddhism, adhering strictly to the original Pali scriptures. There is no all-powerful god in Theravada Buddhism; in contrast to Mahayana beliefs, even the Buddha himself cannot be invoked to intervene benevolently in one's life. It is up to the individual to work out his own salvation. And it is through service to other beings that the individual enhances his own status.

The Sacred Bo Tree And the Tooth Relic: Two very important events in ancient Sri Lankan history had long-reaching effects on island Buddhism and worship patterns, persisting even today.

The first occurred during the residence of Mahinda at Anuradhapura. The sage's father, Emperor Asoka, took a cutting of the sacred *bo* tree under which the Buddha had attained enlightenment and sent it to Sri Lanka as a token of The Enlightened One for the newly converted Buddhists. He planted the sapling in a golden vessel; put it in the care of his daughter (Mahinda's sister), the nun Sanghamitta; and had it transported by ship to the island. It was received with great ceremony by the people of Anuradhapura. King Devanampiyatissa himself saw to the replanting of the tree in his

Sinhalese, like all people, can be activist or pacifist. Left, one of the nation's well-trained servicemen. Right, the serenity of monkhood.

garden, where it remains today – one of the most sacred objects of veneration for millions of Buddhists. As the original *bo* tree no longer stands, this documented cutting is regarded as the most holy of holy trees.

Some five centuries later, early in the 4th Century A.D., another great treasure arrived in Sri Lanka. This was the Buddha's left eyetooth. It was revered that, in subsequent centuries, wars were fought for its possession. Along with a sacred alms bowl that had belonged to the Buddha, obtained during the reign of Devanampiyatissa, the Tooth Relic has come to symbolize the very strength and independence of the Sinhalese nation.

From earliest times to present, the tooth has been enshrined in golden caskets in the capital's Temple of the Tooth, the Dalada Maligawa. Today, it is in Kandy. Replicas of Sacred Buddha Relics are paraded around the city for two weeks every August in the great Esala Perahera festival.

At that time of the Buddha's *parinibbana*, his physical remains were divided among Buddhist faithful throughout South Asia. The tooth had been in the custody of the Kalinga Kings of India for many centuries. When his throne was threatened by a non-Buddhist dynasty, King Guhasiva entrusted the Tooth Relic to his daughter Hemamala, with the instructions that, should he be defeated in battle, she and her husband Dantakumara should carry it to safety in Sri Lanka, where King Sirimeghavanna was on the throne. Thus when Guhasiva's worst fears were realized, Hemamala escaped with the Tooth Relic, concealing it in her hair as she and Dantakumara disguised themselves as religious pilgrims.

Sirimeghavanna received the relic with profound reverence, and housed it initially within the precincts of his royal palace until a suitable new temple could be built.

The history of Buddhism in Sri Lanka is a long and complicated one with many peaks and valleys. At the Aluvihara cave temple, near Matale (north of Kandy), the sacred scriptures, the *Tipitaka*, were first committed to *ola* (palm leaf) tablets about 2,000 years ago. In the 5th Century A.D., the great monk Buddhaghosa Thera came to Sri Lanka from India and compiled the voluminous Pali commentaries that

Everyone likes sweets, Sinhalese shopkeeper in Kandy must meet the demand for *rasakevili*, a rich and sticky sweetmeat.

firmly established Sri Lanka as the home of Theravada Buddhism.

Mahayana Buddhism had moments of predominance; its *bodhisattva* cult, which led to the worship of "Buddhas-to-be" as deities, was particularly prevalent during the period of Polonnaruwa's control of the island. The sexually explicit cult of Tantrism also was important at times.

But by the time the Burmese sent a 15th Century embassy to Sri Lanka to revive its Sangha, Theravada Buddhism had obviously regained its hold. It again suffered serious persecution under the Portuguese colonial rulers, but under the Kandyan rulers and (later) the British, and with a little help from the Sangha in Siam, Theravada recuperated to again become the strongest religion in the land – albeit with mildly Christian touches, such as the creation of the non-sectarian Young Men's Buddhist Association.

The Importance of Caste: The exchanges between ancient Sri Lanka and India brought more than Buddhism to the island nation. They brought the traditional caste system as well. Despite the interdictions of Buddhism, not to mention the later effects of Westernization and modernization, the Sinhalese caste system has persisted to occupy an important place in modern society.

In fact, there are 14 different castes in Sinhalese society; these can determine an individual's ritual status, marriage choices, and to a certain extent his occupational options. To further complicate matters, the Sinhalese generally divide themselves into up-country (Kandyan) and low-country branches, a legacy of centuries when the Portugese and Dutch controlled the coastal areas while the Kandyans clung tenaciously to the hills.

Ironically, the caste divisions are most obvious to the visitor in the place he would least expect to find them: in the Buddhist Sangha, the order of monks.

There are three *nikayas*, or sects, in modern Sri Lankan Buddhism. They differ little or not at all in doctrine, but emphasize their caste differences in ritual subleties and by the way their wear their saffron robes.

The Siyam Nikaya, generally regarded as the "upper-caste" sect, came into being in the mid-18th Century when the Kandyan kings were forced to send to Ayuthaya in Siam for monks to ordain new members of the Sinhalese Sangha. The new order formed into two chapters, the

Asgiriya and Malwatta, both of which have their head monasteries in Kandy today. Royal decree restricted ordination to members of the two highest Sinhalese castes.

In response to this discriminatory attitude, the Amarapura Nikaya was established in 1803 by a lower-caste Sinhalese who obtained his ordination at the Burmese capital of Amarapura and returned to his native Sri Lanka. People of all castes are admitted.

The Ramanya Nikaya was founded in 1835 by a dissident monk who considered the other two sects too materialistic. Lay members do not recognize monks of the other two *nikayas*; and though this sect is small, it wields considerable influence.

Look for the different ways in which members of the various *nikayas* dress. Siyam *bhikkus* cover only one shoulder with their robes, and carry umbrellas. Amarapura sect members also carry umbrellas, but their robes cover both shoulders. The Ramanya monks cover both shoulders with their robes, but opt for traditional palm-leaf shades instead of umbrellas.

Observing *Poya* Days: The Buddha himself cannot properly be worshipped in Theravada Buddhism; he is regarded as an enlightened man, not as a deity. But every *pansala* (temple) has certain objects of worship designed to remind the Buddhist devotee of the Dharma. In order of importance, these are the *dagoba*, which preserves relics of the Buddha's corporeal body or of his personal use; the *bo* tree, of which many temples now have cuttings from the Maha Bodhi in Anuradhapura; and images of the Buddha himself, usually in stone, metal or wood, housed in a *vihara* or image house.

The average Sri Lanka Buddhist visits the *pansala* four times a month on *poya* days, which equate to the phases of the moon. The full-moon day, always a national holiday, is most important. A tray of flowers is offered at each of the three places of worship; small oil lamps are lit (to represent wisdom and enlightenment), and incense is burned (to symbolize purity).

Worship is strictly individual. With the assistance of a *bhikku*, a Buddhist might pledge the Five Precepts (no killing, stealing, lying, sexual misconduct or drinking of intoxicating liquors) that all devout Buddhists are expected to follow. On *poya* days, the lay Buddhist is expected to further vow the Eight Precepts, which require that he abstain from eating after noon, sitting on comfortable seats, or witness-

ing music and dance ("pleasures of the senses"). Two more precepts are added for all monks: abstention from wearing beautifying adornments or from touching money of any kind, cash or coin.

Poya day ceremonies are conducted from dawn until dusk at all temples. This includes Dharma sermons, meditation classes, *pujas* (offerings), administration of the precepts, and *pirit*-chanting of protective *suttas* (discourses). In particular, listening to sermons on the various aspects of the Dharma is considered to be one of the most meritorious activities in which a Buddhist might involve himself.

Earning Merit: Merit-making (*punya karma*) is considered to be the cornerstone of lay Bud-

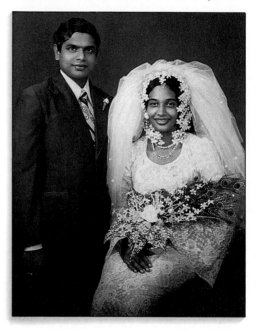

dhism. By following the Dharma and the precepts, by striving for compassion, equanimity and wisdom, and by performing meritorious deeds, one can assure himself a more advanced rebirth on the spiritual ladder toward *nibbana*.

Dana, or almsgiving, is the most visible of merit-making activities. The greater the gifts one gives to members of the Sangha, and the purer and more intense the thought with which they are given, the greater is the merit earned. *Bhikkus* traditionally make their livelihoods by door-to-door begging for their morning meals, so householders have frequent opportunities to gain merit in this regard. *Dana* is also offered in the form of inviting a group of monks to a meal at a family home; this occasion often coincides with an important lay family observance, such as the anniversary of an elder's death.

In addition to *dana*, *sila* (general morality) and *bhavana* (meditation) are high on the list of meritorious action. Of perhaps greatest importance is preaching or hearing the Dharma. Giving or sharing merit, carrying out religious obligations (such as pilgrimage and worship), and paying homage to elders are all considered merit-making deeds.

Devas and Devalas: But the pattern of worship in orthodox Sri Lankan Buddhism has been heavily influenced by animistic cults, Indian Hinduism and Mahayana sects. This is

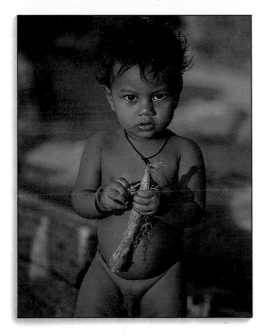

perhaps most obvious in the presence of images of gods as an adjunct to Buddhist objects of devotion.

Buddhism has always been a tremendously accommodating faith. The Buddha himself never forbade the worship of deities; he merely said they provided no release from human suffering. In times of personal crisis, it is not unusual for man to seek help from supernatural deities. Over the centuries, a pantheon of gods and Mahayana *bodhisattvas* grew into the

Left, a Sinhalese wedding portrait, complete with a peacock-feather bouquet. **Right**, the by-product of a similar union in Negombo.

system of Buddhism in Sri Lanka. Today, Sinhalese as well as other Sri Lankans find themselves supplicating non-Buddhist deities at times of drought, flood, family crises ... even crucial school exams!

In the courtyard of nearly every *vihara* is a *devala* (shrine) dedicated to one or more of these deities. Priests called *kapuralas* conduct rites at these shrines and offer prayers on behalf of worshippers. The best known *devalas* are those at Kataragama and at Kandy; the most popular deities are Vishnu, Kataragama, Pattini and Natha.

Natha is a Mahayana deity; according to tradition, he is the Buddha-to-be, Maitreya. As a *bodhisattva*, it is his function to survey the world with great compassion, helping those who qualify to achieve *nibbana*, until his term as Buddha arrives some 2,500 years from now.

Vishnu, the Hindu "preserver," is regarded as the protector of the Buddhist religion on the island of Sri Lanka. Kataragama, known to Hindus as the war god Skanda, is popular because of the great power he is reputed to have. Pattini is venerated as the goddess of chastity and health.

There are also guardian deities, animistic deities (such as Sakra, king of the gods), regional deities (including Saman, whose abode is said to be atop Sri Pada, Adam's Peak), and others.

And there are magico-religious cults, subscribed to by nearly all Sinhalese who does not consult an astrologer before making an important decision. If a horoscope reveals a particularly troubling element, an offering is made to appease the appropriate gods; some Sinhalese go to the extreme of having a *bali* (sacrifical ritual) performed to propitiate planetary deities and thus to avert evil.

Belief in the existence of demons have resulted in the set of ceremonies known as "devil dancing" to control these malevolent spirits. And the wearing of amulets and charms is considered essential to ward off any black magic to which one might be unknowingly subjected.

Common Denominators: Buddhism and religious belief bind together the vast majority of Sinhalese. But there are other common denominators which override all social differences, not to mention political and economic disparities.

Perhaps the foremost of these factors is the lion ancestor itself. The notion of common ancestry, however dimmed by legend it may be, has given the Sinhalese the conviction that they are a branch of the Aryan stock.

Names are another commonality, as Sinhalese names like Jayewardene, Bandaranaike and Senanayake are quite distinct from Tamil or Muslim names – even though many Sinhalese adopted last names like Silva, Fernando and Perera during the era of Portuguese Christianization.

Thirdly, the use of Sinhalese as the nation's official language has increased the distance of the Sinhalese from the Tamil race, although the current government has reaffirmed Tamil, in addition to English, as a national language. Sinhala is derived from the ancient Prakrit tongue of India. It is a language of the common people, unlike the aristocratic Sanskrit language. The Buddha preached his doctrine in Pali, a Prakrit dialect related to Sinhala.

Old Sinhala developed in isolation among all classes of Sinhalese society through the Anuradhapura period of history. During the subsequent Polonnaruwa period, distinctions began to emerge between a Sanskritized court Sinhala, common Sinhala and Pali, the sacred language of Buddhism. But a 14th and 15th Century movement against class differentiation resulted in the translation of Pali *Jataka* stories into common Sinhala and a flowering of Sinhala folk literature. Sanskritized Sinhala made a comeback in the early British colonial period, but as the nationalist movement flourished, so did use of the common Sinhala tongue at most levels of society. Today, it is only among highly educated urbanites, whose home language is English, that Sinhala is not the most understood Sinhalese language.

While urban Sinhalese have largely adopted Western fashions, except perhaps in the comfort of their own homes, dress is an external sign of cultural pride among rural Sinhalese. The ubiquitous *sarama* (sarong) worn by the Sinhalese male is probably of Southeast Asian origin; it is extremely practical for the hot and humid climes of the Sri Lanka lowlands.

The so-called "national dress" – consisting of a white cloth draped from the waist down to the ankles, and a long-sleeved whit Nehru-style shirt – is in fact a slight modification of the traditional dress of Indian males. It was a by-product of Sinhalese nationalism of the late 1950s, championed by the late Prime Minister S.W.R.D. Bandaranaike and later taken up by all Sinhalese politicians, including former President J.R. Jayewardene and present President R. Premadasa. Although still favored as the sartorial symbol of political elites, the masses appear to show an uninhibited dislike for the costume. This is reflected occasionally in newspaper advertisements for marriage partners: one of the frequent specifications for potential bridegrooms is that they wear "the European dress."

In matters of clothing, the Sinhalese female has been more traditional than the male. The typical rural woman wears a wrap-around cloth and jacket at home and at the market, although their 18th Century counterparts are reputed to have gone "topless." The urban Sinhalese woman prefers skirt and blouse for informal wear, and a sari in public. Modern Sinhalese women are highly fashion-conscious, and latest European fashions have a receptive market, especially in Colombo. But in ritual matters, particularly those connected with marriage or funerals, the traditionalism of the Sinhalese female dies hard. The nearly universal preference is for a sari, although the male may be wearing European dress for the same occasion.

Food plays a pivotal role in Sinhalese social life, even deciding the destiny of governments. Politicians, being keenly aware of this fact, give it due place and prominence at election time. What observers refer to as "rice politics" is in fact an outgrowth of the importance of this dietary element among the Sinhalese people.

No day is complete without a meal of rice. What's more, rice is an essential ingredient for treating guests at weddings, for *dana*, and after funerals. Rice cooked with coconut milk is an indispensable item at Sinhalese New Year ceremonies, and is offered to the gods. Among Sinhalese Buddhists, a sampling of the food cooked for the noon meal (excluding fish or meat curries, anathema to orthodox Buddhists) is offered to the Buddha by the housewife.

A description of the Sinhalese would not be complete without some mention of their weakness for the hospitality they warmly extend to friends, relatives, and even to total strangers. A Sinhalese would go out of his way to open his doors to a guest and treat the visitor to the best meal he could afford. The warm reception is a cultural value with intimate ties to the Buddhist ideology of compassion and charity.

A Sinhalese woman of Kandyan ("up-country") heritage. Many younger women today are very conscious of Western fashion.

Tamils comprise about 19 percent, or a little less than three million, of Sri Lankan's population. Two-thirds of these are Sri Lanka Tamils (also known as Jaffna Tamils) whose roots in the island date back nearly 2,000 years. The remaining six percent are Indian Tamils who came from the South Asian motherland only in recent centuries. This distinction is important. It denotes not only comparative length of resident, but also consequent socio-cultural disparities.

While the Tamil language, the Hindu religion, and specific customs and traditions are predominant among both groups, Sri Lanka Tamils pride themselves on the fact that they are descendants of South Indian invaders of the Pandya, Chola and Pallava kingdoms of the 2nd and 3rd centuries A.D.

By contrast, Indian Tamils arrived in Sri Lanka as hired laborers to toil in the tea plantations of the British *raj* in the 19th and early 20th centuries. A majority of them today still reside on tea estates in the Hill Country. They are drawn from poorer regions and lower castes of South India, and thus are considered culturally and politically inferior to their long-established brethren. Even in their religious activities, Hinduism as practiced by Indian Tamils is generally more devotionalistic, including firewalking and other painful-looking forms of penance.

The Jaffna Tamils: Jaffna, the bustling metropolis of the Northern Province, has always been the main center of Tamil culture in Sri Lanka. At various historical junctures in the distant past, Tamil kingdoms occupied sizeable chunks of Sri Lankan real estate; but on every occasion, resourceful Sinhalese kings pushed them back to the lands their descendants currently occupy. Today, a significant number of more militant Tamils have begun to be of more militant Tamils have begun to make demands for an independent state, to be known as Eelaam.

Were this new political entity ever to come about, it would occupy one of the least hospitable regions of the entire island: the Northern Province and upper East Coast. Reddish-brown soil and scrub jungle fade into arid, sandy, flat wastes as one proceeds north through Vavuniya toward Jaffna. Clumps of palmyrah trees are the only living entities to break the monotony.

Yet it is this virtual desert that has shaped the character of the Sri Lanka Tamil. Over the centuries, he has acquired the values and attitudes necessary to survive in a hostile environment. The industriousness of the Jaffna farmer, and the thrift and acumen of the Jaffna trader, are proverbial in Sri Lanka.

The farmer is inevitably found watering his garden plot of vegetables, chilies or tobacco before the sun has climbed high enough to begin its scorching spree. He draws the water from deep wells sunk into the soil by his own hand. His children assist him, getting their first lesson of the day on the harshness of life and the need to temper it with hard work.

Although school is second on the list of daily priorities, Tamil children are continually bombarded with the message that a sound education is essential to their future. This parental policy has resulted in the creation of a Tamil intelligentsia whose numbers outweigh their minority status. In legal, medical, academic and

Left, Tamil girls in their ceremonial best sit on a wall to watch Jaffna's Nallur temple festival, **right**, their southern counterparts drape brightly colored saris at Kataragama, above.

administrative fields, Tamils today are nearly on an even keel with the Sinhalese.

The political unity of the Sri Lanka Tamils does not obscure the many social disparities among them, many of which are premised on the notion of hierarchy. For instance, Jaffna Tamils consider themselves superior by birth and culture to Tamils from other regional centers like Mannar, Vavuniya or Batticaloa. The Tamils of Jaffna maintain that they have maintained their racial "purity," which Tamils of outlying areas have lost through intermarriage. (This is especially the case in Batticaloa, where Tamil-Muslim marriages are common.)

Among the Jaffna Tamils in particular, there are rigid caste divisions. The strictly vegetar-

visitors to Jaffna, who are always surprised by the number of churches in a supposedly Hindu stronghold.

But just as Sinhalese Christians are influenced by Buddhist ethics, so are Tamil Christians affected by their Hindu heritage.

Fundamentals of Hinduism: The source of all religious knowledge is generally considered by Hindus to be the *Vedas*, a collection of more than 1,000 hymns written down about 1700 B.C. by the first Aryan invaders in North India. These hymns defined a polytheistic religion which became known as Brahminism. All men were linked to a god-creator named Brahma. It was said that the priest caste came from his mouth, the warrior caste from his arms, the

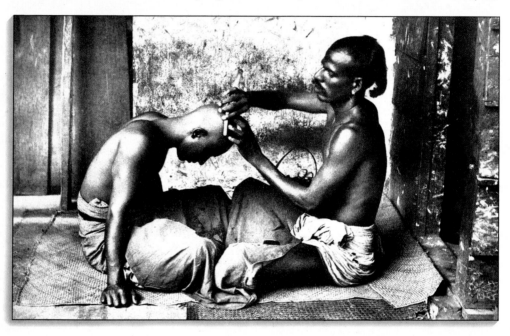

ian *brahmans*, inheritors of priestly knowledge, are regarded as the purest and highest. Next come the *vellala* or farming caste; then craftsmen like goldsmiths, blacksmiths and carpenters. Any of these people have the privilege of entering Hindu temples to supplicate the gods. But inferior castes, including fishermen, toddytappers, barbers and drum-beaters, cannot sit at the same level or dine at the same table as higher-caste Tamils.

Caste differences are further complicated by religious preferences. Perhaps as many as 20 percent of all Tamils in Sri Lanka have embraced the Christian religion, especially Roman Catholicism. This is evident to first-time

artisans and traders from his thighs, and the serfs and low-caste masses from his feet.

As Brahminism evolved into modern Hinduism, people of the subcontinent began to feel increasingly that existence and reality were subjects too vast to be encompassed within a single set of beliefs. The Hindu religion of today, therefore, comprises many different metaphysical systems and view points, some of them mutually contradictory. The individual opts for whichever belief or practice suits him

A Tamil barber shaves another head in this turn-of-the-20th Century photography. Note the cloth used to catch the shorn hair.

and his particular inclinations the best.

Hinduism has no formal creed, no universal governing organization. Brahmin priests serve as spiritual advisers to upper-caste families. But more important is that the individual comply with his family and social group. Obedience to the gods' laws and placation through ritual are a part of every Hindu's daily routine. Each individual partakes in the divine in his personal way. For the common folk, this often involves a matter-of-fact repetition of gestures. But it is part of an all-prevading religiosity.

A majority of Sri Lanka Hindus are Shaivites. That is, they regard the god Shiva as supreme. Shiva is "the destroyer" in the classic Hindu trinity, along with Brahma "the creator" and Vishnu "the preserver." Those who worship Shiva do so not because they love destruction. They recognize that all things must sooner or later come to an end, and from that end will come a new beginning. Shiva is intent on destroying everything, including ignorance. His devotees respect the lack of permanence in life.

"Shiva is happiness and goodness," explains Pandit Markandu Swamikul, a brahmin priest in Jaffna. "In other words, he is wholeness. All is one, all is Shiva. He is smaller than small and bigger than big."

Devotional Practices: The most visible form of Hindu devotion is the *tikka*, the "divine eye." A mixture of sandalwood paste or holy ash is applied to one's forehead, above and between the eyes, as a symbol of sacred presence to help in the search for god.

Puja, ritual offerings, are presented to Shiva and other gods of the pantheon in a variety of forms. Hindus believe that all existence is comprised of five elements: earth, water, fire, wind and *akasha* (ether). Offerings should symbolize each of these elements. "Earth" *puja* may be sandalwood paste, holy ash, incense (in sticks), coconut, or fruits – especially in a fruit salad known as *panchama*, containing five kinds of fruit. "Water" *puja* can be well water, perfumed water, coconut water or milk. "Fire" offerings can be of several kinds; the lighting of oil temple lamps is most normal. Smoke, especially from incense, represents "wind," as do fanning and animal hair. During dawn and dusk *puja* hours at Hindu temples, all four of these offerings will be presented to the accompaniment of drum-beating, bugle-blowing, bell-ringing and the chanting of *Vedas* – sacred sounds said to equate with *akasha*.

Milk is one of the most common forms of *puja*. Temple visitors will frequently be offered warm milk with which the image of a deity has been annointed; this is regarded as particularly auspicious, a medicine of sorts.

When *puja* is administered in private homes, it is done for the family or the self. When performed in a temple, it is for "the world's sake." It takes on special meaning at pilgrimage sites like Kataragama.

Temples and Deities: The *devala* (shrine) or *kovil* (a smaller temple without a resident deity) is organized in such a manner as to resemble the human body. The most visible part of the temple, the multi-tiered Pandyan *gopuram* with its carved and colorful figures at the entrance to the temple, is symbolic of the feet. The temple's main image is installed in the *garbhagrha*, or "head," while offerings are made in the *sthapana mandapam*, thought of as the "stomach."

The full pantheon of gods are worshipped here. Key among them are Shiva's wife, Parvati (Uma), and his two sons, Skanda (Murugan) and Ganesha. Hindus beseech Parvati for fertility and abundance; Skanda (the chief deity of the Kataragama shrine) for the tremendous power and compassion afforded him by his six faces and 12 arms; and Ganesha, the elephant-headed god, for success in intellectual pursuits. It is Ganesha's reponsibility to decide between success and failure, to remove obstacles or to create them as necessary.

Pattini is the very popular goddess of health and chastity. In legend, she is the ideal wife – steadfast, patient and forgiving. Another goddess, Kali, is propitiated by those seeking success on dangerous or risky ventures. In dry farming districts, the deity Aiyanar, who safeguards agriculture and presides over forests, tanks and fields, is of special importance.

And Vishnu, of course, remains a significant deity; there is a sizeable cult of Vaishnavites in Sri Lanka. It is Vishnu's duty to assure the preservation of life and of the world. Vishnu is also called Upulvan, and is identifiable by his blue-lotus skin color. He is traditionally considered to have visited earth in 10 different incarnations – among them as the prince Rama, hero of the classic *Ramayana* epic; the Gautama Buddha, who is said to have corrupted the demons; and as the ever-popular Krishna, central figure of the *Bhagavad-Gita* scripture.

In the *Bhagavad-Gita*, Krishna appears as a charioteer for the warrior Arjuna, who meets an opposing army manned by his friends and relatives. Arjuna is reluctant to strike until convinced by Krishna that he must be true to his own role in life; he goes on to battle and exterminates the well-known opposition.

The idea of "new beginnings," manifested in the doctrine of reincarnation, is what keeps the Hindu caste system strong. Hindus believe they must accept and act according to their station in life, no matter what it may be. Their birthright is a reward or punishment for actions, *karma*, accrued in a previous life. Their behavior in this life will help determine their next one.

Life-cycle Ceremonies: Westernization has had a definite effect upon the life of Sri Lanka Tamils. The absorption of customs, dress, tastes, attitudes not to mention use of the English

language, have brought about major changes in the world views of urban Tamils in particular.

The rural Tamil, however, is generally a strict adherent to tradition. When a Tamil girl comes of age, for example, she is kept in seclusion for at least 16 days in a private hut made of freshly cut coconut leaves. When she is taken out of seclusion, she must immediately undergo a ritual bath, performed first by a washer-woman, then by married women who are close kin. After this, she fed a strict diet of raw eggs, sesame oil, and *pittu* - a steamed breakfast food made from millet or rice flour. (The Sinhalese have a similar ceremony; they feed the girl a spice soup during her seclusion.)

Tamil marriages are consecrated at a Hindu temple. The highlight of a ceremony is the tying of the *thali*, a gold necklace containing a medallion on which are inscribed figures of a conch, a trident and a ring - symbols of the Hindu trinity. Marriage is an event of far-reaching importance, for during the ceremony, the bride becomes the symbolic goddess of the household, and the groom her god.

Ideally, the household is the unquestioned domain of the Tamil wife. She rises before her husband in the morning, and by the time he awakes, has already gone through her morning ablutions, lit the fire, worshipped the family deities, and prepared the morning meal. She does not eat until her husband has been served and treated to the best food. The wife is the last to eat and the last to go to sleep. But this tradition is changing in the face of urbanization, modernization and Westernization.

Tamil funerals vary according to whether the dead person is male of female, married or unmarried. If a married woman dies before her husband, she is considered fortunate and is believed to have gone to a "good place" in the afterlife. "She has gone with the wedding necklace on," the saying goes. A woman who dies after her husband, on the other hand, is regarded as quite unfortunate. In a sense, she has lost her "god," the source of all that gave her life meaning. At her husband's funeral, the widow dresses like a bride as the family barber cuts the gold marriage necklace she wears. After this, tradition says she can no longer wear gold jewelry or brightly colored saris; from this time forth, she must wear white and avoid public events. In modern Sri Lanka, this isn't often practiced.

In matters of dress, Tamil respect for traditional attire remains undiminished, though many Tamils wear European dress to work in urban centers. The traditional wear for men is the *verti*, a long length of cotton draped from the waist to the ankles, with a long-sleeved collarless shirt. The customary Jaffna sari for women is worn in a slightly different fashion than the Sinhalese sari: the end is kept long enough to be taken over the shoulder a second time, brought back tightly around the waist, and tucked to the back of the body.

Symbols of Hindu faith: left, Skanda, the god of Kataragama, sits with his wives astride his peacock, adorning a *gopuram*. Right, Skanda's ornate *vel* (trident) is an object of veneration.

Descended mainly from Arab traders who are believed to have settled in Sri Lanka as far back as the 8th Century A.D., Muslims constitute about seven percent of the island's population, or about one million persons. They are found throughout the country, especially along the southwest and east coasts and in urban areas.

The social landscape of a Sri Lankan town would not be complete without its community of Muslim families occupying a single street or quarter. They form a alliance with an intense feeling of community consciousness, which is symbolized by the mosque with its dominating minarets.

Though racially akin to the Sinhalese and Tamils – by virtue of the fact that the original Arab traders did not bring women with them and had to borrow wives from the native population – the Muslims nevertheless form a distinct ethnic group. The cultural gulf is chiefly attributable to the extreme orthodoxy of their monotheistic religious tradition.

The Ideology of Islam: Of all the major faiths alive and well on planet Earth, Islam is the one that has adhered most closely to the ideology of its founding fathers. The prophet Mohammed, an Arab of the 7th Century A.D., is believed to have been the instrument through which Allah (God) revealed his final truths. These truths were recorded in the Arabic language as the Koran.

Extremely conservative in nature, Islam emphatically prohibits any form of idolatry or magic such as is accepted by Sri Lankan Buddhists, Hindus and even Catholics. The moral precepts of the Koran and the hypnotic voice of the *muezzin* call the devout to prayer five times a day. Men and women are kept strictly separate at times of worship; any form of contact between the sexes is considered too much of a distraction to allow one to fully concentrate on his devotion and prayer.

In fact, the culture of Sri Lanka's Muslims is in many ways more akin to that of their religious brethren in the Middle East and North Africa than to their neighbors is Sri Lanka. Their festivals and their social lives, in general, are defined and regulated by Islamic law and culture. The celebration of the Prophet's Birthday, the month-long festival of Ramazan (during which household members must fast during daylight hours), and the observance of the Haji commemorating the flight of Mohammed from Medina to Mecca – the dates of which are based on the 354-day Islamic calendar – align Sri Lanka Muslims into a sense of brotherhood with other Islamic nations.

There are other factors which underscore the acute parochialism of Islam. There is a taboo on the eating of pork. A rite of circumcision is compulsory for all Muslim males at birth. Foremost, there is the universal Muslim thirst to make a *hajj*, a pilgrimage, to the holy city of Mecca at least once in life. Indeed, those who make the journey are forever after honored with the title *hajiar* before their names.

Sri Lanka Muslims are generally classified into two groups. Those descended from Arab traders are commonly known as Moors. There is also a significant community of Malays. For both groups, Arabic is the language of religious instruction and prayer. But the Moors speak the Tamil language for secular purposes, including education; while the Malays, especially predominant in the Hambantota area (where they are said to have landed in thousands of small boats), still employ their mother tongue.

Muslim food is generally much sweeter from the standard rice-and-curry fare of the Sinhalese and Tamils. What's more, the manner of consumption is radically different, especially at ritual or ceremonial occasions: males eat separately from females and sit in groups of three or more, sharing a single massive plate.

Men are emphatically the providers in a Muslim household. Women are normally restricted to home. When they do go out in public, women drape their saris over their heads and the lower part of their faces.

Yet cultural bridges, and social and economic ties, do cement the Muslim culture into the Sri Lanka ethnic mosaic. For example, the Tamil wedding custom of the *thali*, or sacred necklace, has been adopted by Sri Lankan Muslims. In addition, the majority of Muslims are engaged in trade and commerce, activities that force them to interact with people of other communities.

Muslim men young and old gather for conversation after morning prayers at the Jamiul-Alfar Mosque in Colombo's Pettah district.

THE BURGHERS

The Burghers constitute a tiny but visible fraction of the Sri Lankan population. Strictly speaking, they are the descendants of the Dutch colonialists who occupied the island between 1658 and 1796. But the term "Burgher" – Dutch for "town dweller" – is loosely employed in reference to any Sri Lankan descended from any European colonialist, including Portuguese and British.

Burghers themselves recognize differences in social status, depending on the relative purity of their biological descent – a recognition shared by the rest of the Sri Lankan population. Criteria for "ranking," apparently derived from Sinhalese caste ideology, include differences in skin color, physical stature and lifestyle. Those whose physical appearance and cultural preferences – food, dress, speech, education, residence and recreation – are closest to European are designated "upper class." Lower-class Burghers are paradoxically those who have more in common with the average Sinhalese or Tamil than their upper-class counterparts.

But by and large, Burghers as a community share more characteristics with one another than with other ethnic groups. Typically, they are found in and around urban centers, wear European clothes, and belong to the Christian faith. (Upper-class Burghers are most often Presbyterians.) Marriages tend to be within the Burgher community, although intermarriage with Sinhalese or Tamils is not uncommon. The primary social unit is the nuclear family.

A characteristic often attributed to the Burgher by members of other ethnic groups is his tendency to enjoy "the good life" without any thought to the morrow. This perception of the Burgher as a veritable hedonist with a love for wine and song, good clothes and parties, cannot be entirely true. It does not do justice to the sedate and industrious Burghers who have excelled in the fields of education, the judiciary and civil service in Sri Lanka. Today, many are active in the travel trade.

The current president of the community's Dutch Burgher Union of Ceylon is a Justice of the Supreme Court of Sri Lanka, Mr Percy Colin-Thome.

In spite of the obvious differences in physical appearance and cultural habits, Burghers have traditionally enjoyed a peaceful coexistence with the rest of the island's people. Nevertheless, the wave of Sinhalese nationalism which enveloped the island in the 1950s caught many Burghers unawares. The medium of education and administration was changed from English to the vernacular, and this posed a grave threat to the Burgher community. As long as English had been the *lingua franca*, the

Burghers – as well as other non-Sinhala speaking groups – had been well-integrated with the rest of the nation. The de-Westernization that followed left the Burghers essentially without a country.

The logical outcome was a mass exodus of Burghers to the Western world. Those Burghers who have remained in Sri Lanka have gradually assimilated themselves with the local culture and conditions. It is not uncommon today to come across a Burgher child being educated in the Sinhala language, or a Burgher girl clothed in a sari. To be sure, the late 20th Century Burgher of Sri Lanka is at a crossroads of culture.

Left, Jeff Beling is a leading educator and Biblical scholar in Colombo. **Above**, a member of the younger generation of Burghers.

THE VEDDHAS AND THE GYPSIES

Like most of the world's primitive tribal peoples, the Veddhas of Sri Lanka have come to face an ineluctable choice. Unless they assimilate into the mainstream of society and culture, they will vanish from the face of the earth.

In the course of the past half-century, most of the several thousand Veddhas still living in the island's most remote reaches have opted for the first alternative. Many have abandoned their traditional jungle *modus operandi* of hunting and gathering, and have taken up lives as farmers, living side-by-side with Sinhalese peasantry in the Central and Uva provinces around Mahiyangana and Bibile Similarly, a few hundred of them in the Eastern Province, near Gal Oya, have assimilated with the Tamil population of the area and have adopted Tamil ways and customs.

But some pockets of Veddha resistance to assimilation remain. Two notable ones are Dambana, a settlement about six miles (10 kilometers) from the town of Mahiyangana; and Nilgala, a mountain tipped with thick jungle in the eastern Uva Province.

Veddhas are generally thought to be the remnants of the *yaksa* and *naga* tribes of *Mahavamsa* times. Descended from a prehistoric hunting people dating to Neolithic times, they have racial affinities with Africa's Pygmies and Bushmen, the Australian Aborigines, and the Andamanese of the Bay of Bengal.

Cultural assimilation by the Sinhalese has been going on since the landing of Vijaya. Waves of Sinhalese settlers have whittled away at the Veddhas' forest home. With increasing population pressure, traditional hunting grounds have become prime targets for intrusive settlements, especially by *chena* cultivators.

Today, Veddha features are similar to those of many Sinhalese: short wavy hair, moderately long faces, and broad noses. The spoken language is also similar. There are marked dialectical differences, but the linguistic structure is the same.

The process of assimilation of the Veddha has been most noticeable in his choice of a livelihood. For the most part, he no longer lives by bow-and-arrow. Instead, he cultivates a small plot of jungle-fringe land by the *chena* method of farming. He subsists mainly off the produce of this plot, supplemented by occasional game and honey.

Many Veddhas have given up the worship of ancestral spirits and have embraced Buddhism. Still others have chosen to leave their traditional habitats entirely, and have obtained land in government agricultural settlement projects. Intermarriages with Sinhalese have intensified assimilation and have eroded the tribal social organization, based on matrilineal clans.

But no aboriginal population has successfully withstood the onslaught of an unfamiliar way of life from every conceivable front. The

Veddhas are no exception. A visitor to a modern Veddhas settlement cannot miss seeing the sad and apathetic faces of adults, the makeshift and overcrowded houses, and the look of fear on the faces of children. Not all the well-meant efforts of government welfare officers can possibly compensate for the loss of the old lifestyle and the dread of the unknown future.

The Veddhas is probably proudest when he puts on a "show" for curious carnival-goers. Dressed in his span cloth and in rags rolled up around his waist, carrying his longbow and arrow, with a short axe slung on his shoulder, he faces the "new" jungle of civilization.

A few Veddhas – notably those of Dambana,

haunt of the famed Veddhas chief Tissahami – have gone one step further. The aged Tissahami and his tribesmen not long ago visited president J.R. Jayewardene at his official residence in Colombo. Clad in his Veddha best, the chief urged that his people be allowed to remain in their ancestral lands and not be resettled to an agricultural scheme.

The Gypsies: Sri Lanka's gypsy population had its origin on the Indian subcontinent 2,000 or more years ago. According to ethnologist M.D. Raghavan, they fall into three major

categories – the Ahikuntakaya snake-charmers, the Maddiliya monkey-trainers, and the groups that specialize in tattooing.

Gypsies wander from one end of the island to the other in groups of 15 to 25 individuals, including women and children. Each band consists of several nuclear families living under the supreme authority of a single leader. Donkeys transport their meager belongings – palmyrah leaves to comprise their miniature domed lean tos, chickens, baskets and some

Left, today's Veddha hunter, though rarely seen, prefers a gun to the bow-and-arrow employed by his 17th Century forebears, right.

cooking implements. They set up camps on unoccupied land in villages, small towns or on the fringes of urban centers.

There, they concentrate on their various crafts and specialties. The Ahikuntakaya are known for their ability to snare snakes, especially cobras, and making them "dance" to the tunes of their flutes. In fact, the snakes are responding to the mesmeric movements of the gypsy's knee and flute rather than to the melancholic notes.

Other men practice the art of tattooing and train costumed monkeys to dance. Women make beads, hats and reed baskets, or go from door to door telling fortunes and reading palms. Gypsies are also known as expert hunters; they ferret out field rats or fish in small reservoirs in order to supplement their daily diets.

For a people who spend so much time wandering, the gypsies show a remarkable degree of social stability and disinclination to change. This may be due to their social isolation from the rest of Sri Lankan society. Indeed, they are viewed more as a tolerable nuisance rather than an economic necessity. It is a widely held conception among the Sri Lankan masses that gypsy hygiene is so lacking, should they stay in one location for more than seven days, the place will become infested with worms!

Gypsy social organization is extremely tight. The authority and charisma of the band leader is unquestioned. Furthermore, a tribal judicial system has been set up with its chief justice in Anuradhapura.

An annual corroboree is held in the month of November at a favored spot in the North Central Province. This yearly meeting, which draws members of the clan from throughout Sri Lanka, coincides with the Hindu Deepavali "festival of lights." Matters of common interest to all gypsies are discussed, vows are fulfilled, and plans are laid for each band's travel during the coming year. Decisions are made by band leaders in consultation with gypsy elders.

Despite their social isolation, gypsies revere the same gods as the Sinhalese and Tamils – Vishnu, Kataragama and Pattini. Marriages involve the *thali*, the sacred necklace of the Tamil. The custom of cross-cousin marriage, an ancient tradition among Sinhalese and Tamils, denotes a common cultural ancestry.

Few places on earth can offer such great variety in as compact an area as Sri Lanka. Smaller than Tasmania, this pear-shaped island nevertheless contains extremes of terrain from arid desert and jungle wilderness to frosty mountain peaks. In a single day, the visitor can travel from the ruins of millennia-old civilizations to luxury beach resorts. Or he can experience both the chaotic frenzy of swarming festivals and the serenity of traditional rural villages. Every point on the island can be reached from every other location within just a few hours by car or public transport. This means that even the short-term visitor can sample a true cross-section of Sri Lanka's bountiful beauties.

Most journeys begin in bustling metropolitan Colombo, the modern commercial center and maritime capital. Here there is shipping in the historic Fort and the Pettah bazaar. Here too are the fascinating National Museum, the famous Dehiwala Zoo, and the parliamentary complex at Kotte. The long South Coast, curving some 180 miles (290 kms) from Colombo to Yala, is famous for its numerous beach resorts – places like Bentota, Hikkaduwa and Koggala. It is also the location of the old Portuguese port of Galle (the "Tarshish" of the Bible?), and the frenetic pilgrimage site of Kataragama, sacred to all religions.

North of Colombo, the West Coast road progresses north through the resort town of Negombo, age-old fishing communities and coconut plantations to the great wildlife refuge of Wilpattu.

Sri Lanka's second city is Kandy, last capital of a classical, independent Sinhalese kingdom and still the home of traditional arts, music and culture. The incomparable Perahera celebration, featuring a procession of more than 100 elephants, is held every August. It is only 72 miles (115 kms) by road from Colombo. Kandy is in the foothills of the Hill Country. It is an uphill grind from here, through mile after mile of lush green tea estates, to the one-time colonial hill station of Nuwara Eliya at 6,199 feet (1,889 meters). Even today, the town seems more British than Britain. Some 50 miles (80 kms) west is Adam's Peak with its mountaintop monastery, sacred goal for multitudes of hardy pilgrims. At the mountain's foot is Ratnapura, the "city of gems."

In the arid North Central Province, Sri Lanka's fabled "Ancient Cities" have survived the ravages of time. Anuradhapura, capital of the country for over 1,000 years, proudly displays its *dagobas* and other ruins. Polonnaruwa, its successor, is less expansive but equally impressive. And the citadel of Sigiriya, an indescribable 5th Century palace atop an isolated rock, still awes visitors.

The East Coast is the site of some of the country's finest beaches at Passekudah and Nilaveli. Trincomalee's fine harbor and the elephant sanctuary at Lahugala are among its other points of interest.

The far north is dominated by Jaffna, centuries-old capital of the Tamil culture in Sri Lanka. The land here is excessively dry, but generations of hard-working farmers have made it highly productive.

This, then, is Sri Lanka. Enter the following pages for a closer look.

Preceding pages: Galle Road scene. Left, tourist asea at Negombo.

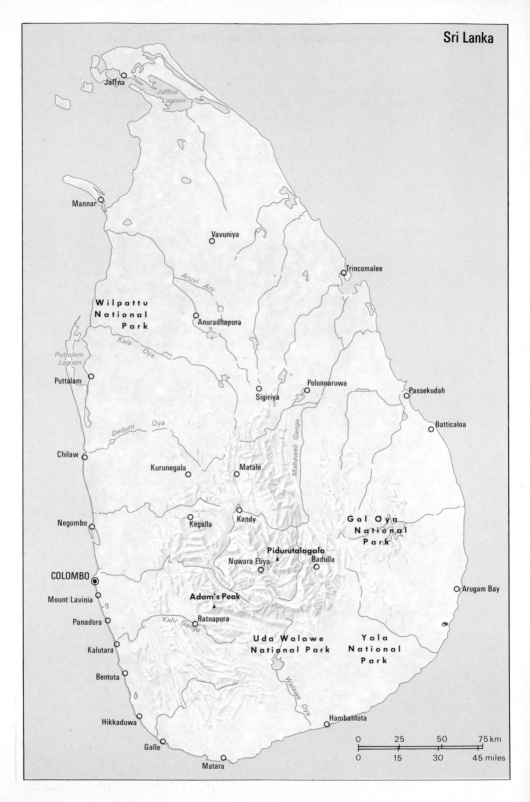

Sri Lanka

Jaffna
Jaffna Lagoon

Mannar

Vavuniya

Trincomalee

Wilpattu National Park

Aruvi Aru

Anuradhapura

Kala Oya

Puttalam Lagoon

Puttalam

Polonnaruwa

Passekudah

Sigiriya

Deduru Oya

Batticaloa

Chilaw

Kurunegala

Matale

Mahaweli Ganga

Gal Oya National Park

Negombo

Kegalla

Kandy

Pidurutalagala ▲

Nuwara Eliya

Badulla

COLOMBO ◉

Arugam Bay

Mount Lavinia

Adam's Peak ▲

Panadura

Kalu Ganga

Ratnapura

Kalutara

Uda Walawe National Park

Yala National Park

Bentota

Walawe Oya

Hikkaduwa

Hambantota

Galle

0	25	50	75 km
0	15	30	45 miles

Matara

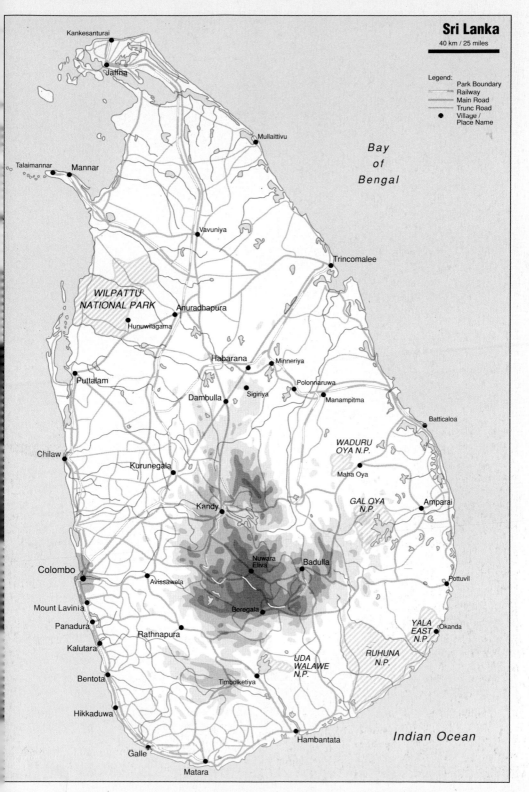

Sri Lanka

40 km / 25 miles

Legend:
Park Boundary
Railway
Main Road
Trunc Road
● Village / Place Name

Kankesanturai

Jaffna

Mullaittivu

Talaimannar   Mannar

Bay
of
Bengal

Vavuniya

Trincomalee

WILPATTU
NATIONAL PARK   Anuradhapura

Hunuwilagama

Habarana   Minneriya

Polonnaruwa

Puttalam   Dambulla   Sigiriya   Manampitma

Batticaloa

WADURU
OYA N.P.

Chilaw

Kurunegala   Maha Oya

GAL OYA
N.P.   Amparai

Kandy

Nuwara
Eliva   Badulla

Colombo

Avissawela   Pottuvil

Beregala

Mount Lavinia

Panadura   *YALA*
EAST   Okanda
N.P.

Kalutara   Rathnapura

Bentota   *RUHUNA*
N.P.

Hikkaduwa   *UDA*
WALAWE
N.P.

Timbolketiya

Galle   Hambantata

Indian Ocean

Matara

97

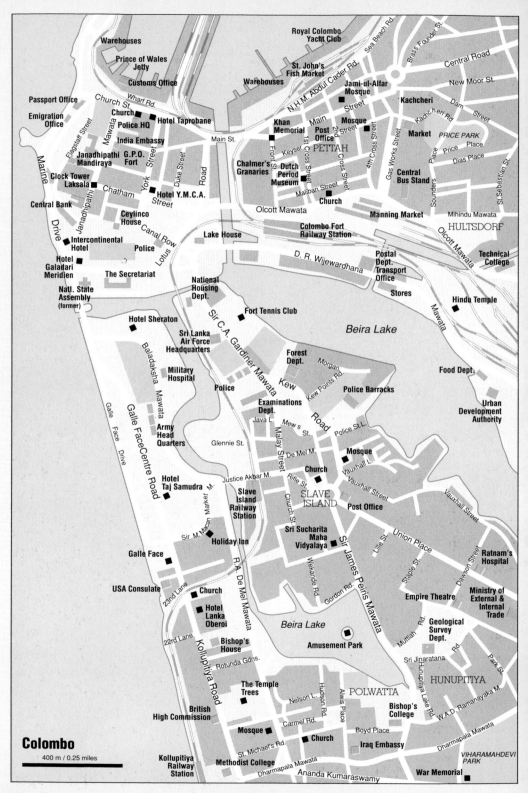

Warehouses
Prince of Wales Jetty
Customs Office
Passport Office
Emigration Office
Church St.
Wharf Rd.
Church
Police HQ
Hotel Taprobane
India Embassy
Janadhipathi Mandiraya
G.P.O.
FORT
Clock Tower Laksala
Chatham
Hotel Y.M.C.A.
Central Bank
Ceylinco House
Canal Row
Intercontinental Hotel
Police
Hotel Galadari Meridien
The Secretariat
Natl. State Assembly (former)
Marine Drive
Janadhipathi
York Street
Duke Street
Main St.
Road
Lotus

Royal Colombo Yacht Club
St. John's Fish Market
Warehouses
N.H.M. Abdul Cader Rd.
Sea Beach Rd.
Brass Founder St.
Central Road
New Moor St.
Jami-ul-Alfar Mosque
Street
Kachcheri
Khan Memorial
Main
Post Office
Mosque
Keyser
1st Cross Street
2nd Street
4th Cross Street
Kachcheri Rd.
Dam Street
Market
PRICE PARK
Price Place
Dias Place
PETTAH
Chalmer's Granaries
Front St.
Dutch Period Museum
Maliban Street
Church
Gas Works Street
Central Bus Stand
Sounders
St.Sebastian St.
Olcott Mawata
Manning Market
Mihindu Mawata
HULTSDORF
Lake House
Colombo Fort Railway Station
D. R. Wijewardhana
Postal Dept. Transport Office
Stores
Olcott Mawata
Technical College
Mawata
National Housing Dept.
Fort Tennis Club
Beira Lake
Hindu Temple
Hotel Sheraton
Sri Lanka Air Force Headquarters
Military Hospital
Sir C.A. Gardiner Mawata
Police
Forest Dept.
Kew Points Rd.
Morgan
Police Barracks
Food Dept.
Baladaksha Mawata
Kew
Examinations Dept.
Java L.
Road
Urban Development Authority
Army Head Quarters
Glennie St.
Mew s St.
Malay Street
De Mel M.
Police St.L.
Mosque
Church
Galle Face Drive
Galle Face Centre Road
Hotel Taj Samudra
Justice Akbar M.
Rifle St.
Vauxhall L.
Vauxhall Street
Sir M. Macan Market M.
Holiday Inn
Slave Island Railway Station
Church St.
SLAVE ISLAND
Post Office
Vauxhall Street
Galle Face
Sri Sucharita Maha Vidyalaya
Sir James Peiris Mawata
Lille St.
Union Place
Staple St.
Dawson Street
Ratnam's Hospital
USA Consulate
R.A. De Mel Mawata
23rd Lane
Church
Hotel Lanka Oberoi
Wekande Rd.
Gordon Rd.
Empire Theatre
Muttiah Rd.
Ministry of External & Internal Trade
22nd Lane
Bishop's House
Beira Lake
Geological Survey Dept.
Sri Jinaratana
Park St.
Kollupitiya Road
Rotunda Gdns.
Amusement Park
HUNUPITIYA
The Temple Trees
Nelson L.
Hudson Rd.
Alvis Place
POLWATTA
Hunupitiya Lake Rd.
W.A.D. Ramanayaka M.
British High Commission
Carmel Rd.
Boyd Place
Bishop's College
Dharmapala Mawata
Mosque
St. Michael's Rd.
Church
Iraq Embassy
VIHARAMAHDEVI PARK
Methodist College
Kollupitiya Railway Station
Dharmapala Mawata
Ananda Kumaraswamy
War Memorial

Colombo

400 m / 0.25 miles

THE METROPOLIS OF COLOMBO

Nearly every visitor to Sri Lanka begins his stay in Colombo. The spirited maritime capital, spread along the shore of the Indian Ocean for some nine miles (14 kilometers), is where business and commerce begin and end in Sri Lanka. It is a spacious city of approximately one million inhabitants, an ethnic stew of the island's diverse races and religions. Here, more than anywhere else in the country, old and new coexist, though not always in harmony. There are high-rise hotels and colonial mansions, supermarkets and street bazaars, flashy Western fashions and traditional sarongs, speedy sports cars and one-man rickshaws.

The city is known to the Sinhalese as Kolomba. There was a settlement here, at the mouth of the Kelani River, as early as the 8th Century A.D. Arab traders used it as a port for shipping cinnamon. They were still here when the Portuguese arrived at the beginning of the 16th Century; by this time, the Sinhalese rulers of Kotte were shipping camphor, sapphires and elephants, as well as cinnamon.

The bountiful spices of Ceilao, as Portugal called the island, were the goods that the Iberians coveted. They carved the Portuguese coat of arms on a rock by the shore and established their first outpost on the spot. The Dutch later rebuilt a fort in the same location, and downtown Colombo still bears the appellation "Fort" from those early days. Otherwise, almost the only structural reminders of Portuguese and Dutch colonialism are some of the churches they left behind.

The Fort: Most of the colonial remnants found in Colombo today are the legacy of the British. They drove the Dutch out in 1796, and held the upper hand here until Ceylon was granted its independence in 1948. During the British era, Colombo reaffirmed its position as commercial center of the Indian Ocean. The city spread south and east, streets were widened, trees were planted, and parks were created. Horse-racing was a regular activity on the seaside Galle Face Green.

Today, most of Colombo's leading hotels are gathered around that same Green, now minus the horses. The Green gives way to "Fort" at the busy bridge across the seaward entrance to Beira Lake.

To your left are a series of old cannons pointing their muzzles toward the open sea, a reminder of uncertain days of the past. To your right are the brown stone buildings of the former **National State Assembly** (better known as "Parliament") and which now house the offices of the Presidential Secretariat. These buildings are now losing their governmental importance as Sri Lanka's administrative capital is moved to suburban Sri Jayawardhanapura Kotte. Standing in front of the Assembly are statues of three of the principal figures in Sri Lanka's fight for independence in the 1940s. In the foreground is the first Prime Minister, D.S. Senanayake. To his right is Sir D.B. (Baron) Jayatillake and to his left is Ponnambalam Arunatchalam.

Straight ahead is the **Lighthouse Clock Tower**, probably the best-known landmark of the Fort. For close to a century, it

performed the dual function of warning ships and telling time, despite being located in the middle of one of the city's busiest intersections. The tower was built in 1857 to a design by Lady Ward, wife of Governor Sir Henry Ward, who named the city "Galle Face Green." Ten years later, it was crowned with the lighthouse; this remained a beacon for the city shoreline, several blocks away, until a new seaside lighthouse was constructed in the 1950s.

The clock was not installed until 1914. Though commissioned in 1872, it was stored in a warehouse for 42 years to avoid the expense of putting it up! By the time its four sets of six-foot dials were raised, it cost £1,200 – £100 more than the structure it was placed in. Today, it tells four different times, depending upon which side of the tower you are facing.

The Clock Tower stands at the crossroads of Chatham Street and Janadhipathi Mawatha, formerly Queens Street. Back toward the Galle Face Green, **Ceylinco House** rises before the twin pillars of the **Ceylon Inter-Continental** and **Galadari Meridien** hotels. The Akasa Kade restaurant on the 12th floor of Ceylinco House offers a fine view of Colombo night and day. Although other high-rises are now starting to get in the way, Adam's Peak can often be seen in the distance between January and April, the clearest time of the year. There is a philatelic exhibition and postage-stamp sales counter (for collectors) on the fourth floor of Ceylinco House. Across the street, in the ground floor of the **Central Bank of Ceylon**, a numismatic exhibition of ancient and modern currency is of interest to coin collectors.

The President's House: Back past the Clock Tower, heading toward the Harbour, you are sure to encounter armed, uniformed sentries guarding a tall iron gate. This is not Buckingham Palace, but it *is* the Sri Lankan equivalent: the **President's House**, Janadhipathi Medura. Built in the late 18th Century by the last Dutch governor of Ceylon, J.G. Van Angelbeek, it became the official residence of British governors. Known first as King's House, and later as Queen's House, it hosted numerous distinguished guests passing through Colombo. Peer

Colombo, circa 1910.

Main Street. Colombo.

through the gates and foliage for a glimpse of the villa's entrance. In front of the house is a statue of Governor Sir Edward Barnes who was responsible for the construction of a Colombo-Kandy road in the 1830s. All trunk road mileage in Sri Lanka is measured from this statue.

On the north side of the President's House are the **Gordon Gardens**, laid out in 1889 by Governor Sir Arthur Gordon in honor of the Jubilee of Queen Victoria. Her imposing statue still stands there. Within the grounds is a *padrao*, a 10-ton boulder on which the first Portuguese adventurers to arrive in "Ceilao" carved a cross, their coat-of-arms and the date 1501. For a time, Gordon Gardens was a public park. Entrance is now restricted because it is enclosed in Republic Square, where the Prime Minister's and Cabinet offices are also situated. Perhaps when the transfer of government to Kotte is complete, the park will again be open to the public.

Opposite the President's House is the 19th Century "White Giant," the elegant **General Post Office**. Around the corner to the right, past the Fort offices of the Tourist Information Center on Sir Baron Jayatillake Mawatha (formerly Prince Street), is **Cargills**, Colombo's oldest department store, established in 1844. A look through this store is a fascinating glimpse into shopper's habits of the past – even if many of the wares and merchandise are from the present.

Shopper's Area: Cargills is at the corner of York Street, downtown Colombo's broadest and busiest artery. A right turn will take you past numerous shops and street sellers to the **Laksala**, a government-sponsored emporium for local handicrafts from throughout the island. Virtually a museum of modern and traditional Sri Lankan arts, all articles displayed are for sale at fair prices. If you proceed directly across York Street and take the second right turn on Duke Street, you will find yourself in the midst of the **World Market**, an Old World street bazaar with various textiles and household goods for sale in the daytime hours, and more illicit services offered at night.

The Harbour Area: A left turn on York Street leads directly to the **Passenger**

York Street in the 1980s.

Harbour Terminal, once the country's busiest port of immigration, now rarely used except for the occasional visits of cruise ships. On the corner facing it is the **Grand Oriental Hotel**. It is not a luxury hostelry that it once was, but the view of the Harbour from its fourth floor restaurant is still grand.

Turn left (west) on Church Street. What is today called the Mission to Seamen was once the **Garrison Church of St. Peter**, consecrated in 1821 on the site of the 1735 Dutch governors' banquet hall. Memorial tablets on the walls commemorate the achievements of early settlers. Under lock and key, but open to inspection under the vicar's watchful eye, is a remarkably handsome set of gilt altar vessels presented to the church as the personal gift of King George III – a large tray, a chalice and paten, a ewer and a pair of candlesticks.

Continue on Church Street, under the massive overhead walkway of the new **National Police Headquarters**. At the west end of the street, where it turns into Marine Drive is the *dagoba* of **Buddha Jayanthi**. It was begun in May 1956 on the 2,500th anniversary of the death of the Buddha, and according to its original conception is the first landmark on the Sri Lankan horizon to be spotted by an arriving ship. Today, its four-legged framework straddles the street, with its its elaborate monument rising 250 feet above street level. Supported entirely by public contributions, the *dagoba* stands as an attractive and curious marine observatory.

Reserve your direction past the Grand Oriental Hotel. Continue along the edge of the Harbour. The breakwaters which enclose this artificial haven were built only in the last quarter of the 19th Century. The 602-acre port handles more than 90 percent of Sri Lanka's seaborne trade.

Pettah – Bizarre Bazaar: Follow Main Street across an obscured canal to the **Pettah** district, Colombo's busiest and most traditional bazaar area. A mosaic of human movement and architectural memories, it is currently undergoing a facelift. Traffic piles up on its streets, pedestrians jostle each other, vendors scream and children play.

"Pettah" is a word of British Indian

Remnants of the past on Galle Face Green.

origin, derived from the Tamil *pettai* for "outside." In Sinhala, it is called *pita kotuwa*, "outside the Fort."

At the entrance to the Pettah there is another clock tower. Jog to the right here, but continue in the same direction down Main Street. This roadway, once effectively blocked by the makeshift stalls of petty merchants, has been reopened to vehicle traffic. There is a proposal to relocate the stalls somewhere near – or in – the St. John's Market on Reclamation Road. These merchants peddle clothing, jewelry, fruits, household goods, toys, leather goods, and almost anything else the customer may want for a fraction of what it might cost in a proper store.

The mercantile district of the Pettah is highly compartmentalized. First Cross Street specialize in electrical and photographic goods. Second Cross Street is lined with jewelers, especially those dealing in watches and gems. Third Cross Street is hardware dealers. Sea Street is occupied by goldsmiths. Main Street itself is dominated by textile dealers. And so on. One of the most fascinating byways is

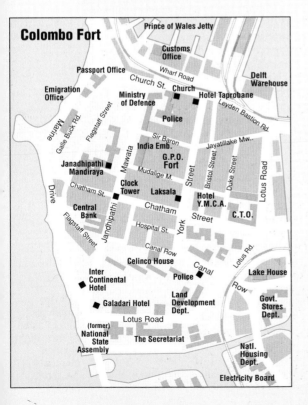

Colombo Fort

Prince of Wales Jetty

Customs Office

Passport Office
Wharf Road
Delft Warehouse

Emigration Office
Church St. Church

Ministry of Defence
Hotel Taprobane
Leyden Bastion Rd.

Police

Sir Baron
India Emb.
Jayatilake Mw.

Janadhipathi Mandiraya
G.P.O. Fort

Mudalige M.
Bristol Street
Duke Street
Lotus Road

Clock Tower
Laksala

Central Bank
Chatham
Hotel Y.M.C.A.

Chatham St.
Street
C.T.O.

Hospital St.
York

Canal Row

Celinco House
Canal
Lotus Rd.

Inter Continental Hotel
Police
Lake House

Row

Galadari Hotel
Land Development Dept.
Govt. Stores Dept.

Lotus Road

(former) National State Assembly
The Secretariat
Natl. Housing Dept.

Electricity Board

Fifth Cross Street, whose resident shopkeepers carry all types of tea, spices and *ayurvedic* medical remedies. The lane is pure paradise to the olfactory sense.

The Pettah has historical attractions, too. Starting at the Pettah Clock Tower walk directly away from the Harbour on Front Street, past the Chalmers Granaries. At Keyser Street, turn left to the remains of the **Kerkhopf**, an old Dutch cemetery. The tombstones piled here were moved from their former adjacent site when it was taken over by commerce.

At the southern end of Front Street is the **Colombo Fort Railway Station**. Besides being Sri Lanka's busiest rail center, it houses a small collection of old railway equipment. See it on weekend afternoons or by prior arrangement.

On Second Cross Street, two blocks south of Main Street at the corner of Prince Street, is the colonnaded **Old Post Office**. At one time a private house, it is the last vestige of an 18th Century Dutch residential community. The front stoop and the tall doors are typical of the architecture of the time. The date over the main door is 1780, but a city map of 1732 shows a building described as a "seminary" on the same site.

Today, the building has been converted into a **Dutch Period Museum**, officially opened by former President Jayewardene in July 1982. Furnishings, household goods and maps have all been carefully chosen. But work still has not been completed, and the museum's opening hours are unreliable.

Near the Harbour end of Second Cross Street is the **Jami-ul-Alfar Mosque**. Built in 1908, the name of this large Muslim holy building means "Congregation of Prayer." It is a startling brick red-and-white in color. Some of its members may be descendants of the early Moorish settlers in Colombo. Prayers are recited here five times daily, as prescribed by the Koran. At other times, visitors are welcome to enter the premises (but not the *maharab*, or prayer hall) to discuss Islam with the *ulama*, the learned teachers.

East on Main Street is **Kaymans Gate**, an old stone belfry on the south side of the road near Fifth Cross Street. In ruins today, it may be the oldest Christian structure extant in Sri Lanka. Tradition says it belonged to the 16th Century Portugese Church of Sao Francis at Kotte, and was moved to its present site by the Dutch. The name it bears is unusual: there never was a gate here, and the nickname *kaymans* – Dutch for "crocodiles" – probably came from the number of reptiles which swam in the fort's nearby moat.

Close to Kaymans Gate, at the corner of Kachcheri Road, is the **Old Town Hall**. Today it is an odorous and many-sided market, selling everything domestic from vegetables and fruit to household utensils.

Sea Street branches north from Kaymans Gate toward the Harbour. About a quarter-mile down, on the left, are a series of three adjacent Hindu *kovils*: the **Ganeshan**, the **Old Kathiresan** and the **Sri New Kathiresan Temple**. The latter, dedicated to Skanda, features a variety of colorful carvings on its *gopuram*, and is the largest Hindu temple in Colombo. The annual Vel procession, the city's major Hindu festival, begins and ends at here.

Outstanding Churches: A short distance further north, Sea Street rejoins the harborfront highway at Kochchikade. Look for the throngs at the doors of **St. Anthony's Church**. Believers of all religions, not just Roman Catholics, beseech a "miracle-working" statue of the popular Portuguese saint for favors at times of personal or family crisis. Tuesdays, for some reason, are most crowded.

Turn right opposite the dull yellow church on Jampettach Street, then turn right again to climb Vivekananda Hill. At the top of the hill, at the junction of Ratnajothi Saravanamuttu Mawatha, is Colombo's best known church, the Dutch-built **Wolvendaal Kerk**. When it was dedicated in 1757 (after eight years of construction), it was the most dominant structure in the city. With its five-foot-thick walls and its four scroll-gabled transepts, it is a noble if severe work of colonial architecture. Inside are numerous period pieces – a canopied pulpit, an intricately carved wooden font, crystal lamps, silver communion vessels, and an illustrated Dutch Bible. Old tombstones and hatchments cloak the floors and walls. Today, regular services are held in English and Tamil.

The only Catholic cathedral in Colombo, **St. Lucia's Cathedral**, stands on a hill a kilometer to the northeast. A massive domed structure featuring open confessionals and ionic columns, it is the focus of Roman Catholicism in the country. The nave holds 6,000 worshippers. It took 34 years to build and was completed in 1906.

The **Paramananda Purana Viharaya**, which like St. Lucia's is in Colombo's Iotahena district, was founded in 1806. Its *vihara* contains murals of the Buddha's life and of Buddhism's history in Sri Lanka, as well as a smaller replica of the great Aukana Buddha. Nearby is the **Dipaduttaramaya** temple, Colombo's oldest by a few months. It also was established in 1806. The architecture shows a distinct Siamese influence. Murals within the *vihara* were painted by a Burmese monk in the 1890s. In the same district, the **Sir Muthumariamman Kovil** on Kotahena Street is dedicated to Pattini, the goddess believed to have the power to prevent and cure diseases. Devotees flock here to make vows.

Heading south from here, Sri Sumanatissa Mawatha takes you to Panchikawatta Road, famous as the area

Left, the Lighthouse Clock Tower in Fort. Right, a young merchant in the World Market.

where any spare part for any vehicle can be found; and past the **Tower Hall** with its white clock tower. This building, one of Colombo's first two venues for traditional theater, was closed in the 1960s, but was restored and reopened in 1978 by President Premadasa when he was Prime Minister. Next door is the **Elphinstone Theatre**, Sri Lanka's first cinema.

Back toward the Pettah is the **Hultsdorf** district. Hultsdorf Street itself winds over a hill cloaked with attorneys offices and law courts. Indeed, this is the most prestigious legal address in the country. Across the street from **All Saints Church** (1860) is the **Supreme Court**, the **Ministry of Justice** and the Bar Association of Sri Lanka's head offices. The imposing structure of the Supreme Court is a recent addition to the Hultsdorf skyline. The complex was a gift from the Chinese government to Sri Lanka, declared open by then President J.R. Jayewardene in 1988.

Slave Island: Wedged between Fort and Pettah on the north, the Galle Face Green on the west, and the railroad tracks on the east, are **Beira Lake** and **Slave Island**. In centuries past, the "island" was just that; today, much of the original lake having been reclaimed, it is merely a well-demarcated district of Colombo.

Neither are there any slaves in Slave Island today, but there once were. It must have been an unpleasant exile. Not only did the late 17th and 18th Century Dutch confine their slaves to quarters on the island (transporting them by boat to their daylight chores); they also stocked the lake with crocodiles, preventing the slaves' escape while giving their fort a moat-like defense! Those slaves who did flee were flogged and branded for a first offense, hanged for a second.

In British times, the crocodiles were banished and the lake became a pleasant place for rowing and sailing. A couple of rowing clubs still use the lake today. For a time, the island was a base for a company of the Malay Regiment: thus its Sinhalese name, Kompanna Veediya, "company street." Today, it contains numerous government offices, the headquarters of the Sri Lanka Air Force, the City Football League grounds, some of the older hotels,

18th Century Colombo, as seen by a Dutch engraver.

LA VILLE COLOMBO SUR LE GRAND ISLE DE CEYLON.

Die Stadt Colombo

La Ville Colombo

cinemas, bookstores. There are also a significant number of *kovils* and mosques, among them the **Sri Siva Subramania Swami Kovil** on Kew Road, built in the early 20th Century mainly for Indian Hindu soldiers in the British army; and the **Military Mosque** and **Akbar Mosque**, primarily for members of the Malay Regiment.

If you follow Sir James Peiris Mawatha south out of Slave Island, you will brush the shore of the southwestern arm of Beira Lake and note two points of particular interest. One is a small island which was once a popular **Amusement Park**, no more than 150 meters off shore. Access is by small skiffs on the shoreline. It has become run down in recent years, but improvements are planned. Second is the modern **Simalaka**, a Buddhist hall built out onto the lake. Its lovely *bo* tree and Buddha image are clearly visible from the shore, and it is especially lovely in the evening, when it is picturesquely lit. Associated with the nearby **Gangaramaya Bhikku Training Centre**, it is intended for monks as a conference hall and place of meditation.

Cinnamon Gardens: The **Cinnamon Gardens** district, better known today by its postal code designation of "Colombo 7," is Colombo's most fashionable residential district, and as such is worth a long stroll. It takes its name, of course, from the tasty spice that originally drew the Portuguese and Dutch to Sri Lankan shores. Once, this whole district was covered with spice plantations. No cinnamon is grown here today, save perhaps in private garden plots, but the name has stuck.

Now many foreign embassies have moved into old colonial mansions; Sri Lankan government offices and Colombo University have taken over others. The district's wide avenues are shaded by huge overhanging trees. Pretty gardens and neatly trimmed lawns surround the old houses. It is this area that has earned Colombo its reputation as a "Garden City."

The greenest place of all is **Viharamahadevi Park**, which demarcates the southern limit of the old Slave Island. Once the largest cinnamon plantation in the region, this expanse of green – the city's largest – was formerly named Vic-

Galle Face personalities: left, hotel doorman; and **right**, Velu, "kiteman" of the Green.

toria Park. It was renamed in 1958 after a great Sinhalese queen of historical legend. As the story goes, Viharemahadevi was cast adrift from the Colombo area by her father, the king of Kalaniya, in the centuries pre-dating the Christian era as a sacrifice for a royal indiscretion. She washed up some time later on the shore at Kirinda, in Ruhuna (near Yala), and was taken as queen by King Kavantissa. They became the parents of the great King Dutugemunu, who on his mother's urging regained Sinhalese possession of Anuradhapura from the Chola conquerors and united Sri Lanka under one crown for the first time.

Viharamahadevi's statue can be seen amidst the park's lush vegetation. Ebony, mahogany, lemon, fig, sal, eucalyptus, and other trees make their homes here. There are also lotus ponds, fountains and an orchid house. Look for the flocks of songbirds and the flying foxes, large fruit bats which can be seen roosting in the daylight hours, hanging upside down from tree branches. An open-air theater here offers frequent, and free, theater and mu-

sical shows. There is a Children's Park on the southeastern side of the greater park, featuring a small train and a zoo with numerous "baby" animals. Near the northeast corner of the park is located the **Town Hall** (1928), bearing architectural similarity to many state capitol buildings in America. An impressive Buddha statue faces it from across the street. Beyond, near De-Soysa Circus, is the striking century-old **Devatagaha Mosque.**

Green Path: Ananda Kumaraswamy Mawatha, better known by its former name of Green Path, cuts through the middle of Viharamahadevi Park. As you enter the park on this street from the west, you pass the **Public Library** (1978) on your left, marked by a Boy Scout statue in front. Just north is a **War Memorial** to servicemen killed in the world wars. The memorial was first raised in 1914; additional plaques were added after the defense of the island in the Second World War. Every November 14, a military parade and wreath-laying service is held here. The nation observes a full minute of silence following a two-gun salute.

Movie posters, Slave Island.

A short distance further along Green Path, on the right, the **Mahaweli Exhibition and Royal Asiatic Society Library** building, featuring traditional Kandyan architecture. It exhibits the classical genius of ancient Sri Lankan tank-builders and the comparable abilities of modern engineers working on the Mahaweli River Development Scheme. Near the east end of the park is the **Art Museum**, the frequent venue for temporary exhibitions of paintings and handicrafts by both local and foreign artisans.

The National Museum: The south end of the park is dominated by the **National Museum**. Established in 1877 by Governor Sir William Gregory, it is a treasure trove of articles depicting Ceylon's historical and cultural past and present. Among the articles of special interest are the regalia of Sri Wickrama Rajasingha, the last King of Kandy. Artifacts and antiques allow one to trace Sri Lanka history from prehistoric times, through the classic periods of Anuradhapura and Polonnaruwa, up to present times. Note the ancient bronze and steel implements,

the carved ivory, the Sinhalese banners, the ritual masks, and the Dutch colonial furniture. One of the more interesting displays is a collection of gifts of state presented to former Prime Minister Sirimavo Bandaranaike. The museum library contains more than a half-million volumes on Sri Lanka, including several thousand *ola* (palm-leaf) manuscripts, painstakingly inscribed.

South of the museum on Guildford Crescent is the **Lionel Wendt Art Centre and Theatre**. Wendt (1900-1944) was an accomplished lawyer, pianist and photographer who gained international acclaim in the latter field in the 1930s. This gallery-theater, his memorial, offers various art, graphics and photography exhibits, as well as providing a head office for the Ceylon Photographic Association.

The old **Turf Club** is located on Reid Avenue south of Guildford Crescent. Although the horse-racing track was closed in 1956, the grandstands still remain. For a time the buildings were used by the art curriculum of Colombo University, much to the delight of Sinhalese punsters, who

noted the similarity between the words for "art" and "horse." A new sports stadium is proposed on the site.

Colombo University is across Reid Avenue from the Turf Club, sharing a triangle of land with **Royal College**. The University Library and the **Planetarium**, a wigman of pre-stressed concrete 23 meters (75 feet) in diameter, are just to the south of the old race track.

Independence and Remembrance: On the east side of the Turf Club is the **Independence Memorial Hall**. It is constructed of reinforced concrete and pillared in the style of medieval Kandyan audience halls. On Feb. 4, 1948, the Duke of Gloucester – on behalf of the British Crown – formally opened Ceylon's first Parliament here. Bas-relief bronze panels depict scenes from Sri Lankan history; a separate gallery of paintings and sculptures is proposed for the basement of the hall.

Across Independence Avenue from the hall is the **Sports Ministry**; various cricket, rugby and football (soccer) clubs have their home fields in this area. The **Sri Lanka Foundation Institute**: an academic research and seminar facility, faces Independence Hall from the west; it was donated by West Germany. Offices of the Sri Lanka Broadcasting Corporation and the Ceylon Institute of Scientific and Industrial Research are south of the hall.

Opposite a replica of the Aukana Buddha on Bauddhaloka Mawatha is the **Bandaranaike Memorial International Conference Hall** – best known to Colombo residents by its acronym, "BMICH." The huge octagonal building, raised in 1971 at a cost of about US$1.5 million, was a gift of the People's Republic of China. The main assembly hall accommodates 1,500 persons, making it one of the finest convention facilities in South Asia. Inside is a small museum commemorating the life and times of former Prime Minister S.W.R.D. Bandaranaike, assassinated in 1959.

Some distance east, on Dudly Senanayake Mawatha, the road to Kotte, is the **College of Indigenous Medicine** and **Ayurvedic Hospital**. The traditional healing arts of Sri Lanka, which include herbal treatments and baths, are preferred **Independence Memorial Hall.**

over Western techniques by many Sri Lankans today. One famous ayurvedic practitioner used to advertise the cure of "Sprains, Fractures, Bow Legs and All Other Skin Diseases."

Just to the north of the college is the **Gotami Vidyalaya**, a Buddhist temple notable for its remarkable modern murals. They were executed by the well-known artist George Keyt, assisted by Manjusri Thera, then a Buddhist monk, later famed as an artist in his own right.

Galle Road South: The Galle Road runs like a ribbon of tar along Colombo's western seaboard, continuing for some 70 miles from the Galle Face Green to the port of Galle. Impressive buildings and business centers nudge overlooked slums for want of space. If the city has any one road that can be considered its main artery, this is it.

Start your exploration in the **Galle Face Green** itself. This kilometer-long treeless expanse was established by Governor Ward in 1859 as a promenade "in the interest of the ladies and children of Colombo." Today, as winds and sea whip across the Green from the Indian Ocean,

there are those who maintain it should be renamed the "Galle Face Brown." But after heavy monsoon rains, it regains the color of its name.

Once known as the "Hyde Park of Colombo," the Green saw not only horse-racing, but also colonial army parades and other activities. Now it is a place where occasional public events are held, including political rallies. On weekends, sandlot cricket or football games are a common occurrence.

More popularly, it is a place to go fly a kite. Colorful native kites, sold on the lawn in front of the old Galle Face Hotel, flutter and twirl with the ubiquitous crows in the stiff sea breezes. At the north end of the Green, on a low hill overlooking the sea, stands statue of former Prime Minister S.W.R.D. Bandaranaike, donated by the Soviet Union.

Behind the Bandaranaike statue, on the shore of Beira Lake, is the proposed site for the new **Sheraton Hotel**. Beyond the headquarters of the **Sri Lanka Army**, is the Indian-owned **Taj-Samudra Hotel**. The **Holiday Inn** stands near the south

end of the Green, a half-block from the **Galle Face Hotel**. The latter hotel, once operated by the Regent Hotels group of Hong Kong, proudly calls itself the first hotel in Asia, having been constructed on this site in 1856. The Hotel Lanka Oberoi – the lobby of which features four huge Ena de Silva batiks, each worth over U$3,500 – stands next to the **St. Andrew's Scots Kirk** in the Kollupitiya district (Colombo 3) south of the Galle Face. St. Andrew's was Sri Lanka's first Presbyterian Church, built in 1842. Directly opposite the Hotel Lanka Oberoi is the main **Tourist Information Center** and offices of the Ceylon Tourist Board.

The British High Commission and the new American Embassy are just down the street from the Oberoi. Across from them is the frangipani-fringed **Temple Trees**, official residence of the Prime Minister.

At the corner of Ananda Kumaraswamy Mawatha, Kollupitiya junction beckons wanderers to the large and fascinating **Kollupitiya Market**. It is a kaleidoscope of sights, smells and sounds, well worth a visit of an hour or two.

The Way to Bambalapitiya: Small businesses, shops and restaurants line Galle Road for the next several miles. Keep an eye open on your right for **Mumtaz Mahal**, a seaside colonial mansion, now the official residence of the Speaker of the National State Assembly.

About three miles from Fort, you come to the big Bambalapitiya Junction at the corner of Bauddhaloka Mawatha. This is the beginning of the mile-long Bambalapitiya district (Colombo 4).

At the bottom of the small lane, namely Glen Aber Place, heading seaward from the junction, is the **Borah Mosque**, place of worship of the small Islamic community of Borah's.

One of the Colombo's most important and popular Buddhist temples is the **Vajiraramaya**, in the midst of Bambalapitiya on Vajira Road, a short walk from Galle Road. It is one of the nation's recognized seats of learning, and is a frequent venue for English-language sermons on Buddhist doctrine and philosophy.

Almost opposite Dickmans Road, a small lane called Melbourne Avenue turns **Kollupitiya Market.**

toward the ocean. Here you will find the international headquarters of the **Colombo Plan Bureau.** Established in 1950 to provide financial and technical assistance to underdeveloped member countries, the Colombo Plan is said to have been the brainchild of J.R. Jayewardene, then Ceylon Finance Minister and former Sri Lanka president, and Australian Foreign Minister Percy Spender. Great Britain, Canada, New Zealand, India and Pakistan were also among the original signatories to the "Colombo Plan for Cooperative Economic Development in South and Southeast Asia." Today, the leading donors to the plan are the United States and Japan. In all, there are 26 member nations.

Dickmans Road heads almost due east from Galle Road. One block before its intersection with Havelock Road, turn left onto Anderson Road. A few hours down on the right is the **Ratnapura Gem Bureau and Museum's** Colombo showroom. Beside the minerals and gems displayed here; there are also collections of brass and silver handicrafts, and a gallery of predominantly religious paintings.

Across Havelock Road, Dickmans Road becomes Isipatana Mawatha. Here you will find the pretty little *dagoba* and impressive *vihara* of the **Isipathanaramaya** temple. The frescoes here are of special note. One block north, the **Asokaramaya** is also noted for its murals. The **Lumbini Theatre**, south on Havelock Road, is a favorite arena for traditional Sinhalese theatrical performances.

The Galle Road proceeds south through the district of Wellawatta – sometimes known as "Little Jaffna" for its concentration of Tamils – to Dehiwela, best known as the site of the **Zoological Gardens.** Reputed to be one of Asia's finest, the Zoo was among the first to introduce the "open concept" in animal habitats. It has a fine collection of mammals, birds, reptiles and fishes from Sri Lanka and the Indian subcontinent. Densely foliated and well landscaped, the 11-acre site is also thoughtfully organized.

Perhaps its most famous attraction is the daily elephant show at 5:15 p.m. The mammoth beasts perform a variety of acrobatic (for elephants) maneuvers. One

Mount Lavinia Hotel.

big pachyderm even plays a harmonica, the others skipping along behind! Signs will direct you inland from the Galle Road to the Zoo.

Also in Dehiwela is the **Subodharmaya** temple, on a small lane to the left just after the main junction. There is an impressive Buddha image here; the mystic author Ouspensky made it famous as "the Buddha with the sapphire eyes." In fact, *pol-thel* (coconut oil) lamps give it the glow.

The beach resort of **Mount Lavinia** is next. A one-kilometer detour off the Galle Road, **Mount Lavinia Hotel** preserves another dash of colonial splendor. Sip an *arrack* cocktail on the poolside deck while watching the sun set over the Indian Ocean and the evening lights come on in Colombo Fort, eight miles north.

Several smaller inns and numerous restaurants and souvenir shops have sprung up along Hotel Road in recent years, making this area – once the suburban residence of a British governor – into a little resort within the Colombo metropolitan limits. But be cautious if you bathe here. The undertows claim several tourists' lives each year.

Kotte and Kelaniya: Just east of the city are two points of particular interest. At Kotte, renamed **Sri Jayawardhanapura Kotte**, seven miles (11 kilometers) from Fort, is Sri Lanka's new parliamentary complex and administrative capital. Surrounded by the waters of Lake Diyawanna Oya, the new **Parliament Building** is a study in simple oriental architectural beauty. The new US$43 million center will eventually include all other government offices plus the various amenities of a planned city. The nation's business and commercial center will stay in Colombo proper.

The most important center of faith for Colombo Buddhists is at Kelaniya, seven miles northeast of Fort and a short detour off the Kandy Road. Indeed, the **Kelaniya Raja Maha Vihara** is said to be one of the three places on the island that the Buddha himself made a special point of visiting.

According to the *Mahavamsa*, the unusual "paddy-heap" shaped *dagoba* at Kelaniya marks the spot where the Buddha, on the request of a *naga* king, sat on a "gem-studded throne" to preach the Dharma to his subjects and convert them. It is ascribed to King Yatala Tissa of the 3rd Century B.C.

The modern *vihara*, built earlier this century, has a distinct elegance. Frescoes, by the late artist Soliyas Mendis, decorate its walls, telling stories of the Buddha, Buddhism in Ceylon, and Kelaniya Temple history. Geometrically patterned ceiling paintings in the main hall are fascinating. There are also three important Buddha images, one reclining and two seated. Rows of comical dwarfs and elephants, copied from Polonnaruwa's Tivanka Image House, adorn the outer walls.

The annual *perahera* at Kelaniya, held during the January full moon (in the Sinhalese month of *Duruthu*), celebrates the Buddha's visit. It is perhaps second only to the Esala Perahera in Kandy in spectacle.

The town of Kelaniya itself is a center of traditional Sinhalese pottery. Characteristic of the local terra-cotta work is incised decoration. Painted clay animals range from naive to grotesque.

Outside (left) and inside the Kelaniya Raja Maha Vihara.

116

SIGHTS OF THE SOUTH COAST

Sri Lanka's South Coast is a region of great variety. Here are many of the country's famous beach resorts; the focus of the rubber and toddy-tapping industries; the old Portuguese and Dutch stronghold of Galle; the island's last remaining primeval forest; ancient ruins; great pilgrimage centers; and a large national park. A good road follows the coast like a ribbon for the 150 miles (241 kilometers) from Colombo to Hambantota.

Head south on the Galle Road out of the capital city, past the beach resort of Mt. Lavinia and the domestic airport at Ratmalana. **Lake Bolgoda**, located between Moratuwa and Panadura, is very popular among boating and water-skiing enthusiasts.

Kalutara, 27 miles out of Colombo, boasts the **Gangatilaka Vihara**, which can be seen from miles away. This huge new *dagoba*, just south of the Kalu Ganga bridge, marks the site of an ancient Buddhist temple. Not a reliquary like most *dagobas*, it is hollow with a beautifully painted interior.

Outside the *dagoba*, by the side of the road, stands a small Buddhist shrine and a *bo* tree, in front of which is a *pin-kate* (or till) to which passing drivers make offerings to ensure the success of their journeys.

Kalutara was once a major center of the island spice trade, particularly cinnamon. The Portuguese, Dutch and British in turn had small fortifications here to guard the river entrance to the interior. Today, the town is perhaps most famous for its mangosteens. Though this delectable fruit – introduced from Malaya in 1813 – is plentiful all over the island, Kalutara is reputed to have the highest quality and most reasonable prices. Purple and grenade-shaped, it is in season from May through July.

Some of Sri Lanka's finest basketry is made in Kalutara's **Basket Hall**. Fine geometrical patterns and a variety of colors are woven into the work.

The Rubber Industry: Kalutara is also the center of Sri Lanka's most thriving rubber district. At **Agalawatta**, 14 miles (23 kilometers) inland, the Rubber Research Institute has a model estate where studies are carried out in botany, soils, chemistry and pathology. The rubber plantations of Sri Lanka are among the oldest in the world. Dartonfield Estate, founded in 1934, has been in the forefront of research groups battling all kinds of plant diseases and developing new strains of rubber.

Rubber is obtained from the milky sap exuded by the rubber tree. This sap is released by making a slanting spiral cut in the tree's bark with a special V-shaped knife. The sap drains into a small receptacle, usually a coconut shell, suspended below the cut. Every second or third day, for 10 months, about 0.03 of an inch is shaved off the lower side of the cut. During the two-month period of the year when the tree drops its leaves, it is given a "rest" from this tapping.

The sap, called latex, is collected in buckets and carried to a factory. There it is strained through a fine brass sieve, "standardized" (with the addition of water) to a mixture of 1½ pounds solid rubber per

Preceding pages: river scene near Bentota. **Left**, Bentota Beach. **Below**, the beach at Polhena.

gallon, and poured into troughs to co-agulate. Then the now-spongy mass is passed through a series of rollers, reducing it to a desired thickness and imprinting a raised pattern which prevents the sheets from sticking together. Crepe rubber is produced by adding sodium bisulphate to the latex at this stage.

After rolling, the sheets of rubber are hung in hot-air houses (which enhance the drying process) or smokehouses (said to provide the rubber with a more effective preservative). The sheets that emerge can be marketed as translucent raw rubber.

Most rubber plantation superintendents will be happy to show unannounced visitors around their factories. To be certain, however, obtain permission prior to arrival.

Beaches of Bentota: The most popular beach stretch begins several miles further south of Kalutara at **Beruwala**. From this point south and east, tourist hotels and small resorts spring up every few miles along the coast.

Beruwala is believed to be the first Moorish settlement on the island, established by Arab traders in about the 8th Century A.D. A large population of Sri Lanka Moors, many of them gem traders, still live in this area, especially in the so-called "China Fort" district.

On a rocky headland is the most famous Muslim shrine in Sri Lanka, the **Kachchimalai Mosque**. At the end of the fasting month of Ramazan, thousands of Muslims make a pilgrimage to its white minarets. More specifically, they visit the tomb of Sheik Ashareth, a saint whose rock coffin is said to have floated ashore here 1,000 years ago.

Alutgama, a bus-depot center and fish-market town, separates Beruwala from the tourist resort of Bentota. Inland from Alutgama, about five miles by twisting and sometimes paved road, is the five-acre private garden called "**Brief,**" home of septuagenarian landscape artist Bevis Bawa. The sprawling house in the midst of this tranquil oasis is a veritable museum of art, containing Bawa's own works (he is a well-known sculptor), the works of friends (such as George Keyt and Donald Friend), and fine antique furniture from home and abroad.

At **Bentota** is the 100-acre **National** **Holiday Resort** complex, containing several major tourist hotels, a market place and shopping center, cultural displays and exhibitions. The **Bentota Beach Hotel** was built on the site of the old Portuguese fort-cum-British rest house. The beach here is lovely and calm except during the southwest monsoon; October through April are the best months for swimming.

The **Bentota Ganga**, which forms the river boundary between Sri Lanka's Western and Southern provinces, is navigable upstream for light craft for 20 miles or more. About three miles upriver from the tourist settlement is the **Galapata Vihara**. This 12th Century temple has few remains, save a carved gateway and a long private inscription recording a gift of lands and slaves to the monastery on the site. If you plan a boat trip, ask your hotel to arrange it for you, and pack a lunch. Reject offers from strangers on the beach; some trusting tourists have reported frightening incidents.

Tapping Toddy: Throughout Sri Lanka, especially along the coastal strip from Colombo to Galle, ropes running between the palm-leaf toupees of coconut trees draw the attention of observant visitors. These are the roosts of "toddy-tappers," young men who climb high into the trees to obtain the sweet, milky sap of the coconut blossom. Perhaps the greatest concentration of these tappers is along the coast south of Bentota.

Toddy is big business in Sri Lanka. It provides the favorite alcoholic beverage of the working man, both in its raw fermented form and distilled, as *arrack*. In order to obtain "toddy" sap, the buds of coconut flowers are bound to prevent them from flowering. Twice a day for two weeks, the pods are knocked upon with a bone; at the end of this two-week period, the tips are cut and a pot is fastened over the pods to collect the dripping nectar. An individual tapper harvests 100 or more trees a day by tying groups of trees together with strong coir (coconut-fiber rope). After climbing a single tree, he can stay 30 to 40 feet in the air tapping one tree after another, until a complete circuit has been made. Then he returns to earth, emptying his clay pot full of toddy sap into a 65-gallon barrel at ground level. Toddy carts travel **Today tapper, Balpitiya.**

Ambalangoda Rest House, and a pleasant bathing beach nearby. Rocky offshore islets provide a sanctuary for seabirds.

Less than 10 miles inland, the village of **Meetiyagoda** is the center of Sri Lanka's primary district of mining for the softly beautiful gem called the moonstone. Clear or slightly milky white in color, the moonstone is not considered a precious gem, but nevertheless is popular in jewelry.

Hikkaduwa, a town teeming with life, exudes a character almost of its own. It is patronized largely by low-budget travellers attracted here by the lovely beach and the pre-ponderance of cheap rest houses and eating places. Many of them are located at the south end of town in **Narigama**, Sri Lanka's answer to Bali's Kuta Beach. Bright batiks, masks, jewelry and other crafts are sold all along Hikkaduwa's Galle Road strip. But several higher quality establishments, catering to the more moneyed visitors, are also located in this town.

Surfers find the break at Hikkaduwa to their fancy. A larger number of visitors take to the water with snorkel and mask to view the underwater attractions of the country's best-known **coral gardens**. Although not as impressive as they were before hordes of visitors began picking them over, the gardens are still beautiful. Glass-bottomed boats are available for hire to those not inclined to make a dive.

On **Dodanduwa Lake**, off the main road south of Hikkaduwa, is a serene Buddhist **island hermitage** that must rank as one of the Sri Lanka's most peaceful spots. This hermitage has a fine reputation of scholarship. It can be visited by prior arrangement.

The Port of Galle: The South Coast's major city is **Galle**, whose oldest landmark is the massive Portuguese and Dutch fort in which the central city is contained. But the city may be much older. Some scholars believe it to be the "Tarshish" of the Old Testament, to which King Solomon sent his merchant vessels, and to which Jonah fled from the Lord.

Galle's geographical location on world sea routes certainly made it an important port of call for centuries between the Middle East and the Orient. The city thus became an emporium of foreign trade with a wealthy, highly cosmopolitan

Galle.

population. The Portuguese first came ashore in 1505 when they were blown off course pursuing a Moorish spice fleet toward the Maldives. They established a stronghold in 1589 after an attack on their Colombo fort by the Kandyans. The Dutch stormed the fortress in 1640 with 12 ships and 2,000 men, and captured it after almost four days of unremitting battle.

Today, the 90-acre **Galle Fort** shows no evidence of its Portuguese founders. The Dutch incorporated the Portuguese northern wall in a great rampart in 1663. A second, taller wall was built inside of it. Between the two walls, a covered passage connected the central bastion with the fort's two half-bastions overlooking the sea. The Dutch also installed a sophisticated drainage system, complete with brick-lined underground sewers that were flushed twice a day by the tides.

A walk around the ramparts that surround the modern city of Galle is a pleasant way to pass a morning or afternoon. Try not to be offended by the lace and coral vendors who assail you; instead, enjoy studying the old cannon mounts and watching the surf fishermen standing in the water below.

The original gate to the fort was by the harbor. It is still there, marked by the old Dutch V.O.C. (for "Vereenigde Oost Indische Compagnie") arms with a rooster crest. The **Main Gate** was opened in the wall by the British in 1873. Not far from the gate is the old **Government House**, dating from 1683.

Churches and Graves: Several important churches are within the fort, including the **Groote Kerk**, the oldest Protestant church in Sri Lanka. Originally constructed on the site of a Portuguese Capuchin convent upon the Dutch conquest in 1640, the present church was raised in 1755. The interred remains of Dutch were moved here in 1853; their gravestones pave the floor, and coats-of-arms coat the walls. Outside the fort walls is the **Kerkhopf** (1786). On the gates of its interesting cemetery are the Latin words: *memento mori*, "remember death."

Close to the Groote Kerk is one of Sri Lanka's leading remnants of the colonial era, the **New Oriental Hotel**. It is neither

Street scene, Galle.

new nor oriental. Constructed early in 1684 as the Dutch command headquarters, it later served as quarters for British troops and was converted to a hotel in 1865. It has been in the ownership of a single family, the Brohiers, since 1902. The hotel boasts lovely gardens, quaint bedrooms, and a massive dining hall.

In Galle, as perhaps nowhere else in Sri Lanka, the memory of fine old colonial mansions is preserved even if their fabric is fast crumbling. Most of these great homes survive as private residences – **Eddystone, Armitage Hill, Mount Pleasant, Mount Airy**, and **Garstin Hill**. Possibly the best preserved is **Closenberg**, formerly the home of a shipping line captain, now a quiet guest house on a point of land overlooking once-lovely Closenberg Bay with its cement factory. Another "great house," **Buona Vista**, affords a fine view of the region from a hill behind Closenberg.

Beyond Galle, Route A17 wends its way inland, first east, then north, toward the Rakwana Massif and the Hill Country. At **Deniyaya**, about 50 miles (80 kilometers) from Galle, the best approaches can be made to the **Sinharaja Forest**, Sri Lanka's last remaining primeval rainforest. A single faint foot-path cuts through the heart of its 50 square miles (130 square kilometers). Vegetation is many-layered, as in the Amazon or Congo. One walks in a cathedral gloom. Rare orchids blossom and cicadas chirp. Otherwise, the suffocating silence is broken by the sound of rain: 200 inches fall annually here, spread throughout the year. The sheer discomfort of rain-bred leeches, pullulating on the floor of dank and rotting leaves, is as great a discouragement to the would-be intruder as the danger of wild animals and venomous snakes.

There are no such dangers down the coast from Galle, where a beach resort has been developed at **Koggala**. Here also is the new **Martin Wickramasinghe Museum of Folk Art and Culture**. Koggala Lake was of great importance on the British in their Second World War defense of Sri Lanka against the Japanese: it was used as a base for seaplanes and Catalina flying boats. It was from here that Squadron Leader L.J. Birchall, a Canadian, had taken off when he discovered a large Japanese fleet steaming toward Trincomalee. His prompt radio alert – prior to his being shot down and captured by the enemy – was largely responsible for the subsequent Japanese failure to annex Ceylon. This was a major turning point in the war in the Indian Ocean.

Fishing on Stilts: The stretch of shoreline from Koggala through Ahangama to Weligama is famous for its "stilt" fishermen. In fact, these anglers do not perch on stilts at all. They sit on crossbars tied athwart forked branches of trees, planted in the sea bed. This unique method of fishing is highly photogenic.

Inland about 1½ miles from **Ahangama** is the **Kataluwa Temple**. Its marvelous wall paintings were recently featured on Sir Lankan postage stamps. Four different styles of painting are represented; they describe legends and depict dancers and musicians.

At **Weligama,** the main road branches. The marine drive follows a lovely, sandy beach, protected in part by a lush and paradisiacal island a couple of hundred

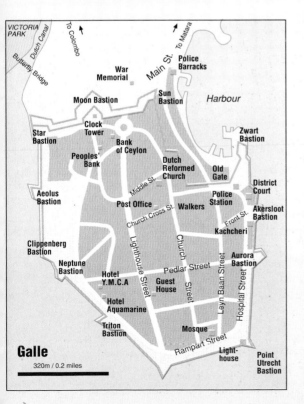

Galle

320m / 0.2 miles

VICTORIA PARK

To Colombo

Dutch Canal

Butterfly Bridge

Main St.

To Matara

War Memorial

Police Barracks

Moon Bastion

Sun Bastion

Harbour

Clock Tower

Star Bastion

Bank of Ceylon

Zwart Bastion

Peoples' Bank

Dutch Reformed Church

Old Gate

District Court

Aeolus Bastion

Middle St.

Post Office

Walkers

Police Station

Akersloot Bastion

Church Cross St.

Front St.

Kachcheri

Clippenberg Bastion

Neptune Bastion

Lighthouse Street

Pedlar Street

Aurora Bastion

Hotel Y.M.C.A

Guest House

Church Street

Leyn Baan Street

Hospital Street

Hotel Aquamarine

Triton Bastion

Mosque

Rampart Street

Light-house

Point Utrecht Bastion

meters offshore. Some call this piece of land **Taprobane Island**; others know it as Yakinige Duwa, "She Devil's Island." It has also been dubbed Count de Mauny's Island, after the French expatriate who bought it in the 1930s and fulfilled his vision of Eden by converting a scrub-covered islet into an exquisite garden. His small but jewel-like house, decorated with eclectic local handicrafts, has had a variety of owners since the Count's death. There are persistent unsubstantiated rumors that the small estate may someday be turned into a hotel.

The highway's inland branch passes through the main town of Weligama. Keep your eyes open for curb stands (some say this buffalo-milk yogurt is tastiest here) and numerous pottery shops. The road winds past the **Kusta Raja Image**, an impressive ancient sculpture in a rock wall. It is believed to be that of the Mahayana Buddhist *bodhisattva* Avalokitesvara. Legend holds, however, that it represents Kusta Raja ("Leper King"), a foreign potentate afflicted with a dreaded skin disease. He sailed to Sri Lanka and was cured by subsisting for three months on *thambili*, the juice of the King Coconut.

Exactly 100 miles (161 kilometers) from Colombo is **Matara**, another old fort town built around the banks of the Nilwala Ganga. It is the southern terminus of the rail line from Colombo and the site of the new **Ruhuna University**.

Matara is an ancient settlement, occupied long before the Portuguese raised a stockade here in the early 16th Century. **Matara Fort**, erected by the Dutch, cuts off a section of land between the sea and the river; within lies most of the old town. Matara's rest house incorporates portions of what once were elephant stables. The old church, built in 1769, is still in use.

After Matara Fort was seized and badly damaged by a Kandyan army in 1761, the Dutch commander constructed the little **Star Fort** two years later. A fine example of military architecture, it has double walls with a moat between them. It was converted to civilian use under the British, and today houses the public library. Look for this fort – and on its gateway, the coat-of-arms

Stilt fishermen, Weligama.

of Baron van Eck, the Dutch governor – about 100 meters north of the old fort.

On the streets of Matara are sideless wooden carts called *hackeries*. Traditional bullock-cart races are held all over rural Sri Lanka on Sinhalese New Year day, but these *hackeries*, designed for speed, are peculiar to the Matara area.

Two miles west of Matara is a superb bathing beach at **Polhena**. East of Matara, a short detour inland will bring you to the **Weherehena Temple**, notable for its colossal Buddha statue and its underground shrine room illustrated in comic-book style with scenes of Buddhist stories.

'City of the Gods': Dondra, about three miles past Matara, is the southernmost point of Sri Lanka. Beyond its lovely octagonal white lighthouse, there is nothing but open sea all the way to Antarctica. Other than the lighthouse (Sri Lanka's tallest at 176 feet) and a thriving cashew industry, it is religion that draws people to Dondra.

No more venerated shrine was ever revaged by the Portuguese than the far-famed **Maha Vishnu Devala**, whose roof of gilt copper shone far out to sea. This shrine was originally constructed about the 7th Century A.D., and was known from China to Morocco. The city around it was "Devi Nuwara," "City of the Gods." Today, there is only a restored stupa, a small and austere stone shrine, and a row of almost pathetic square chapels.

Despite the shortcomings of the site, thousands of pilgrims still flock to the shrine annually for the Dondra Fair and Perahera in the month of *Esala* (July-August). This fair is a throwback to typical *devala* festivals of times long past: Vishnu is the chief deity, and worship of the Buddha is secondary. The 10-day *perahera* is similar in many ways to the great Kandy Perahera, with which it coincides.

Continue through Dondra, and at **Dikwella**, take the cutoff toward Beliatta. Follow it for about a mile to the **Wewurukannala Vihara** – site of the largest Buddha statue on the island. One hundred sixty-five feet (50 meters) high, it was constructed only in 1970. Much like the Weherehena Buddha, this image is seated, painted and surrounded by an eight-

Weherahena temple near Matara.

story building to emphasize its size. In the adjacent vihara are many more images and murals telling Buddhist stories.

Mawella, about four miles past Dikwella on the coast road, features a blowhole, the second largest of only a half-dozen known in the world. "**Ho-o-maniya**," as it is onomatopoeically called, spouts as high as 60 feet (18 meters) into the air, especially in June when the southwest monsoon is worst. Water is trapped in a fissure in a sea-level cave, then forced by wave pressure 75 feet (23 meters) straight up through a chimney in a flat rock! The path to the blowhole leads off the main road at the 117th mile.

Tangalla, the next sizable town, is blessed with a four-mile-wide bay that is a pleasure to swimmers, a paradise to divers. An offshore reef extends like a wall to break the surf. Some major hotels have sprung up recently to take advantage of the clean white sands.

North of Tangalla 13 miles (21 kilometers) by road is the imposing rock of **Mulgirigala**, at 692 feet (211 meters) almost as isolated and sheer as Sigiriya.

There is a *dagoba* rather than a palace atop the rock. Its cave temples (some dating to the 2nd Century B.C.) are of great historical significance: here in 1826, George Turnour, a British colonial officer, found in monastic library the *olas* which enabled scholars to translate the *Mahavamsa* from archaic Pali.

East of Tangalla, there is an immediate change of landscape. You have left the island's "wet zone," graced by the southwest monsoon, and entered the "dry zone." From here to Yala, the road passes a number of brackish water lagoons (called *kalapuwa*).

Hambantota, the largest town on the southeastern coast with a population of about 9,000, is a well-sheltered fishing port. Its lovely rest house hangs on reddish cliffs, which overlooks a white beach backed by sage-green jungle. Just outside the town are salt pans where sea water is left to evaporate, then carried by rail to salt factories.

Hambantota has Sri Lanka's largest proportion of Malay Muslim population. Ancestors of the Malays arrived in sam-

Beach scene near Tangalla.

pans from the Indonesian archipelago during the period of Dutch colonization. More Malays were imported by the British as army mercenaries; today they are fishermen, salt workers and farmers.

Self-drive tourists may be relieved to reach Hambantota, which has the only reliable mechanics for many miles around. The town also boasts the best curd this side of Matara, and numerous stalls line the road just northeast of town.

Don't miss the turnoff seaward into the **Bundala Sanctuary**. Flamingoes are often seen here during the northeast monsoon. Elephants sometimes retreat to the Bundala salt pans during times of drought. Ten miles beyond Bundala, the **Wirawila Sanctuary** encompasses two *wewa* – Wirawila and Tissa. Many aquatic species of birds and several jungle types, including hornbills, make their homes here.

The Ruins of Ruhuna: Now you enter a fascinating region where history, religion and wildlife share top building. **Tissamaharama**, on Tissa Wewa's banks, was the ancient capital of the province of Ruhuna, to which Sinhalese patriots rallying support against Indian invaders invariably fled. No systematic excavation of the known (and unknown) archaeological sites of Ruhuna has yet been undertaken.

One of the few excavated structures is the **Maha Thupa** in Tissamaharma. It dates from the 2nd Century B.C. or earlier, and is believed to have been the largest *dagoba* in Sri Lanka at that time. A **"palace"** – more likely the chapter house of a monastery – has been excavated near the Tissa Wewa bund.

Here also is the **Yatala Dagoba,** where recent diggings have unearthed a fine elephant wall, a great 17-foot moonstone, and a rock-cut inscription. A huge **monolith** stands nearby; marks on one face are said to have been made by chains with which the royal elephants were kept tethered.

Seven miles (11 kilometers) southeast of Tissamaharama is **Kirinda**, the seaside community where Queen-to-be Viharamahadevi is said to have come ashore after her perilous drifting voyage from Kelaniya. A white *dagoba* stands on the rocky cliff, commemorating the safe ar-

Curd stand near Hambantota.

rival of the princess.

'The Holiest Place': In modern Sri Lanka, Tissa and Kirinda carry far less importance to the average person than **Kataragama**. Author Paul Wirz called this jungle site on the Menik Ganga "the holiest place in Ceylon." Hindus, Buddhists and Muslims alike flock to the shrines – about 13 miles (21 kilometers) from Tissamaharama – to worship and make offerings. The largest throngs come during the July-August Kataragama Festival, but the day never passes that the temples are not packed with devotees.

The deity most often associated with Kataragama is Skanda, known here simply as Kataragama Deviyo. Although Buddhists travel to Kataragama ostensibly to visit the **Kirivehera**, a great *dagoba* one kilometer west of the main shrine, where the Buddha is said to have sat in meditation on his third and final visit to Sri Lanka; and although Muslims come to pray at the **Masjad-ul-Khizr** mosque, said to mark the burial place of an important Muslim saint; the followers of all religious can be seen making offerings of

fruit and flowers to Kataragama Deviyo himself!

Unlike festival times, when self-mortification in the fulfilment of vows to the gods seems to be the rule rather than the exception, daily worship at Kataragama is much more tame. Pilgrims purchase offerings at numerous stalls beside the menik Ganga, bathe in the river's waters, then stroll the few hundred meters to the sacred shrines.

The **Maha Devala**, principal shrine of the Kataragama complex, is a simple white stone structure, unornamented except for an elaborately carved door at its main (east) entrance. It contains no image of the Kataragama Deviyo; the place of honor is given to Skanda's *vel*, or lance, which none but the highest priests have ever seen. Within the central shrine complex are *kovils* dedicated to Ganesha and Vishnu, the goddesses Kali and Pattini, and the *deviyo* Mangara. The **Seven Hills of Kataragama** rise two miles south of the holy shrines.

The eastern limit of the South Coast is marked by the **Ruhuna National Park**, best known simply as "Yala." Established in 1899, it is the most popular place in Sri Lanka for viewing wild elephants and other wildlife. The main entrance to the park is at **Palatupana**, about 12 miles (19 kilometers) east of Tissamaharama.

There is a very large number of archaeological sites within the park. Most interesting is **Sithulpahuwa**, which is a wild rocky site near the banks of the crocodile-riddled **Katagamuwa Wewa**. More than 60 inscriptions at Sithulpahuwa identify it as one of the greatest 2nd Century B.C. monastery of celebrated piety and scholarship.

Offshore of Yala are two sets of rocky islets, each marked by a lighthouse. They offer what is reputed to be the finest skin diving anywhere in Sri Lanka. Known as the **Great and Little Basses**, these long red-sandstone reefs, swept by fierce currents and only barely awash, have spelled doom to many ships. Only in the 1860s did the British succeed in raising the prefabricated lighthouse on the Great Basses. Some eight miles (13 kilometers) offshore from Kirinda, its red beacon can be seen flashing far out to sea.

Offerings (left) and blessings at Kataragama.

NEGOMBO AND
THE WEST COAST

The region generally referred to as Sri Lanka's West Coast stretches for some 100 miles (160 kilometers) from Colombo to Wilpattu National Park. Traveling north from the capital, Route A3 to Negombo branches off from Route A1, the Kandy Road, just beyond the **Kelani Ganga** bridge. Residents of the country between here and Negombo, a distance of 18 miles (29 kilometers), are heavily Roman Catholic. Pastel churches line the highway, beckoning travelers with their small shrines to saints and madonnas. The Feast of St. Anne is celebrated here in late July in a carnival-like atmosphere.

A turnoff west (toward the coast) just beyond the fifth milepost leads past the **Pegasus Reef Hotel**. A fascinating but little-used back road to Negombo, it follows an old **Dutch canal** for many miles to the south end of the Negombo Lagoon, then proceeds up a narrow neck of land populated largely by Catholic Tamil fishermen. Known as the *karava*, these fisherfolk claim to be descendants of a North Indian warrior caste who first migrated to Sri Lanka about 1,000 years ago. During the Portuguese colonial era, the *karava* embraced Catholicism almost without exception. Mass baptisms, during which all who attended were given the same surname, resulted in a preponderance of *karava* with names like Fernando, Pereira, de Silva, de Mels and Mendis.

Rubber's Asian Birthplace: The trunk route to Negombo is not without its interesting stops. Just past **Ja-Ela**, across the **Kalu Oya** bridge, turn right on the road toward Gampaha; follow it about six miles (10 kilometers) to the **Henaratgoda Botanical Gardens**. Replaced on most tourist itineraries by the Peradeniya Gardens near Kandy, Henaratgoda's foliage is nonetheless magnificent. It features trees from every corner of the tropical world, and especially from Brazil.

Brazil's most notable contribution to the Sri Lankan economy was the Para rubber tree – *Hevea brasiliensis*. Here at Henaratgoda, in 1876, the first seedlings ever planted in Asia grew and flourished. A British colonial agent had smuggled 70,000 rubber seeds out of the Amazon jungle. London's Kew Gardens succeeded in the cultivation of 2,700 of them. About 2,000 seedlings were then transported to the warm, moist climatic conditions at Henaratgoda. These little trees sired the rubber industry throughout Southeast Asia – in Malaya, Indonesia and South India as well as in Sri Lanka.

Look for a grove of tall, straight-stemmed trees with wounded bark, situated alongside the Palm Circle on the garden's Central Drive. These trees are labelled. No. 6 was the first rubber tree to be tapped in Asia for its rich white latex. No. 2 offered so generous and regular a yield that it convinced all skeptics of the wisdom of establishing a rubber industry here. At its peak, this one tree produced 18 pounds of latex in a single month.

Back on Route A3, take note of the **Free Trade Zone** as you approach **Katunayake International Airport**. More than 22,000 Sri Lankans are employed in this 160-square-mile (414-square-kilometer) in-

Preceding pages: fishing fleet at sea off Negombo. Left, a fisherman unravels his nets. Right, Roman symbol of Catholic faith south of Negombo.

dustrial zone, which opened in 1978. Garment factories and electrical firms forms the majority of the 47 industries operating here with foreign investment support.

A short distance before the airport road, near **Kandawala**, notice a simple survey tower off to the right side of the highway. This and a similar tower in the Hambantota district are the only monuments to one of colonial Ceylon's greatest public servants, Major Thomas Skinner. From 1833 to 1845, as Civil Engineer and Commissioner of Roads, he surveyed the Hill Country on foot and erected his towers as baselines for triangulation.

Negombo's Colonial Charm: The major beach resort on the coast north of Colombo is **Negombo**. Here, in an Old World atmosphere of 17th Century churches and forts, dozens of hotels, guest houses and restaurants have sprung up along the beach on Lewis Road. They run the gamut from luxury hotels to tiny "travellers halts." Negombo's beach is far from the best on the island, but its proximity to the airport makes it an ideal first-night or last-night stopover in Sri Lanka.

Like many other coastal towns in this country, Negombo was an important spice port long before the Portuguese set foot on the island. The enterprising Moors set up a trading system, whereby native labor hauled cinnamon to the coast here. The Portuguese took possession of Negombo about 1600 and raised a small **fort**. The Dutch claimed the stronghold in 1640 and refortified it, providing their initial foothold in Sri Lanka. The British found the fort abandoned in 1796; they tore down most of it to put up a large jail, still in use. All that survives today are the main gate and parts of two bastions.

A few other Dutch relics exist. The canal system, which stretches almost 80 miles from Colombo to Puttalam, is the most evident. A **rest house** facing the lagoon is an old Dutch building; there is a **Dutch cemetery** opposite and to the left of the fort gate.

Negombo Lagoon is a good place to watch the *karava* fishermen at work. Their principal craft is the *oruva*, a dugout outrigger canoe whose pre-historic evolution can be traced from the Comoro Islands off

Karava cemetery on coast south of Negombo.

Mozambique, Africa, to the South Seas. It has been here in Sri Lanka for a long time: the Roman historian Pliny of the 1st Century A.D. called this vessel a typical sight off Taprobane's coast. These fishermen bringing their daily catch of crabs and prawns, seer and other fish, to the fish markets. During the day, they are seen mending their nets on the beach. Many make their homes on the small island of **Duwa**, across the lagoon from Negombo, but connected by motorable causeway.

Duwa's Roman Catholics host the island's only Passion Play throughout the Christian Holy Week, from Palm Sunday to Easter. Far from being an Oberammergau, this naive pageant is presented in simple fashion with strong faith. It is a curious mixture of puppetry and live theater, combining straight prose dialogue with a stylized song-drama form called *nadagam*. Much of the action takes place off stage in the streets of the village. The Good Friday climax, when the crucifixion of Jesus Christ is reenacted, is indeed a moving scene.

Along the shopping streets of Negombo are many establishments selling religious medallions and artifacts. But these are balanced by a proliferation of toddy and *arrack* taverns – proof of the merry pattern of life that the population has adopted.

Coconuts and Batiks: From Negombo to Mundal Lake, coconut estates line the highway, crowding villages for space. Near the community of **Lunuwila**, about 10 miles (16 kilometers) north of Negombo and a short distance inland, is the **Coconut Research Institute**. This government-supported agency, founded in 1929, conducts experiments in breeding, planting and fertilization techniques, pest control, and in the development of industries based on coconut by-products.

The coconut plays a major part in the everyday lives of Sri Lankans. They drink its sap and use the liquid squeezed from the grated kernel for making curries. The plaited fronds become roofing material for village huts and the fruit's fiber goes into the making of coir rope. Coconut grows throughout the coastal regions of the island, except in parts of the north where the palmyrah palm has taken over.

Roman Catholic Church, Negombo.

Perhaps the finest coconut grows in this district, between the Negombo coast and Kurunegala.

The management of coconut is relatively easy. Only periodic fertilization is required. A tree can be plucked in a 50-day cycle using a long pole from the ground, or by the age-old method of shinning up the tree trunk and taking the fruit by hand.

Commercial concerns process coconut into copra (the dried kernel of the nut) and desiccated coconut. Both forms are exported. Also extracted is the highly fatty coconut oil, a household word in Sri Lanka when it comes to frying something.

A stretch of several miles along the main road between **Marawila** (20 miles from Negombo) and **Mahawewa** is famous for its batik factories. The largest of many textile craft centers is the **Buddhi Batik Factory**, which employs 350 girls in the various phases of batik manufacture – tracing, waxing, dying in chemical baths, washing and rinsing in boiling water. The quality of batiks in this area is as good as anywhere on the island, and prices are generally a bit lower. If you buy, make sure your fabric is colorfast.

The Riderless Horse: Just over the bridge at the entrance to the town of **Madampe**, on the shore of a small tank, stands the **Tanniyan-valla Bahu Devala**. You may be startled by the crude though arresting effigy of a rearing horse. Local legend claims that when a Madampe citizen of the last century rode his horse past this *devala* without making an offering, the steed shied and bolted, throwing him to the ground. Badly hurt, the rider vowed that if he lived, an effigy of his horse would decorate the *devala* courtyard. Today, every wary passer-by pauses to offer a few coins or a broken coconut!

The fishing town of **Chilaw** perches picturesquely at the mouth of **Chilaw Lake**. A humped-back bridge over the lagoon leads past the bustling fish market to the **rest house**, recommended by the incredible portions of delicious baked crab and seafood served up for travelers' lunches.

A couple of miles inland from Chilaw, on the road to Wariyapola and the brief-lived ancient capital of Panduvas Nuwara, *Oruva* boats prepare to set sail.

the temple of **Munnesvaram** is on the banks of a *wewa* of the same name. It is the southernmost of Sri Lanka's age-old Shaivite *isvarams*, residences of the supreme god. Devotees claim the god Vishnu worshipped at this site in person eons ago, and that the shrine was established by the epic hero Rama, himself an *avatar* (incarnation) of Vishnu. It was destroyed by the Portuguese and reerected during British times. For two weeks in early September of every year, a temple festival featuring fire-walking is celebrated.

Entering the 'Dry Zone': As you cross the **Deduru Oya** and proceed north, the terrain suddenly becomes markedly drier. You have left the Sri Lankan "wet zone" behind. The fishing community at **Udappuwa**, about four miles west of the main highway on the small neck of land between Mundal Lake and the sea, is a *karava* settlement – but Hindu *karava*. The village *kovil*, dedicated to the worship of the goddess Draupadi, includes firewalking in its annual festival. For 18 days, devotees maintain a strict vegetarian diet. Each day, a temple official reads them passages from the Buddhist *Jatakas* (!) for strength. Then on the eighteenth night, after a ritual washing at sea, men, women and children alike tread on a bed of coals. They believe they are protected by the flowing hair of the goddess Draupadi, a joint consort of five Pandyan princes of the *Mahabharata* tale.

Mundal Lake itself is a palm-fringed sheet of water navigable all the way to the Puttalam Lagoon, 15 miles (24 kilometers) north. It is deceptively shallow, however, with a bottom of dangerously sticky mud.

At the 78th milepost, turn west (left) at the village of **Palavi**, two miles before Puttalam. A 24-mile (39-kilometer) road will take you up the west bank of the seafood-rich **Puttalam Lagoon** to the old fort town of Kalpitiya.

Two-thirds of the way there, break your journeys at the community of **Talawila**. The Roman Catholic church is a site of pilgrimage, especially during the Feast of St. Anne on July 26. Even Muslims come here to worship the Virgin Mary's mother, whom they call Hannah Bibi. The church is said to have been founded by a 17th Century Portuguese who had a divine vision of St. Anne herself. The shrine has a reputation as a place of healing.

Kalpitiya, guarding the western entrance to the Puttalam Lagoon, was established by the Portuguese in the early 17th Century. The Dutch raised an improved fortification on the site in 1676; this was surrendered to the British in 1795, and a British garrison occupied it for about three decades before it was abandoned. A four-sided building with 20-foot scarps, the **fort** is now roofless but is still in good condition. **St. Peter's Kerk**, about a half-mile west of the fort, owes its unique architecture to the British, who rebuilt the gabled and thatch-roofed Dutch church in 1840. Inquire for the caretaker, who lives in Kalpitiya, to enter the fort and church.

Puttalam Lagoon is Sri Lanka's second largest lagoon (after Jaffna). It is deep and widely navigable. In **Dutch Bay**, at its oceanward mouth, the island of **Ipantivu** is often occupied by migrant coconut pickers of fishermen. Some miles further north is the seldom-visited island of **Karativu**, a strip of sand eight miles long and half to three-quarters of a mile wide.

Negombo Fort.

Its only permanent residents are deer, but fishermen set up *vadis* (temporary camps) all over the island as monsoons dictate.

Return to Palavi and proceed to **Puttalam**, the terminus of Route A3. Puttalam is an arid fishing settlement with nothing in particular to recommend it, although it was known to Arab traders as early as the 14th Century.

An old road leads north from Puttalam to the **Kala Oya** and the frontier of **Wilpattu National Park**. A suitably equipped Jeep can traverse the park and continue all the way to Mannar. **Pomparippu**, within the bounds of the park about 22 miles (35 kilometers) from Puttalam, is notable for its Stone Age graveyard. Fields of funerary urns, many buried with skulls and pottery, have been discovered.

Route A12 begins in Puttalam and runs across the island, through Anuradhapura to Trincomalee on the East Coast. There is a turnoff to Wilpattu National Park at the 27th milepost. Famed for its leopards, the park is easily accessible from Anuradhapura.

Traveling along the Kandy Road: Travelers proceeding from Colombo to Kandy

have enough points of interest enroute to make their journey last two days! There is a mandatory stop at Kelaniya Temple, just outside Colombo. At Miriswatta junction, less than 17 miles from the capital, a road leads through Gampaha to the Henaratgoda Botanical Gardens.

A turnoff to the right at the 22nd milepost (Tihariya junction) takes you two miles to the **Varana Vihara**, a series of cave templed dating perhaps from the 3rd Century B.C. Some of the caverns appear to have been artifically cut from huge boulders. *Dagobas*, murals and a reclining Buddha are among the temples' treasures. A monastic library is its greatest pride.

A few miles away at **Attanagalla**, the **Attanagalu Vihara** has been a place of worship since the 3rd Century A.D. It may have been the island's earliest *vatadage*, a circular pillared temple enclosing a *dagoba*. Today, a small stupa exists beneath the building's octangular roof; there is a larger 13th Century *dagoba* on the temple grounds.

Back on the main highway, near **Nittambuwa**, 25 miles (40 kilometers) from Colombo, the tomb of the former Prime Minister **S.W.R.D. Bandaranaike's** is simply set in the grounds of his father's Horagolla mansion, not far from the roadside. He was assassinated in 1959.

You can't miss the "cashew capital" of **Pasyala**, near the 29th milepost. A banner stretched across the highway proclaims "Cadjugama," "**cashew city**." Several dozen makeshift stalls, managed by colorfully clad young women, comprise a wayside snack bar. The fresh cashews (in fact a species of mango) are delicious, and the *thambili*, King Coconut water, is thoroughly refreshing.

The villages of **Bataliya** (named for *bata*, split bamboo) and **Weweldeniya** (for *veval*, split cane) are famous for their basketware and weaving. Cane-work is also sold by the roadside in the bazaar town of **Warakapola**.

At **Ambepussa**, you are in the Kegalla District. The highway branches here. Route A6 proceeds north through Kurunegala to Trincomalee. Route A1 continues straight to Kandy.

Left, painted stork at Wilpattu National Park. Right, husking coconuts.

RICHARD GABRIEL

behind Barefoot

A TASTE OF KANDY: THE HILL CAPITAL

Nestled in the foothills of the Hill Country on the banks of a lovely tree-lined lake, the city of Kandy is the center of traditional Sri Lankan culture. Perhaps more than anywhere else in the island, this comfortably cool home to nearly 100,000 people represents the living past.

The sacred tooth of the Buddha, symbolic of sovereignty over the island, is preserved here in its own temple. Every August, it is paraded around the city on the back of an elephant in what may be Asia's biggest celebration. Traditions of Sinhalese music and dance, arts and crafts may be forgotten in Colombo, but they flourish in this hill city. Monasteries of Sri Lanka's two leading Buddhist sects are long-established centers of learning here. Indeed, the functions which once fell to the ancient cities of Anuradhapura and Polonnaruwa are as much alive in Kandy today as they have been for some 400 years.

Preceding pages: **Kandy city and lake.** **Left**, modern Kandyan chief in Perahera procession. **Below**, an Asgiriya monk displays palm-leaf scriptures.

To many Sri Lankans and visitors alike, Kandy is the sweetest city on the island. But its name did not derive from any confection. Simply, *kanda* is the Sinhalese word for "hill" – an appropriate label for this settlement at 1,600 feet (488 meters) elevation. Kandy was originally known as Senkadagala, after a hermit who is said to have lived here. It became a religious center in the 13th or 14th Century and a political center in the confused days following the decline of Polonnaruwa. When the Portuguese took a firm hold on the low country during the 16th Century, the Sinhalese rulers of Kotte and Sitawaka retreated inland eventually setting up their capital at Kandy in 1590.

For the 225 years that followed, the Hill Country rulers doggedly maintained their independence. They defied the Portuguese, Dutch and British alike, and remained a thorn in the side of all three colonial powers until the British once and for all subdued the Kandyans in 1815. It remained in British hands until Ceylon achieved its independence in 1948, but not before it had served a spell as Lord Mountbatten's Second World War headquarters. Today, many Sinhalese known Kandy as *Maha Nuwara*, "the great city."

The city is centered on serene Kandy Lake, a 19th Century creation of independent Kandy's last king. A densely foliated residential district covers the hills on the lake's south side, while the main town occupies the streets to the west and north. Highway A1 from Colombo, the Kandy Road, becomes Dalada Vidiya as it runs along the north lake shore past the colonial Queens Hotel and the famous Temple of the Tooth, known as the Dalada Maligawa. D.S. Senanayake Vidiya, formerly Trincomalee Street, conjuncts Dalada Vidiya at the Queens Hotel and proceeds north as route A9.

The Temple of the Tooth: Any visitor to Kandy will want to start his or her tour at the **Dalada Maligawa**, the unmistakable moated pink building standing almost alone near the lake shore.

Ever since the 4th Century A.D., when the Buddha's tooth was brought to Sri Lanka hidden from sacrilegious hands in an Orissan princess' hair, the relic has grown in repute and holiness in Sri Lanka and throughout the Buddhist world. It became not only Sri Lanka's most prized possession, but the very seal of sovereignty. The national capital was regarded as the place where the Tooth Relic was permanently housed.

The tooth came to Kandy in 1590. King Wimala Dharma Suriya I built a two-story shrine on the site of the current temple. Three generations later, King Narendra Sinha raised a new two-story temple. It survives today as the Inner Temple.

Improvements were made by later kings. Early in the 19th Century, Sri Wickrama Rajasinha added the octagonal Pittirippuva at the corner nearest to the lake. This provided a place from which he could address his subjects on important occasions. The British for a short time converted the lower chambers of the Pattirippuva into a Garrison room for troops but it now houses the temple's priceless library.

Few persons ever see the Tooth Relic itself. What they see instead, behind a gilt railing a table of silver, is the great *dagoba*-shaped *karanduwa*, a gold-plated reliquary. This is only the outermost casket of seven. Within, it is said, are six increasingly smaller shrines of similar shape, all of pure gold and ornamented with precious gems. When the tooth is displayed (on rare occasions) at exhibitions, it rests in a loop of gold that rises from the heart of a golden lotus.

At one time, the inner sanctum was accessible only to the king and certain monks. Today, during *puja* hours, visitors can penetrate two antechambers and view the reliquary from the "Hall of Beatific Vision." *Pujas* are held at dawn (about 6 a.m.), mid-morning (about 11 a.m.) and dusk (about 6:30 p.m.). The temple itself is open to visitors from dawn to dusk.

There are many other treasures within the temple. A miniature Buddha carved from a single three-inch-by-two-inch emerald, is protected in the 'Karanduva into the inner-sanctum, while a sitting Buddha cut from a chunk of rock crystal, is exhibited in the lower shrine below the Octagon. Fine woodcarvings, painted ceilings, and silver-and-ivory doors adorn the Inner Temple. In the library are exquisite *ola* manuscripts, hand-etched on sheets

Left, balloon vendor on streets of Kandy.

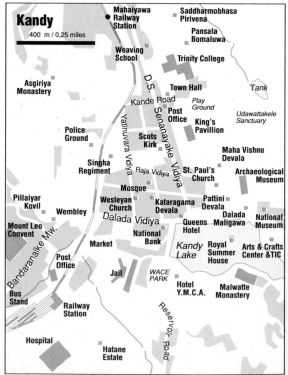

of palm leaf, bound within boards of gilt silver, intricate lacquer and carved ivory.

On the south side of the temple, facing the lake, is an open courtyard where elephants are caprisoned and prepared for the two-week Esala Perahera in July-August. This festival should not be missed. (See the feature on festivals).

The Royal Palace Complex: The Dalada Maligawa was part of a tremendous complex of buildings that extended from the King's Palace (north of the temple) past the Queen's Palace (behind and uphill from the temple). It included the royal **Audience Hall**, slightly behind and to the north of the Temple of the Tooth.

Quintessential of Kandyan architecture, this pillared opened hall had its foundation stone laid in 1784. It was not completed until the British were in control of Kandy. But the Audience Hall was in use even before the elaborately carved columns of teak and *halmilla* were in place in the stone floor. For in 1815, this was the venue of the conference of Kandyan chiefs who agreed to surrender the kingdom to the British. Today, the Audience Hall is

kept in top condition. At one time, the Hall was occasionally used for ceremonial sittings of the Supreme Court.

The only portion of the **King's Palace** existing today is the public sector which served as the British government agent's residence. The private rooms have vanished. The palace is thought to have been built by King Wimala Dharma Suriya I in the late 16th Century. The influence of Portuguese prisoners of war is seen in its design and construction. Today it is occupied by the **Archaeological Museum**, open 8 a.m. to 4 p.m. except Tuesdays.

More interesting is the **National Museum**, housed in what used to be the **Queen's Palace**. It is just east of the Dalada Maligawa, on a small hill over-looking the lake. Rooms and cloisters open onto a small central courtyard. The museum contains a good collection of Kandyan royal regalia and an extensive display of jewelry and household articles. It is open 9 a.m. to 5 p.m. except Fridays.

Within a single block of the royal palace complex are three of the four historic *devalas* which play a key role in The Esala

The Queen's Hotel.

Perahera. Almost directly across the street from the Temple of the Tooth is the **Pattini Devala.** Though purely Hindu in origin, this popular goddess of chastity and health is a favorite among Buddhists as well. Her small and simple shrine is probably second in antiquity only to the **Natha Devala,** the oldest surviving building in Kandy. Its enclosure adjoins the Pattini shrine to the north. This *devala* was probably the center of a Mahayanist cult of Natha worship in the 13th or 14th century. The shrine's style is Dravidian, consisting only of a porch and sanctum built on a walled platform; but its Buddhistness is asserted by a *dagoba*-shaped *sikhara.*

The **Maha Vishnu Devala** is the most important of Kandy's four major *devalas.* The worship of Upulvan, as Vishnu is known to Buddhists in his role as protector of isle Buddhism, originally was centered on Dondra. During the wars with the Portuguese, the deity's image was removed first to Alutnuwara in the Kandyan foothills, then to the safety of Kandy. The *devala* is located across Raja Vidiya from the Natha Devala, close to the King's Palace. It has a double roof and lantern, and colorful *makara torana* gateway at the top of a flight of steps. Vishnu is regarded as lord of elephants, so the *mahout* of each elephant taking part in *peraheras* must stop and salute at this point on the route.

Christians, Hindus, and Buddhist Monks: At the nearest street corner to the *devalas,* on Raja Vidiya, is **St. Paul's Church.** Built of brick in 1846, it still has regular Anglican services featuring a 115-year-old pipe organ. The Rev. Neil Van Dort, a Burgher, until recently used to conduct services in English and Sinhalese, incorporating traditional Kandyan drumming as well as rice and flower offerings into his program.

Near the church, back toward the lake shore, is the government-run **Laksala,** featuring handicrafts created all over the island. The selection is not exclusively Kandyan, but the range is quite wide and the prices fair.

The so-called **King's Pavilion,** at the foot of the hills, has its main entrance off Raja Vidiya about a half a block west of St. Paul's Church. Built not by a king but by the indefatigable Governor Edward

Temple of the Tooth, circa 1864.

Barnes in 1834, this splendid house is now kept as a Kandy residence for the President of Sri Lanka. (Barnes' other two palatial mansions became hotels – one in Mt. Lavinia, the other in Nuwara Eliya.)

If you continue on Raja Vidiya for about 1½ blocks, then turn left on Kotugodalle Vidiya for another block or so, you will discover the **Kataragama Devala** on your right. The most recent of Kandy's four important *devalas*, it is one of the most popular Hindu temples in the city. The persistent ringing of a bell is a sign that a ceremony is in progress. Visitors without hats and shoes may freely enter and observe.

Another block west, on Yatinuwara Vidiya, the **Sinha Regiment** maintains its headquarters. The private regimental collection of the forces may be of interest to military buffs. The officer-in-charge can arrange a showing.

The **Asgiriya Monastery** is a short uphill walk from here. Head north on Yatinuwara Vidiya to the railroad tracks. Cross, take the right-hand fork, and continue for about one-quarter mile to this mother temple of the Siyam Nikaya sect of Sinhalese Buddhism.

Together with the lakeside Malwatta Monastery, Asgiriya exercises spiritual control over the vast majority of Buddhist communities in Sri Lanka. In general, communities north of Kandy look to Asgiriya for guidance, while those in the south look to Malwatta. There is little difference between the two. They share equally in the ritual service of the Tooth Relic. And each is a classic example of the proper complex surrounding a monastery.

Asgiriya was established in the 17th Century. Solid hingeless doors and fine woodcarvings are among the monastery's treasures. It also has ancient *ola* manuscripts and styli, plus an 18th Century king's chair of carved ivory and painted wood. Inside the meditation room are a number of gold and ivory objects.

A Walk Around the Lake: A pleasant way to spend a couple of morning or afternoon hours is to stroll around **Kandy Lake**. Leaving the Queens Hotel and heading south along the embankment, you'll pass a boat jetty jutting into the lake. For a few

Temple of the Tooth, circa 1980s.

rupees, small outboard-powered craft will take visitors for brief spins around the lake, perhaps for closer looks at cormorants and water monitors.

Sri Wrickrama Rajasinha saw Kandy Lake completed in 1807, just eight years before he surrendered his kingdom to the British. It was not exactly a popular project among 19th Century Kandyans. Although the lake's great aesthetic beauty was indisputable, Kandyan commoners argued that it served no practical purpose. Built with compulsory and unpaid labor, it irrigated no fields. But the British loved it. Nineteenth Century governors laid out the promenade around the lake and added a parapet to its rim. And Rajasinha himself took rather a fancy to it. Offshore from the Dalada Maligawa he built an islet, and on it he constructed his Royal Summer House. Some say he kept his harem there year-round. On the site of the summer house, the unromantic British built a powder magazine no prettier than a coffin. It was not demolished until the 1960s.

Not quite halfway down the south shore of the lake, is the **Malwatta Monastery**, which is even older than its hilltop counterpart, the Asgiriya. Its old *vihara* may date from the 16th Century. In ancient times, Malwatta's *sangharaja* was regarded as the ruler of the brotherhood of monks.

The first historic mention of the Malwatta Monastery was in 1597, when King Wimala Dharma Suriya I brought monks from Burma to revive the Ceylonese Sangha through ordination. For centuries since, the monastery has held annual ordinations of its own. The ceremony (called *upasampada*) takes place in June; visitors may be admitted to witness this occasion of rare solemnity.

Malwatta's chapter hall, built in 1753, is a typical Kandyan-style building with tall columns, carved lintels and a painted ceiling. Its treasures include magnificent Kandyan chests, *olas* and furniture.

Further down the lake shore is the **Hotel Suisse**, another old colonial mansion now converted to lodging. Near the east end of the road fringing the lake's north side is the **Buddhist Publication Society's** new headquarters. There is a small bookstore and an extensive library. Lay Buddhists

Kandyan dancers.

and sometimes English-speaking *bhikkus* are on hand to assist visitors. This is where you should inquire if you are a potential student of meditation or have other interests in Theravada Buddhism.

Further along the return route to downtown, only 100 meters from the Dalada Maligawa, the **Kandyan Arts and Crafts Association** and the **Tourist Information Center** share the same building facing the lake. Ignore the touts and snake charmers who hang out on the sidewalk in front, and wander into the Art Association's exhibit halls. Founded in the early 1880s to protect and encourage genuine Kandyan arts and crafts, the association was the first enterprise of its kind in Sri Lanka. Silver and brass metalwork, lacquerwork, wood and ivory carving, pottery and weaving are all represented here.

North of the lake, behind the Temple of the Tooth and the royal palace complex, is the lush and relatively untouched vegetation of the **Udawattakele Sanctuary**. Some 160 acres of tropical rainforest provide a haven to fascinating flowers, birds and monkeys. A poor dirt road is motorable

Silver and brass in a metal worker's shop.

only in good weather, but there are several walking paths.

Perhaps the most pleasant view of Kandy town is from **Castle Hill Park**, sometimes also called Wace Park. From this height, easily reached by following the main uphill road from the southwest corner of the lake, the main section of the city – from Asgiriya to Tooth Temple – is spread out below. D.S. Senanayake Vidiya aims straight as a flung spear at the Matale Hills in the distance.

Kandy's **Municipal Market** is only a couple of blocks west of the lake jetty. In close quarters are the **bus depot** and the **railway station**. Just across the tracks from the station is the main **post office**, in a building that once housed the Grand Hotel. Like many other businesses in this part of town, the hotel failed financially. Some maintain this neighborhood is ill-omened because it was the torture ground of the Kandyan kings. Impalements, dismemberment by elephants, and other atrocities took place here in the 17th and 18th centuries.

About four miles (6½ kilometers) from

Kandy on the main highway to Colombo are the **Peradeniya Botanical Gardens**. Established in 1816, they were initially planted only with coffee and cinnamon; but the scope was soon expanded to include all Sri Lankan flora, and later to encompass overseas species as well.

Visitors can walk or motor through the 147-acre gardens. Special features include the Avenue of Royal Palms; the bamboo-fringed Riverside Drive; and Bat Drive, with a vast population of flying foxes spending their days hanging upside down. There are also a spice garden, an herb garden, and orchid house, a cactus house and a glass house of anthuriums, begonias, African violets and other species. Admission is charged.

Across the Mahaweli River from the gardens, connected by suspension bridge, is the **Gannoruwa Agricultural Research Station**. Botanical problems ranging from acclimatization to entomology are studied by scientists here. Once the private coffee estate of Governor Edward Barnes, it became a research station in the 1890s.

The **Mahaweli River** draws three sides to the Botanical Gardens which are situated in a major meander in the stream. In fact, the geography of the entire Kandy area is dominated by the Mahaweli. By far the largest river in Sri Lanka, the Mahaweli is 206 miles (332 kilometers) in length. It rises high in the Hill Country near Adam's Peak and flows across two-thirds of the island's length and breadth to the sea near Trincomalee. More than 40 tributaries augment its course.

The Mahaweli's greatest value to Sri Lanka has always been in irrigating farmlands, and the late 20th Century is no different. The Mahaweli Diversion Scheme, now nearly complete, will alter the agricultural pattern of about half of the island's land area, bringing green fields to the dry north. Throughout the Mahaweli basin, both east and west of Kandy, teams of international experts are erecting new dams and undertaking related projects.

The **University of Peradeniya**, Sri Lanka's largest institute of higher education, is south of the Botanical Gardens. About 6,500 students are enrolled in arts,

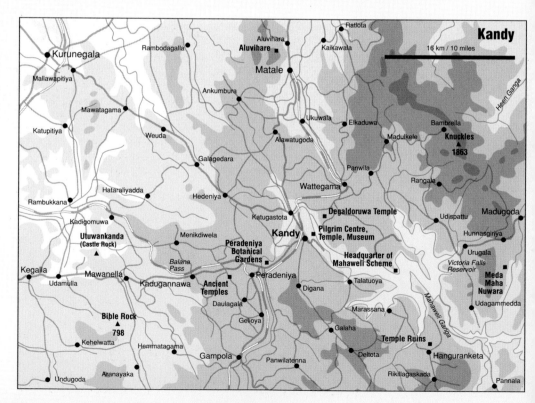

sciences and medical curricula. The spacious green campus is laid out near the banks of the Mahaweli.

Elephants and Jatakas: The river figures in another of the most popular visitor attractions in the Kandy region – the **Elephant Bathing Place** at Katugastota. At the foot of the main bridge on the highway heading north, *mahouts* lead their great beasts to the river to cool off after (or during) a day's labor. Mid to late afternoons are usually the best time to watch. Don't be surprised when the *mahouts* demand payment for photographing their elephants!

A half-day motor tour through the Dumbara Valley east of Kandy will take you to several more interesting sites. Follow Route B38 out of town toward Teldeniya. Cross the Mahaweli, turn right with the highway, and take the next left turn toward Medawala.

It is no more than a half-mile to the **Kalapuraya Craftsmen's Village**. A variety of skills in metalwork and woodcarving are displayed in this artificially created community. About one-quarter

mile further on the right, the **Galmaduwa Gedige** is an unfinished 17th Century Buddhist temple with a pyramidal tower of stone and brick, highly reminiscent of a Hindu *gopuram*.

Another two miles up the road is the **Degaldoruwa Cave Temple**, which dates from the mid-18th Century. It contains wall paintings of great interest and rare quality. Into depictions of the Buddhist *Jataka* tales are worked details of monastic, court and village life of the time. It is a documentary of customs, manners and social conditions, down to fine points of costume and utensils.

The **School of Kandyan Dance** at **Gunnepana** village is one of the most famous centers of dance instruction. Near this community, which is located about one mile north of Degaldoruwa, is a second village, **Amunugama**, equally well-known for its proliferation of drummers. Another two miles is **Medawala**, where several families specialize in traditional metalworkers' craft of repousse. From here, you can return to Kandy via Katugastota.

Paddy field on the outskirts of Kandy.

SHORT TRIPS FROM KANDY

There are many interesting attractions within hours of Kandy by road. They include impressive vistas, important ancient temples, craftsmen's villages, and even an orphanage for elephants. Many of these points of interest are easily accessible from Route A1, the principal highway link between Kandy and Colombo. In particular, three 14th Century temples of great importance are a short distance beyond Peradeniya.

Turn south at Embiligama. Junction, some 2½ miles (four kilometers) beyond the botanical gardens, and proceed a short half-mile to the **Gadaladeniya Vihara**. Built almost exclusively of stone in 1344, it is situated on a hilltop commanding views of the surrounding countryside. The architecture is Dravidian. The entrance porch features large stone pillars which support a roof of huge stone slabs. Within the *vihara*, an ancient stone-and-plaster

Buddha image looks down upon milk-rice pots that have collected food offerings for centuries. The 638-year-old *jak* wood doors still exhibit their original paintings.

In the immediate vicinity, the village of **Kiriwavula** has a traditional brass foundry. Metalwork is carried out by the *cire predue* (lost wax) method; the finished art is displayed in a small showroom. Crude spectacle lenses are also ground here, using pure rock crystal.

About 2½ miles south of Gadaladeniya is the **Lankatilaka Vihara**, also completed in 1344 but in a more traditional Sinhalese style. Situated atop a gray crag amidst fertile highland green, it justifies its name: "the beauty spot on Lanka's brow." The shrine contains an ancient Buddha image of brick and plaster, plus *devalas* to the four guardian deities of the island, each with his consort. A Pali language rock inscription at the site records the valuable gifts to craftsmen who toiled on the temple. Woodcarvers still work at the foot of the rock on which the temple stands.

Another mile away, by motorable road or footpath, is the **Kataragama Davala** at

Lankatilaka Vihara.

Embekke. Famed for its woodcarvings, the *devala* is attributed to King Wikramabahu III or Gampola (1357-1374). A timbered roof is supported by superbly crafted columns their carved panels displaying a great variety of designs. Figures include swans, a double-headed eagle, a lion, a lotus, wrestlers, soldiers, dancing girls, musicians, and many others, including a village mother suckling her infant.

North of the Kandy-Colombo highway, on the road to Murutalawa, the **Dodanwela Devala** preserves the golden crown and steel sword of Kandyan King Rajasinha II. The nearby village of **Manikdiwela** was founded in the early 1950s by textile expert Edith Ludowyk as a weaving center; sophisticated hand-loom fabrics are produced here.

The View From Kadugannawa: About six miles form Peradeniya, the town of **Kadugannawa** sits at the top of a steep descent. A 125-foot (38-meter) lighthouse-like **monument** to roads engineer W.F. Dawson celebrates the completion of the 72-mile Colombo-Kandy road in 1827.

Asia's first mailcoach service was inaugurated along this route in 1932. Just below Kadugannawa is a large boulder. Dawson made a point of tunneling through it to fulfill an old Kandyan prophecy - that the kingdom should never fall "unless an enemy pierced the living rock" to reach it.

The view as you descend the steep road is remarkable. The flat-topped rock in the distance is known as **Bible Rock**; colonial religionists felt it resembled a partially opened book placed spine upward. To the north is **Alagalla** (3,390 feet; 1,033 meters), whose southwest face drops off sharply some 2,000 feet. The main Colombo-Kandy rail line winds around its base.

Utuwankanda, or Castle Rock, is a forested hill to the north of the highway near Mawanella. The rock pinnacle at its peak gives it the appearance of a fortress. In the 1860s, this became the hideout of an outlaw named Saradiel. Such a legend has grown around this murderous robber and highwayman that many folks today regard him nostalgically as a sort of Robin Hood. In fact, there is no evidence that he

Gadaladeniya Vihara.

ever "stole from the rich to give to the poor." He once returned twice the sum he had stolen from an old man when he learned that it was life savings intended as dowry. But he killed 18 men in as many months before he was captured in Mawanella and hanged.

Mawanella is today a town of spice gardens. Signs in English, German ("Gewurz Garten") and French ("Jardin des Spices") line the highway, enticing visitors to sniff and sample such scents and flavors as cinnamon, ginger and cardamom.

There are many little-known ancient temples in the hills, rocks and caves of this region. One of the most important is the **Maha Vishnu Devala** in Alutnuwara, a couple of miles south of the main highway, west of Mawanella town. In the early 14th Century, a red-sandalwood image of the god Upulvan (Vishnu) was brought here for veneration from the *devala* at Dondra. Later, when the image was removed to Kandy, a great God who causes women to fall into hysterical trances became the center of worship. A *perahera* is held here annually during the month of *Esala*.

A short distance before the highway enters Kegalla, a road leads north toward **Pinawella**. Here a government-supported **Elephant Orphanage** is located on the banks of the Maha Oya. Some 15 elephants, many of them babies less than a year old, are raised to maturity after having been found abandoned or injured in the country's jungles. They are trained to work, and eventually are sold to companies or temples. It is most interesting to visit at feeding or bathing time.

Near the 42nd milepost, a road winds several miles north to **Beligala**, one of several places said to enshrine the Bowl Relic of the Buddha. **Beligala Vihara** may date as far back as the 2nd Century A.D. Its entrance gate is large enough to admit an elephant, and its moonstone is of rare design. The Tooth Relic was once kept here in the 13th Century.

Another mile down Route A1, a road turns south three miles to **Dedigama**, a fascinating archaeological site and the birthplace of the great King Parakramabahu I of Polonnaruwa fame. This noted ruler constructed the *dagoba* known as

Left, cinnamon, Mawanella. Below, wrestlers on carved column at Embekke's Kataragama Devala.

Kotavehera to commemorate himself in the 12th Century. Truncated in style, it possesses at least 10 relic chambers, instead of the usual one. Nearby is an **Archaeological Museum** (closed Tuesdays), whose treasures include a delightful "elephant lamp" found within the *dagoba*. The bronze elephant is an oil reservoir, standing a shallow dish from which burn the usual wicks. When the supply of oil in the dish sinks below a certain level, the elephant replenishes it in much the same manner as the famous "Mannikin Piss" replenishes the Brussels fountain.

At Ambepussa, Route A1 is joined by A6 from Kurunegala and Trincomalee. Colombo is about 38 miles (61 kilometers) southwest of here.

The Aluvihara Rock Temple: North of Kandy, the modern town of **Matale** owes its existence chiefly to the erection in 1803 of **Fort MacDowall** by the British. All that remains of the fort today is a gateway. There are traces of earthworks where the Anglican church now stands.

East of here, off Route B36, the village of **Palle Hapuvida** specializes in lacquer work of the *niyapotuvada* or "nailwork" variety. This cottage industry is several centuries old.

Aluvihara is situated just north of Matale, about 18 miles (29 kilometers) from Kandy. Here, in the 2nd Century B.C., the Buddhist scriptures (the *Tipitaka*) were first committed to writing, a chore that required the devout attention of about 500 senior monks. The library was totally destroyed in 1848, along with a large part of the rest of the temple complex, when the British pursued a notorious rebel leader to a hiding place in the rock caves here. Since that time, monks have been painstakingly re-inscribing the *ola* (palm leaf) manuscripts. The 550 *Jataka* tales (stories of the Buddha's many births) have been recorded in Sinhalese; and the first of the "three baskets" of the *Tipitaka* was completed in 1982. The rock caves were formed long ago by boulders tumbling down a nearby mountain. They contain various icons and frescoes. One cavern graphically depicts a sinners' hell.

The most prominent landmark on the road east from Kandy is **The Knuckles**,

Orphaned elephants, Pinawella.

whose unmistakable profile looms 6,112 feet (1,863 meters) above the Dumbara Valley. But their beauty gives only a taste of what is to come along the narrow, winding road to the great *dagoba* of Mahiyangana, 46 miles (73 kilometers) east of Kandy. For Route B38 is arguably the most grandly scenic on the island.

East of Kandy: About eight miles east of Kandy, keep your eyes open for a turn to the left leading to the village of **Henawala**. Craftsmen here are famous for their mat weaving. Produced from vegetable fiber rather than palm leaves or reeds, the mats have beauty and durability.

A turnoff to the left before the town of Teldeniya leads to the headworks of the **Mahaweli Diversions Scheme** at **Polgolla**. There is not a lot to see here; a 530-foot (162 meter) long dam impounds a small lake. Just downriver, are the **Victoria Falls**. Only 33 feet (10 meters) high, they are impressive for the way in which they shoot through a rock-bound corridor. Nearby, British and Swedish engineering firms have constructed hydroelectric projects.

Teldeniya, a village nearby, once renowned for producing cotton, tobacco, coconuts and vegetables, now lies buried under several hundred tons of water. The village had been in the way of the waters from the Mahaweli Diversion Scheme. Beyond this, the road gets more rugged. Hamlets perch on steep hillsides and ridges. Tiny roadside shops display bananas, mangoes, breadfruit, *jak* fruit, pomelo, jungle fruit (like a tiny red crabapple) and the orange fruit of the cashew.

Twenty-four miles (39 kilometers) east of Kandy, the ridgetop highway passes the great hump of **Hunasgiriya Peak**. Centuries ago, below it, was a secret citadel of Kandyan kings at times of foreign attack and occupation. On more than one occasion, the Tooth Relic was harbored here. The massive ruin of Medamahanuwara, "the great city in the middle," can still be seen on its summit.

Past Madugoda, the road begins to descend, first gradually, then rapidly, to the Mahaweli River at Mahiyangana. In one five-mile stretch, there are 18 switchbacks, and driving can be a bit hazardous. The perils include wild monkeys who insist on occupying the middle of the highway.

The view on descent is awesome. You can see many miles in all directions, except the one you've just come from. Ahead of you lie the lowland plains and jungle known as the **Bintenna**. This is Veddha territory, the "last stomping grounds" of Sri Lanka's Stone Age race.

Just a couple of miles beyond the base of the hill, a half-mile south of the main highway, is the ancient *dagoba* of **Mahiyangana**, one of the most holy of Buddhist monuments on the island. The devout believe it was erected over locks of the Buddha's hair even before His death. According to the *Mahavamsa*, the Buddha visited this site during a Veddha festival and levitated, at once terrifying and converting the island's inhabitants.

It is said that a collarbone plucked from the Buddha's funeral pyre was later added to an expanded *dagoba*. Successive rulers, including Dutugemunu in the 2nd Century B.C. and up to the present, have improved upon the *dagoba*, covering it with layer after layer like a lily bulb, until it reached its present impressive proportions.

Left, Mahiyangana *dagoba*. **Right, roadside fruit sellers.**

THE VERDANT HILL COUNTRY

Tea. The glistening green leaves of this lovely shrub, and the colorfully clad women who pluck it, provide lasting impressions of Sri Lanka's Hill Country for most visitors. Neat rows of green cloak ridges and valleys. Nowhere else on earth is tea more important to the economy on the palate than here.

But the Hill Country is much more than tea. With average heights well over 3,000 feet (914 meters), and several peaks above 7,000 feet (2,134 meters), this region has a cool, crisp climate unknown elsewhere in Sri Lanka. Unusual plants, birds and animals thrive. Here are impressive natural features like waterfalls and caves. Here, too, are such unique locations as the old British hill resort of Nuwara Eliya, the gem capital of Ratnapura, the holy mountain of Adam's Peak, and the great rock sculptures of Buduruvagala.

Route A5 is the principal highway from Kandy through the Hill Country. It follows the Mahaweli River south from Peradeniya to **Gampola**, national capital for a brief period in the 16th Century, then climbs steeply for 36 miles (58 kilometers) to Nuwara Eliya. The highway switches back and forth through **Ramboda Pass** tea estates, passing enroute the 329-foot (100-meter) **Ramboda Falls**. The **Labookellie Estate** at 5,200 feet, invites passers-by to stop for a refreshing cup of tea and a factory tour. As elsewhere in the country, most estate workers here are Indian Tamil migrants who toil for wages under US$1 a day – but whose room and board, not to mention health, education and welfare, is guaranteed by the tea estate management.

Climbing Through Hanguranketa: An alternate route from Kandy to Nuwara Eliya, equally beautiful but less traveled, is Route B39 through **Hanguranketa**. Eighteen miles (28 kilometers) southeast of Kandy, Hanguranketa was a sacred refuge for the 17th Century Kandyan King Raja Sinha II. Its **Potgul Maliga Vihara** is of great importance. **Potgul** means "library," and this ancient building contains a fine collection of *ola* manuscripts, with gorgeous handcrafted covers of chased brass and silver. There is also a beautiful moonstone and an "inside-out" *dagoba*, whose outer walls display the murals usually locked within the relic chamber.

The *potgul* is one of many holy buildings facing a central green in Hanguranketa town. Across is a Vishnu *devala* with a frieze of sculptured stick dancers. A nearby Pattini *devala* has similar sculptures. Fallen stones behind the *devala* mark the site of Raja Sinha II's palace-in-exile.

About three miles south of Hanguranketa, at Rikiligaskada, Route B39 meets Route B40 from Peradeniya. Eight miles down this highway is the **Loolecondera Estate**, site of Ceylon's original tea factory. Scotsman James Taylor lived and worked in a small bungalow, now a washerman's quarters. He made the earliest Loolecondera tea on his own veranda. There are impressive views from here across the Great Valley toward Hunasgiriya.

The rest of the long, winding route to Nuwara Eliya, through Maturata and Ragala, is mainly one of the tea estates and hill scenery. **Kurundu Oya Falls** drop 620

Preceding pages: Hill Country at dawn. Left, tea plucker at work. Right, plowing a paddy field.

feet (189 meters) above the Mulhalkela Bridge on Route B39, but is a difficult uphill scramble.

A Touch of England: The alternate upland routes meet in **Nuwara Eliya**, nestled in a wooded basin at 6,128 feet (1,884 meters) – at the foot of Mt. Pidurutalagala, Sri Lanka's highest peak. Even today, 3½ decades after the British left Ceylon, the town seems like a piece of the English Lake District. Tudor-style and Victorian homes look across a pretty blue lake; colorful flowers blossom in parks and gardens; hunting and fishing trophies adorn the walls of the old hotels.

The first Westerners to stumble upon the site of modern Nuwara Eliya were members of a British colonial hunting expedition in 1819. Six years later, a health resort and military sanitorium were established in the cool climate. In 1846, Sir Samuel Baker, the British explorer best known for his Nile discoveries, spent two weeks in Nuwara Eliya convalescing from malaria. He enthusiastically returned two years later to establish "a little English village." Not one for wasting time, Baker immediately imported everything he would need to carry out his plan: his hounds, his vast arsenal of sporting firearms, his domestic staff, farmhands, artisans, a bailiff, chosen sheep and cattle, farming machinery, a blacksmith and forge, and a horse-drawn carriage. Everything and everyone came up the Ramboda Pass in bullock wagons and elephant carts. Only the carriage didn't survive. Baker's coachman explained in a letter:

Honord Zur: I'm sorry to hinform you that the carriage and osses has met with a haccidint and is tumbled down a preccipice and its a mussy as I didn't go too ...

Although his eight-year experiment was abandoned in 1856, several of his farmers and artisans stayed on as pioneer settlers. Baker's legacy includes the vegetables – beets, cabbage, tomatoes, leeks and potatoes – that flourish in this climate, the pedigreed Hereford and Durham cows that he first brought, and the brewery that he established.

The real landmarks of Nuwara Eliya today are its hotels, and none more so than the archaic **Hill Club**. This gray stone

Left, Olde English-style bungalow in Nuwara Eliya.

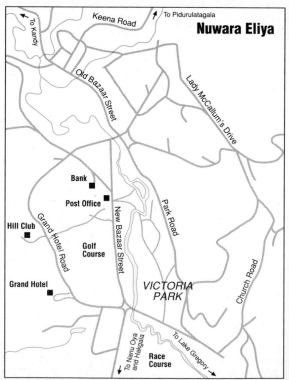

Nuwara Eliya

mansion, on a hill overlooking the 18-hole golf course, is like a page from a 19th Century history book. The Club was founded in 1876 and the present premises was built in 1927. Its library still stocks some original encyclopedias and other books, and its billiard table is a true antique. Mounted heads of leopards, boar and other wild animals stare down from the walls.

Guests are admitted to dine in this private club, but gentlemen must wear ties. (If you don't have one, you can borrow one from the bartender's collection – but don't expect it to match your wardrobe.) Non-member Sri Lankans are admitted only as guests of the members of the club.

Practically next door to the Hill Club is the **Grand Hotel**, a fine Elizabethan-style inn. Across town is the **St. Andrew's Hotel**. The **Queen's House**, now the President's House, is another great colonial-era estate. There are other architectural monuments to the English. The post office with its charming clock tower, the serene Anglican church, the private residences with their gabled roofs and dormer windows - all speak of a time now past.

Post Office, Nuwara Eliya.

Victoria Park, in the middle of town, is a lovely place for a stroll or a picnic. Seasons may be absent elsewhere in Sri Lanka, but here you can read them by the flowers, which bloom in the spring (March to May) and the fall (August and September). These are the "seasons" when low-country folk flock to Nuwara Eliya to escape the sea-level heat and humidity.

The **race course**, south of the park, comes alive with pony races once a year in April. The racing of thoroughbred horses has been recently re-introduced in Nuwara Eliya, promising a revival of this glamorous and exciting sport. Golfers consider the **golf course** in Nuwara Eliya as one of the finest, and certainly among the most picturesque, in Asia. There is boating on **Lake Gregory**, a bit south of the race course; and fishermen find the trout-filled lake and streams to be delightful. Trout are not native to Sri Lanka, but they have been stocked in these Hill Country streams for just over a century. Twenty live brown trout survived the passage from England in 1882. In 1896, the Nuwara Eliya Trout Hatchery, operated by the Ceylon Fishing

Club, was opened, and stocked with rainbow trout as well as browns. After release, they grow to considerable size – over 14 pounds (brown) and 12 pounds (rainbow) are the record catches in Lake Gregory. Unfortunately, in recent times Lake Gregory has fallen to neglect. Much of its expanse is covered by weeds. But public concern which highlighted its sorry state has resulted in the initiation of restoration work which is currently underway.

Hikers find the walk up rounded **Mount Pidurutalagala** a pleasant day's outing. Mt. Pedro, as it is sometimes called, is the highest point on the island at 8,281 feet (2,524 meters). It takes about two hours of walking to reach the summit, crowned by Sri Lanka's first television transmitter. Nuwara Eliya looks like a fairyland village at Mt. Pedro's foot. The view from the summit extends from Adam's Peak (southwest) to Kandy's Knuckles (north) to the Bintenna plains (east).

The Hakgala Gardens: Four miles southeast of Nuwara Eliya is another prominent peak, Hakgala. At its foot lie the **Hakgala Botanical Gardens**, and beyond, the Hakgala Strict Natural Reserve. The gardens are smaller and less exotic than those at Peradeniya, but at 5,600 feet (1,707 meters) elevation the species of flora quite different. Opened as an experimental cinchona plantation (for production of the malaria antidote quinine) in 1860, the pride of the gardens is now roses and ferns.

The sheer rock of Hakgala ("Jaw Rock"), which rises 1,500 feet straight up above the gardens, is said to have been carried here from the Himalayas in the jaws of Hanuman, the mythical monkey general who helped Prince Rama rescue Princess Sita from the demon King Rawana in the *Ramayana* epic. Legend says the **Sita Amman Kovil**, less than a mile back toward Nuwara Eliya on the east side of the highway, is where Sita was imprisoned.

The **Hakgala Strict Natural Reserve** contains several unique species of animal and bird life, among them the bear monkey or "wanderoo," which grows to four feet standing erect. His deep "hoo-hoo" bellow often echoes through the gardens.

The terrain around Hakgala is dominated by small vegetable farms, cultivated

Left and below, two of the many beauties of Hakgala.

in terraced plots on steep slopes. About 15 miles (24 kilometers) west (on Route A7 via Nanu Oya, the nearest rail depot to Nuwara Eliya), the **Sri Lanka Tea Research Institute** maintains headquarters at the St. Coombs Estate near Talawakele. On this model estate and factory, research is carried out in all fields related to the health and development of the tea plant. A scientific library of 20,000 volumes is maintained, and a quarterly journal is published and distributed worldwide.

Two impressive waterfalls flow from the hills within sight of one another near here. Devon Falls, 281 feet (86 meters), is tall and narrow, while St. Clair Falls, 241 feet (73 meters), is a broad double cascade.

Perhaps the most awesome and forbidding region of Sri Lanka is the **Horton Plains**. Located on a high windswept saddle at 7,000 feet (2,134 meters) elevation, these plains are hard to reach but well worth the effort. Until a few years ago, there were only foot trails to this region. Today, three roads make the steep winding ascent. From the west, there is a rough Jeep track through the Agrapatna tea es-

tate. From the north (via Pattipola), a once-paved road with frighteningly large potholes skirts the summit of Mount Totapola at 7,746 feet (2,361 meters). From the east, the best of the three accesses rises from the rail junction of Ohiya.

The Horton Plains are an expanse of misty grassland interrupted by scraggly trees and ice-cold rivulets. Nearly uninhabited, they are lonely yet exhilarating. There is a Department of Wild Life Conservation bungalow called **Anderson's Lodge** and a guest house, appropriately named **Farr Inn**, which offers meals and lodging to hungry wanderers. Otherwise, there are birds and rhododendrons, and other flora and fauna.

Many visitors come to the Horton Plains to see **World's End**, considered the finest view in all of Sri Lanka. It is a three-mile (five-kilometer) walk from Farr Inn. The terrific escarpment drops vertically for about 1,000 feet (328 meters) and falls away almost as steeply for another 4,000 feet (1,312 meters). In the early morning, a crescent of silver – the Indian Ocean – rims the horizon 50 miles (81 kilometers)

Terraced vegetable plots along the road to Nanu Oya.

to the south. Later in the day, a heat haze can obscure the view. During the southwest monsoon, the only view is of boiling, vaporous clouds in all directions.

The Horton Plains form the eastern extremity of the **Peak Wilderness Sanctuary**, extending through the alpine ruggedness for some 25 miles (40 kilometers), west of Adam's Peak. Black eagles, blue magpies and other rare birds are found here, also occasional leopards, deer and jackals. There were once elephants here, but none were seen since the 1930s.

East of Nuwara Eliya, the major Hill Country market center of Badulla is about 33 miles (53 kilometers) beyond Hakgala on Route A5. Typically scenic hill towns like **Keppitepola** and **Welimada** dominate this route, along with vegetable farms and tea estates. The **Istripura Caverns**, several miles north of Welimada, are the longest and most complicated underground labyrinths on the island – a huge series of interconnected chambers at many levels, some of them extraordinary deep. These caves take their name, which means "City of Women," from the myth that each cavern was the private home of one of the wives of an ogre, who maintained an enormous harem!

Badulla is the terminus of the rail line from Kandy and Nuwara Eliya. The rail route closely parallels Route A16, and has many points of interest. The **Idalgashinna** station is situated on a ridge with a view that approximates that of World's End.

The town of **Haputale** is perched on a similar ridge; looking down the main street of town, you can see all the way to the Hambantota Lighthouse. **Diyatalawa**, site of an army training camp, is favored by some as a hill-station escape. Even more popular is **Bandarawela**, 4,036 feet (1,230 meters), some 700 feet lower than Haputale. A charming if unspectacular town and a seasonal fruit-growing center (especially pears and strawberries), its climate is drier and milder than Nuwara Eliya.

Three miles out of Bandarawela on the highway to Badulla, the **Dowa Cave Temple**, near an old wooden bridge, attracts visitors with its ornamental gateway. The cave is situated by a stream at the bottom of a hill; it has a 13-foot (four-

Misty Bandarawela.

meter) Buddha image sculpted into rock, and some interesting paintings.

The train from Bandarwela makes a stop in Ella (to which we will return); proceeds through the **Demodera Loop**, where the track descends so rapidly that it doubles back beneath itself; and continues to its final stop at Badulla.

Badulla's Elephant Slayer: When the Badulla Blanket, a humid mist that often fills this town's hill hollow, is not oppressively near, Badulla is a pleasant stop. Among the points of interest are the **Kachcheri**, the British government residence standing on the site of the palace of the Kandyan Prince of Uva; and a **pillar inscription**, describing a 10th Century legal code by King Udaya III of Anuradhapura.

St. Mark's Church has a roofed lychgate which commemorates Major Thomas W. Rogers, former assistant to surveyor Thomas Skinner. Although Rogers covered most of the southeastern part of Sri Lanka on foot during the course of his years of service, he is usually remembered for his questionable prowess as an elephant hunter. He lost count, he said, after having shot and killed his 1,300th beast. Perhaps it was divine retribution that he was struck and killed by a bolt of lightning on the veranda of the Haputale Resthouse.

The **Mutiyangana Vihara** is considered one of Buddhism's 16 holiest places in Sri Lanka. Its origins, as well as most traces of its ancient buildings, are lost, but tradition ascribes it to King Devanampiyatissa of the 3rd Century B.C.

The **Dunhinda Falls**, about 3½ miles out of Badulla, including a 1½-mile walk, are sometimes called Sri Lanka's most awe-inspiring cascades. Their Sinhalese name means "smoking water," and the spray gives them that appearance. They drop 190 feet (58 meters) down a rocky cliff.

Towering over Badulla is the mountain called **Namunukulla** ("nine-peaked"). Easily seen by ships approaching Sri Lanka from the distant Bay of Bengal, it offers an easy climb to its 6,679-foot (2,036-meter) summit, through the Spring Valley tea estate. The view reaches from Batticaloa to the Basses reefs.

Leaving the Hill Country from Badulla, there are two choices of routes. One can

Ella Gap.

proceed east through **Passara** to the hot plains of the East Coast, and eventually to the ocean shore. Or one can travel south, preferably through the Ella Gap.

Probably the most beautifully situated rest house in Sri Lanka is the one in the village of **Ella**, 12 miles (19 kilometers) south of Badulla. From its front garden, the terrain falls away some 3,000 feet (over 900 meters) to the south coastal plain. Framed by towering Ella Rock on the right and a wooded ridge on the left, the spectacle of **Ella Gap** is one that invites rest house visitors to laze and gaze.

Ella Rock is notable for the gaping cave it contains – the **Cave of Rawana**, according to *Ramayana* enthusiasts. It was the cave where the Sinhalese paleontologist Deraniyagala discovered 10 skeletons of the cannibalistic *Homo Sapiens Balangodensis*. Properly known as Rattaran Guhava, this cave requires a rope or rope ladder for entry, as the floor is several feet below its mouth.

The new (1969) highway through Ella Gap passes **Rawana Ella Falls** between the 12th and 13th mileposts. Only 27 feet (eight meters) high, these falls are wide and handsome. Eleven miles below Ella, a roadside marker at the community of **Randeniya** denotes the battlefield where the Portuguese suffered a major defeat at the hands of the Kandyan army in 1630.

Welawaya, as its name implies, is well away from nearly everything else on the island. But it does lie at the important junction of Route A2 (to Hambantota) and Route A4 (to Colombo and Batticaloa). And only about three miles south is one of the most fascinating and mysterious sites in Sri Lanka – the great Mahayana Buddhist rock sculptures of **Buduruvagala**.

The Buduruvagala Buddha: Perhaps because Sri Lanka has considered itself the home of Theravada Buddhist doctrine, comparatively little has been chronicled on Mahayana history in the island, despite its obvious influence at various times of history. Thus, the seven colossal figures sculpted into a rock face here are a source of controversy. Authorities generally date them to the 9th or 10th Century.

The central figure of the group is the Buddha, standing 51 feet (15½ meters)

Left, Rawana Ella Falls. **Below**, bodhisattva Avalokitesvara carved in rock at Budduruvagala.

from head to toe – the largest standing Buddha on the island. He is attended on either side by figures of two *bodhisattvas*, each 40 feet (12 meters) in stature. Each of them in turn has two attendants. On the Buddha's right, the figure is thought to be Avalokitesvara. The one on the Buddha's left is believed to be either Maitreya, the future Buddha, or Vajrapani, a Tantric *bodhisattva*. With Avalokitesvara are his spiritual consort – the bare-breasted goddess Tara – and (probably) his constant companion Sudhanakumara. The attendant figures in the other group have not been identified. One holds in his hand the *dorje* or thunderbolt symbol common to Tibetan Tantrism. The figures are all carved in high relief. Traces of stucco and paint, as well as twin holes (perhaps for a protective platform) above the heads of the major figures, indicate that they were well-tended in centuries past.

A bit off the beaten track, Buduruvagala can be reached by car or bus and foot. A dirt road leaves the junction of Route A2 and proceeds through a rural community, up a steep slope to a dead end where vehicles can park almost within sight of the sculptures. Until the recent completion of an extended access road, the approach was much more adventuresome. A boatman conducted visitors across a tank (now drained), from where local children led the way down a half-mile path through elephant country. Suddenly, the rock face dramatically revealed itself through a dark arch of forest. There is some fear now that commercialization may creep in.

West to Ratnapura: The most remarkable sights in the 75 miles (121 kilometers) of highway between Welawaya and Ratnapura are water-associated. Close to Koslanda, near Milepost 124, are the **Diyaluma Falls**, whose drop of 560 feet (171 meters) is the highest single leap on the island. It is impossible to miss them: they seem to leap out at the traveler on this road. A short sidetrip from the Beragalla road junction (at about Milepost 119) leads to rock pools at the top of the falls.

Contrary to popular belief, the Diyaluma Falls are not the highest (in total drop) in the island. That honor falls to the **Bambarakanda Falls** near Kalupahana,

The great sculptures of Buduruvagla.

1½ miles off Route A4 at Milepost 102, west of Haldummulla. (An estate road to the West Haputale tea factory brings them into view.) The total drop is 790 feet (241 meters); the lowest of the three drops is 461 feet (141 meters). These falls, however, are highly seasonal. Spectacular when fed by monsoon rains, they are unimpressive during drought.

At **Belihul Oya**, the streamside resthouse allows one to cool off from hot days of driving. Several deep pools in a mountain stream flowing from the Horton Plains offer clean, clear water for bathing.

Cave fanciers may want to digress at **Balangoda** and follow the side route toward Uggalkaltota for 15 miles to the **Hituwalena Cave** at Kurugala. Considered by Muslims to be part of the holy place Daftur Jailani, it is said that an Iraqi holy man once spent 12 years here in meditation. A deep pit which drops off abruptly 100 feet into the cavern is said to be the mouth of an underground passage to Mecca, though no one has followed it that far. An annual Muslim pilgrimage is made to this cave. Across a ravine is a Buddhist cave over 2,000 years old, called Budugala. It is now a temple.

'The City of Gems': Sixty-three miles (101 kilometers) from downtown Colombo, **Ratnapura** is the most famous gem-mining locality in Sri Lanka. That reputation is well-deserved. Travelers between Pelmadullaa and Avissawella on Route A4 can hardly miss the gem pits excavated in the middle of paddies and other fields just off the road. Miners may be approached without hesitation to watch them work. (See the feature on gems.)

There are several museums and galleries in Ratnapura town to enlighten the curious. The **National Museum**, off the main highway east of town, features a model section of a typical gem pit (showing the geological strata) and a display of fossils from the Balangoda district, a paleontological treasure chest. The nearby **Gemmological Museum** is interesting for its metallurgical displays of precious gems.

Not as highly commercial, and with a wider range of exhibits, is the **Ratnapura Gem Bureau and Museum** in the Gatangama area, a mile or two from downtown.

Ratnapura, the city of gems.

Owner Purandara Sri Bhadra Marapana runs a training center for youthful artisans, not only in gem work but also in painting and brass and silver work. Marapana specializes in adapting traditional elements to modern artistic demands. **Hotel Kalawathie**, on his personal Polhengoda Village estate, has a rare herb and vegetable garden just a mile northeast of the city; in late 1982, Marapana also introduced indigenous herb and oil baths at his estate.

Ratnapura is Sri Lanka's gem capital, but it is also a holy city. A new standing Buddha statue, built by the **Viniharama Vihara**, stands on a hill overlooking the city. More important, the ancient **Maha Saman Devala**, dedicated to the tutelary deity of Adam's Peak, is about two miles outside Ratnapura. Built by Parakramabahu II in the 13th Century, it reached the height of its glory during the Kotte period two centuries later. The Portuguese destroyed it in the 1620s; ironically, when the *devala* was restored in late Dutch times, it incorporated a Portuguese church! The troupe of dancing girls once maintained by the *devala* has disappeared, except

Some of the riches of Ratnapura.

perhaps during the annual fair and *perahera* in the month of *Esala*. This *perahera* is among the largest in the country. One of its main features is the *maha baha*, a giant effigy who like the Roman Janus has two faces – one pink-cheeked and smiling, the other dour and black-visaged.

The Adam's Peak Pilgrimage: Ratnapura is the "classical" gateway for the pilgrimage climb up 7,360-foot (2,243-meter) Adam's Peak. It is 16 miles by foot (or nine by vehicle and seven by foot) to the top of the pointed peak by this arduous route through the Carney Estate. The other route, from Maskeliya via the Dalhousie Estate, begins at a much higher elevation and is a much easier ascent of about 4½ miles (seven kilometers).

All four major religions of Sri Lanka claim Adam's Peak as a holy mountain. Buddhists call the mountain Sri Pada ("the sacred footprint") and say it was visited by Gautama Buddha himself. To Hindus, the peak called Shivan Adipatham ("the creative dance of Shiva") preserves Lord Shiva's footprint. Muslims insist it is the

place where Adam first set foot on earth. And Roman Catholics say the footprint impressed in the boulder at the summit is that of St. Thomas, the early Christian apostle who preached in South India.

An earlier name given to the mountain is Samanala Kanda, "Saman's Hill." Since before Buddhism arrived in the island, the deity Saman has been regarded as supreme here. The clouds of yellow butterflies which converge on the mountain for a short time each year are called *samanalayo*.

Since the 11th Century, the mountain has been a goal of pilgrims. King Vijaya-bahu I and King Nissanka Malla of Polon-naruwa both recorded their pilgrimages here. The *Mahavamsa* made reference to the Buddha's footprint atop the mountain.

Pilgrimage season begins in December and continues until the Wesak festival in May. It is at its height in March. At other times, the mountain is bleak and rains make the trail dangerous. Tens of thousands of pilgrims make the journey every year. Most of them climb at night up a staircase illuminated by electric lamps. Frequent *ambalanas* (pilgrims' rests) and refreshment stalls make the climb easier. Those who reach the summit by dawn witness an almost supernatural spectacle: the magnified, triangular shadow of the peak itself superimposed on the awakening countryside. On very rare occasions, one may see the "Specter of the Brocken" –one's own immensely magnified shadow borne on distant wraiths of mist, looped by a rainbow halo.

Adam's Peak pilgrims follow a number of unique traditions in their ascent. It is customary for first-time climbers to pile great turbans of white cloth on their heads. On both main routes, the Indikatupana ("place of the needle") demands the devout to stop and fling a threaded needle into a shrub by path's side, marking a spot where the Buddha is said to have paused to mend a tear in his robe. At the summit, a bell clangs unceasingly, reverently tolled by old man and toddler alike, to signify a pilgrimage completed. (The current journey may not be tallied, for it is not complete until the return home.) It is bad form, by the way, to ask how far it is to the top. Instead, just exchange the greeting *karunavai* – "peace." If you're not taking

the Ratnapura route to the top of the mountain, you must approach **Maskeliya**, at the foot of the northern Adam's Peak path, by side road off Route A7 between Avissawella and Nuwara Eliya. Turn off through Hatton (at Milepost 82) and proceed about 15 miles (24 kilometers) past the **Mousakellie Reservoir**, which drowned the old town of Maskeliya in 1969. The town was relocated just uphill.

On your return trip to Colombo, pass through **Norton Bridge**, center of operations for several new Mahaweli Scheme projects. Ironically, the **Laksapana Reservoir**, soon to be completed, will eliminate the lovely **Laksapana Falls** (377 feet; 115 meters) by the roadside. **Aberdeen Falls** (296 feet; 90 meters), three miles north of Norton, will continue to exist, but the flow will be controlled.

From **Gingiathena Pass** (Milepost 70), which offers a clear view of Adam's Peak on a bright day, a series of switch-backs wind rapidly downhill through **Kitulgala**, a little Kelani River community and site of filming of *Bridge Over the River Kwai*. On a hill above this town, a prehistoric cave was recently discovered containing large middens of shells from some unknown civilization. Excited paleontologists are researching the find.

At **Avissawella**, the highways to Ratnapura (Route A4) and Nuwara Eliya (Route A7) join and proceed together the final 45 miles (72 kilometers) to Colombo. Near here are the scattered ancient ruins of **Sitawaka**, a stronghold of Sinhalese nationalism against the Portuguese in the 16th Century. Many claim it dates some 2,000 years prior to that. No buildings stand here today, but the remains of the **palace walls** have been identified and marked. This site is on the south side of the Kelani Ganga. Across the river is the **Berendi Kovil**. Built by King Rajasinha I (1578-1597) to try to waylay divine retribution for his dual crimes of patricide and murdering Buddhist monks (by burying them up to their necks in a field and plowing their heads off). Stone columns with wonderful designs are strewn about the ruin. The temple was probably never finished, as the court moved to Kandy upon the King's death, and Hinduism fell from royal favor.

Sri Pada: Adam's Peak summit.

ANURADHAPURA: ANCIENT CAPTIAL

Centuries before the birth of Christ, while the Greek Empire was flourishing in the Mediterranean and other regions were emerging from the late Stone Ages, Sri Lanka was a land of highly advanced civilization. Well-ordered cities, linked by fine roads and nourished by a marvelous irrigation system, made this tropical island one of the trade centers of the world.

But in contrast to the ruins of Greece, Rome, and other occidental civilizations, Sri Lanka's ancient cities lack an obvious plan. Sole remains are of scattered palaces and temples. As the only aspect of existence considered worthy of permanence was the Buddhist religion, only those structures devoted to the Buddha's honor were given the perennial medium of stone. For the layman, wood and clay sufficed.

In this time, Anuradhapura was the greatest city of all. Its ruins today display infinite details of rare beauty, delicately set in the world's mightiest masses of monumental masonry, second only to the Pyramids of Egypt.

Excavations on the site of Anuradhapura verify that human settlement began here about 500 B.C. According to the *Mahavamsa,* there were three "Anuradhas" involved in the founding and development of this city. Appropriately, the settlement became known as Anuradhapura, "the city of Anuradha." The first was a general of Prince Vijaya, legendary forefather of the Sinhalese race; the second was a nephew of the king. In the 4th Century B.C., when King Pandukabhaya established his capital here, he did so at an auspicious time under the constellation "Anuradha."

Anuradhapura remained the capital of Sri Lanka for about 1,400 years, until the 10th Century A.D. At the height of its glory, this civilization spread its influence from the Tiber to the Yellow Sea. It covered some 20 square miles (52 square kilometers) and had a population variously estimated at several tens of thousands. Houses two and three stories high, and perhaps two stories underground, were common. Minor streets were organized according to classes of artisans. Industry was thriving. The king lived in a bejeweled palace of 1,000 chambers, and gold-pinnacled shrines rose hundreds of feet into the air.

For about two centuries after the fall of Anuradhapura, the kings of Polonnaruwa attempted to restore some of its buildings. But for the next eight centuries, the city was left to the dry-zone jungle. Only the sacred Bo Tree itself, the Sri Maha Bodhi, the one living relic of past splendor, was continually attended, generation after generation, by hereditary guardians. The tradition continues to this day.

In the 1820s, a young British civil servant named Ralph Backhaus mounted a private expedition and rediscovered many of the ruins of the old capital. But it was not until 1871 that official interest began to be taken; and it was 1890, after the appointment of H.C.P. Bell as Archaeological Commissioner, that zealous if amateurish efforts at excavation began.

Suddenly, Sinhalese nationalism and Buddhist fervor were struck by the symbolism of the heritage seen in the ancient

Preceding pages: an Anuradhapura panorama. Left, a Thuparama guardstone. Right, Buddha image at Ruwanweli.

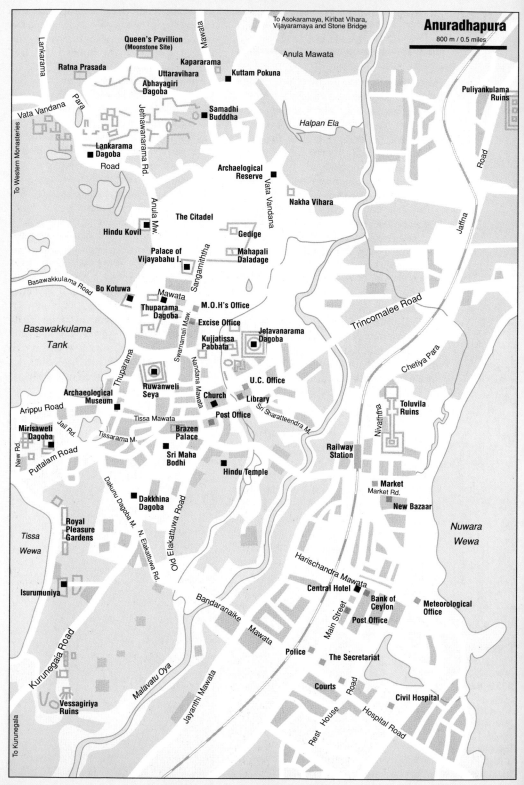

Anuradhapura

800 m / 0.5 miles

To Asokaramaya, Kiribat Vihara,
Vijayaramaya and Stone Bridge

Lankarama

Mawata

Anula Mawata

Queen's Pavillion
(Moonstone Site)

Kapararama

Ratna Prasada

Uttaravihara

Kuttam Pokuna

Puliyankulama
Ruins

Abhayagiri
Dagoba

Vata Vandana

Para

Samadhi
Budddha

Halpan Ela

To Western Monasteries

Jethawanarama Rd.

Road

Lankarama
Dagoba

Archaelogical
Reserve

Vata Vandana

Nakha Vihara

Anula Mw.

The Citadel

Jaffna

Road

Hindu Kovil

Gedige

Palace of
Vijayabahu I

Sangamiththa

Mahapali
Daladage

Basawakkulama Road

Bo Kotuwa

Mawata

Trincomalee Road

Thuparama
Dagoba

M.O.H's Office

Basawakkulama
Tank

Excise Office

Chetiya Para

Thuparama

Kujjatissa
Pabbata

Jetavanarama
Dagoba

Nandana Mawata

Swarnamali Maw.

Archaeological
Museum

Ruwanweli
Seya

U.C. Office

Nivaththa

Toluvila
Ruins

Arippu Road

Church

Library

Tissa Mawata

Post Office

Sri Sharatteendra M

Mirisaweti
Dagoba

Tissarama M.

Brazen
Palace

Railway
Station

Jail Rd.

Puttalam Road

New Rd.

Sri Maha
Bodhi

Market

Market Rd.

Hindu Temple

New Bazaar

Dakunu Dagoba M.

Dakkhina
Dagoba

Nuwara
Wewa

Tissa
Wewa

Royal
Pleasure
Gardens

N. Elakattuwa Rd.

Old Elakattuwa Road

Harischandra Mawata

Isurumuniya

Central Hotel

Bank of
Ceylon

Meteorological
Office

Kurunegaia Road

Bandaranaike

Mawata

Main Street

Post Office

Police

The Secretariat

Malavatu Oya

Road

Courts

Rest House

Hospital Road

Civil Hospital

Vessagiriya
Ruins

Jayanthi Mawata

To Kurunegala

stones. The British government envisioned the political prestige involved in turning a restored ancient capital into a regional administrative center. So a new town grew up amidst the ruined temples and palaces.

For Buddhists, there are eight places of particular sanctity within Anuradhapura where devout pilgrims are obliged to worship. These are the Sri Maha Bodhi, the Ruwanweli Seya, the Thuparama Dagoba, the Jetavanarama Dagoba, the Abhayagiri Dagoba, the Lankarama Dagoba, the Mirisaweti Dagoba, and the Isurumuniya Vihara.

The best time to visit Anuradhapura, if also the most crowded, is during the *Poson poya* in June. This celebrated the advent of the Buddhist religion to the island, and a huge influx of pilgrims fills the city.

The Oldest Tree: No spot in Anuradhapura is more sacred than the **Sri Maha Bodhi**. Worship at the *bo* tree has continued unbroken for 23 centuries. In fact, this is the oldest historically documented tree on earth. It was carried here as a sapling of the *ficus religiosa* beneath which the Gautama Buddha himself attained enlightenment. Today, the importance of this tree is so great and so widely known that in 1950, when a blight attacked the tree and its life was imperiled, a botanical expert from the Smithsonian Institute made a special trip to Anuradhapura to treat the plant, with obvious success.

Today, iron crutches must support the venerable boughs of this holy tree, which is surprisingly slight for its ancient age. It stands amidst other younger trees upon a special platform, a *bodhighara*, encircled by gold-plated railing. Most of the *bo* trees in Sri Lanka, and some in Burma and Thailand, have been nurtured from Sri Maha Bodhi's seeds. Its leaves are said to have provided the shape according to which Sri Lanka's *dagobas* are designed.

The **Brazen Palace**, or Loha Prasada, was originally built by Dutugemunu in the 2nd Century B.C. as a monks' residence adjacent to the *bo* tree. According to the *Mahavamsa*, it was nine stories high and 150 feet (46 meters) in width, length and height. There were 1,000 rooms adorned with silver and precious gems. Its roof was covered with plates of copper: thus its name. But it was apparently a wooden structure, for it burned down during the reign of Dutugemunu's successor. Sadhatissa reerected a seven-story building on its site, but it was razed by the Cholas in their 11th Century sack of the city. The present forest of 1600 stone columns, in 40 rows of 40 each, is apparently a survival of its final restoration by King Parakramabahu I in the 12th Century. The pillars are of several styles, some ornamental and some rough-hewn.

West of the Brazen Palace and the Sacred Bo Tree, near the banks of the **Basawakkulama Tank**, is the fine **Archaeological Museum**. Housed in the former "residency" of a British government agent, it explains many of the unique architectural features of the city.

Pride of Dutugemunu: The **Ruwanweli Seya**, the "Great Stupa" (Mahathupa) raised in the 2nd Century B.C. by Dutugemunu, is popularly regarded as the greatest of the *dagobas* at Anuradhapura. Indeed, it was completed as Dutugemunu lay on his deathbed in 144 B.C. Nineteenth and 20th Century restoration work failed to regain the perfect "water bubble"

Worshipping at Sri Maha Bodhi, the sacred *bo* tree.

shape that the king sought; but the main features were reinstated, incorporating the modifications of countless rebuilders throughout Anuradhapura history.

Today, gate houses at each of the four cardinal points mark the *dagoba's* outer walls. From a sand courtyard, the impressive elephant wall upholds the *dagoba* platform in the same way that elephants hold up the earth in Buddhist cosmology. Walk clockwise around the *dagoba*. Note the four 8th Century limestone statues of Maitreya, the future Buddha. A model *dagoba* on the southwest side of the stupa shows how the Mahathupa may have originally looked in its pure "water-bubble" shape. A larger-than-life statue of a man, probably Dutugemunu himself, stands respectfully facing the great *dagoba*. On the grounds beside the Ruwanweli Seya are several **monastic buildings.**

Across the road to the west, the Basawakkulama Tank is probably the oldest work of its type in Sri Lanka, positively identified with King Pandukabhaya in the early 4th Century B.C.

The **Thuparama Dagoba**, north of the Ruwanweli Seya, is the oldest *dogoba* in the country, and is believed to enshrine the Collarbone Relic of the Buddha which was sent by Emperor Asoka after Mahinda's conversion of Anuradhapura. King Devanampiyatissa erected it in the 3rd Century B.C. and called it "the monastery with the stupa." The *dagoba* was of "paddy-heap" design, and of earth alone. In the 2nd Century B.C., King Lanjatissa enclosed it in wooden pillars as a *vatadage*; in the 7th Century, Agbo II improved the *vatadage* with stone pillars and a conical roof. Some of the pillars still stand. The present "bell" shape of the *dagoba* is the result of an 1862 restoration.

The Giant Jetavanarama: A small moundlike *dagoba* southeast of the Thuparama, the **Kujjatissa Pabbata**, dates from the 8th Century. But it was probably built on an earlier site, and may be the tomb of Elara, the great Chola king vanquished in the 2nd Century B.C. by Dutugemunu.

Due east is the **Jetavanarama**, the mightiest mass of its kind on earth. It was

Ruins of the Brazen Palace.

originally more than 400 feet (122 meters) high, and the crystal finial of its modern restoration will glitter 500 feet (152 meters) above the beholder. Its base, 370 feet (113 meters) in diameter, stands upon a brick foundation 26 feet (eight meters) in thickness, which in turn rests on a raft of concrete. The entire structure occupies some eight acres of land. It is larger than all but two of the Pyramids.

The Jetavanarama was begun by King Mahasena in the late 3rd Century A.D. during a period of schisms between different monastic sects. In December 1982, 9th Century gold plates – containing Sanskrit text of a Mahayana *suttra* – were discovered by archaeologists during excavation work.

Near the southwestern corner of the Citadel, on your left as you enter by road from the south, is the 11th Century **Palace of Vijayabahu I.** The ruins of this comparatively humble building, together with its marked resemblance to similar buildings at Polonnaruwa, suggest that it was hurriedly erected by Vijayabahu for his coronation in the ancient royal city, before he departed to make Polonnaruwa his seat of power.

A park area to the east of the road, about 100 meters north of the palace, contains the ruins of the **Mahapali Refectory** (an alms hall), the ancient **Dalada Maligawa** (Temple of the Tooth), and a pair of sacred shrines. The Dalada Maligawa, distinguished by its tall stone columns, was the first home of the Tooth Relic in Sri Lanka after its imperiled 4th Century A.D. flight from Kalinga, in South India, in the hair of a princess.

Further to the east, beyond the Citadel walls, a track leads to the unusual **Nakka Vihara**, a square brick *dagoba* of the later Anuradhapura period. Along one wall, in stucco, are a profusion of figures of Mahayana deities and objects.

The road continues north beyond the Citadel, and proceeds through a crossroads to several monasteries and *dagobas*. A short distance on the right (east) is the **Kapararamaya**, a 7th Century monastic structure whose buildings are arranged in quincunx (a symmetrical five, as on a playing card or die) within a parapet wall.

The Thuparama Dagoba.

Nearby is the **Asokaramaya**, a group of 10th Century monuments which includes two *viharas*, a bathing pavilion whose roof was supported by 84 pillars, and a broken seated image of the Buddha in the rare *abhaya* mudra posture, bestowing protection.

The Abhayagiri Complex: One of the earliest of all Sri Lankan *dagobas* is the **Kiribat Vihara**, probably built around the 3rd Century B.C. It may enshrine one or more of the alms-bowlful of relics provided by the Indian Emperor Asoka. The image house includes a magnificent fallen Buddha sculpture. It is situated several hundred meters north of the Asokaramaya. Just before the end of the motorable road north, a track to the left (west) leads about 800 meters to the **Vijayarama** monastery. Thought to date from the later Anuradhapura period, its *dagoba* is of conventional circular shape. Yet surviving sculptures show clearly that it was a Mahayana shrine.

Return to the crossroads north of the Citadel. This area falls within the bounds of the **Uttaravihara**, or northern monas-

tery, surrounding the great Abhayagiri Dagoba. On the east side of the crossroads are the **Kuttam Pokuna**, or Twin Ponds. This pair of 3rd Century A.D. monks' bathing pools are archaeologically perfect. Although they are called "twin," one is half again as long as the other. The water which feeds the ponds flows first into an enclosed filtration basin, then through a beautiful *makara* gargoyle and lion's head spout into the smaller tank. A sub-marine conduit feeds the larger tank.

West, beyond the crossroads, is the **Samadhi Buddha**, also dating from the 3rd Century A. D. This limestone image, apparently one of four originally seated around a *bo* tree, depicts the Buddha in the serene state of *samadhi*, or deep meditation. Its nose – a later restoration of a broken piece of the image – is obviously of a different age and demeanor than the rest of the statue. Indian statesman Jawaharlal Nehru found solace and strength in a photograph of this statue when he was imprisoned by the British.

Straight ahead on this road, the **Abhayagiri Dagoba** was founded as a

Left, the famous moonstone of Abhayagiri monastery. **Right**, the Samadhi Buddha.

monastery by King Vattagamini Abhaya in 88 B.C. The *dagoba* on the site was constructed in the early 2nd Century A. D. by King Gajabahu. With a height of 370 feet (113 meters), and an almost identical diameter of 360 feet (110 meters), it was the second largest *dagoba* on earth, after the Jetavanarama. Today its pinnacle has crumbled, but even at 249 feet (76 meters), it is a massive structure.

Northwest of the Abhayagiri is the **Ratna Prasada**, or Gem Palace, of the 2nd Century A.D. This handsome ruin's gigantic columns were once the domain of a heretical abbot.

At the entrance to the Ratna Prasada is the finest **guardstone** in Sri Lanka, both in terms of execution and preservation. A guardian spirit, a *naga* king, holds a vase of plenty and a flowering branch to symbolize prosperity. Above him is a *makara torana*; behind him, a cobra hood; and at his feet, a dwarf attendant.

Slightly to the northeast of the Ratna Prasada, in front of the ruins of an image house, is a **moonstone** that is often considered the finest in the country. Sur-
rounded by an iron fence to protect it from possible vandalism, this perfectly executed sculpture symbolically portrays the transcendence from desire (flames) to *nibbana* (represented by the lotus in the stone's center). Dwarfs hold up the steps above the moonstone in this 8th or 9th Century shrine; at the top of the steps are two more deities and a pair of Sinhalese lions.

South of the Ratna Prasada are a series of minor sites which include a former *bo* tree shrine, the Abhayagiri refectory, and a seated Buddha of the 7th Century in the *vitarka* (teaching) *mudra*. The **Lanka-rama Dagoba**, yet further south, was founded by Vattagamini in the 1st Century B.C. Three concentric circles of surrounding pillars show that it was contained in a *vatadage*.

The Western Monasteries: West of the main city of Anuradhapura, easily accessible from the Abhayagiri complex, are a series of 6th to 9th Century hermitages collectively known as the **Western Monasteries**. Monks who lived in these 14 forest hermitages had a reputation of extreme asceticism. The main component

The Abhayagiri *dagoba*.

of the hermitages was the *padhanaghara* or meditation hall. This consisted of a pair of east-west oriented platforms, based on living rock and surrounded by a rock-cut moat, connected by a monolith as a bridge over the moat. The western platform was covered, the eastern open to the sky. The effect was one of tremendously austere and uniform discipline. Only the monks' urinal stones were highly decorated; for what reason is unknown.

The road past the hermitages returns to the city again near the **Tissa Wewa**, a large tank ascribed to King Devanampiyatissa in the 3rd Century B.C. He made it Anuradhapura's chief source of water, a role it still discharges. In the 5th Century A.D., King Dhatusena built a great canal, the Jaya Ganga, from the Kalawewa to here.

North of the Tissa Wewa Rest House is the **Mirisaweti Dagoba**, built by Dutugemunu between 161 and 158 B.C. to commemorate his victory over Elara and his assumption of the kingship. Now in restoration, the Mirisaweti exhibits the best preserved terraces at its base of any ancient *dagoba* in Sri Lanka. Over 200 feet (61 meters) high, it was the prototype for the Mahathupa.

The **Dakkhina Dagoba**, east of the rest house and south of the Sri Maha Bodhi, was probably built over the cremated ashes of King Dutugemunu. Indeed, traces of charcoal and ashes were found in the center of this circular brick mound, and were dated to the 2nd Century B.C.

Lilies and Lovers: The **Royal Pleasure Gardens**, also called the Ran Masu Uyana, cover some 400 acres below the bund of the Tissa Wewa. Through their length are scattered great boulders, many of which were once capped by summer houses. At the southern end of the grounds, near the **Isurumuniya** rock temple, are a group of three ponds, two of which are decorated with lovely bas-reliefs of elephants playing in the water lilies.

Isurumuniya was built in the 3rd Century B.C. as part of a monastic complex called Issiramana, which also included the Vessagiriya site to the south.

From the non-religious point of view, this temple may be the most interesting site in Anuradhapura. Built around two

Left, Kuttam Pokuna, the 'Twin Ponds.' Right, 'The Lovers' of Isurumuniya.

vast boulders below Tissa Wewa, Isurumuniya is beautified by the pool in front of it and embellished by Anuradhapura's most famous rock carvings.

The best known is called "The Lovers." The somewhat naive official description of this 6th Century Guptastyle carving is: "The woman, seated on the man's lap, lifts a warning finger, probably as a manifestation of her coyness; but the man carries on regardless." The figures may represent Dutugemunu's son Saliya and the low-caste maiden whom he loved.

Above the pool, in bas-relief, is a Disneyesque group of elephants frolicking in the water; the natural shape of the rock creates a three-dimensional effect. Nearby is a splendid carving in high relief of a male figure, seated in a relaxed royal pose, while the handsome head of his horse peers over his right shoulder. These are described as being of the 7th Century Pallava style of South India.

The **Vessagiriya** caves honor 500 members of the *vaisya* caste who were ordained by Mahinda.

The majority of the ancient monuments of Anuradhapura are situated west and north of the modern town. But a few important ruins are located on the east side of the city. Just north and east of the railway station, the **Toluvila** ruins are connected with an unknown monastery built in about the 6th Century. Somewhat more than 100 buildings were grouped on either side of a central avenue with symmetrical precision. Two miles north, on the road to Jaffna, the Tantric ruins of the **Pubbarama** monastery exhibit a raised and moated central platform with a building at each corner, one of them an angular *dagoba*.

East of Anuradhapura, about 1½ miles on the road to Mihintale and Trincomalee, is the **Paccinatissa Pabbata Vihara**. A quadrangle of some 775 by 120 feet (236 by 37 meters) enclosed by a moat, it was built in the 3rd Century.

The **Nuwara Wewa**, on the city's eastern flank, is the largest and most modern of Anuradhapura's tanks. It was created in the 2nd Century A. D., but fell into ruin, and was only restored by the British in the 1890s.

The Rock temple of Isurumuniya.

MIHINTALE AND OTHER SITES

Anuradhapura was and is a great Buddhist capital. But it was not the place where the Buddhist religion first overwhelmed the people of Sri Lanka. That honor goes to **Mihintale**, a rocky hill about seven miles (11 kilometers) east of Anuradhapura. For it was here, in the year 247 B.C., that King Devanampiyatissa became converted to Buddhism in his encounter with that first missionary of the Dharma.

Mihintale – the mountain of Mahinda – soon became a great monastic city encompassing not one but four rocky, forested hills. In the 10th Century, regulations were established to preserve the forests and wildlife. Today, the feeling of seclusion still exists, despite a thriving bazaar at the foothills and the presence of tens of thousands of fervid pilgrims, especially on the full-moon of *Poson* in May.

Whether Buddhist pilgrim or visitor, one must climb 1,840 steps to reach the *dagoba* at the summit of this very sacred mountain. The **staircase** was built by King Bhathika Abhaya (22 B.C. to 7 A.D.). An ancient paved road, 1,500 years old, now cuts that number in half by ascending to a terrace halfway up the 1,019-foot (311-meter) hill.

At the foot of Mihintale Kanda (hill) is a **hospital**, so denoted by an inscription and by the presence of a stone cistern for medication by immersion in herbal oils. A nearby **vihara** of unknown age probably marks the remains of a monastic complex.

To the right of the stairs, about half-way up the first long flight, is the 2nd Century B.C. **Kantaka Chaitiya**. Not excavated until 1934, it was found in an almost perfect state of preservation, displaying some of the finest architecture of the early Anuradhapura period. Standing 39 feet (12 meters) high, with a 426-foot (130-meter) base, it has four *vahalkadas* (altar-piece panels) with beautiful ornamental friezes of captivating dwarfs.

The **Mandapaya**, or pavilion, set on the terrace halfway up Mihintale Kanda, is the point at which all main paths from various parts of the complex converge. Just west of here is the **Lion Bath**, a stone cistern carved to resemble a lion whose mouth spewed water. North of the Mandapaya is a 10th Century **vihara** with inscriptions laying out monastic rules; and nearby, the 6th Century **Bhojana Salawa**, an eating hall.

The spacious glade at the top of the main stairway is the site of the **Ambasthala Dagoba**, a charming stupa said to mark the spot where Mahinda appeared to Devanampiyatissa instead of the deer that the king had been hunting. (The name recalls the *amba*, or mango, tree of their dialogue). It may have been built shortly after Devanampiyatissa's death. It was converted to *vatadage* style in the 3rd Century A.D. Near it is the **Aradhana Gala**, the "rock of convocation" from which Mahinda first preached.

At the pinnacle of Mihintale Kanda, clearly visible from all surrounding points, is the 1st Century B.C. **Maha Seya**. This *dagoba* is said to enshrine a single hair of the Buddha. There is a superb view toward the great *dagobas* of Anuradhapura.

A large boulder east of the Ambasthala Dagoba is called **Mahinda's Bed**. The

Mahinda's Bed looms above the Ambasthale Dagoba at Mihintale.

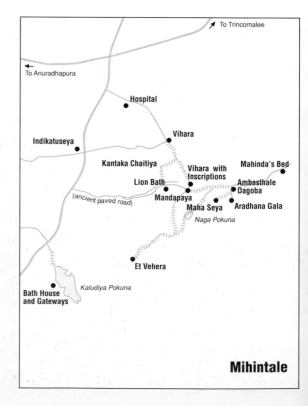

Mihintale

190

saint slept or meditated (or both) on a meticulously smoothed slab, over which the boulder arches. The highest point in the Mihintale hills is crowned by the **Et Vehera**, the "distant" *dagoba*. Completely ruined, it may be the repository of Mahinda's cremated ashes. A rock pool along the path to this mountain from the Mahdapaya is called the **Naga Pokuna** because, on its back wall, a seven-headed cobra has been hewn from the rock.

A secluded pool, the **Kaludiya Pokuna**, was the center of a cave-dwelling monastic community about one-half mile southwest of Mihintale Kanda, at the foot of Anaikutti Kanda. And near the base of the fourth (and westernmost) hill, Rajagirilena Kanda, the **Indikatu Seya** *dagoba* has enshrined several copper plaques bearing Tantric inscriptions.

The Aukana Buddha: There are numerous other important ruins within easy driving distance of Anuradhapura. Among those of major interest are:

• The **Aukana Buddha**, undoubtedly the most magnificent undamaged ancient image in the island. This 5th Century

statue, ascribed to King Dhatusena, is 42½ feet (13 meters) high, standing beneath a recently constructed brick shelter, a reconstruction of an image house said to have contained it 1,000 years ago. Aukana means "sun-eating," and the image is best viewed when the sun rises. It is situated 32 miles (51 kilometers) southeast of Anuradhapura via the great tank of Kalawewa.

• The **Sasseruwa Vihara**, seven miles (11 kilometers) west of Aukana by back roads, reached by a climb of 280 stone steps. Ancient monks occupied nearly 100 caves between the 3rd Century B.C. and 2nd century A.D. It is best known today for its rough-hewn Buddha image, carved from a sheer rock face. About three feet (one meter) shorter than the Aukana, it is cruder and less discreet in style. Some say it is a 5th Century prototype of the Sukana or the creation of an apprentice to the Aukana sculptor. Both are directly facing the old Kalawewa sluice.

• **Yapahuwa**, a rock fortress that was a 13th Century Sri Lankan capital. Unlike Sigiriya, the palace was not built at the summit of the 300-foot (91-meter) table-topped crag. Instead, two semi-circular walls and moats protected the royal palace complex, standing on a ledge at the top of striking staircase. The stone ruins of the steps, reminiscently Cambodian, are among the handsomest on the island. Friezes of jubilant musicians and dancers decorate the stairs and the porch above them. To reach Yapahuwa, travel south from Anuradhapura on Route B63. 40 miles (64-kilometers) to Maho, turn east and look for the massive rock to the south.

• **Tantirimalai**, about 35 miles (56 kilometers) northwest of Anuradhapura via Medawachchiya, which has ruins of an ancient forest monastery. Two superb Buddha images, one seated and one reclining, are carved out of solid rock. A small stupa atop the hill, overgrown by a *bo* tree, dates from the 9th or 10th Century. Caves at the site contain prehistoric drawings.

• **Ritigala**, a range of wooded mountains 25 miles (40 kilometers) southeast of Anuradhapura off the Polonnaruwa road. "Meditation paths" wind across stone bridges at this 2nd Century B.C. forest hermitage site.

Left, a vintage car on the road to the 39-foot Aukana Buddha, right.

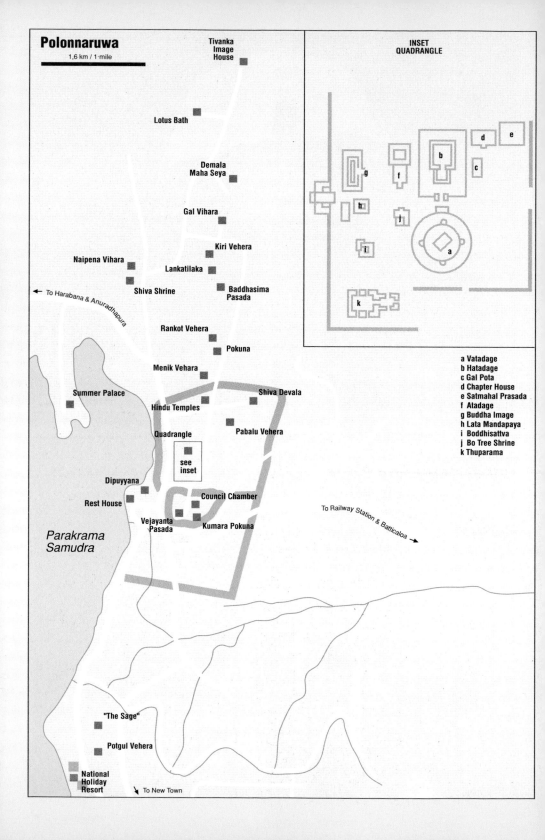

Polonnaruwa

1,6 km / 1·mile

Tivanka Image House

Lotus Bath

Demala Maha Seya

Gal Vihara

Kiri Vehera

Naipena Vihara

Lankatilaka

Shiva Shrine

Baddhasima Pasada

To Harabana & Anuradhapura

Rankot Vehera

Pokuna

Menik Vehara

Shiva Devala

Summer Palace

Hindu Temples

Quadrangle

Pabalu Vehera

see inset

Dipuyyana

Rest House

Council Chamber

Vejayanta Pasada

Kumara Pokuna

To Railway Station & Batticaloa

Parakrama Samudra

"The Sage"

Potgul Vehera

National Holiday Resort

To New Town

INSET QUADRANGLE

a Vatadage
b Hatadage
c Gal Pota
d Chapter House
e Satmahal Prasada
f Atadage
g Buddha Image
h Lata Mandapaya
i Boddhisattva
j Bo Tree Shrine
k Thuparama

THE GREAT RUINS OF POLONNARUWA

The 11th to 13th Century capital of Polonnaruwa has more to see and less to conjecture than the older metropolis of Anuradhapura. With its comparatively brief and uncomplicated history (two centuries and a dozen rulers, in contrast with 1,400 years and 123 kings of Anuradhapura) and its far more completely preserved ruins, much more recently exposed to the ravages of time, Polonnaruwa (say Poh-loh-NA-roowah) has a particular fascination for the average visitor.

The age of the city's foundation is not known with any certainty. A military garrison from Anuradhapura may have been stationed here in the early years of the Christian era. By the 6th Century, it was a military camp of some importance, strategically located guarding the Mahaweli River crossings from Ruhuna, the southern province where rebellions continuously fomented.

'The Saga,' probably Parakramabahu I.

After their conquest of Anuradhapura, the 11th Century Cholas set up their capital in Polonnaruwa, from which they could more effectively control the outlying regions of the island. But the Sinhalese regained the upper hand under the leadership of Vijayabahu I, who defeated the Cholas in 1073. He was formally consecrated to the kingship in Anuradhapura, but kept his capital in Polonnaruwa. Vijayabahu then devoted his reign to rebuilding the country with an improved irrigation system and a strengthened inner core of Buddhism. The work was carried on in the latter part of the 12th Century by Parakramabahu I, under whose guidance the fortifications, the great tank, and a large number of the buildings were erected.

The century after Nissanka Malla's death in 1196 consisted of continual invasion and devastation from India and Malaya. When a semblance of order was restored late in the 13th Century, the capital was moved to the western part of the country, and Polonnaruwa returned to the jungle. The Portuguese seem to have found and looted the site, but it was lost to the Dutch, and was not rediscovered until the 19th Century British became involved in excavation.

The huge lake upon whose northeastern shore Polonnaruwa rests is an inland sea known as the **Parakrama Samudra**. The largest irrigation tank of Parakramabahu I, it was the life-blood of the ancient city in the same way that it is the lifeblood of the region today, providing water for the growth of thirsty rice crops and other foodstuffs. Its 5,600 acres of water irrigate an estimated 18,200 acres of paddy land. Five minor lakes were incorporated in the building of the Parakrama Samudra, whose 8½-mile bund contains 4½ million cubic yards of earth. One thousand men employed in the hand labor of the period, working 24 hours a day, could scarcely have completed the job in 12 years.

The Quadrangle: Polonnaruwa's centerpiece is the **Terrace of the Tooth Relic** (1), best known today as "The Quadrangle." Twelve magnificent buildings stand on this platform in the heart of the ancient city. Enter from the east through a **gatehouse**. This structure must have been at least two stories high. At the bottom of the steps is a water trough in which worshippers could wash their feet.

The **Vatadage** (a) – the circular building on your left as you enter – is probably the oldest monument in Polonnaruwa, preceding by several centuries the establishment of the capital. Every other *vatadage* known in Sri Lanka dates from around the 7th Century, and this one is no exception: an inscription traces it to King Sila Meghavanna of Anuradhapura. The *dagoba* around which it was constructed, too, apparently was part of an early monastery. The floridly decorated stonework is a legacy of Nissanka Malla.

At the building's northern entrance is a guardstone (one of a former pair) preventing evil from entering. The moonstone at the second flight of steps is the best preserved in Polonnaruwa. In the center of the Vatadage, within the concentric stone columns that once supported a conical roof, four Buddha statues face the cardinal points, their backs to the sacred mound of brick – all that remains of the *dagoba*.

Directly opposite the Vatadage is the **Hatadage** (b), a Temple of the Tooth built either by Parakramabahu or Nissanka Malla in the 12th Century. Solid, stone walls surround the lower story while, an upper story of wood, in which the Tooth Relic would have been kept, has long since disintegrated. The walls of the building are inscribed with a self-gratifying account of Nissanka Malla's deeds. On the entrance porch, dancers and musicians are portrayed in stucco.

To the east of the Hatadage is the **Gal Pota** (c) or "Stone Book," the most grandiose of all Nissanka Malla's grandiose inscriptions. This enormous stone slab, 26 feet (eight meters) long and 14 feet (4½ meters) wide, was dragged here from Mihintale. The inscription expounds on the king's invasion of India and his relations with other foreign states.

A 7th Century **chapter house** (d) is against the Quadrangle's northern wall, next to the fascinating **Satmahal Prasada** (e). Neither the builder nor the original name of this structure is known. Its current label translates simply as "Edifice of Seven Stories." The simple stepped design has been compared to that of the

The Vatadage in the Quadrangle.

Mesopotamian ziggurats, but this "angular stupa" is similar to one found in northern Thailand (at San Maha Phon). The technique of masonry dates it to the 12th Century; it may originally have been octagonal in shape. Deistic figures in niches denote a Mahayana Buddhist influence.

To the west of the Hatadage is the **Atadage** (f), the original Temple of the Tooth at Polonnaruwa, built by Vijayabahu I in the 11th Century. The ground floor, decorated with ornamental pillars, resembles a traditional image house. The now-vanished (wooden) upper story apparently held the Tooth Relic as well as other treasures, for Atadage means "house of eight relics."

Lotus-stem Pillars: On the northwestern corner of the Quadrangle is a platform that once housed a **reclining Buddha image** (g). A long brick outline is all that remains. To the south is the late 12th Century **Lata Mandapaya** (h). A lovely pavilion with curving, vinelike pillars, it was King Nissanka Malla's "flower scroll hall," where he listened to the chanting of religious texts. The pillars represent lotus stems. The entire

The Thuparama image house.

pavilion is surrounded by a simple railing and gateway of squared stone. The image of a **bodhisattva** (i) stands in the center of the terrace, perhaps to remind onlookers of this last stage of perfection before achieving Buddhahood. The remains of a **bo tree shrine** (j) are marked by a small building west of the Vatadage.

The **Thuparama** (k), in the southwest corner of the Quadrangle, is the best preserved building in Polonnaruwa. Possibly constructed by Parakramabahu, its brick walls are about seven feet thick, and are corbelled overhead to form a vault, or *gedige*. The main image area is a square chamber, reached from a rectangular vestibule. In the inner sanctum is a ruined Buddha image much older than the Thuparama itself; this image may have been installed from a deserted early shrine nearby. On the outer walls of the Thuparama, architectural models in fine stucco give an excellent idea of what contemporary buildings of Polonnaruwa looked like.

Below the terrace, just south of the Quadrangle, is a 13th Century **Shiva De-**

vala dating from the period of Pandyan reign. The stonework is of fine quality and profuse ornamentation. So magnificently fitted as to require no mortar whatever, it rivals that of any South Indian shrine of its period. But the roof, with its brick *sikhara*, has crumbled away. In this *devala* were found most of the Polonnaruwa bronzes on display in the National Museum in Colombo.

The Inner Fortress: The road past the Quadrangle travels south through a gateway into the **Citadel**, the inner fortress and administrative capital of Parakramabahu's ancient city. The largest building standing within its still-clearly-visible walls was the **Vejayanta Pasada** (2), the royal palace of Parakramabahu I. The King named it in honor of the palace of the god Indra. The ruins of three stories (of a total of seven, according to the chronicles) can be seen today; empty sockets in the great brick walls show where wooden beams upheld higher stories. Most of the ground floor is taken up by a large hall, 102 by 42 feet (31 by 13 meters), probably an audience hall. Many smaller chambers and the remains of stairway can also be seen.

Parakramabahu's **Council Chamber** (3) is situated directly east of the palace. This great hall, on its three-tiered stone platform, was evidently connected with the palace by a covered colonnade. The stone carving is particularly note-worthy; the bas-relief protrayals of elephants around the base are a triumph of naturalism. Two flights of steps, each with a moonstone, are at the building's entrance. This building was the king's formal center of government and legislation.

Just below the Citadel walls, to the east, is a large but exquisite stepped bath of cut stone. This **Kumara Pokuna** (4), the royal bath, is of intricate geometrical design. Underground stone conduits feed it from the Parakrama Samudra. In the 12th Century, it stood in the midst of a lovely garden of flowering bushes and fruit trees.

Reverse direction, returning up the road past the Quadrangle, and turn right (east) at the first crossroads. Notice, as you travel this direction, the ruins of the ancient main street of Polonnaruwa, running straight east-wards. Turn right onto the **The Gal Vihara.**

grounds of the **Pabalu Vehera** (5), a small *dagoba* of brick which may have been built by Parakramabahu's Queen Rupavati. Image houses on the site, containing *bodhisattva* statues, may have been moved here from outlying areas in the 10th or 11th Century.

At the end of this eastern road is another **Shiva Devala** (6), an 11th Century structure properly known as the Vanam Madevi Isvaram. This temple, the only all-stone building in Polonnaruwa, is named after the queen of Rajaraja I, the Chola conqueror who established his capital here. It is in an almost perfect state of preservation.

Return to the crossroads and turn right. The ruins of other **Hindu temples** (7) stand near the ancient stone slabs of the city's northern gateway. Just outside the northern gate, a footpath leads to the **Menik Vehera** (8). This ruined *dagoba* is of note for the terra-cotta lions on its base. An image house with standing Buddha sculptures is nearby.

Most of Polonnaruwa's great monastic complexes stood to the north of the city. The first to be encountered along this road is the **Alahana Pirivena**, whose most notable monument is Nissanka Malla's 12th Century **Rankot Vehera** (9). It currently is being extensively restored under the auspices of the Cultural Triangle project. More than 180 feet (55 meters) high and about the same dimension in diameter, it is the largest *dagoba* in Polonnaruwa and the largest built in Sri Lanka since the 400-foot Jetavanarama was raised in Anuradhapura in the 4th Century. Its name means "golden pinnacle," which it must have once been capped by. It was modeled after the water-bubble-shaped Ruwanweli of Anuradhapura. A small path leads from here to a **pokuna** (10) in which monks bathed.

North of the *dagoba* is a rocky crag containing four caves. Known as the **Gopala Pabbata**, it is the earliest known site at Polonnaruwa. Inscriptions in the cave have been dated from the 2nd Century B.C. to the 5th Century A.D.

The **Baddhasima Pasada** (11), or convocation hall, is the highest structure of the Alahana Parivena complex. Here were celebrated the solemn rites of the monastery, and here was enforced the

Left, the serene face of the Gal Vihara's seated Buddha. Right, the Lankatilaka image house.

strict disciplinary code of the Sangha, the order of monks. The abbot's throne can still be clearly recognized in the center of the building. Around it were cells occupied by individual monks.

By far the most striking of the Alahana Pirivena ruins is the image house called the **Lankatilaka** (12). This massive brick building stood (and stands) 170 feet (52 meters) long, 60 feet (18 meters) wide and 58 feet (17½ meters) high. Within the great nave, whose interior walls still show traces of the brilliant murals that once decorated them, a gallery ran around three sides. But the worshipper entering the image house is left with an unobstructed view of a gigantic brick standing Buddha which still dominates the shrine, though headless. A vaulted dome above the inner sanctum has collapsed.

To the north of the Lankatilaka is the **Kiri Vehera** (13), a *dagoba* thought to have been the gift of Queen Subhadra, one of Parakramabahu's wives. This is the best preserved *dagoba* in Polonnaruwa. Its original plaster is largely intact. Small brick mounds around the platform of the *dagoba* are probably funerary *dagobas* for the cremated remains of important monks or members of the royal family.

In 1983-84, archaeologists made several new discoveries at Alahana Pirivena, including a cemetery, a fascinating ancient hospital site, and the toilet and shower area of the monastery.

Glorious Gal Vihara: Of all the brilliant structures at Polonnaruwa, the best known are the Buddha sculptures comprising the **Gal Vihara** (14). Once known as Uttararama, the "northern shrine" of Parakramabahu, its modern name means simply "rock shrine." The four mid-12th Century statues, cut from a single granite wall, rank among the true masterpieces of Sri Lankan Art.

The southernmost statue is a seated Buddha in deep meditation. His throne is adorned with lions and thunderbolts, and behind his head is a halo. The second sculpture is within a cave artificially hewn from solid rock. Various deities, including Brahma and Vishnu, surround the image of the seated Buddha; remains of bright murals that once decorated the cave

An ancient Buddha image in the Thuparama.

walls can still be made out.

The third figure depicts a standing Buddha in a rare cross-armed pose. Twenty-three feet (seven meters) high, it was once believed to represent the Buddha's favorite disciple, Ananda. The face is serene and the body relaxed. The northernmost statue is a 46-foot (14 meter) reclining Buddha shown at the moment of entry into parinibbana. Note the slight depression in the pillow under His head, and the marks on the soles of His feet.

At one time, the Gal Vihara Buddhas were enclosed by brick buildings, as sockets in the rock walls around them testify. The Cultural Triangle project is making plans to restore these protective structures in much the same manner as at the Aukana Buddha.

The Northern City: A road travels north from near the Gal Vihara to several additional points of interest. To the right (east) of the road, the **Demala Maha Seya** (15) is a vast artificial hill offering a beautiful view south across the Alahana Parivena. An enormous mound of brick, this hill marks a failed attempt by Parakramabahu to build the world's largest *dagoba* – a proposed 600 feet (183 meters) in height. Work on the building was done by Pandyan prisoners-of-war captured during Parakramabahu's South Indian campaign. A small *dagoba* of later date crowns the mound.

Further up this road, to the left, is the late 12th Century **Lotus Bath** (16). A unique stone bath, it is built in tiers of eight-petaled lotuses. It is one of few surviving ruins of the **Jetavana Monastery**, estimated to have consisted of some 500 buildings, and important enough to have hosted an annual Esala Perahera-style procession for the Tooth Relic.

The most important Jetavana building known today is the **Tivanka Image House** (17) at the end of the northern road. Sometimes called the Northern Temple, its main image was a standing Buddha in the *tivanka* or "thrice-bent" position. In this posture, hips and neck were bent opposite directions, setting the body in three flowing diagonals. The pose denotes ease in a male or grace in a female. Time-worn wall paintings within the image house display *Jataka* scenes of the Buddha's

The 12th Century Lotus Bath.

previous lives. Stucco ornamention on the outer walls depicts dwarfs and lions in infinite amusing poses. The dwarfs of the Kelaniya temple near Colombo were based upon these figures.

Return to the main road separating the Gal Vihara from the Kiri Vehera, and proceed to a T-junction. Almost opposite are two Hindu temples. The northern of the two is called the **Naipena Vihara** (18) or "cobra shrine" because the figure of a many-headed cobra adorns its fallen brick *sikhara*. The cobra is associated with Vishnu, the "preserver" of the Hindu trinity. His image may have stood on a stone pedestal in the inner sanctum. Immediately south is a **Shiva Shrine** (19). Its central chamber contains a finely executed stone *lingam* and *yoni*, the phallic male-female symbol associated with Shiva and his consort Parvati. Several fine bronzes were found on this site.

Parakramabahu had a **Summer Palace** (20) across the lake from his capital, on a peninsula jutting far into the water. Traces of painting still survive on the plastered walls of the sumptuous mansion. Today,

however, its residents are water birds. It can be reached by turning south on a side road off the Habarana highway, about a half-mile northwest of the main entrance to Polonnaruwa.

Nissanka Malla's 'Island Garden': Nissanka Malla was a vain man. He insisted on constructing new residences and monuments whenever possible, rather than using those built by others. When he rose to power, he eschewed the palace and council chambers of Parakramabahu for his own **Dipuyyana** (21) or "island garden" on a promontory by the lake. It is easily found today, directly north of the **rest house** (22).

Parakramabahu actually built the gardens as his royal pleasure gardens. These included the **baths**, which lie in a hollow just a stone's throw from the rest house. Circular and square pools were fed through stone cisterns and spouts from the great lake above them. The ruins of Nissanka Malla's **palace**, on an adjacent site, are unimpressive. Reputedly erected in seven months, the palace was a huge wooden-columned building. Remains of the **audience hall** and a windowless stone building called **"the mausoleum"** are north of the baths.

Nissanka Malla's **council chamber**, however, is among the most interesting of Sri Lanka's plethora of ruins, for here may be understood some of the pomp of Sinhalese royalty. On each pillar of the building, where the king and court assembled in state, are carved the designations of the ministers and other officers who took their places there. The King sat on a lion throne at the head of the chambers. On his right hand stood (in order) the heir apparent, the other princes, the generals of the army, the prime minister and cabinet, the finance ministry and the record keepers. On the king's left, facing the prime minister, were the regional governors, then businessmen and lesser nobles.

Close to the rest house, a new **Archaeological Museum** is under construction. It will display a number of artifacts found at Polonnaruwa, previously exhibited at other museums.

The Southern Monastery: The highway follows the bund of Parakrama Samudra south from the rest house to the **Potgul Vehera** (24), or Southern Monastery. Just

Left, Stilt-walking Polonnaruwa children.

north of the monastery is a 12th Century statue often called **"The Sage"** (23). There are few secular statues in Sri Lanka, and none has caused so much controversy as this one. Most persons believe it represents Parakramabahu I, holding an object which represents the yoke of kingship. Others maintain that it is a Buddhist sage holding a bundle of *ola* manuscript.

The Potgul Vehera lies about 100 meters south of the statue. It is unique in structure – a central circular (and formerly domed) building surrounded by four small *dagobas* on its central platform. Traces of color decoration remain on the outside; the acoustics within are excellent. It may have been a library (*potgul*) or a story-telling chamber.

Nearly opposite the Potgul Vehera is Polonnaruwa's **National Holiday Resort** hotel complex (25). Three modern hotels on the site overlook the *samudra*.

Medirigiriya and other sites: Twenty-four miles (39 kilometers) north of Polonnaruwa, via secondary road through Hingurakgoda, are the important ruins of **Medirigiriya**. The *vatadage* atop a low rocky point, built in the 7th Century by King Agbo IV, is considered one of the finest examples of this architectural form. There are three concentric rows of pillars (a total of 68 pillars) surrounding four large seated Buddhas facing the cardinal directions. A granite staircase leads up to it. A 3rd Century A. D. image house stands nearby. An early carved brick molding at the base of the present stupa has led some scholars to believe this could have been a place of worship as early as the 1st Century A. D.

Northeast of Polonnaruwa about 25 miles (40 kilometers), a large wildlife refuge surrounds the **Somawathie Chaitiya**. Here there are a monastery, a *dagoba* and other ruins.

Southeast of Polonnaruwa, the rock spire of **Dimbulagala**, also known as Gunner's Quoin, rises from the scrub jungle. From earliest Buddhist times, this has been a hermitage for meditating monks. About 500 rock caves are cut into the mountain; they have been occupied almost continuously since the 3rd Century B.C.

The **Medirigiriya** *vatadage*.

THE CITADEL
OF SIGIRIYA

The sight is stupendous even today: a massive monolith of red stone rises 600 feet from the green scrub jungle to accentuate the lucid blue of the sky. How overpowering, then, this rock fortress of Sigiriya must have been when it was crowned by a palace 15 centuries ago.

Sigiriya (say see-gih-REE-yah) was no gloomy and forbidding fortification, as many other citadels are. At the brief height of its glory – a flowering of only 18 years in the late 5th Century – it was one of the loveliest royal cities that ever graced the earth. And today, it is perhaps the single most remarkable memory for visitors to Sri Lanka.

Ruins of the fabled palace spread across the very peak of the "Lion Rock" – so-named, perhaps, because visitors formerly began the final harrowing ascent through the open jaws and throat (*giriya*) of a lion (*sinha*) whose likeness was once sculpted halfway up the monolith. Only the gigantic paws remain today. Within a grotto on Sigiriya's sheer west face, beautiful bare-breasted maidens still smile from incredible fresco paintings. Surrounding the foot of the rock, extending for several hundred meters, are Asia's oldest surviving landscape gardens, incorporating lovely ponds around Sigiriya's plinth of fallen boulders.

The Parricide King: The site of Sigiriya was known from ancient times. Inscriptions on boulders confirm that it was a hermitage for Buddhist monks from an early date. Its importance as a seat of royalty began and ended in the last quarter of the 5th Century, under the direction of a mad genius named Kasyapa – who conceived and perfected this masterpiece under a shadow of paranoiac fear.

Kasyapa was the eldest son of Anuradhapura's King Dhatusena, the great tank builder. Fearing that he would be supplanted in the royal succession by his younger half-brother Mogallan whose mother was of royal blood while Kasyapa's was a commoner – Kasyapa seized the throne and imprisoned his father. Mogallan fled to India.

Kasyapa demanded that his father reveal the wealth he was convinced had been hidden. Dhatusena took the young usurper to the bund of the Kalawewa, the greatest of his irrigation works, below which lived a venerable monk who had been his teacher and companion of many years. "There," said Dhatusena, pointing, "are all the treasures that I possess."

"Slay my father!" cried an outraged Kasyapa. The former king was walled alive within his tomb.

Fear, arrogance and a delusion of divinity drove Kasyapa to construct his palace on Sigiriya rock. Seven years after his ascent to the throne in 477 A.D., Kasyapa moved into his fabulous new palace. Eleven years after, in 495, he descended from his impregnable stronghold to meet Mogallan – returned from India with an army of combined Chola and Sinhalese troops – on the treacherous plains near the modern village of Habarana.

At the height of battle, Kasyapa's elephant, sensing a hidden swamp before him, momentarily turned aside. His army, fearing their leader had turned in retreat,

Left, Sigiriya, the 'Lion Rock.' Right, gardens extend from the foot of the monolith.

broke in confusion. Kasyapa was left defenseless. Flamboyant to the last, he drew his dagger, cut his own throat, raised the blade high in the air, and stuck it back in its sheath before falling.

Sigiriyan graffiti: Although Mogallan immediately moved his capital back to Anuradhapura, Sigiriya was not instantly forgotten. For at least 500 years after the death of Kasyapa, sightseers scaled the citadel to gawk at the Sigiriya Maidens and admire the view. Sri Lanka's oldest graffiti verifies this. Incised in tiny pearl-like script into the so-called **Mirror Wall**, beneath the frescoes pocket, are prose and poems more than 1,000 years old.

Today, most of the three-meter (10 foot) high Mirror Wall has fallen, and no one is likely to mistake for the original that portion rebuilt by the Archaeological Department. The true wall is distinguished by the extraordinary coating of polished lime which still today, 1,500 years later, gleams and reflects like glass.

The Mirror Wall held the astonishing walkway called the **Gallery** against the rock face. Visitors pass this route immedi-ately after they have climbed the caged spiral staircase to the phenomenal fres-coes pocket of the **Sigiriya Maidens.**

No one quite knows whom the seductive beauties, painted in tempera in brilliant colors on the rock wall, represent. It is easy to think of them as *apsaras*, heaven-dwelling nymphs from a realm or radiant light – above whom, perhaps, lived the "god-king" in his rock-top palace. Perhaps they were only ladies of the court on their way to the temple. The graffiti speak of 500 "damsels", there are but 18 today, pro-tected from sun, wind and rain erosion in this sheltered grotto. In 1967, a vandal obliterated several of these priceless treasures. Fortunately, they were restored by Dr. Marenzi, sponsored by the Smithsonian Institute.

The pathway toward the rock's summit leads from the frescoes along the Mirror Wall; past a **lookout** where a *galdunna*, or boulder-catapult, still waits to be loosed on an attacker's head; and up to the **Lion Terrace**. Bounded on three sides by a low parapet and on the fourth (the south) by sheer cliff, it is a beautiful site. The gigantic

Left, one of the 18 Sigiriya Maidens.

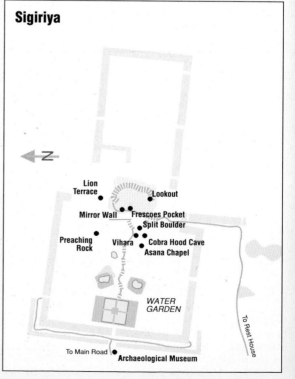

Sigiriya

Lion Terrace
Lookout
Mirror Wall
Frescoes Pocket
Split Boulder
Preaching Rock
Vihara
Cobra Hood Cave
Asana Chapel
WATER GARDEN
To Main Road
Archaeological Museum
To Rest House

lion which once crouched here, half-emerged from his den, was a magnificiently romantic architectural concept; the conceit of having the one path to the climax of this fantastic city lie through the jaws of the menacing beast provided an intimidating military advantage as well. Today, one climbs through two clawed paws to reach the steep stairwell and wind-blown railing leading to the summit.

The entire summit of Sigiriya, nearly three acres in extent, was occupied by buildings. Running water trickled through channels beneath the floor of the moated, colonnaded **Royal Summer House**. Bathing pools were cut out of the living rock. Below and to the east, a canopied divan or "throne" was carved from naked rock. At the base of the rock are the fascinating rock and water gardens. Especially note one enormous **split boulder**. On the half still standing, a water cistern has been cut. On the fallen half, a rock throne faces a square, leveled floor which may represent a council hall.

Several Buddhist religious sites can be identified among other rocks. In the **Co-**bra Hood Cave, so named because of the way the rock looms over it, an inscription dates to the 2nd Century B.C., and faint remains of ancient paintings can be discerned on the ceiling. A **cave vihara** contains the undated torso of a Buddha statue. There are more traces of paintings on the ceiling of the **Asana Chapel**; its empty stone slab is believed to have been a throne for an absent Buddha, on which early monks meditated. To the north, the so-called **Preaching Rock** held tiered platforms for orating monks. A multitude of miniature niches are carved into the rock; on *poya* days, these held the flickering lights of 100 oil lamps.

At the main western entrance to the Sigiriya compound, beckons the **Water Garden**. The symmetrically planned ponds may have been purely ornamental.

After many neglected centuries lost in the scrub jungle, Sigiriya was rediscovered by an incredulous British hunter in the mid-19th Century. From 1982 to 1987, under UNESCO and Cultural Triangle Project sponsorship, extensive digs and restoration were underway. Finds are ex-

The Lion Terrace's portal to the summit.

hibited at the small **Archaeological Museum** just west of the water garden, outside the main walls of the fortress.

The Dambulla Cave Temple: By far the most impressive of all the many cave temples in Sri Lanka is the series of five caverns comprising the **Raja Maha Vihara** at the village of **Dambulla**, a mere 12 miles (19 kilometers) southwest of Sigiriya. Climb up a huge sloping rock face that rises more than 350 feet (over 100 meters) above the village and admire the view across the plain to Sigiriya rock.

The largest cave, the fourth on your right after you pass through a gateway, is the most interesting. The ceiling of this cavern is fully illustrated with paintings that follow the natural folds of the rock so closely that many visitors have taken the surface to be of cloth! Among the cave's numerous statues – are images of Upulvan (Vishnu) and Saman. Dating from the 12th Century, they may be the earliest *devala* statues to appear in a Buddhist image house. The cave's history dates to the 2nd or 1st Century B.C., when King Valagam Bahu took refuge here after be-

ing driven out of Anuradhapura by invading armies.

Bring a flashlight, preferably with a diffuse beam, to inspect the paintings in these temples. Bear in mind that because this *is* a temple, visiting hours (8 to 11 a.m. and 2 to 7 p.m.) are somewhat restricted.

Other Ancient Sites: A sampling of other ancient points of interest south and west of Dambulla includes the following:

•**Nalanda Gedige**, the earliest known all-stone building in Sri Lanka (dating from the 8th Century) and one of the most remarkable examples of the amalgamation of Hindu and Buddhist architecture. Probably a Mahayanist shrine, its stones, now being reassembled, contain rare Tantric carvings of sexual theme. It is located on the bund of a tank just east of Route A9, 12 miles (19 kilometers) south of Dambulla.

•**Ridigama**, a 2,000-year-old cave temple some 11 miles (18 kilometers) east of Kurunegala. In its Maha Vihara is a heavily gilt sedent Buddha, a large reclining Buddha, and an intricate ivory-paneled door frame.

•**Arankele**, a 6th Century forest hermitage 15 miles (24 kilometers) north of Kurunegala.

•**Kurunegala**, now a thriving regional center, and for a brief period centuries ago, the national capital. Jumbled ruins with carved stairs and door jambs are on **Ibbagala**, one of a series of huge granite outcroppings known as the Animal Rocks.

•**Dambadeniya**, national capital for about 100 years after the fall of Polonnaruwa in the 13th Century. Some 19 miles (31 kilometers) west of Kurunegala on Route B27, its principal surviving ruins are a two-story Dalada Maligawa (Temple of the Tooth Relic) and a *dagoba*, within a crude *vatadage*, which locals revere for the 60 corporeal relics of the Buddha it is said to contain.

•**Panduvas Nuwara**, a 12th Century capital located about midway between Kurunegala and Chilaw off Route B33. It features a well-preserved walled **Citadel** about 1,000 feet (305 meters) on a side, containing an enormous moated palace and audience hall. It was built on an earlier site by Parakramabahu I prior to his conquest of Polonnaruwa.

Left, the painted ceiling of Dambulla's Maha Vihara cave. Right, exterior view of the Dambulla temple.

EASTERN REACHES, SANDY BEACHES

Sri Lanka's Eastern Province stretches some 200 miles (about 320 kilometers) along the seacoast from the Kokkilai Lagoon to Ruhuna (Yala) National Park.

It is justly famous for its beaches. Tourist centers have sprung up in the Nilaveli area, 10 miles north of Trincomalee, and around Kalkudah, 20 miles north of Batticaloa. Less well known but pleasant beaches are found up and down the coast.

Most of the East Coast is in sharp contrast to the luxury beach resorts, however. Except when the northeast monsoon makes its annual assault between October and January, it is a parched, dry area, with poor soil that requires constant attention. Tamil Hindus and Muslims, many of them farmers and fishermen, forms the majority of the population. Reminders still abound of a devastating 1978 cyclone that complicated their already difficult lives.

There are two major cities along the East Coast – Trincomalee, whose harbor is considered one of the best sheltered on earth, and Batticaloa, which like "Trinco" was a key Dutch and British colonial outpost.

In recent years, the eastern coast of Sri Lanka has been largely inaccessible due to ongoing civil strife, and many of the seaside resorts and hotels have fallen to neglect. Normalcy is however, slowly returning to these areas along with the tourist. It is likely that before long the eastern coast will once again become the focus of tourists from the world over.

'Trinco' and Its Harbor: Back in 1775, a teenaged midshipman named Horatio Nelson arrived in **Trincomalee Harbour** aboard the *H.M.S. Seahorse*. Later, as admiral of the British Navy, he remembered it as "the finest harbour in the world." Indeed, with its 33 miles (53 milometers) of shoreline locked in by hills on three sides and protected by islands on the fourth, it is hard to argue. In size, Trincomalee is the world's fifth largest natural harbor; but despite its potential, it has remained of secondary economic importance to Colombo. Sri Lanka has started on plans to make Trincomalee the country's No. 2

container port, perhaps with a free-trade zone. "Trinco," as its friends call it, was well-known so Sri Lanka's inhabitants many centuries ago. This may have been the port where Mahinda landed on his way to Mihintale to convert the Anuradhapura Kingdom to Buddhism.

The first recorded European landing was made in 1617 by a Dutch-sponsored Danish vessel. The port switched hands back and forth between the Portuguese, Dutch, British and even French until 1795, when England finally secured a grip on Trincomalee as its first possession on the coast of Ceylon.

During the Second World War, Trincomalee Harbour was the home base for the combined East Asian fleets of all Allied powers. It remained a British Royal Navy base for many years after.

The Japanese staged an all-out air assault on the harbor on April 8, 1942. But the Allied forces – having been previously alerted to the raid – had sent the fleet to sea, and only two ships, one a merchant vessel, were destroyed in the harbor by Japanese bombs and gunfire. About five

Preceding pages: the Tirukonesvaram Kovil in Trincomalee. *Left,* fishing boats near Kuchchaveli. *Right,* the lover's leap at Swami Rock.

miles out to sea, the aircraft carrier *Hermes* plunged burning into 30 fathoms of water, riddled with bombs. (It was rediscovered in the 1970s by diver Rodney Jonklaas, who followed the tales of fishermen to locate its hulk, teeming with marine life.) Despite the setbacks, the British succeeded in turning the Japanese away.

Today, Trinco is far removed from the sleepy market center it once was. Civil unrest has taken its toll. The visible military presence and uncertainty of terrorist attacks, have dispelled the town's easygoing character. Trinco occupies a finger of land that protects the harbor from the open sea.

Visitors to Trinco commonly begin their sightseeing at **Fort Frederick**, which sits on a promontory at the east side of Trincomalee town. The site was first used by the Portuguese (1624) and later by the Dutch, whose gateway bears the date 1676. The British named it in honor of Frederick, Duke of York, in 1803. A century and a half of British fortifications can be found around the fort grounds – vaults, gun emplacements, and other such necessities, both above and below ground.

The remnant of a herd of spotted deer still lives on the fort grounds. Shady banyan trees spread over the *kachcheri* (the former government secretariat) and the adjacent **Wellington House** – so-named for the Iron Duke himself, Arthur Wellesley, 1st Duke of Wellington. Stricken with malaria after a great victory in South India in 1799, Wellington convalesced in this house and missed the ship that was to carry him to a new command in Egypt. But the *Susannah* went down with all hands lost in the Gulf of Aden, and the Iron Duke was saved for his historic encounter with Napoleon at Waterloo.

At the northeasternmost tip of Fort Frederick's promontory is a cliff known as **Swami Rock**, dropping about 360 feet (110 meters) directly into the sea. On its topmost pinnacle is the **Tirukonesvaram Kovil**, rebuilt on the site of the fabled "Great Pagoda" – the Dakshana Kailayam, the Temple of 1,000 Pillars – destroyed by the 17th Century Portuguese. It was, and is, one of the great Shaivite *isvarams*, already considered famous and ancient when King Mahasena of Anuradhapura

established a Buddhist monastery in its stead in the 3rd Century A. D.

A *kovil* restoration was completed in 1963. Three ancient bronze images and a Shiva *lingam*, the latter found by divers at the bottom of the cliff beneath the temple, were installed for worship. *Puja* services are especially colorful at dusk on Fridays.

Trincomalee may take its name from the site of this temple – perhaps from the Tamil words *tiru kona malai*, "mountain sacred to Konesvara (Shiva)."

One pillar from the Great Pagoda still stands at the top of Swami Rock. It perpetuates an apparently unfounded Dutch legend about a **lover's leap**. According to the inscription, a beautiful Dutch maiden named Francina Van Rhede cast herself from the cliff as she watched her faithless lover, a seaman, sail away. In truth, this lady was known to have been happily married to a second husband eight years after the date on this pillar!

Across the peninsula from Fort Frederick, **Fort Ostenburg** overlooks the entrance to the Inner Harbour from the top of Eastern Hill. It was originally built by

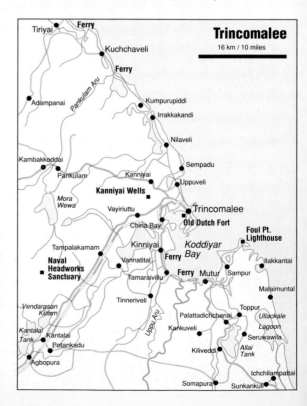

the Dutch, but only British fortifications are visible today. The **British Dockyard** below has been taken over today by the Sri Lankan Navy; this entire peninsula is thus "off-limits" to visitors unless special permission is obtained. Also restricted are visits to **Admiralty House** and **Pepperpot Cottage**, a great house and a bungalow designed by a ship's carpenter and surrounded by picturesque gardens. A banyan tree on the grounds is said to be the biggest on the island.

Among other points of interest in Trincomalee, the **Archaeological Museum** has a noteworthy collection of Buddha images and other antiquities of the East Coast.

The Beach at Nilaveli: North of Trinco, a 20-mile strand of beach runs uninterrupted up the coast past Kuchchaveli. One of Sri Lanka's premier beach resorts, **Nilaveli**, is the center of this strip, geographically as well as in terms of tourist interest. When the southwest monsoon strikes the opposite shore of Sri Lanka for several months beginning (usually) in April, this coast is the place to be. With the exception of the Club Oceanic at **Uppuveli**, about four miles out of Trinco, most of the beach hotels and guest houses are between the 9th and 13th mileposts of the road north. The major recreation is sun-bathing; deep-sea fishing, skin diving and shell collecting are excellent. But watch out for sea urchins and skates at all times of year, and for stinging jellyfish especially in July and August.

Hotels along this strip tout **Pigeon Island**, just a few hundred meters offshore from most of the Nilaveli hotels, as an ideal location for half-day snorkeling excursions. It's only about a 15-minute trip by outboard motorboat. But visitors often find this tiny accumulation of sand, shells and rocks to be highly overrated. The underwater scenery is better on coral reefs a little further off-shore. Pigeon Island takes its name from its importance as a breeding ground for the blue rock pigeon. It is also a breeding ground for poisonous snakes, which sleep through the sun-scorched days but crawl out of their dens at dusk. The British navy once used the island for gunnery practice.

Trincomalee scenes: left, a tooth-powder vendor; right, the Fort Frederick gateway.

Back on the mainland, **Red Rocks Bay** (near Milepost 16) has excellent swimming and even better shell-collecting. **Kuchchaveli**, another five miles north, requires a crossing of a lagoon mouth by vehicular ferry. Again, there is fine swimming and fishing available, but currents are unpredictable near the headland.

The most important ancient site in the region is the *vatadage* at **Tiriyai**, a modern village just inland from Milepost 28 (after a second ferry crossing). This circular, pillared temple crowns a prominent rock with a view of the sea. An inscription dates it to the 7th or 8th Century, records it as Girihandika Cetiya, and claims to enshrine hair relics of the Buddha. Its Mahayana origin is confirmed by an inscribed statement that the **bodhisattva** Avalokitesvara resided here. The *vatadage* is being restored by archaeologists and monks.

Pulmoddai is further north still, some 35 miles beyond Trincomalee. A third ferry crossing is involved; these vehicular craft get slower and more archaic as one moves north. A "mineral sands dressing plant" at Pulmoddai separates the mineral particles of beach sand by using magnetism and flotation techniques. More than 75,000 tons of the mineral ilmenite are produced annually at this plant.

Five miles north of Pulmoddai is **Kokkilai**, where a vast, shallow lagoon has become a sanctuary and a paradise for bird watchers. Wild ducks, pelicans and flamingoes share the waters with a variety of migrants. A rubber raft is recommended for avid avifauna followers.

Off the Trinco-Anuradhapura highway, at the 105th milepost, is an important ancient Buddhist temple known as the **Velgam Vihara** or (to Hindus) as the Natanar Kovil. It was built approximately 2,000 years ago in the vanished village of Velagama by King Bhatika Tissa (22 B.C. - 7 A.D.), according to an inscription, and was renovated and enlarged by 11th Century Chola invaders. There are guardstones outside and a Buddha image within a ruined image house. It represents one of the most interesting amalgams of Hinduism and Buddhism in Sri Lanka.

An alternate route to this *vihara* or *kovil* (take your pick) comes more directly from **Club Oceanic, Uppuveli**.

Nilaveli, but requires a final approach by foot for the final mile beyond the picturesque **Periya Kulam** tank. This is a pleasant spot for a picnic anytime except between February and May, when the malodorous *mi* trees are in bloom.

About seven miles (11 kilometers) west of Trinco, just south of the Anuradhapura road, are the **Kanniyai Hot Springs**. Hindus consider them the creation of Vishnu, and there is a small shrine near the site. Each of the seven springs offers water of a slightly different temperature, ranging between about 85°F and 115°F, (29°C to 46°C). Each well is contained in an individual enclosure, and the whole small space in which they occur – about four by eight meters – is again enclosed by a stout wall. Bathers draw up buckets of water from the wells, and occasionally pull up small fish with it!

From Trinco to Batti: The main highway south from Trincomalee to Batticaloa, Route A15, is handicapped by the six ferry crossings it requires, including four within 10 miles where the **Mahaweli River** empties into **Koddiyar Bay**. Patient travelers are rewarded with beautiful scenery, close looks at oyster fishermen, and low-tide glimpses of mud-hopper fish.

Near the village of **Muttur**, between the third and fourth crossing, a plaque beneath the **"White Man's Tree"** marks the spot near where Robert Knox (then aged 18) and 15 English companions were taken captive by Kandyan King Raja Sinha II in 1660. Placed under a sort of "house arrest" in different rural parts of the island for the next 20 years, Knox and a companion eventually succeeded in escaping to a coastal Dutch fort and then back to England. His book, *An Historical Relation of Ceylon* (published in 1681), is still considered the most perceptive foreign work ever written on Sri Lanka, untainted by the acrimony of captivity. Together with Alexander Selkirk's account of shipwrecked solitude on one of the Juan Fernandez islets west of Chile, Knox's book became the basis for Daniel Defoe's classic, *Robinson Crusoe*.

An Alternate Route: Travelers who are willing to journey a few miles further to avoid time-consuming ferry crossings can head southwest from Trincomalee to

Left, windsurfing in calm seas at Nilaveli. **Right**, bathing at the Kanniyai Hot Springs.

Kantalai, a distance of about 25 miles. A secondary road then turns east for a similar distance to rejoin Route A15 near the Allai Tank at the Alioluwa Junction.

The **Kantalai Tank** is one of Sri Lanka's more important bodies of inland water. Thought to have been built in the 7th Century, this 4,725-acre reservoir is the life blood of a large agricultural colony as well as the source of water for Trincomalee and its nearby beach resorts. The Kantalai colony raises rice and sugar cane, the latter for a sizable refinery and distillery.

The road between Kantalai and Alioluwa Junction skirts the northern border of the **Somawathie Chaitiya Game Sanctuary**. It is not unusual for travelers to see wild elephants on the road.

It is a worthwhile five-mile detour from the Alioluwa to the **Seruwawila Dagoba**, along the eastern shore of the Allai Tank. Both the tank and the *dagoba* are attributed to the 3rd Century B.C. King Kavantissa. With a classic touch of Buddhist politics, he secured the allegiance of the buffer state of Seru – at a time when his Ruhuna kingdom was challenged by the northern Tamil invaders – by presenting a frontal bone of the Buddha for enshrinement in a *dagoba* in the ancient Seru Capital city.

As Route A15 continues south, the turbulent Mahaweli outlet at **Verugal** requires another ferry crossing. A man-eating crocodile was active in this stretch of river as late as 1982. Visitors should be warned not to go bathing from the ferry! At **Panichchankeni**, 35 miles north of Batticaloa, the island's longest bridge spans the mouth of the Upaar Lagoon. **Chenaikkuda Beach**, protected by an offshore islet, has lovely holiday bungalows but an overabundance of sea snakes.

Twenty miles north of Batticaloa is **Valachchenai**, a large market town and site of Sri Lanka's largest paper factory. It is reached by an usual rail-cum-motor bridge across the Valaichenia Aru. Route A11 connects west from here to Polonnaruwa. Around the 70th mile-post, travelers should keep their eyes open for wild elephants (this is a crossing on the **Nelugala Corridor**) and maybe even leopards. Between 1921 and 1923, a man-

Strolling along the sands of Kalkudah.

eater took the lives of 20 persons before she was finally shot and killed near the village of **Punani.**

Kalkudah and Passekudah: Valachchenai is the gateway to what many visitors feel are the finest beaches on the island. **Kalkudah Bay**, facing east, is protected even from the northeast monsoon by a headland of pink and tawny boulders. **Passekudah Bay**, which opens to the north, has an offshore reef sheltering the sandy beach and keeping the water calm, clear and shallow – except during the northeaster. There is no place better for children. Windsurfers and water-skiers find it a delight.

This lower East Coast region was heavily devastated by the 1978 cyclone, and tourist development plans have lagged a bit as a result. Generally, higher-priced accommodations are a short walk across the headland in Kalkudah. Prices of all lodgings climb significantly when the "season" begins in April, just as they do in South and West Coast resorts at opposite times of the year. From here for many miles south, the coast is heavily populated.

Route A4 runs south to Pottuvil along the beach-front strip much as the Galle Road does along the southwest coast. One village runs into the next, divided only by lagoons, as *cadjan* fences crowd the road for room.

The market center of the southeast coast is **Batticaloa**, better known simply as "Batti." The Dutch established their first foothold in Sri Lanka here in 1602, traveling overland from Batti to meet the king in Kandy. The Portuguese erected a fort here in 1627; the Dutch claimed it in 1638, handed it over to the Kandyans in 1643, but reoccupied it in 1665. In 1795, three weeks after the capture of Trincomalee, Batticaloa surrendered without a battle to the British. After 1836, it was converted from military to administrative use. The **Dutch fort** of 1665 still stands today by the banks of the shallow and muddy **Batticaloa Lagoon**. Its exterior is in excellent condition with unbroken square walls, a bastion in each corner, and a moat that still holds water. But the buildings within are 20th Century government offices.

The most famous feature of Batticaloa is not its fort, but its "**singing fish.**" Es-

Pulling in the *ma-dela* fishing net.

pecially on full-moon nights, a multitude of faint but distinct sounds, like a distant orchestra playing a full range of musical chords, rises from the depths of the lagoon's waters. Louder in some places than in others, it is perhaps best heard from a boat at the town end of the **Kalladi Bridge**, with one ear to an oar dipped into the water, greatly enhancing the quality of the sound.

There are many theories about the source of this sound, but none yet has a scientific confirmation. Most fishermen of the area believe that the "singers" are species of mollusks which dwell on the floor of the lagoon. Many divers insist that shoals of top-sail catfish, occurring in great numbers in the lagoon, are the culprits. The less romantic suggest that the sound is due to water flowing past holes in the coralline rocks; high tides under full-moon conditions would see this flow at its maximum.

Batti Lagoon is navigable for a longer distance than any other Sri Lanka, about 35 miles (56 kilometers) from Chenkaladi to Kalmunai. Fishing is good and bird life plentiful. But bathing is discouraged by the number of "razor mussels" in the wa-ter, most notably just offshore from the Batticaloa rest house. In slicing swimmers' feet, the mollusk also injects an anticoagulant, causing dangerous wounds.

It is possible to head back inland toward the Hill Country on Route A5 from **Chenkaladi**, a few miles north of Batticaloa. About 25 miles along this route is the **Maha Oya** hot spring; it is located two miles from the rest house by Jeepable track. The **Rugam Tank** north of here is a favorite watering hole for wild elephants. This route connects with Kandy via the holy site of Mahiyangana, or with Badulla via Bibile in the heart of Veddha country.

A second route turns inland at **Karativu**, 28 miles (45 kilometers) south of Batti on Route A4. This highway winds directly into Gal Oya National Park, passing through the town of Amparai and close to several other interesting sites. The first point of interest is the **Digavapi Dagoba**, one of Buddhism's 16 holiest places in Sri Lanka. The *Mahavamsa* says the Buddha meditated at this spot after having left his footprint atop Adam's Peak. Tradition says the *dagoba* was raised by Saddhatissa,

Bullock cart near Chenkaladi.

younger son of King Kavantissa of Ruhuna, in the 3rd Century B.C. to enshrine fingernails of the Buddha. It is located south of the Gal Oya river, about 10 miles off the main road to the national park.

At **Amparai**, the largest town in the Gal Oya valley, there is an **Archaeological Museum** containing artifacts discovered in the valley, among them ancient terracotta figures. The **Gal Oya Valley** was the site of Sri Lanka's first major post-independence irrigation project, and its success helped lay the groundwork for the modern Mahaweli scheme. Its main reservoir, the **Senanayake Samudra**, now the centerpiece of the **Gal Oya National Park**, remains far and away the largest inland body of water in Sri Lanka. About 350 square miles (906 square kilometers) of irrigated land was opened to development, industrial as well as agricultural, by the Gal Oya project. A sugar refinery and distillery at **Hingurana** is the largest in the country, although the cane harvest is difficult to organize: soldiers are often called in to put their bayonets to work as pruning knives.

Buffaloes wallow in mud near Amparai.

Veddha Country: One of the Gal Oya scheme's obstacles rested in the fact that much of the jungle land it was opening was traditional Veddha territory. No less that six former Veddha settlements lie today beneath the waters of the Senanayake Samudra. Many of these aboriginal people were relocated to the new agricultural colonies, but many more resisted this threatening new lifestyle, preferring instead to hold out against progress in the remaining Bintenna jungles.

Perhaps no Veddha community has received greater attention than the isolated hamlet of **Rathugala**, a good 20 miles by rough jungle track from the Gal Oya headquarters town of **Inginiyagala**. Even here, bark huts have replaced traditional caves, and bows and arrows are often neglected. But clans are still based on matrilineal descent, and the Veddha language – a Sinhala patois – is spoken.

The 234-square-mile (606-square-kilometer) Gal Oya National Park is still under development. Elephants and water birds are its chief attractions, and are commonly visible from launches on the great

Senanayake Samudra. The expansive view from the bund of the reservoir is impressive, especially following the wet season, when the blue of the water strikes a muted contrast to the distant purples of the jagged Uva hills and the towering square peak called Westminster Abbey, almost due south. The reservoir, 19,200 acres in size, was modeled on the Tennessee Valley Authority's work in the United States. It takes the name of its chief mover, D.S. Senanayake, Minister of Agriculture in the late British period and the first Prime Minister of independent Ceylon.

A Fallen Buddha: The highway south terminates in **Siyambalanduwa**, where it T-junctions into Route A4. A turn to the right (west) leads after about 22 miles (35 kilometers) to **Monaragala**, and from there back into the Hill Country or on to Colombo. Some 15 miles south of Monaragala, off a back road via Okkampitiya, is **Maligawila**, one of the Ruhuna's most remarkable ruins. A great fallen Buddha image, 34 feet (10½ meters) high and 10 feet (three meters) across the shoulders, was carved completely in the round from

a single stone and then transported and raised here on a lotus pedestal, which still lies nearby. It dates from the early 7th Century, and is tentatively identified with an enormous monastic establishment called the Ariyakari Vihara by the *Mahavamsa*.

East of the Siyambalanduwa junction, Route A4 leads after about 11 miles (18 kilometers) to the **Lahugala Sanctuary**, probably the likeliest place in all of Sri Lanka, including the national parks, to find a wild elephant. Located directly on an elephant migration corridor, Lahugala Tank (also called Mahawewa) draws entire herds of elephants to feed on its lush *beru* grass for days at a time. A smaller nearby tank, Kitulana, is the home of little climbing perch; during August and September droughts, these fish can be seen skittering across dry ground, including roadways, to reach the larger tank.

Guardstones and Surfers: About 2½ miles further east, a short distance south of the highway by easily motorable track, the **Magul Maha Vihara** is one of the most interesting ruins on the island. Within a small area, there are monuments in several distinctive styles from diverse periods of history. Guardstones and moonstones are in abundance and variety. Parts of the complex are thought to be 2,000 years old, others perhaps less than 1,000. There is a *dagoba*, a well-preserved *vatadage*, some good-sized pavilions, and a recently uncovered large Buddha image. Less than a kilometer further south are the remains of a circular structure thought to have been an elephant stable.

Route A4 reaches the seacoast and turns north toward Batticaloa at **Pottuvil**, Milepost 202 from Colombo. There are ancient ruins of a *dagoba* on a bluff here, and a resthouse overlooking the thundering sea waves. Visitors to this area prefer to continue another 1½ miles south to **Arugam Bay**, which boasts what is considered the best surfing beach in Sri Lanka. The sweeping, sandy bay has dangerously crashing waves, however. The fishing village here is noted for its prawns, a real taste treat.

The coast road continues south another 11 miles **Panama**; from there, a Jeep track leads to **Okanda** and the **Kumuna bird sanctuary** on the northeastern fringe of Ruhuna (Yala) National Park.

JAFFNA AND THE NORTH

The Jaffna Peninsula and the rest of Sri Lanka's vast Northern Province comprise the country's driest region. Its inhabitants' industriousness and, in recent decades, a variety of government-sponsored agricultural development schemes have saved it from being a virtual wasteland.

In ancient times, this area carried great importance. Mannar Island, Sri Lanka's "gateway" to the Indian mainland, was the first landfall of Vijaya, the legendary founder of island civilization. Jaffna, the center of Sri Lanka's Tamil and Hindu culture, was the capital of an independent medieval kingdom and later a key colonial outpost for the Portuguese and Dutch.

About three-quarters of a million people today make their homes on the Jaffna Peninsula. Some 999 square miles (2,587 square kilometers) in size, the peninsula is saved from being an island only by a half-mile-wide strip of sand at its far southeastern end. Its flat, dry land is interspersed with shallow lagoons, and a number of interesting offshore islands extend the geographical pattern.

Legend has it that a wandering minstrel with extra-sensory perception was Jaffna's founder. He came to Sri Lanka to escape a shrewish wife. When he appeared before the king playing his *yal*, or lyre, the monarch tested the minstrel's mental abilities with a series of questions. The results were so positive that the delighted ruler made him a gift of the barren Jaffna Peninsula. The *yal* is today the symbol of Jaffna, which sometimes is also called "Yalpanam," "city of the lyre."

Just as with the eastern coast, so has much of northern Sri Lanka fallen to disruption and destruction due to fighting between the Sri Lankan armed forces and the separatist factions. Jaffna, the stronghold of the militant groups has taken a heavy toll. Access to the north is heavily restricted and inadvisable. But, when better times comes, Jaffna and the north will offer the discerning traveler a glimpse into a land of stark beauty, that is rich in culture and history.

Preceding pages: the frenetic Nallur festival. Left, Jaffna schoolboys. Right, a Shiva devotee.

Jaffna Fort: Archaeological digs on the Peninsula have uncovered evidence aplenty of civilizations over 2,000 years old. From the 13th Century, when Polonnaruwa was in decline, until 1619, when the Portuguese established a foothold, Jaffna was an independent Tamil kingdom. The Dutch captured the city in 1658 after a three-month siege. They surrendered the fort to the British East India Company without a battle in 1796. The magnificent fort still stands in the heart of Jaffna city. A classic of Dutch military architecture, it is probably the best preserved fortress on the island of Sri Lanka, and as such is still in use as a prison and police headquarters.

The Dutch fort was built over the earlier Portuguese stronghold. Its main work is a five-pointed star with a classical bastion at each point. The outwork, completed only in 1792, is a bigger star still, enclosing altogether 55 acres – though the sea to the south allows full development of only three of its points. Between the inner fort and the outwork lies a wide moat.

The drawbridge at the land gate to the fort is guarded by armed police. Techni-

cally, visitors must obtain an entry permit from the nearby police station; but the guards will often grant permission to enter in exchange for the taking of a photograph!

Among the buildings in the fort's grassy interior are the **Groote Kerk**, a Dutch church dating from 1706; the **King's House**, former residence of the Dutch and British commanders; and a small house once occupied by author Leonard Woolf.

The four-gabled, cruciform church was a model for Colombo's larger and more pretentious Wolvendaal Kerk. It is under the aegis of the Archaeological Department; if locked, the curator of the Jaffna museum will open it during working hours. Inside, an impressive pulpit faces the stately governor's pew. On the floors and walls are tombstones and family insignias. One of the fine monuments set into the floor contains the following quintessential example of graveyard humor in its inscription:

Fui quod es
Sum quod eris

In other words: "What you are, I was; what I am, you will be."

Behind the church, on the fort ramparts, is a lofty structure with large beams that self-appointed tour guides (usually off-duty policemen) will tell you, with ghoulish relish, was once a gallows where public executions were performed. In fact, it was the belfry which called Jaffna Christians to worship.

The King's House is another excellent example of Dutch period architecture. Rambling in plan, it has vast rooms, a high-pillared veranda more than 200 feet long, and doors so tall a stepladder was required to fasten their upper bolts. Few worthwhile pieces of furniture remain within. Note the enormous beds, provided with movable steps for climbing into them!

A Stroll Through Town: Jaffna Park, occupying two square blocks above Main Street, is the focus of civic activities in Jaffna. Surrounding the greenery are municipal offices, the post office, and the Moghul-style public library. Another two blocks east on Main Street, past the rest house, is the **Archaeological Museum**. Contained in a fine traditional house (of which there are several on this street), the

Nallur Kandaswamy Kovil.

museum includes numerous Sinhalese-Buddhist artifacts found at the nearby Kantharodai excavations, as well as fine exhibits of Tamil-Hindu life and culture.

Turn up first Cross Street, then take a left on Hospital Road into the main commercial section of town. At the **Municipal Market**, head first for the mango sellers' stands. The Jaffna mango is famous throughout the country for its peculiar sweetness. Its high season is June to September. Palmyra-leaf mats, baskets and hand-rolled cigars are other popular purchases.

Around the corner and up Kannathiddy Road is the **jewelers' district**. In days gone by, this stretch of street was so full of gold bullion, it was like a scene from the Arabian Nights. Today, few of the shops remain. Once Jaffna was known throughout the world for a particular type of filigree. Now the Jaffnaite thinks of gold only in terms of weight.

As you wander through Jaffna's narrow streets and side lanes, you'll be unavoidably aware of the *cadjan* fences which surround nearly every house on the peninsula. These barriers of woven coconut or palmyrah (the species of palm almost a trademark of the Jaffna Peninsula) ensure privacy. But this shouldn't lead you to thinking that Jaffna's Tamils are introverted. In fact, you'll find friendly smiles almost everywhere.

The community of Nallur, an integral part of Jaffna city lying two miles (three kilometers) from Jaffna Fort on the Point Pedro Road, was where the last capital of the independent Kingdom of Jaffna was. It was founded by Sempaha Perumal in the mid-15th Century, and remained the center of the kingdom until Sangili Kumara was defeated by the Portuguese in the battle of Vannarponnai in 1619.

Nallur: Temple and Toppu: Today, all that remains of the royal palace complex is the **Sangili Toppu**, a roadside archway which may have led to the king's residence. Beyond the gateway is a small stone-built pond called the Jumnari, said to have been filled with water from the sacred Jumna Ganga in India. Far more impressive today is the **Nallur Kandaswamy Temple**, site of the largest annual festival in Jaffna. The original temple, dedicated to

Vespers at a Catholic church.

Murugam (Skanda, the Hindu war god), stood in the royal compound, but was burned to the ground along with the rest of the city by its Portuguese conquerors. It was rebuilt on its current site in 1807, and has been continually renovated and improved upon since.

Punctual *pujas* are offered several times a day, and a regularly recited liturgy invokes not only Murugam, the eldest son of Shiva, but also King Bhuvanaika Bahu, regarded as the founder of the temple.

During the so-called "Nallur season" of July and August, this temple puts on its most colorful face. For 26 days, concluding with the August new moon, there is an aura of sincere spirituality. Attend an evening *puja*, taking off your shoes (and men, your shirts) before entering the temple. Partake of the ritual, with its strident music of drum, bell and oboe, with its mystic incenses and scents of jasmine, sandalwood and turmeric.

At night, after a long and eager suspense, the temple *ratham* (chariot) makes its appearance. The *ratham* is a towering, fabulously decorated "car" whose archetype was the terrible juggernaut that so appalled British colonialists. (Devotees, then, in a climax of ecstatic devotion, flung themselves beneath its wheels.)

From Nallur, the Kachcheri-Nallur Road leads after about 1½ miles (two kilometers) to the Chundikuli district at the junction of the Kandy Road. At this site is located the **Kachcheri** – the former secretariat of colonial government – in a complex of buildings known as the Old Park.

Percival Acland Dyke, a mid-19th Century British administrator whose autocratic manner earned him the moniker "Rajah of the North," built this now-neglected complex in a great ellipse. His palatial residence is on one side; the *kachcheri*, as well as other domestic offices and the stables, are on the other. Dyke "ruled" Jaffna from 1829 to 1867. He was the man responsible for the planting of Honduras mahogany trees in Jaffna, thus providing shade for generations to come.

Colombutturai Road leads east from here to **Colombutturai Jetty** on Jaffna Lagoon. The fishermen here draw a grudging living from the shallow sea.

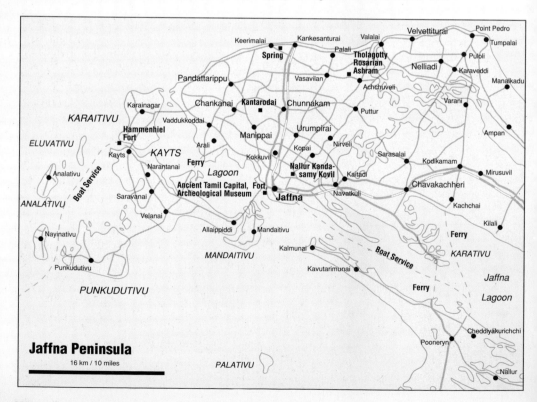

Jaffna Peninsula

16 km / 10 miles

Many of them fish from gaily painted diesel-driven craft, but others still opt for the traditional single-hulled *kattumaram*, quite different from the twinhulled vessels that the West knows as "catamarans." In the Tamil language, *kattumaram* means, literally, "logs lashed together." That is exactly what these sophisticated rafts are: no metal is used in their construction.

Around the Peninsula: Outside of Jaffna city, the peninsula is dry and flat but fastidiously farmed and meticulously tended. Deep wells drilled into the limestone shelf provide a source of irrigation, with the help of heavy buckets on large pivoted poles. Onions, chilies, rice and tobacco are the chief crops, but farmers produce an amazing variety of other vegetables, fruits and grains from the unwilling soil, almost like magicians pulling rabbits from hats.

Start a tour of the Jaffna Peninsula by leaving the city in a northwesterly direction. The town of **Vaddukoddai** is noted for its old colonial church which started as a Portuguese Catholic shrine, later was taken over and modified by the Dutch, then was occupied by American missionaries. Nearby **Jaffna College** was founded by American missionaries.

A causeway spans the lagoon which separates the peninsula from **Karaitivu Island**. Densely populated and heavily farmed, the island's chief interest to visitors is **Casuarina Beach** on its north shore. The water is extremely shallow and coral-strewn, but the beach is wide and clean, and is shaded by casuarina trees, otherwise known as ironwoods. The road east from the causeway passes through the hamlet of **Chankanai**, where a Portuguese church of note still stands in a state of partial recognition. Its walls and chancel are intact, and it has a unique vaulted stone roof.

One of the most fascinating stops for a visitor is the ruins at **Kantharodai**, located near Chunnakam west of the main Jaffna-Kankesanturai road. Ask directions locally to reach the site. Discovered in 1916, serious excavation began under the auspices of the Ceylon Archaeological Department only in 1966.

So close and crowded are the miniature *dagobas* on the site that nearly 100 have

Peninsula farmland near Chankanai.

been excavated in an area of only about two acres. As the largest stupa is no more than 12 feet in diameter, it is likely the *dagobas* are votive in nature. Perhaps 2,000 years old or more, they are a reminder of the strong Sinhalese-Buddhist influence in the Jaffna area prior to the 8th Century A.D. Some of the findings at this site are now on display in the Archaeological Museum in Jaffna city.

The North Coast: Turn left on the main highway and head north toward the Palk Strait separating Sri Lanka from India. About one mile beyond Tellipalai is the **Maviddapuram Kandasamy Kovil**, whose annual July festival draws pilgrims from India and further lands. Maviddapuram means "city where the horse face vanished," and a legend explains this odd appellation. An 8th Century Chola princess named Marutapiravikavalli was ladened not only with an unpronounceable name but also a face like a horse. She beseeched a Shaivite sage to help relieve her condition, and he advised her to bathe in the freshwater springs at Keerimalai, 1½ miles northwest of this *kovil*. Daily obeisance and submergence helped cure her, and in gratitude she arranged to have this temple, honoring Skanda, constructed.

At the **Keerimalai Spring** where the miracle cure occurred, statues of the horse-headed princess overlook the beachfront springs. They pour into an artificial bathing pool beneath the small **Naguleswarm Shivan Temple** just off the road. There was a *kovil* here since ancient times; Hindus consider it one of the original five *isvarams* (divine residences) of early Shaivism.

Beyond **Kankesanturai**, of interest chiefly as the site of a government cement factory and the Palaly Airport, the road proceeds along the peninsula's north shore toward Point Pedro. South of the coast road, near the airport, can be seen the charming ruin of the **Portuguese church** at Myliddy. Its architecture is distinctively Romanesque and its floor plan a Latin cross. A few miles further, the fishing village of **Val-vedditurai** is conspicuously affluent. Many persons claim this is because the community's major income source is smuggling goods from India. The bustling town of **Point Pedro** is a

The ruins of Kantharodai.

232

major fishing port. Its lighthouse is situated close to Sri Lanka's northernmost point. A short distance southeast of Point Pedro is the long stretch of shifting sand dunes known as the **Manalkadu Desert**. This miniature Sahara is occasionally interrupted by oasis-like hamlets which provide splashes of green between the steep dunes and the sea or lagoon. Nestled in the dunes four miles from Point Pedro is the village of **Vallipuram**, reputed to be an ancient Tamil capital known as Singai Nagar, capital of the Kingdom of Jaffna before Nallur. It also is the site of the **Vallipura Alvar Kovil**, one of the country's most important Vishnu temples, especially honoring the incarnation of "The Prescrver" as Krishna.

A short distance off the road back toward Jaffna (leaving Point Pedro in a west-southwest direction) is the village of Achchuveli with its ruined **Dutch church**. Of greater interest is the **Nilavarai Tidal Well** near Puttur, on the main Jaffna road. The most marked example of the geographical curiosities created by Jaffna's limestone shelf, the water in this "bottom-less well" reaches a depth of 145 feet (45 meters)! An underground connection with the sea is apparent, as the bottom third of the water in the well is extremely salty.

In sharp contrast to the well water is the wine made at the **Rosarian Ashram** in Tholagatty. Produced from grapes harvested from the monastery's own vines, the wine won't please too many trained palates, but it does suffice for the brothers' communion ceremonies, as well as provides a little extra income to the ashram with public sales. Tastier and more refreshing by far are the homemade fruit juices made by these self-sufficient monks for the consumption of themselves and guests. The thriving monastery was founded early this century.

Cruising the Islands: Some scholars maintain the name Sri Lanka derived from *laksa-dvipa*, meaning "hundred thousand islands." This label may be poetic flight, but there are not far short of a hundred isles off the Jaffna Peninsula alone. They hang like a necklace and pendant in a long southwestward loop. The largest of the Jaffna islands is **Velanai**, often called

Left, drying fish at Point Pedro. **Right**, a Rosarian monk at Tholagatty.

Kayts after the name of its chief town. Only a half hour's bus ride (via causeway) from Jaffna city, the island retains an old-fashioned atmosphere. There are dainty wildflowers and huge Roman Catholic churches; most notably, there are forts and fishermen.

The **Urundi Fort** in Kayts is an untouched example of Portuguese workmanship, left to decay by the Dutch. A public road runs through the horse shoe-shaped fortress, with two apparently unconnected halves. Far more impressive is **Fort Hammenhiel**. This island stronghold guards the western entrance to the Jaffna Lagoon. Built as Fortaleza Real (Fort Royal) by the Portuguese in the mid-17th Century, it was rechristened Hammenhiel (Heel of the Ham) by the Dutch. (They felt the map of Ceylon resembled a ham, and this fort fell right at the knuckle!) The fort was constructed of quarried coral on a sandbank. It was extensively altered and strengthened by the Dutch. The British employed it as a jail and hospital; and during the Second World War, it became an air-sea rescue station.

The fort is now the property of the Archaeological Department. Visitors can travel there by boat, in the company of the caretaker (who lives in Kayts), between 8 a.m. and 6 p.m. daily.

Kayts Harbour is the most ancient ships' haven in the Jaffna area. Some scholars say the ships of King Solomon traded here for apes and peacocks: the Hebrew words are identical to the Tamil.

The island of **Nainativu**, easily reached by boat from Kayts, boasts an internal bus service that plies what must rank as the shortest regular route in the world: two miles. But it is a route of great importance to both Buddhist and Hindu pilgrims.

Throughout the year, Buddhist devotees throng to the **Nagadipa Vihara**, site of one of the Buddha's three reported visits to Sri Lanka. So well-known is this story that this *dagoba* and image house have expropriated the name Nagadipa – given by the *Mahavamsa* to the entire Jaffna Peninsula – as their own.

Hindus are attracted to Nainativu's **Naga Pooshani Ammal Kovil**. Tamil parents carry newborn children here to **The Manalkadu Desert.**

ask the blessings of the Naga goddess Meenakshi, the "fish-eyed" consort of Shiva. Some 60,000 pilgrims attend the annual temple festival in June or July.

On the south beach of Nainativu is a community of chank fishermen. The chank (*turbinella rapa*), a shell similar to the conch, is used as a ritual instrument in Hindu and some Sinhalese religious ceremonies; there is also a limited industrial demand.

Delft Island (also called Neduntivu), the outermost and second, largest of the Jaffna islands, about 20 square miles (52 square kilometers) in size, has a population of approaching 10,000. Delft has a bleak and bitter beauty: sparse wind-blown grass on parched plains, gaunt trees in blazing sun, fretted limestone carved in myriad caves. Wild ponies roam the island; they are of a breeding stock maintained from Portuguese times.

Points of interest include a two-story **Portuguese castle** with a strange chamber that may have been a dungeon. **Nolan's Bungalow**, a small home with a fine masonry cote for carrier pigeons, was the residence of an early 19th Century British lieutenant, whose Irish blood can still be seen in some of the island's residents. Stables and watering-troughs (at Sarapiddi), probably built by Lt. Nolan, held 60 to 80 breeding horses. The **Vediresan Koddai** is the apparent ruin of an ancient *dagoba*. Morning and afternoon launches ply the waters back and forth to Kurikadduvan Jetty on Punkudutivu island, connected to Velanai via a causeway.

Even more isolated than Delft are two tiny islets, normally uninhabited, that are of great seasonal significance to Roman Catholics. **Kachchaitivu** hosts its festival in March (usually), drawing pilgrims from India as well as Sri Lanka. **Palaitivu**, closer to the mainland, is host to celebrations during the calm of February seas. Fishermen flock to the Church of St. Anthony for the colorful three-day festival.

The overland journey from Jaffna to Anuradhapura involves a passage of some 120 miles (193 kilometers) through Sri Lanka's most forboding wasteland, The Vanni. Leave Jaffna via the Kandy Road. In the midst of white sand dunes and black palmyrah palms some 23 miles (37 mi-

Talaimannar lighthouse.

lometers) east of the city is the **Naga Thambiran Kovil** near Pallai. Every October, the 10-day Kappal Thiruvila (Festival of the Ship) reenacts the triumph of the *naga*, the serpent deity, over the sacrilegious Portuguese marauders.

The **Chundikkulam Sanctuary**, southeast of here, is a paradise for water birds of all types, especially flamingoes, who gather in large migrant flocks beginning in September-October. The main highway avoids the sanctuary, instead crossing **Elephant Pass**, a lagoon across which elephants used to wade.

At Paranthan, a rough road turns west for 15 miles to **Pooneryn**. The small moated **Dutch fort** here is known chiefly for its invisible equestrian ghost. The specter gallops up to the walls with jingling harness and horse-hooves pounding, thunders over the non-existent drawbridge and disappears. There is daily launch service between here and Colombutturai Jetty in Jaffna.

The vast Vanni region which comprises most of the Northern Province is dry scrub land. Agriculture is centered mainly around a few ancient tanks, notably the **Iranaimadu Wewa**. Streams from the tanks feed village rice fields, while drier fields on higher ground support seasonal crops of gourds and grain. **Vavuniya,** some 30 miles (48 kilometers) from Anuradhapura, is the administrative capital of this region.

About 25 miles west of Vavuniya, a detour off the Mannar road, is the sanctuary of **Madhu**. A "miracle-working" statue in the Church of Our Lady of the Holy Rosary is the goal of the most popular pilgrimage of the Sri Lankan Roman Catholic year. It is climaxed by the Feast of the Visitation on July 2. As many as 100,000 people attend.

The Mannar Region: As you approach the causeway to Mannar Island, the large **Giant's Tank** (4,547 acres) is on your right. Designed by Parakramabahu I in the 12th Century, it was restored in 1897. It offers a wonderful place for picnicking and bird-watching when full. But in recent times of drought, it has been parched and dry. North of the Mannar highway, on the coast, is the ancient town of **Mantai** (Mahatittha), considered by most scholars to have been the landing place of

Vijaya, legendary ancestor of the Sinhalese. Nearby is the **Tiruket Isvaram**, one of the most famous of all Shaivite shrines of the pre-Christian era. Excavations have uncovered ancient Shaivite images and numerous Roman coins which bear evidence to the age and celebrity of the port of Mantai.

Mannar Island is Sri Lanka's biggest – other than the mainland itself. It is about 50 square miles (130 square kilometers) in area, and accommodates a population of nearly 20,000. A highway causeway and railroad connect it to the mainland.

Mannar is perhaps best known for its baobab (bottle) trees. Outside of isolated examples in Jaffna and Delft, they are the only ones in Sri Lanka. Said to have been introduced by early Arab traders, these East African trees have enormous, bulbous, usually hollow trunks which may surpass 30 feet in circumference, plus wrinkled elephantine bark and tapering, sparsely foliated branches. Legend says it was condemned by God to grown upside down, with roots for branches. But the odd tree contains a reservoir of water, and it can live over 1,000 years.

The **Mannar Fort** was erected by the Portuguese in 1560 under the name Sao Jorge. The Dutch strengthened but did not alter it. In fact, Anglican services are still held in the old Portuguese chapel within its walls. South of Mannar Island, extending for several miles, are the well-known **Peral Banks**, breeding grounds of the true pearl oyster. The Mannar beds have not been commercially productive for many years. But recently, plans were announced to resume commercial pearling here.

Near the westernmost tip of Mannar Island is the town of **Talaimannar** – literally, "Head of Mannar." From this pier, a twice-weekly ferry crosses the Palk Strait to Rameswaram, India. It is a crowded crossing, not recommended for any but the adventurous. West of Talaimannar, a series of reefs, shoals and tiny uninhabited islets sweep west to connect with India. Known as **Adam's Bridge**, this series of stepping-stones were used by the monkey general Hanuman, legendary hero of the *Ramayana* epic, to follow the demon king Rawana after his kidnapping of Princess Sita.

Death in The Vanni: drought hits the Ma Villu tank.

The people of Sri Lanka have always been inclined toward ritual and ceremony. Almost everything, domestic or professional, demands some ritual. Leaving home on a long journey, the first day of attending school, a new job, laying the foundation for a new building, moving to a new house, the sowing of paddy, and the harvesting of grain – among other things – have traditionally been occasions for ceremonies, either simple or elaborate, with as much pageantry as possible.

But the most important occasions demanding ceremony are religious. In certain instances, religious ceremonies have grown to massive proportions, taking on the nature of festivals that time has helped to elaborate. If one looks at a festival calendar of Sri Lanka, it is obvious that a festival of one type or another is taking place nearly all the time.

This mentality is perfectly reflected in the grand Esala Perahera that takes place over two weeks every August in Kandy, the ancient hill capital.

The Kandy Perahera: The beginnings of the Kandy Perahera were very small and simple. King Megavanna (ruled 301 to 331 A.D.) decreed that the Tooth Relic of the Buddha, which was also the symbol of sovereignty, should be brought out from its enshrined place so that public homage could be rendered in a *perahera* (procession) once a year. Today this ceremony has grown into one of the most splendid sights in Sri Lanka and indeed one of the most spectacular pageants in Southeast Asia or perhaps the whole world.

The proper Kandy Perahera, however, began during the reign of King Kirthi Sri Rajasinha of Kandy in the 18th Century. During his reign, he invited a number of Buddhist monks from Siam to Lanka to help restore the island's monasteries and its Theravada orthodoxy, then degenerating in the face of foreign war and ill discipline from within. The visiting monks protested to the king that the predominant religious activity of Kandy's Hindu *devalas* was unseemly in a Buddhist royal capital. The king

Preceding pages: a turn-of-the-century Esala Perahera; caparisoned elephants; night and day dancers. **Left**, Raja, the tusked elephants, bears the relic casket. **Above**, a senior official.

accordingly ordered that a solemn annual procession of the Tooth Relic be forthwith instituted, and that a procession of Kandy's four *devalas* be incorporated in the open homage. The Perahera maintains this tradition today.

The *devalas* follow next. First comes the Natha Devala; Natha, the tutelary deity of the city of Kandy, is identified with Maitreya, the Buddha-to-be. Next comes the procession from the temple of Vishnu, the deity to whom special care of the welfare of Buddhism is entrusted. Close behind are the columns from the *devalas*

of Skanda, the Sinhalese war deity of Kataragama, and Pattini, the female deity of health and chastity. Each is followed by a train of colorfully caprisoned elephants.

The procession is led by the Maligawa Perehara which proceeds from the Dalada Maligawa (Temple of the Tooth). The magnificent tusked temple elephant (known as the "tusker") is adorned with colorful cloth, lined with tiny electric bulbs. He carries on his back an illuminated howdah with the golden *karanduwa* – a replica of the *dagoba*-shaped casket in which the sacred tooth is enshrined. The genuine Tooth Relic was once carried in the Perahera, but this is now considered unsafe and inauspicious. Then follows another train of dozens of elephants.

Behind them, attired in the garish but traditional attire of office, walks the Diyawadana Nilame, the chief trustee of the temple and the holder of the highest lay office in the island. Walking in pace behind are the other officials of the temple.

The others that constitute the Perahera are the Kandyan dancers, devil dancers, whip crackers, stick dancers, lines of school-children, costumed dancers, and an assortment of acrobats and flame dancers.

Splendor of the Randoli: For the first five nights, this procession is known as Kumbal Perahera; it shows only a shadow of its climactic

of the Kataragama deity's sword. After the last of the night processions, the ceremonial howdah containing the symbolic *karanduwa* is deposited until morning in the Asgiriya Vihara, a mark of signal honor to the mother of King Kirthi Sri Rajasinha. At dawn, a small procession leaves for the river at Getambe, a Kandy suburb about two miles south of the city. Here the water of the river is parted with a circular sweep of the sacred sword, and four clay pots – one from each of the *devalas* – are filled from within the circle thus demarcated. These pots are preserved throughout the ensuing year. Should any of them run dry before the next Esala festival, it is considered a sign of impending misfortune. At noon of that day, the

splendor. But on the sixth night, the Randoli Perahera begins. The *randolis* ("golden palanquins") which bear the deities' consorts join the *devala* ranks, each borne immediately behind the elephants carrying the emblems which represent the respective deities. The circuits gradually increase in length and the trappings in grandeur, until after five nights of the Randoli, the Perahera reaches its magnificent and colorful best. This climactic Randoli Perehera may include 100 or more elephants, ranging from majestic bulls to half grown calves.

To conclude the Perahera, a final *devala* ceremony is enacted. Known as the water-cutting ceremony, it is a ritualistic purification

final Perahera, the only daytime procession, begins.

Almost all Buddhist temples in Sri Lanka have their own *peraheras* once a year. Participation is generally confined to the villagers of the little hamlets in which they are situated. Everyone in the village contributes something toward these little *peraheras*. It is indeed a very pretty sight to see small processions, consisting mostly of school-children, drummers and dancers, weaving their way through paddy fields at dusk.

In January every year, the Duruthu festival begins at Kelaniya Temple, about seven miles east of Colombo. The various religious formalities that take place for about a week culminate in the Duruthu Perahera, second in grandeur only to the great Esala Perahera in Kandy. This *perahera* is held to commemorate the visit of the Buddha to the site of Kelaniya.

Wesak: Full Moon in May: Temple bells all over the island announce the dawn of Wesak. Pilgrims garbed in austere white, in towns, and villages alike, slowly wend their ways to the temple to observe *sila* – that is, to spend the day in meditation, reading religious books, and listening to the words of the Master recounted by a monk. These two days of Wesak, the full moon day of the month of May and the day following it, are the two holiest days in the Buddhist calendar all over the world. This is

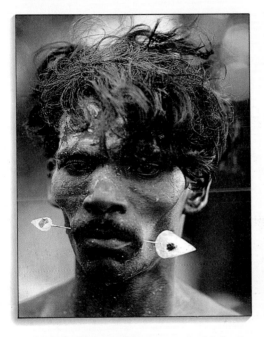

when Buddhists commemorate the birth, the enlightenment and the death of the Buddha.

All major towns become places of gaiety at Wesak time. The celebrations in Colombo are unmatched. Large *pandals* (bamboo frameworks) are erected along the streets, hung with paintings depicting the Buddha's life or some Jataka tale, and illuminated with a myriad of pulsating colored bulbs. Every Buddhist home has some form of lighting, from a lovely bucket lamp to Chinese lanterns or homemade paper

Left, *kavadi*-carrying dancers at the Kataragama festival. **Right**, a Hindu devotee pierces his cheeks to fulfill a vow.

lanterns of various shapes and sizes.

But the finest illumination of all is the flickering flame of the tiny *pol-thel pahana*, the coconut oil lamp which lines the driveways of some houses and the courtyards of temples. Its simple ancient charm is unmatched.

Pantomimes telling Buddhist tales are played out on sidewalk stages. Groups of musicians in mod clothes cause massive traffic jams as crowds gather in the streets to hear them rap out the rhythms of rock music.

Another unique feature of Wesak is the *dansela* or alms hall. These little sheds are put up by the roadsides and furnished with tables and chairs. Here local people give out food, ranging from rice and curry to sweet meats, free to all souls weary and footsore after long walks looking at *pandals* and decorations. *Danselas* are usually organized by a small group of people living in the same area, assisted by contributions from neighbors.

All major towns in Sri Lanka have their share of Wesak activity, but the visitor is advised to stay in Colombo to see the real grandeur of the holiday.

Poson – the advent of Buddhism: More than 2,000 years ago, the reigning monarch of Anuradhapura, King Devanampiyatissa, was chasing deer in the forest of Mihintale when someone called out: "Tissa!" For a moment, the mighty king was aghast. Which man in his realm would dare call him by name? On looking up he saw, standing on a rock, a figure in a saffron robe with six companions, one of whom was in lay attire. The mendicant was none other than Arahat Mahinda, the son of Emperor Asoka of India. Mahinda converted the king to Buddhism, thus introducing the faith to Sri Lanka. It was the full moon day of June, now known as Poson, a day which Buddhists in Sri Lanka revere second only to Wesak itself.

Although Poson is celebrated throughout the island, the major ceremonies are confined to Anuradhapura and Mihintale. The temples are crowded, the streets illuminated and decorated. Long lines of people climb the many steps to the plateau of Mihintale, to the temple and then to the *dagobas* that lie atop the nearby hillocks. Most visitors climb the dizzying heights to the top of the rock, to the very spot from which Arahat Mahinda delivered his initial discourse.

If the full impact of the Poson festival is to be felt, the visitor must go to Mihintale. The crowds may be an inconvenience, but it is well worth the effort.

The Kataragama Festival: In July and August, almost at the same time as the Esala Perahera, the awesome Kataragama festival takes place over a two-week period. A celebrated ancient place of pilgrimage, Kataragama not so long ago was nestling in deep jungle. The jungle has been cleared along the Menik Ganga (river), and Kataragama has become a place of worship not only for Hindus, but for Buddhists, Muslims and some Christians as well. Still, the major part of devotees who actively participate in the festival are Hindus, as the proceedings honor Skanda (also known as Murugan), the main deity of Kataragama.

The most remarkable feature of the celebration is the penchant of devotees to self-morti-

of their feet. These acts of self-mortification are, however, confined to a minority. Most pilgrims are involved in less flamboyant religious activities such as worshipping at the temples of the many deities, fulfilling vows, giving alms to beggars, or worshipping at the Buddhist *dagoba* known as Kirivehera.

While these activities take place on a daily basis throughout the year at Kataragama, there is an added dose of pageantry at festival time. Everywhere one can see colorful flags and lights. The constant blowing of conch shells, beating of drums, and chanting of pilgrims fill the air.

The climax, of the festival is a grand *perahera* which, though much smaller in scale than the

fication, generally in repayment of vows. These include minor acts, such as rolling half-naked around the *devala* precincts' hot scorching sand, and major feats of penance. Some foot pilgrims may carry on their shoulders the decorated arched framework known as the *kavadi* for 100 miles or more. Others skewer their cheeks and outthrust tongues with miniature spears or are suspended from trestles on hooks which bear the entire weight of their body.

One of the most famous spectacles of Kataragama is the fire-walking. Devotees, from old men and women to small children, walk over a bed of burning embers without any visible sign of discomfort or injury to the soles

ones of Kandy and Kelaniya, does not lack splendor and ceremony. The final touch is a water-cutting ceremony similar to that seen in Kandy during the Esala festivities.

The Vel Procession: Vel is the name given to the trident of Skanda, the god of war. In Sea Street in Colombo, one of the largest and richest of the city's Hindu temples is dedicated to the Kathiresan, an aspect of Skanda. Three and four miles to the south at Bambalapitiya and Wellawatte, respectively, stand two *kovils* dedicated to Pillaiyar, another name for the elephant-headed deity, Ganeswara (Ganesh).

Every year, the *vel* of Skanda is carried in procession to one or the other, alternatively, of the two outlying *kovils* and back again to Sea Street. This constitutes the Vel festival, and the temple whose turn it is to receive the sacred symbol is for three days *en fete*.

Merry-go-rounds and souvenir stalls (those selling cheap bangles made of colored glass or plastic are particularly fascinating) are set up in the temple grounds. Hawkers line the streets offering sweets and enormous stacks of sugar cane which seems to bear an almost ritual significance.

The processions to and from the *kovils*, beginning and ending the festival, are colorful affairs. A great gilded temple cart is drawn by hundreds of devotees – some of whom, although dressed in the egalitarian simplicity of

a white waistcloth, shawl and smears of holy ash – are among the wealthiest citizens of Sri Lanka. They are assisted by two magnificent white bulls.

The outward journey is by day, and is tortuously slow. In addition to its crawling pace, the cart makes many predetermined stops for religious observances and to receive welcomes from various reception committees. In all, the four miles take almost a day to cover. The

Jaffna Hindus draw the Nallur temple chariot with enormous ropes, left; while Colombo Hindus carry the Vel chariot through the streets of the metropolis, above.

return journey, however, is much faster, and is very colorful by night, with hundreds of electric bulbs and other decorations lining the route.

The visitor who wishes to observe the procession can best see it along Galle Road at any point between Fort and Bambalapitiya or Wellawatte, as the case may be. The day *perahera*, though not matching the night one in splendor, should not be missed in order that the entire essence of this splendid festival is captured.

Other Hindu Celebrations: Thai Pongal, in January, is kept in honor of the Hindu sun deity. There is obligatory worship at the *kovil*, but special observances are also held at home. The most important of these is the making and ceremonial consumption of the traditional spiced and sweetened rice called *pongaal*, a sacramental feast.

In Hindu rural areas, a charming sequel known as Madu Pongal (the Pongal of the cattle) follows a day or two later. Each household's domestic animals – from the sacred cow and the great draught-oxen to the family herd of goats, and sometimes even little puppies – are washed and specially fed, marked on the forehead with an auspicious smear of red, and garlanded with marigolds.

Maha Sivarathri day in February is perhaps the most important wholly religious festival of the year among Shaivites, who comprise by far the majority of Ceylon Hindus. It is a deeply symbolic occasion celebrating the union of the great deity Shiva with his consort Paravathi. All-night *pujas* are offered in the temples, and every house keeps an all-night vigil.

The Festival of Lights, called Deepavali, while no less rich in symbolism, is a more joyous occasion. At this time in late October or early November, Hindu houses are refurnished, new clothes are worn, and lamps are burned everywhere to welcome Lakshmi, the goddess of wealth. For the Hindu business community, this festival marks the beginning of the financial year.

In August of every year, there is a spate of Hindu festivals in the Jaffna Peninsula. The most impressive of these take place at the following locations: Kandaswamy Kovil, Nallur; Vallipuram; and Sellasaunathi Kovil, Thondamannar. At the last-named site, firewalking takes place.

Muslim Observances: Muslim festivals, on the whole, are distinguished by their lack of public ostentaion. At most, public meetings are held for corporate prayer or open proclamation of the faith. At home, there is always prayer and reading of the Koran.

The Milad-um-Nabi festival commemorates the birth of the Prophet Mohammed. The dates of Islamic religious functions vary each year because Muslims follow the Lunar calender in which a year is 11 days shorter than in the Roman calender.

Id-ul-Fitr (popularly known as the Ramazan Festival) marks with feasting the end of the long discipline of the month of Ramazan. Devotees observe Ramazan by strict fasting for four weeks during which, but for a single daily meal before dawn, a devout man will not even swallow his own spittle.

Id-ul-Azha (the Haji Festival) recalls the ultimate triumph of faith of the biblical Abraham in his proffered sacrifice of Isaac, his son. It honors all those Muslims who have made the pilgrimage to Mecca and thereby become *hajis*.

Christian Ceremonies: Of Christian festivals little need be said, for they are familiar all over the world. There are, however, a few peculiar to Sri Lanka, most important of which are the Festival of Our Lady of Madhu and the Feast of St. Anne at Talawila. Both lack the color and pageantry associated with the Buddhist and Hindu festivals, and concentrate more on religious observances.

The Madhu festival goes on for two weeks, during which time large numbers of Roman Catholics gather in campsites surrounding this church near Mannar on the northwest coast of the island.

It is climaxed by the Feast of the Visitation on July 2. The destination of the pilgrimage is a miracle-working statue, said to be that of Our Lady of Healing, carried to Madhu from a Portuguese church which once stood at neighboring Mantai.

The Feast of St. Anne, dedicated to the mother of the Virgin Mary, takes place every year on July 26 at the small settlement of Talawila, halfway up the Kalpitiya Peninsula west of Puttalam. The church, while flooded with pilgrims at this time, is a magnet throughout the year because of its reputation as a place of healing.

Sinhalese New Year: Another very significant festival in Sri Lanka is the Sinhala Avurudu or Sinhalese New Year, which falls in April. This is also the Tamil New Year; it is a non-religious festival celebrated by all Sri Lankans, and associations merely with Buddhist Sinhalese are totally incorrect.

Sinhala Avurudu marks the completion of the solar circuit. It does not begin at the customary hour of midnight on the designated day, but is astrologically determined. Thus it could be that the new year might begin at 10 a.m., for instance. There is also an astrological determination of the conclusion of the old year. More often than not, the new year does not begin at the time the old year ends. The few hours' time between the new and old year is known as the *nona gathe* or "neutral period." This period is reserved for religious activity, whatever one's religion might be.

The festival is celebrated in all its orthodoxy in rural areas, and if one really wants to observe traditional customs, one should be in a remote village during the days immediately preceding and following Avurudu. On the eve of the new year, family members clean up their dwelling and at a specified time light a small lamp in the garden. At the commencement of the neutral period, all activities stop, including eating and drinking. Even visiting is not done by the orthodox.

With the start of the new year, a fire is lit in the kitchen, new clothes are worn (of a color determined by the almanac), and fresh activities begin. A person may make a token gesture of starting work by touching for a few moments the tolls of this trade.

Then comes the *gana-denu*, literally meaning "give-and-take." Before making any new transactions, a Sri Lankan would exchange money with someone close to him, or someone considered a good customer. An orthodox family would not dare to give money to a fishmonger or beggar, however generous or charitably inclined they might be, prior to the initial *gana-denu*.

The New Year practices reach a climax with the annointing ceremony. Oil is mixed with an herbal paste; then, at an auspicious moment, a respected family elder rubs a spot of oil on the head of each family member. Annointees sit on chairs facing a direction specified by the almanac, trampling a white cloth beneath their feet, under an awning from which hangs various types of leaves.

Sinhalese New Year in the villages is also the time for various sports and games.

A Sinhalese woman lights the traditional oil lamp to celebrate the start of the new year. The Avurudu falls in the month of April.

FRENZIED MOODS OF DANCE AND DRAMA

Lavishly costumed performers leap and swirl in frenzies of acrobatic movement. Their feet bounce off the ground in intricate patterns that reflect the complex rhythms of the drum beats. Hips swing, hands sway, shoulders shrug. Heads, heavy with masks or make-up, tilt. Torsos, fringed with frills and fancy ornaments, move constantly. Such is the essence of dance and drama in Sri Lanka. In all its verve and color, it dazzles the eye and excites the senses. It remotely resembles two forms of classical Indian dance – the Bharata Natyam and Kathakali. But the dances of Sri Lanka are inimitable inventions of the Sinhalese soul, unique in the repertoire of the world.

The Elements of Sinhalese Dance: The famous Sanskrit treatise on dance and music composed by the sage Bharata, sometime between the 2nd Century B.C. and the 3rd Century A.D., distinguishes between a pure dance form (*nritta*), expressive dance (*nritya*) and drama (*natya*). By Bharata's definition, Sinhalese dance can be considered *nritta*. That differentiates it from Kathakali and Bharata Natyam, which fit into the category of *nritya*.

The two Indian dance forms are primarily employed as media for story-telling and for expressing a wide variety of emotions through the use of symbolic gestures and facial expressions familiar to the audience. In contrast, Sinhalese dancing relies on the use of symbolic body movement, expert footwork and strenuous acrobatics to tell its tales.

Bharata also classified dance into two other categories: *tandava*, its vigorous, masculine manifestations; and, *lasya*, the graceful, feminine form. Sinhalese dancing more closely fits the description of *tandava*, since it is usually performed by males who can do justice to its dynamism.

Sinhalese dance separates neatly into two styles. "Low-country dancing" refers to the form practiced throughout the coastal belt south of Colombo; this is often broadly called "devil-dancing" because of its exorcistic nature. "Up-country dancing," also known as the Kandy

school, flourishes in the provinces of the former Kandyan kingdom.

While both forms exhibit the vigorous movements common to all dance in Sri Lanka, Kandyan dancing has been taught to girls as well as boys. Today it is often performed, particularly for tourists, by women – a development that has softened some of the masculine moves integral to a successful performance.

The Kohomba of Kandy: Both forms of Sinhalese dancing originated in the folk rituals of the island and still exhibit those roots. The dances of Kandy date back to the Ritual of the

God Kohomba, an all-night ceremony for the purpose of appeasing that god and his spiritual associates.

The aesthetics of Kandyan dance, and the meaning of its movements, can be most fully appreciated during performances in its original setting: the Kohomba Kankariya, an assortment of ceremonies in honor of Kohomba. In a magnificently decorated pavilion, about 50 dancers fill the stage. Attired in frilled costumes – their beads and breastplates glistening and their anklets and headdresses sparkling in the mysterious light of torches – the dancers pirouette, skip and whirl to the beat of 10 drums, executing astonishing acrobatics in mid-

Preceding pages: Kandyan dancers exhibit grace and splendid attire. Left, a Kandyan drummer displays intensity. Above, a conchshell blower announces a ceremony.

air. The performance culminates in a gesture of obeisance performed with hands folded in worship before the altar of the god. In this scenario, the dancer doubles as a shaman or priest, the *yakdessa*, who has expressed his devotion to his god in terms of rhythm and movement.

Such ritual dances gave rise to a kind of secular dance entertainment known as *vannama*. As the appellation suggests, these are descriptive dances named after the animals and birds whose movements they mimic. In theory, it appears this form denotes a leap from *nritta to nritya*. In reality, the form remains pure rather than expressive dance.

The *vannama* usually marks only a superfi-

lumbering gait of an elephant.

The other 17 traditional *vannamas* follow the same peculiar pattern. The opening rhythm imitates the trot of gallop of a horse or the swoop of a hawk, but the dance that follows leaves the beat behind in a delirious fit of pure, ecstatic movement. Interludes of *vannama* dancing often accompany performances of a traditional Kohomba Kankariya. Dancers from various schools that practice differing interpretations of the *vannama* often compete with one another during these sessions, providing exhibitions of rare virtuosity.

Kandyan dance can be enjoyed in all its primitive grandeur at the Esala Perahara, the annual festival in Kandy.

cial attempt to portray the movements of the animal or bird for which it is named. The Gajaga Vannama or Dance of the Elephant is a perfect example of this idiosyncrasy. The dancer begins by singing the "Song of the Elephant." The words describe a fabulous beast that has eight long tusks and 16 trunks and lives in heaven. As he sings, the dancer moves his arms in the sweeping style characteristic of Kandyan dance. He does little actual dancing. The slow, dignified rhythm of the song suggests the majestic gait of the elephant. But when the song ends, the dancer vaults into action, bounding and bouncing to a frenzied rhythm in a manner that bears no resemblance whatsoever to the

These dance forms reached perfection in part because of the patronage of the court of the Kandyan kings and its feudal chieftains. The classical influence of the Bharata Natyam also inspired the dancers of Kandy to perfect their own style. Evidence indicates that Bharata Natyam was popular with the Sinhalese kings of the 15th Century and later. Friezes found at Yapahuwa, thought to belong to about the 13th Century, depict dancing women in poses recognizable as those of the Bharata Natyam.

Devil Dances of the South: Sri Lanka is basically a Buddhist country. Buddhism is a nontheistic religion which asserts that man must attain salvation through his own efforts, not through the aid or intervention of a god or gods. Thus, folk rituals aimed at appeasing evil spirits and exorcising demons might appear out of place in Sri Lanka. But over the centuries, Buddhism blended with folk cults in which super-natural beings are believed to influence good and evil.

The Sinhalese divided these entities into demons, who cause disease and pestilence; and benevolent gods, who bestow good will when properly appeased. This categorization subsequently produced two types of ritual ceremonies conducted by two classes of priests: the god-priest, or *kapurala*, and the lower-caste demon priest, *kattadiya* or *yakadura*.

These rituals gave rise to the so-called "devil dramatic dialogue and impersonation. Usually, they take the form of an authentic folk ritual complete with a chief priest who impersonates the king of demons, Vesamuni, and coadjutor priests who act as assistant demons.

Exorcism, Sri Lanka Style: The setting of a ritual in southern Sri Lanka takes on all the trappings of theater. There is a circular arena where dancers perform, and an ornamental altar with several cages for offerings and serves as a kind of backdrop to the action. Masks worn by the dancers take on a range of weird expressions as they flicker in the light of coconut flares. Finally, exotic rhythms fill the air – it is the beat of the *yak bere* or "demon drum," different from the *gata bere* drum of Kandy.

dances" of south Sri Lanka. Like the dances of the Kandy school practiced in the island's hilly interior, the "low-country dancing" evolved from folk rituals. The rituals aimed to exorcise demons from ailing individuals and asked blessings of prosperity from the gods. But the differences of "low-country dance" are readily apparent even to the layman.

Dances of the south are characterized by pronounced theatrics. In addition to pure dance movements, they incorporate elements of mime,

Left, street dancers during Colombo's Vel Festival. <u>Above</u>, a traditional curved horn leads a women's drum corps at Anuradhapura.

The drum beats build suspense before each demon enters the arena. Generally, an exorcism ceremony begins with an invitation to the demons to appear. The performers chant in time to the drums. The shrill note of chant in time to the drums. The shrill note of a reed flute occasionally pierces the air.

The priest addresses each demon by name and implores him to stop harassing the afflicted subject of the ceremony. He speaks to each demon with endearing terms like *massina* or *malliya*, cousin or brother – an attempt to win the demon's favor. Later, he adopts a humble, imploring tone; finally, the priest begins to threaten the demons in the name of the Buddha and King Vesamuni. The demon enters the body of the afflicted and begins to speak through him. A conversation between the priest and the possessed person ensues.

Priest: Tell me, what demon has possessed you?

Demon: Maha Sohona has possessed me. I am Maha Sohona.

Demon: He ate a certain kind of food without giving me my share of it.

Priest: We are prepared to give you an offering if you leave this human being.

Demon: I want a human victim.

Priest: That is impossible. We cannot give you anything you ask for. You have been given permission by Lord Buddha and King Vesamuni

to do certain things. Have they allowed you to take human sacrifice?

Demon: No. Well, then, give me a four-footed offering.

Priest: That is also impossible.

Demon: Give me a two-footed offering.

Priest: Yes, we will give you this cock. Take it and go away. By the way, how are we to know that you have really left?

Demon: I will break the twig of yonder tree. It will be a sign that I have gone. Or I will shout "hoo" as I go.

The priest gives the patient a live cock. On rare occasions, he may even wring the neck of the bird and drink its blood. Although demons are fond of blood and flesh, they are forbidden to eat it and must be content merely to look at it – an obvious tempering influence of Buddhism on primitive rites.

The Ritual of the 18 Demons: The visitor who wishes to witness a typical exorcism in the low country of Sri Lanka should try to attend a *sanni yakuma*, the ceremony for dealing with demons of disease. There are 18 such demons, but all are manifestations of a powerful, single entity, the Maha Kola Sanni Yaka.

The demons of Sri Lanka are, of course, invisible to man. But the ancient choreographers, dramatists and mask makers of the island painted them as black-skinned monsters with bulging eyes, snake-like tongues and fangs. They often assume the shape of men or animals. They can cause fits of fainting, cholera, dumbness, deafness, blindness, the disease of the three humors – phlegm, wind and bile – even madness and death. They take the form of apparitions to frighten men, particularly in the morning, at midday and in the evening.

The ceremony is performed in a circular arena. Behind it is the *sanni vidiya*, an altar where worshippers place offerings to the demons. The ailing patient for whom the ritual is being performed lies on a mat or bed overlooking the action.

The ceremonies begin at dusk and continue until dawn the next day, a period judged by the Sinhalese to be 30 hours. Chanting and preparatory rites consume the first few hours. Exorcists don their vestments. The chief exorcist wears the grab of Vesamuni, the chief of demons, so that he can command the other demons. The priests light flares and "eat" the flames by breathing in the cleansing fumes of incense.

Gradually, the atmosphere grows thick with the sound of incantations, the beat of the drums, the smell of incense. As the tumult reaches a deafening pitch, a demon jumps out of the *sanni vidiya* and begins to dance. He spins around and around and leaps high in the air, executing the *adauwas* – movements in which he stands in one place and twirls the upper part of his body, from the waist up, with increasing rapidity, until it becomes impossible for the eye to follow. Then he squats in front of the musicians and engages in an impromptu dialogue with one of the drummers.

Left, a proliferation of colorful devil-dancing masks in an Ambalangoda shop. **Right**, one such mask is used in a staged performance.

Discussion With the Devil: In typical performances of the *sanni yakuma*, 18 dancers perform, each representing one of the spirits' attendants. Each holds a particular object in his hand – a pan of burning coals, a burning flare, a pot of saffron-water, a shawl, a pink coconut, a betel box, and so on. Each dancer wears a distinctive costume, one more grotesque than the next, and each exhibits a peculiar idiosyncrasy. One behaves like a circus clown, another amuses spectators with ribald jokes, others laugh incessantly.

The *sanni* demons, who later follow these attendants on stage, can be distinguished only by their masks. Otherwise, they wear the same dress – a garment of *burulla* leaves at the waist, a fur wrap around the shoulders, and a black wig and beard. The erratic, almost abstract, movements of each dancer mimic the disease that each demon has the power to inflict upon mortals. For instance, Kana Sanniya is blind, Golu Sanniya is dumb, and Maru Sanniya gestures and jumps like a raving madman.

The latter is the most monstrous and highly feared demon. Maru Sanniya roars as he enters the arena, shakes the *vidiya*, then climbs onto the crossbeam above the stage door while he glares at the spectators.

The priest eventually addresses him and the conversation that follows is spiced with a humor that relieves the air of tension:

Demon: My dear Gurunnanse (Teacher), as I was reflecting on the virtues of the Buddha and the might of Vesamuni, I heard somebody saying: "My good cousin, my good friend, come from the Eastern Mountain. We will give you a two-legged prey, a cock, instead of a four-legged prey." I could not help coming here when I heard it.

Exorcist: We are the people who invited you.

Demon: Why did you invite me?

Exorcist: You have been inflicting a disease on a certain person. That is why we called you here.

Demon: Where is the sick person?

Exorcist: Here he is. You can ask him all about it.

Demon: Well, let us see. (To the patient.) Does your body ache, sick man?

Exorcist: (Replying on behalf of the sick man.) Yes, it does.

Demon: Do your limbs bend at every joint?

Exorcist: That is nothing unusual. *My* limbs ache at every joint.

Demon: Does your head turn?

Exorcist: Yes, it does.

Demon: Is your stomach soft as a ripe *jak* fruit?

Exorcist: Everybody's stomach is soft. Mine, however, is hard.

The conversation continues in a manner similar to the one previously described. The demon eventually agrees to cure the ailing man in return for an offering of rice, vegetables, curries, curd and treacle – and after the exorcist threatens to burn him to ashes. The devil dancer then holds the offering over the smoke that rises from a pan of live coals, mutters some incantations, and promises the patient's recovery.

Forms of Folk Theater: While such exorcistic rituals exhibit definite theatrical qualities, they are rarely performed for the sole purpose of entertaining an audience. Their goal is to actually facilitate the healing of the ill. Devout Sinhalese believe that any deviation from that goal can have disastrous effects on the exorcist's power over demons.

Sri Lanka's folk theater is firmly rooted in such rituals, however. The resemblance of the masked drama called the *Kolam* to the ritual of *sanni yakuma* is unmistakable.

Four varieties of folk drama have evolved in Sri Lanka, each characteristic of a particular part of the country. The *Sokari*, an offshoot of rituals once performed to assure the fertility of the rice crop and an abundant harvest, is the most primitive. Authentic performances are rare and are confined to hilly regions of the island like Laggala, Hanguranketa, Uda Peradeniya, Hewaheta, Meeruppe, Talatu Oya and Matale. Its theme revolves around the goddess Pattini, patron of purity and fidelity.

Two other styles of folk drama, the *Nadagam* and *Kavi Nadagam*, have all but disappeared from the repertoires of modern Sri Lankan treater, but have left their mark on contemporary drama.

The best preserved of the folk dramas is the *Kolam Natima*. Performances are regularly given in the village of Ambalangoda, 80 kilometers (50 miles) south of Colombo, and in Mirissa, further down the coast. It is in *Kolam* that Sri Lanka's rituals, dance and drama have been combined in a spectacle tantamount to a movie epic. Its dancers wear the most imaginative and outrageous masks, some of an enormous size. They represent gods, demons and other mythical creatures of Sinhalese folklore. The character masks are more subtle, often humorous, and are superbly carved.

Masks and Moods of the Kolam: Performances of the *Kolam* occur at night under the light of coconut torches. The circular arena is similar to those used in exorcistic rituals. A structure of palm leaves is usually erected on one side of the arena to serve both as a backdrop and as a dramatic entrance. A narrator and two drummers stand by the side of the entrance. Sometimes a *horana*, a shrill pipe similar to the oboe, accompanies the chanting of the narrator.

The origin of the *Kolam* drama is legendary,

probably based on a story about a mythical queen who desired to become pregnant. The dances that compose the performance are thus exotic and sexually symbolic.

Various characters appear on stage – policemen, clerks, washermen, and others associated with the court of the king. One highlight of the performance is the appearance of the king and queen in their magnificent, enormous masks.

The entire performance eventually revolves around these masks. One of the most notable is that known as the Five-Women-Pot. It consists of a base mask of a woman, crowned by the figures of five more women posed in a kind of womb shape. The carving of these masks is in itself a distinctive form of artistic expression in Sri Lanka.

The stories that follow the introduction of these many masked characters run the gamut of Sri Lankan dance, mime and drama. The stories have been developed from some of the masterpieces of island Buddhist and secular literature, including popular *Jataka* stories like "Maname Katava" and "Sandakinduru Jatakaya."

Kolam can be best enjoyed as folk art. It expresses the uninhibited attitudes of the rural people towards life, and plays on the foibles of human nature with sympathy and humor.

Vidane Arachchi and the Illusion of Power: Each character or group of characters in these performances is introduced by a narrator in a four-line chant. The character then moves to center stage while executing the dance movements always associated with him. For instance, one scene depicts the village headman, Vidane Arachchi, and the illusory nature of his power. The first performers to appear, usually to represent a group of excited policemen, dance onto the stage in black uniforms with a red cap attached to their masks. Inevitably, Vidane appears to find out what the commotion is all about. He dresses much like a headman of the 19th Century in a sarong and long coat buttoned up to his neck. His hair is tied in a knot at the back of his head and kept in place by a horse-shoe-shaped comb. He is accompanied by his clerk who holds a stylus and a palm-leaf umbrella over Vidane's head, not as a mark of genuine respect, but in feigned subservience. Each time Vidane turns away, the clerk becomes a free-willed human being who is no longer obliged to play his vassal's role. His dance depicts an attitude of mock servility toward Vidane, a routine that provokes much laughter among the audience.

Then there is Nonchi Akka, the aged wife of the king's crier. She casts lustful glances at the men of the court in the belief she can still attract them. The characterization is done solely through the medium of mime and movement, in conjunction with comic expressions cleverly carved on the masks.

Thus is *Kolam* a burlesque of life in the simple setting of a Sinhalese village.

Performances of the exorcistic *sanni yakuma*, left, featuring fierce-looking demons, differ markedly form the *Kolam* folk dramas, right, often characterized as burlesque theater.

A LEGACY OF FINE CRAFTSMANSHIP

Sri Lanka's kings were the traditional patrons of the arts. Grand palaces and elaborate pleasure gardens required the skills of the best craftsmen. Lavish temples and stupas called for proper ornamentation, as did the costumes of the people who worshipped at them.

Fine craftsmanship was not confined to royalty and religion. It touched the lives of commoners as well. Beautifully designed pottery, intricately carved spoons, fine woven baskets and mats, lacquered bows and arrows - all are examples of aesthetically fine yet utilitarian items that a commoner might own.

Today, many artisans carry on the tradition of fine craftsmanship. It often takes a visit to a workshop or a search through stacks of tourist kitsch, but top quality items are readily available if you look.

Woodcarving is one of the oldest crafts still actively practiced. Classical artisans had a preference for low-relief chipwork, which lends itself well to decorative wooden panels, tables and boxes. Today, many panels are carved with age-old designs, providing an interesting cultural link with the past. Kandy and the surrounding district have a large concentration of craftsmen and artists. Near the Lankatilaka Temple and Embekke Devala, woodcarvers recreate some of the famous Embekke carvings, as well as produce their own new designs.

Mask carving uses very light woods and employs more relief work and modeling in order to bring "life" to the demonic representations and characters. Ceremonial devildancer masks traditionally were carved by the dancer himself according to strict specifications and were carefully stained with the proper dyes. Master carvers also produced masks for the folk drama called *Kolam*, sometimes with articulated jaws, rolling eyes, and thick bushy beards. Mask-making remains a specialty in the Ambalangoda district, where it is easy to find mask-makers at work. Today most masks are produced for the tourist trade using enamel paints. Quality ranges from intricate works of art to gaudy atrocities.

Preceding pages: a "Sigiriya Maiden" finds her way onto a low-relief chipwork plaque. Left, brasswork at a Sigiriya souvenir stand. Above, a Kelaniya potter adds final touches.

With Western influence and the growth of the tourist trade, many woodcarvers have taken to three-dimensional carvings. Wooden elephants abound throughout the land, as do religious images – particularly of the Buddha.

Sri Lankan lacquer work utilizes colored lac to decorate a variety of wooden articles. Lac is a resin exuded from certain trees after its bark has been punctured by a "lac" insect. The resin is then plucked from the bark, melted down, strained through muslin, and worked like "pulling" sugar. While the lac is still soft,

pigment is pounded in to produce the desired color. The lac is then dried.

Two principal techniques are employed in Lankan lacquer work. *Biraluvada* or spool-work is used to decorate wooden objects spinning on a lathe. A stick of lac is applied to the turning object; the heat of friction causes the lac to melt onto the wood and to a slight extent into the grain. The second technique involves the drawing of heated and softened lac into a fine thread. It is then laid in a pattern over a basic background color. This method is called *niyapotuvada* or nailwork since the thumbnail is used to guide and break off the filament of lac. Some artisans today also produce lacquer work by painting the object and covering it with layers of clear protective varnish.

The village of Angalmaduwa near Tangalla is known for *biraluvada*, while Palle Hapuvida near Matale is famous for *niyapotuvada*. A good selection of finished pieces in both styles can be seen at the government-run Laksala shops in Colombo and Kandy as well as at the Arts and Crafts Association in Kandy.

Another ancient Sinhalese craft is ivory-work, once important in royal and religious objects. Today, the tusked elephant has become rare. Most Sri Lankan ivory is obtained by illegal poaching. In response to this problem, many Western countries – as well as Sri Lanka itself – have banned the import of new

were important to all strata of society. The National Museum in Colombo houses a collection of metal articles dating back at least 2,000 years. The collection runs the gamut from axe blades, statuary, coins and lamps to intricate filigree jewelry and a gem-encrusted royal trunk.

Today, nearly every woman in Sri Lanka owns at least one piece of gold jewelry. This serves as a form of insurance as well as a banking account and symbol of wealth. When times are good, many people buy gold in the form of rings, earrings, chains, nose studs, etc., and wear it for safekeeping. When times are bad, the gold can be sold off as needed. With such a constant demand, it is not surprising to

and undocumented ivory products. It is best to leave the tusks on the magnificent elephant.

Tortoise-shell work is another craft still practiced despite the cruel and illegal method of obtaining the shell. The Hawksbill turtle, from which the shell comes, is an endangered species. Many countries enforce a ban against the importation of all turtle products.

Marvelous Metalwork: Sri Lanka has a long history of metalwork utilizing gold, silver, copper, tin, lead, iron and their various alloys. Gold and silver were usually restricted to the jewelry and decorative articles of the "three Rs" – royalty, religion and ruling class. More utilitarian metal objects made of baser metals

find goldsmiths throughout the country, even in some of the most rural areas.

Jewelry designs in Sri Lanka vary from the ridiculous to the sublime, as do the quality and price. Some jewelers specialize in setting Sri Lanka's famous gems, while others specialize in pure metalwork or in intricate filigree. Every large town and hotel has its jewelry shops. The Galle area has a number of small workshops that welcome visitors to watch artisans at work. If considering a major purchase, it is best to compare prices and buy from a reputable dealer.

Silver and Brass: Silver, being a precious malleable metal, is the favorite medium for filigree artisans. Filigree necklaces and bracelets, somewhat resembling those of India, usually follow traditional designs. Silver is also a popular medium for candelabra, serving trays, tea sets, spoons, and a wide variety of other wares. Artisans employ classical Sinhalese as well as European designs. Price varies with the amount of silver and complexity of design. Beautiful silver-plated pieces, often using the same design as pure silver articles, cost considerably less.

Brass is the most common ornamental metal used outside of jewelry. The alloy used in Sri Lanka, famous for its quality, is excellent for castwork, cutwork or repousse.

Castings in brass are usually done by *cire perdue*, the "lost wax" method. A full-sized

model is sculpted in wax, covered with a tough clay, then baked to form a mold. Molten brass is poured into the empty mold, assuming the shape of the original wax model. This method permits small as well as large objects to be cast. Popular castings include elephants, Buddha images, vases, bowls, lamps and candlesticks.

In cutwork, the artist cuts the desired pattern directly into a flat sheet of metal. Engraving, hatching or repousse further embellishes the

Left, the woof and wrap of handloom weaving has added a new dimension to Sri Lankan textiles. **Above**, an Ambalangoda artisan puts the bright colours on a devil-dancing mask.

metal. Cutwork is popular for trays, plaques and lamps: it gives the finished product a lacy effect.

Repousse – in brass, copper, silver, or all three combined – is the most characteristic type of Sri Lankan metal-work, preserving a wide range of traditional designs. In repousse, the metal object, usually a flat article such as a tray or plaque, is placed on a resilient pad. The artist hammers the desired pattern from the reverse side by carefully using punch-like dies. The front side then reveals a raised pattern set against a recessed background. Repousse is often done in conjunction with applique. Here thin sheets of copper or silver are carefully fitted into grooves on the front of the article. After the applique is in place, the design is hammered through from the reverse. The seams are carefully smoothed down, creating an interesting pattern in relief as well as color.

The Potters' Craft: Pottery is a living craft that permeates life in Sri Lanka. It has come to represent the fundamentals of rural life – small votive lamps for worship, graceful water jugs, and versatile cooking vessels.

Several government-sponsored pottery centers have introduced new equipment and ideas to the craft. Yet throughout the island, there are scores of potters' villages where craftsmen still employ the traditional methods. Most of the pottery is thrown on low wheels that the potter keeps turning. A lump of clay is placed on the wheel and the potter forms a vessel from the spinning mass. The work consists largely of simple undecorated pieces, but there is a growing demand and supply of decorated pottery as well.

Decoration is usually done by incising patterns or stamping with a wooden die while the clay is still wet. Sometimes a glaze is painted on the spinning pot prior to baking. Most pots are fired in a primitive kiln built of brick or stone and covered with a vaulted wattle-and-daub roof. Small holes at the top of the kiln act as flues while openings at the base allow firewood to be inserted. After baking, the kiln is dismantled to reveal the baked pottery. Some pottery might then receive further decoration: some incised patterns might be filled with a contrasting clay, while other pieces might be painted. But most of the pottery is left with its newly baked beauty intact.

Sri Lanka has a variety of handicrafts that fall under the broad category of textiles – batik, weaving, embroidery and lace.

Batik is one of the most visible of Sri Lankan

crafts. Galleries and factories line the major highways while every tourist destination and hotel offers batik clothing for sale. Batiks are also hung as works of art. They are available from simple single-color designs to intricate multicolored masterpieces.

Batiks are created through a process of waxing and dyeing. A pattern is drawn on a plain piece of material, then molten wax is applied to those areas of the cloth that are *not* to be dyed. This is done by pouring it in fine lines through a tiny funnel-like device, stamping with a die or painting with a brush. After waxing, the material is dyed in the desired color; then it is set and washed. If more colors are desired, the material must be rewaxed and redyed. This process is repeated until the artist achieves the desired color combinations. Originally only one artist created the entire batik from start to finish. Today in assembly-line factories, young women carry out each step of the process separately. The finished product is still handmade, but it passes through many hands on the way to completion. A few traditional artists still prefer to carry out the entire process alone; their creations are often outstanding.

Although hand-woven materials have lost their preeminence in society to machine-made textiles, high-quality handloom goods are still available. The old pit loom has been replaced by the "flying shuttle" type of handloom, capable of producing longer and wider bolts of cloth, usually cotton.

In 1950 Edith Ludowyk pioneered texture weaving at the Menikdiwela Weaving Center near Kandy. Another weaving center, Nayakakande near Colombo, is known for its artful use of color. Barbara Sansoni, a champion of the handloom industry, has established several outlets that deal exclusively in handloom products; her Colombo "Barefoot Gallery" probably has the most extensive selection.

The making of lace, believed to have been introduced by the Portuguese, is centered in the old colonial seaports of Galle, Colombo and Jaffna. Lacemaking is a tedious affair, requiring many careful hours of moving and rearranging spindles of thread among a myriad of pins. In more intricate patterns, months might be required to finish a few inches. Not surprisingly, with the advent of machine-made lace, the handmade variety is slowly fading away as a craft.

Today, lacemaking survives in the skills of septo-and octogenarians. Galle is the center of the craft: there is even a style of lace named after the town. Visitors can't fail to be assailed by youngsters selling their grand-mothers' lace as they stroll along the ramparts of the old fort.

Mats and Baskets: Basketry and mat weaving also have a long history. At one time, mat weaving was considered a necessary domestic accomplishment as mats provided both floor coverings and beds. Today they are still important, especially among villagers.

Mat weaving is a cottage industry that has few established sales outlets. However, at almost all festivals and pilgrimage sites, villagers from miles around bring their mats to sell. During the annual Kandy Perahera, hundreds of mats, rolled in a variety of patterns, line the sidewalks awaiting customers. Mats can also be found in village markets and in the dozens of basket shops that line the Colombo-Kandy road near the town of Warakapola.

Dumbara mats are the most famous. They are woven in the village of Henawela near Kandy, and take their name from the province of Dumbara. These mats are traditionally woven on a primitive loom using fibers from the bow-string hemp. They often are decorated with stripes or patterned bands, animal or floral motifs, using techniques and patterns that have remained unchanged for centuries.

Basketry is another functional craft. Heavy baskets made of split bamboo or cane (rattan) are used for hauling produce, grain, chickens, and an endless variety of other goods. One special type of woven basket is used to measure paddy, while another is used to separate the chaff from the grain.

More delicate and artistic basketry is also popular. The village of Kalutara is one of the best known basket centers and even has a "Basket Hall" where the town weavers may be watched at work. Sedge, pandanus and several types of palm leaves are favorite materials. In Jaffna, the palmyrah palm leaf – seen everywhere in the construction of boundary walls – is also woven into a variety of baskets such as nested boxes.

Each area of Sri Lanka has its own specialty and style of craft. The variety is immense, but is often so scattered that many people remain unaware of the diversity of Sri Lanka's handmade treasures.

Baskets, anyone? A proliferation of these products, made of woven split bamboo or cane, are sold along the Colombo-Kandy road.

Throughout history, Sri Lanka has been known as a land of gems. King Solomon was said to have procured a great ruby for the Queen of Sheba from Ceylon. Marco Polo wrote of wonderful gems, especially of the great ruby that once graced the Ruwanweli Seya Dagoba in Anuradhapura – a "flawless ruby a span long and quite as thick as a man's arm." He may have been exaggerating a bit, but the gems plucked from the earth here have attained worldwide attention and acclaim.

Today, the ruby is quite rare. But its royal brother, the blue sapphire, is the king of Sri Lankan gems. The 400-carat blue sapphire called "Blue Belle," which adorns the British Crown, is from Sri Lanka. The beautiful star sapphire misnamed the "Star of India" (on permanent display in the Museum of Natural History in New York) is another Sri Lankan treasure. Besides rubies and sapphire, the *illama* soil also bears cat's eyes, alexandrites, aquamarines, tourmalines, spinels, topaz, garnets, amethyst, zircons and a variety of other stones.

Mining in the Pits: Most Sri Lankan gems are mined from pits. A unique feature on this island is that a variety of different gems may be found within the same pit. For millennia, nature has washed minerals from their original mountain locations to the lowlands and valleys. This precious cargo of gems has been deposited in coarse water-borne gravel called *illam*, which ancient streams buried beneath a layer of alluvial clay. Alluvial deposits have made the district surrounding Ratnapura – literally, "city of gems" – the most important gem-bearing region of Sri Lanka.

To reach the gem-bearing *illam*, workers must dig through the surface alluvium. The pit, ranging in depth from a few feet to 30 or more, is excavated and its walls supported by a framework of stout logs or planks arranged in crisscross fashion. Long poles, pivoted on scaffolding, act as windlasses to hoist the gravel out of the pit.

The *illam* is then placed in basket-like sieves which are swirled in water, with a rotary mo-

tion, so that the clay and lighter material are washed away. The remaining soil must be hand-picked.

Gemming is a cooperative enterprise in Sri Lanka, not meant for individualists. Each participant gets an appropriate share of any gems sold. There is a landowner and there is someone willing to finance a pit. Another man must pay the government for the right to dig for gems, and obtain a permit. The men hired to dig out the *illam* must be trustworthy; unreliable persons have been known to swallow gems to hide them from other workers. Other employees must stand waist-deep in water to wash off the adhering clay. A man is required to operate (and repair) the pump that keeps water out of the pit. And of course there is the gemmer, the man who recognizes which pebbles are true gems.

The gemmer takes the prizes of the pit to a dealer, with whom he haggles over an acceptable price. In buying a stone, a dealer must decide the best way to liberate a beautiful jewel, either by cutting or polishing. Both operations are traditionally carried out on primitive wheels coated with an abrasive paste, hand-spun like bow drills with stick and string.

Preceding pages, a collection of precious sapphires and rubies in Ratnapura. **Left**, a traditionally styled gem-studded armlet. **Above**, toiling in the mud of a Ratnapura gem pit.

The polisher uses a horizontal wheel of brass or copper, while the cutter – if not replaced by a modern machine – employs a vertical wheel of lead. After "liberation," the stone is ready to be sold unset, or to be set into jewelry by another craftsman.

How to Judge a Gem: The chief criteria for judging a stone are its color, transparency and luster, and freedom from flaws. Generally speaking, the deeper and purer the color of a stone, the better its quality. But by the same token, depth and purity of color are rare, and may even conceal a flaw.

Transparency goes a long way toward indicating a perfect stone. If it does nothing else, it shows up the flaws. But even more important is luster, self-evident only if one is familiar with the sort of luster peculiar to a given stone. (Amateurs beware!)

Gems are often flawed. Common flaws are ill-pigmentations or uneven color distribution; inclusions, which can be bubbles of gas or liquid, or other solid particles; and fissures or cracks. While flaws normally diminish the value of a stone, they may be advantageous if they are regular enough or highly unusual. The much-sought "silk" of the star sapphires and star rubies is actually a uniform pattern of flaws, the inclusion of minute filament or microscopic tubes.

Sri Lanka is ranked among the top five gem-bearing nations of the world. The others are Burma, Brazil, South Africa and Thailand.

Corundums are the most important gem minerals in Sri Lanka. Second in hardness only to diamonds (which are not found in Sri Lanka), they comprise sapphires and rubies. Those stones that come in shades of blue, green or yellow are classified as sapphires. Their cousins, the rubies, are corundums ranging through pinks, violets and reds to the treasured "pigeon-blood red."

The most prized sapphires are those in shades of royal and cornflower blue. Prices for a flawless, deep-hued stone go as high as US$5,000 per carat.

The "star" effect of some corundums is the result of the "silk" inclusions catching outside light. The asterism, usually in the form of a six-rayed star, comes alive when gently moved under the light. Many people find this effect captivating.

The best-known member of the beryl family, the emerald, is absent from Sri Lanka. But related gems abound. The aquamarine is softer than the corundums, and varies in color from a sea-green to ocean blue.

Chrysoberyls come in shades of yellow, green and brownish, with all intermediate variations. The best-known types of chrysoberyl are the cat's eye and the alexandrite. The cat's eye is especially important to Sri Lankans as a protective charm, and fetches a high price. When a chrysoberyl containing a chatoyancy is cut, it displays a clear, iridescent ray that resembles a cat's eye: thus the name.

Alexandrites have the rare property of changing color, and are highly prized for that reason. In daylight they appear green; under artificial light, they turn red. They are found only in Sri Lanka and in the Ural Mountains of

the Soviet Union.

Chrysoberyls are the third hardest mineral known, ranked after diamonds and corundums.

The yellow topaz is a hard stone that takes an exceptionally high polish, giving it a slippery touch. Color varies from almost clear to a fairly deep yellow. This moderately-priced stone is popular in jewelry, but beware when buying: there is no such thing in Sri Lanka as "smoky topaz." Any dealer who offers it is merely trying to pass off quartz at a higher price.

Quartz is found in a variety of colors and can be either transparent, translucent or opaque. Amethyst is a purple quartz of fairly high price; it is a beautiful stone often set into striking jewelry. Smoky quartz ranges in color from light to dark brown and is often set into "cocktail rings."

Garnets are a common, relatively inexpensive stone of often-deep color. Hues range from pale cinnamon to dark reddish brown. They are softer and lighter than rubies and lack the luster of corundums.

Sri Lankan tourmalines come in a variety of colors: yellows, greens, reds and blues. Classified as semi-precious stones – a completely arbitrary classification based on demand and availability – they are relatively inexpensive.

Zircons have a brilliance and fire similar to diamonds, but are a much softer stone. They exhibit a double refraction and vivid luster that

into attractive bracelets and necklaces. Those moonstones which have a blue luster are very popular but are considerably more expensive.

Choosing a Dealer: There are few fields in which the non-expert is at such a disadvantage as in the gem trade. Fake gems, synthetic or paste, are easily manufactured; they can be strikingly beautiful and are often passed off as the real thing. Flaws can sometimes be hidden, colors altered or faked, and last-minute switches made.

The best protection is to compare prices, shop round, and find a reputable dealer. Beware of "bargains" and peddlers. That shiny, polished, perfectly colored sapphire in the street seller's pocket couldn't be genuine, or long ago it

have enabled the colorless variety to be passed off as "diamonds" to the naive. Zircons also possess hues of yellow, orange and brown.

Another popular semi-precious stone is the spinel. Quite common, they come in blue, green, red and orange. In some areas, spinels are "baked," thus changing the natural color.

Probably the least expensive of abundant Sri Lankan gems is the moonstone. These milky-looking stones, a variety of feldspar, are made

Left, a craftsman turns a piece of jewelry into a thing of glimmering beauty. It can then be marketed in a Sri Lankan jewelry shop such as the one at right.

would have been sold in rough form to a gem merchant. Traditionally, gemming was a royal monopoly, with the king going to great lengths to protect his interests. Some of that proprietary attitude survives today: unmined gems are considered to be owned by the state.

The government maintains its own gem dealership, the State Gem Corporation. As a public service, this agency will test any gem, regardless of where it was purchased, to verify its authenticity.

Gems – the basis of legend and cause for adventure, the almost-sensual minerals that have captured men's fancies for eons – still sparkle with a romance of their own.

Over the centuries, Sir Lanka's historic preoccupation with artistic pursuits has transformed the island into a Tolkienesque wonderland of temples, palaces and shrines. Fanciful sculptures and paintings further enhance this fantastic landscape.

Even a visitor whose main interests lie in the pleasures of beaches or wildlife parks can't help but realize he has stumbled into a veritable museum of classical art. The treasures range from the great *dagobas* and moonstones at Anuradhapura to the colossal Buddha sculptures of Buduruvagala, Aukana and Polonnaruwa. Some works startle the viewer with their size and immensity. Others soothe the senses with the subtle simplicity of their execution. All exemplify this complex culture's quest for perfection.

Cosmic Mountains: The most prominent and obvious examples of a classical art form in Sri Lanka stud the hills and plains of the island like arms stretched to the heavens. And that in simple terms, is exactly what what the *dagoba* is – a glorious monument that soars into the sky in celebration of the Sinhalese devotion to Buddhism.

In its most primitive form, the stupa (called *dagoba* in its more developed Sinhalese form), was a mound of earth with a wooden mast embedded in its core. Art historian Benjamin Rowland interpreted it as a model of Mount Meru, the cosmic mountain at the center of the South Asian universe. The mast represented the axis of the universe.

In time, this mound of Meru acquired a funerary, or at least a memorial, significance. One parasol, the ancient Eastern symbol of royalty, was added to the mast above the summit; another parasol stood off to the side to shade another part of the structure. A ring of stones built around the base of the *dagoba* prevented the earth-works from washing away, and a square palisade at the summit enclosed the projecting shaft.

The first *dagobas* housed venerated objects believed to have been personally connected

with the Buddha, like his begging bowl and his teeth. In time, they came to surpass the prominence of the *bo* tree beneath which the Buddha attained enlightenment, offering greater scope for pious grandiosity than the *bodhi-ghara* designed to house cuttings from the original *bo* tree. Nowhere else in the Buddha's world-wide realm has the *dagoba* or stupa achieved the sublimity in size, elegance and symbolism that it has in Sri Lanka.

Fusing Instinct and Dogma: Examples of the primitive *dagoba* no longer exist in Sri Lanka. Those early structures were enlarged and beautified by latter-day engineers of the royal courts. They added ornamentation that fused architectural instinct and dogmatic intuition. They encased the ancient earthen cores in layers of masonry like the tunicate of an onion.

As early as the 2nd Century B.C., Dutugemunu built his great *dagobas*, Mirisaweti and Ruwanweli, of brick masonry. The inherent stability of that construction technique was ensured by foundations that reached far below ground level. It was painstakingly compacted by elephants wearing boots of leather, according to the *Mahavamsa*. Dutugemunu's magnificent creations initiated the age of the giant *dagobas*. In sheer size, they were unique to Sri Lanka and culminated in the construction of Jetavanarama of King Mahasena, 450 years after the reign of Dutugemunu. At 367 feet in base diameter and 160 feet in height, it is taller than London's St. Paul's Cathedral and nearly as large as the Great Pyramid of Cheops.

In its latter-day state of repair, 19th Century writer James Emerson Tennant calculated that Jetavanarama would still hold "twenty millions of cubical feet ... sufficient to raise eight thousand houses each with twenty feet frontage ... line an ordinary railway tunnel twenty miles long, or form a wall one foot in thickness and ten feet in height, reaching from London to Edinburgh." Even the small Ruwanweli Seya at Anuradhapura "would need ... five hundred bricklayers, working English union time for fourteen years to build," surmised the more topical Harry Williams during the long union hours before World War II.

Art Unseen by the Eye: It is not merely the size of a *dagoba* that impresses, but its grace in

Preceding pages: dwarfs, no two alike, line the walls of Kelaniya Temple outside Colombo. Left, the bubble-shaped Rankot Vehera at Polonnaruwa under reconstruction.

balancing form and mass. The edifice took the form of six standard shapes: the early "paddy-heap" represented *dagoba* at Kelaniya; the "bubble" type epitomized by Ruwanweli and the Kirivehera at Polonnaruwa; the "bell" shape that can still be seen in the Thuparama at Anuradhapura; and the "water-pot," "lotus" and *amalaka* (similar to "bell"), which there are no existing prominent examples.

The most notable architectural development that crowned these ancient giants was the *kotkarella* or spire. Its invention has been traced back as far as a 2nd Century A.D. reliquary that can be viewed at the Ruwanweli Seya. Its superstructure reflects the early styles, but it sports an octagonal pillar with a rounded top.

and mass. The Sinhalese have surrounded it with a courtyard sprinkled with white sand and a parapet with four gateways called the *vali-kangana*. Flights of steps opposite the gateways have been furnished with stone water troughs for ablution. The steps often lead to a stone-based platform retained by an "elephant-wall," as can be seen at the Ruwanweli Seya. From this has risen the dome itself, clasped by three concentric ledges – rings of stone masonry called *pesavalalu*.

Evidence indicated that the lowest of the *pesavalalu* were adorned with 16 representations of the Buddha's footprint, stations where the devotee would pause in his clockwise circular movement of worship around the *dagoba*.

Nothing is more suggestive of the evolution from the simple stupa to magnificent *dagoba*, from cosmic model to a *pyx* for a holy relic, than the disappearance of its stone shaft. The whole monument now warrants adoration. In the heart of each mighty pile, built to last for eternity, is a chamber decorated with paintings and sculptures never intended to be seen by the human eye. Here are sealed the holy relics still illuminated by burning lamps, according to tradition. The vast cone of umbrellas above honors the entire shrine.

Today's typical *dagoba* is the climax of centuries of architectural and religious change and experimentation, a vast complex of space

The top and secondary terraces held flower offerings. Other flower altars rose before great screens called *vahalkadas* at the four compass points, facing the worshipper as he ascended the stone platform.

Variations on the Dagoba: Early Indian architects developed the custom of enclosing a small *dagoba* with a circular building. Its roof was supported by concentric circles of pillars. The spire of the stupa rose into a central dome. In Sri Lanka, the only surviving examples of

The revered *dagoba* at Nagadipa, on the island of Nainativu off the Jaffna coast, is a fine example of a traditional bell-shaped stupa.

this practice are rock-cut shrines. Illustrations in bas-relief at Sanchi, India, provide a look at the spectacular free-standing circular relic houses called *vatadages*. They were first built by King Vasabha beginning about 67 B.C. until the 15th Century.

The first *vatadages* were of wooden construction, which hastened their extinction. Ruins of the stone variety that date from the 7th Century can be viewed at Medirigiriya and Tiriyai. The best-known example is at Polonnaruwa, where one of the columns from the two inner rings of roof pillars still stands. The porch of this *vatadage* was added in the 12th Century and other embellishments are the handiwork of King Nissanka Malla.

Stupas that differ in style from the traditional *dagobas* include the square Nakha Vehera at Anuradhapura and the onceoctagonal Satmahal Prasada at Polonnaruwa. In addition, there was a pattern popular around Kandy of arranging five traditional-style stupas in a quinouz: four small *dagobas* surrounding a large central one.

All in all, the *dagoba* is undoubtedly the greatest architectural achievement of Sinhalese. View them at Anuradhapura, Mihintale and Polonnaruwa, and at the museum of Dedigama.

Temples for Images: Although the *dagoba* remains the crowning testament of the Buddhist religion, today the image house is the chief place that worshippers bring their offerings of flower and incense. There is evidence that figures of the Buddha existed in Sri Lanka's earliest years; scholars believe they were not worshipped as images but as containers of precious relics. Buddha himself rejected image worship.

It was not until the reign of King Vasabha in the 1st Century A.D. that the *Mahavamsa* describes the construction of a "temple for images." The deistic attitudes encouraged by early Mahayana influences probably encouraged homage to images of the Buddha.

The buildings that housed these figures ranged from simple shelters to majestic palaces. They became known as *patimagharas*. Early examples found at Anuradhapura generally comprised two types. The foundations of one type near Kiribat Vehera indicate it had a small antechamber that led to the larger sanctuary. It was sometimes surrounded by an ambulatory accessible only from the antechamber. An example of the other type is located in the ruins south of the Thuparama Dagoba. It is a kind of oblong rectangle accessible from a porch on the longer side. This second version always seems to occur as the central unit of a quinoux of smaller structures enclosed within a walled quadrangle.

The most recent examples of the classic *patimagharas* are at the Gadaladeniya and Lankatillaka temples near Kandy. Their design is more complex, each having acquired attachments of one or more *devala* shrines.

The perfection of this unique architectural art form, however, are the three partially preserved image houses of Tivanka, Thuprama and Lankatillaka at Polonnaruwa, popularly called the *gedige*. Constructed of brick from base to roof, they formed vaults topped with an arch. Each course of bricks projected slightly more inwards, a technique that produced long, leaning slopes with a sense of intricate construction and sheer altitude. Externally, a *gedige* achieved superb proportions. Its massive walls were as ponderous as mountains.

Other examples of *gediges* include the primitive one at Jetavanarama and the Galmaduwa near Kandy, with its inner chamber circumscribed by a stone arcade and its corbelled spire of bricks. Numerous cave temples also glow with the same prodigal but cryptic splendor: Dambulla, Degaldoruwa and Mulgirigala. It is unknown when these caves were transformed into image-houses.

The Eclectic Devala: The decline that marked the post-Polonnaruwa period also marked a decline in the splendor and size of the *patimaghara*. This was a time when sanctuaries were raised high on pillars like that at Ambulugala. Even during the grinding struggles of the Kandy period, there still built tiny image houses like those at Medawala. They testify to the survival of Sinhala sovereignty and Buddhism in the face of invaders from the West. These latter styles were simple descendants of the country granary store, little boxes of wattle-and-daub standing on grids of heavy timber raised above the termites' reach by stubby stone piers. They were brave structures, gloriously decorated inside with intricate carvings and bright wall paintings.

A more direct effect of the foreign influence on classical Sinhalese architecture was the rise of the *devalas*, deistic shrines strongly influenced by Hinduism. In fact, the earliest *devalas* were small Hindu temples. But they bore more resemblance to the Buddhist *patimaghara*, than to the fully evolved Hindu *kovil*.

Examples include the Shiva Devalas No. 1

and No. 2 at Polonnaruwa, built by the Chola dynasty of South Indian when they occupied that city in the 10th Century. Temples built to the Buddha, but with the eclecticism so characteristic of Hinduism, can be seen still standing at Velgam Vihara near Trincomalee.

Devalas with Buddha statues, as well as with shrines to deities subservient to the Buddha, peaked in popularity and architectural elegance during the 14th Century. The exemplary *devala* of the period is at Embekke. Ground plans included three halls. The innermost, the *garbhagrha*, was the *sanctum* which contained the god, was usually represented by his insignia or *abharana*. Priests chanted in honor of the deity in another room called the *digge*.

of Sri Lanka. The first manmade monastery was the Maha Vihara at Anuradhapura. Even the smallest monasteries included an *avasa* for the monks, usually individual residential cells arranged around a quadrangle or in rows connected by a cloister-like veranda that opened into a courtyard.

Other features of the monastery included the rectangular *poyage* hall where the *poya* day ceremonies took place, erected upon a consecrated area demarcated by boundary-stones embedded in the earth; the *bodhimaluwa*, a raised terrace where the sacred *bo* tree grew; a preaching pavilion called the *banamaduwa*; and a *dagoba* and image house. The most important monasteries also included baths like the mag-

The grandeur of the *devalas* also eventually declined. They became mere adjuncts to regular temples of the Buddha like the ones at Gadaladeniya and Lankatillaka. Those that remained separate adopted the wooden-floored wattle-and-daub design of the late Kandyan period. In primitive villages, they became a kind of shed beneath a tree.

Other classic structures of ancient Sri Lankan architecture included the religious monasteries (*pirivena*), the meditation unit (*padhanaghara*), various palaces and secular structures and travelers' rests known as *ambalamas*.

The sage Mahinda and his companions used caves in the Mihintale forest as the first *pirivena*

nificent Kuttam Pokuna at Anuradhapura and the Lotus Bath at Polonnaruwa.

On the other hand, meditation units were generally confined to ascetic settlements and forest monasteries. They comprised a walled-in area containing two stone-faced platforms. The westernmost stood upon a hump of natural rock surrounded by a stone-faced moat, an asylum evidently symbolic of the jungle refuge of a hermit. A great monolithic bridge over the moat connected this platform with a second one at the main entrance to the enclosure.

The main gate was always at the eastern end and usually sported a handsome porch with a stone roof and couches. Other amenities included bathing ponds. A good example of these intriguing *padhanaghara* can be seen at Ritigala.

Palaces – 'Merits of the King': The few classic secular structures still discernible among the ruins of the Sri Lankan kingdoms are chiefly royal palaces, some military structures, and a few civil works. Tiled roofs and lime walls were expressly reserved for religious and royal buildings. Their use in other structures could be grounds for treason.

The earliest, identifiable palace is, of course, at the summit of Sigiriya rock. It was built by Kasyapa in the 5th Century. The only palace still recognizable at Anuradhapura itself dates back to the Polonnaruwa period and pattern.

The royal residences of the 12th Century still

reveal features characteristic of the reigning family. The two built by King Parakramabahu I at Panduvas Nurwara and Polonnaruwa are particularly good studies of this architectural form. This Polonnaruwa palace had a central structure for private apartments with brick walls 10 feet thick designed for a superstructure several stories in height. Beam holes in the walls at tow levels still show where the floors rested. This mass of masonry was crowned by

Left, the elephant wall at Mahiyangana is typical of many that surround ancient dagobas. **Above**, The Kandyan-style Buddha images of Dambulla differ from earlier statues.

the sumptuous chamber described in the *Mahavamsa*.

"The height of its splendor was reached in the royal sleeping apartment which was ever-resplendent with a thick bunch of pearls suspended at its four corners, white as moonbeams and gleaming so that they laughed to scorn the beauty of the divine Ganga. (The sleeping apartment) was adorned with a wreath of large golden lampstands which breathed out continually the perfume of flowers and incense. With the network of tiny golden bells suspended here and there and giving forth a sound like the sound of five musical instruments, the palace made known, as it were, the richfulness of the merits of the King."

Most of the ground floor was a vast foyer that led through a smaller hall and vestibule. The building was encased in a great pillared hall and large open courtyard that was in turn surrounded by a vestibule, four sets of galleries with barracks for palace officials and attendants, and a wall. The king's residence was flanked by ancillary buildings for state and private uses. During the reign of Parakramabahu II in the 13th Century, the Temple of Tooth also became an essential and hallowed part of these palace complexes.

The palace still standing in Kandy reflects Western architectural influences imported by the Portuguese and Dutch. It was built in 1595 by King Wimala Dharma Suriya I. It underwent further change after a visit by Dutch Admiral van Spilbergen in 1602. Its most authentic-looking feature is the audience hall which was not built until the British had taken Colombo. The Queen's Palace was also a late addition.

In retrospect, the royal palaces may have been elaborate manifestations of the *ambalama*. These wayside shelters were free to travelers and were still in use until the motor bus arrived. Those that still stand are already the haunt of vagrants. Contrast this sad fact with the description of an *ambalama* in a 15th Century poem: "People gather from diverse ways to rest here. Some recite poetry, and vie with each other; one challenges another at riddles ... foreigners learn and repeat the Buddha's teaching ... "

The most outstanding example of an *ambalama* is at Panavitiya. It stood on an ancient route between Dambadeniya and Kurunegala and probably dates from the 18th Century. It is a mere pavilion with a roof held up by wooden columns and stout beams, artless but for the delightful carving of these beams. This *ambalama*, as others, is genuine Sinhala architecture stripped of pretension and sophistication. Only its charm and taste remain.

Shapes of the Buddha: Sculpture was the other major mode of classic artistic expression in ancient Sri Lanka, a medium often used to complement architectural masterpieces. In its most common form in the island, sculpture took the shape of the Buddha.

Sculpture was the other major mode of classic artistic expression in ancient Sri Lanka, a medium often used to complement architectural masterpieces. In its most common form in the island, sculpture took the shape of the Buddha.

The Buddhas of Sri Lanka were sculptured in a variety of materials. One Chinese reference of the 5th Century A. D. even describes a magnificent image sculptured from jade that inspired great admiration. Fa Hsien, the Chinese traveler of that same period, also talks of seeing an image of jasper at Anuradhapura that rose to an astounding height of 22 feet.

Although it was not always customary to use indigenous materials, the earliest statues were invariably carved from limestone, an abundant resource of the island. Unfortunately, limestone is susceptible to weathering, hastening the disappearance of most of these ancient art works.

Other mediums included marble, used for the Buddha sculpture at Maha Illuppalama; rock crystal and emerald, from which the Buddha at the Temple of the Sacred Tooth in Kandy was fashioned; and pink quartz, which produced the Buddha at Panavitiya. Ivory, coral and even wood were sometimes used, but clay Buddhas were rare.

Gneiss as a material used to sculpt the Buddha image entered the picture later. The earliest use appears to have been in the Aukana Buddha attributed to King Dhatusena's 5th Century reign. Others include the giant recumbent, standing and seated figures of Gal Vihara at Polonnaruwa.

Metal images are rather modest. The best is a 5th or 6th Century relic found at Badulla that is on exhibit at the National Museum in Colombo. Many Kandyan period figures are of brick and stucco. The inferior alabaster Buddhas frequently seen in contemporary Sri Lanka are generally of Burmese manufacture.

Buddha's Postures: The Buddha images of Sri Lanka can be classified into three important postures. The seated form undoubtedly was inspired by the vision of the Buddha seated on the throne of victory under the *bo* tree, simulating the scene of enlightenment. In fact, the earliest mentions of Buddhist sculptures refer to one made during the reign of King Devanampiyatissa in the 3rd Century B.C. It may have been placed near the *bo* tree at Thuparama. The earliest existing image of a seated figure – with feet rigidly interlocked and each instep resting on the opposite thigh – was found at the Abhayagiriya *bo* tree shrine; it is now on display at the Anuradhapura museum. Others include the figures at Yapahuwa and Seruwila where the *bo* Tree can be seen in the background. Colossal figures of this type sit at the Gal Vihara (Polonnaruwa) and Tantrimalai.

With the passage of time, the Buddha statue

rose in importance, from a mere appurtenance to the *bo* tree to an object of veneration in itself. This rise in stature may have coincided with the rise of the image to a standing position. The earliest standing images are probably those found in the courtyard of the Ruwanweli Seya at Anuradhapura. The style of these images subsequently perservered for nearly 1,000 years. Lesser known examples are found at Medirigiriya and at the Thuparama in Polonnaruwa.

A variation of this kind found at Gal Vihara in Polonnaruwa is known as the Tivanka posture. Its arms are crossed and its body flexed into an almost relaxed stance. This pose is common in India. Scholars believe the ancient sculptor's aim was to play down the divine nature of the Buddha and to emphasize his benevolent side.

Finally, there is the recumbent pose of the Buddha. Barring more recent bronzes, these sculptures are all of colossal dimensions. Depending upon the positioning of the feet, these Buddhas can be considered to be either reclining (toes together) or in the process of attaining *parinibbana* (toes slightly apart). Recumbent statues of the Buddha sculpted in stone are found at Ataragollawa, Dambulla, and Polonnaruwa. There are brick and stucco versions in other parts of the island.

Another identifying characteristic of Bud-

course or teaching. The equally rare *bumisparasa mudra* is when the fingers of the right hand stretch to touch the ground.

The styles of the hair and robes in Buddha images changed through the centuries, probably a result of different craftsmen working in different media in different historical periods. But whatever variations the figures took, both India and Sri Lanka utilized a canon of measurements and proportions, the *Sariputra*, that was followed for centuries.

Ultimately, it was the painting of the sculpture that proved particularly significant. The painting of the eyes during an eye festival, a *netra mangalya*, turned each work of stone or clay or metal into a sacred and divine Being.

dha images is the attitude and gesture of the hands, the *mudra*. The *dhyana mudra* describes hands lightly cupped and resting naturally on the center of the lap. The feet are in the yogi position. The *abhaya mudra* displays an attitude of reassurance or the bestowal of protection. Its right hand is raised from the elbow, fingers together, the palm outward. The rare *vitarka mudra* is identifiable by fingers raised (index finger touching thumb) to indicate dis-

Left, the stone carving of a Hindu goddess in the National Museum in Colombo. **Above**, guardstones and moonstone are common features of temples throughout the country.

Individuals, including the artists themselves, were prohibited from receiving the first glance from these holy eyes. They had to be viewed through a mirror while protective incantations were continually chanted.

Hindu Deities and Symbols: The Buddha was not the only one immortalized in classical Sri Lankan sculpture. Many deities worshipped in the island, some belonging to the Hindu pantheon and others peculiar to certain parts of the country, were also committed to stone for worship.

Vishnu, guardian of the entire island, took the form of a painted figure with dark skin. His hands bear a bow, a quoit used in war called a *chakra*, a *pasa* or lasso and a conch shell that was used as a war trumpet. He rides the *gurula* (garuda), the mythical eagle.

Similarly, the god Saman stands on the *minnihalanga*, the seat of power where Buddha always sits. He is accompanied by a white elephant and holds a bow and arrow. Vibeheshana, generally worshipped in the western end of the country, is the subject of the main shrine of Kelaniya. He is accompanied by two singular birds. Kataragama *deviyo* or god Skanda has many hands to symbolize his power. Each holds weapons of war like the *trisula* (trident), a bow and arrow, a *pasa* and flag. His vehicle is the peacock.

An architectural feature that is basically a

horse, a symbol of death. Some also have a band of geese which represents the distinction between good and evil. To some, the moonstone is symbolic of transcending worldly temptations and achieving *nibbane*.

At the heart of many moonstones is a lotus petal. Buddhists regard the lotus as a sacred flower, a symbol of the male and female creative forces that prevails throughout Sri Lankan art, architecture, sculpture and literature. It figures in the legend attached to the birth of the Buddha, when seven lotuses sprang into bloom at his feet as he took the first seven steps of his life. The lotus bloomed again in profusion at the moment he reached the state of Enlightenment. In the moonstone, the lotus usually rep-

mass of fine sculpture is the Sinhalese staircase. It includes an intricately decorated flight of steps flanked by ornate balustrades with a frontal stand formed by a pair of guardstones.

The Moonstone And the Lotus Petal: The elaborate mooonstone at its base is in itself a distinctive element of ancient sculpture in the island. These semi-circular slabs of granite or gneiss acquired increasingly complex bands of decorations over the years. They range from the near abstract – tongues of fire and bands of creeper vines – to symbolic interpretations of the four perils of life. The latter consists of the elephant, a symbol of birth; the bull, indicative of decay; the lion, representing disease; and the

resents the central crowning seat of success. The total effect, then, of mounting the stairs begins with the devotee at the lotus, his back to the world, preparing to ascend to the shrine of wisdom and insight.

The *Mahavamsa* describes a "step shaped like the half moon" in a passage concerning a *vatadage* of the *naga* world. Some of the earliest examples of decorated moonstones can be seen on the ground of the *bo* Tree Temple at Anuradhapura. Other good examples are found at the National Museum in Colombo, the Temple of the Tooth in Kandy, and at various locations in the city of Polonnaruwa. Excavations in 1983 revealed the first rectangular moonstone ever discovered, at Polonnaruwa's Alahana Pirivena.

Golden-colored ladies: Other decorative features of Sri Lanka's fanciful ancient staircases include the guardstones carved with figures like that of the *naga* king standing in an easy posture as if to greet the visitor. Other figures include the dwarf attendants of Kuvera, the god of wealth; and the elaborate *nagaraja* (snake king) guardstones. The *makara* (dragon), the eternal beast of time, enhances the balustrade. This composite animal has the trunk of an elephant, the feet of a lion, the ears of a pig, upturned teeth and a splendid tail.

The ancient Buddhist attitude towards painting is best illustrated by a popular story. It tells

of a saint of Sri Lanka who lived in a cave adorned with religious paintings. But it wasn't until 60 years after he moved in that he noticed the paintings – and then only after it was pointed out to him by people who stood on a lower spiritual plane. Those on the lower levels are traditionally endowed with much greater aesthetic sensibility.

The story is not intended as a condemnation of painting. It merely underlines the fact that

Left, a painted human elephant graces the ceiling of the Temple of the Tooth in Kandy. **Above**, the gem-studded chest of the last Kandyan king is in the Colombo Museum.

any art that was gratifying to the senses was frowned upon by orthodox Buddhists. Ancient artists were commissioned by their kings to produce works for the good of society. Their main focus, then, was to render the concepts of Buddhism to stone and slate. Codified texts known as the *silipasastras* were developed to govern their works. Still, the artist could take the liberty of interpreting those codes as he wished.

Given such constraints, it is remarkable that ancient art, particularly painting, grew into as creative a pursuit as it did. Sinhalese painting is a related yet distinct form of Indian art. In that respect, it is at odds with the "naturalism" of Western schools. This fact is evident in the best known of Sri Lankan painting on the walls of King Kasyapa's 5th Century fortress atop Sigiriya.

Inscriptions on the wall that leads to the picture gallery describes 500 paintings of "golden-colored ladies" of which 29 have been discovered. All but one depict beautifully adorned women, many with bare bosoms. Experts speculate these ladies may have been wives or concubines of Kasyapa. Buddhist convention could simply interpret them to be devotees on their way to worship at the temple. More importantly, these early paintings reveal that the Sri Lankan artists were masters of the line drawing.

Red men on cave walls: Later paintings are found in the Pulligoda cave about 1½ miles from Dimbulagala. Green and red men are painted against a white background on the cave walls. They are in the act of worship and display a developed sense of modeling. Experts believe they were drawn about 900 A.D.

Other paintings that stem from about the same period include the scroll designs of the Ruwanweli *vahalkada* and the divine beings that adorn the walls of the inner relic chamber of the Mihintale *dagoba*. The Enlightenment of the Buddha and the figure of Vishnu found on the walls of the 10th Century *dagoba* at Mahiyangana confirm the *Mahavamsa* record that inner relic chambers of *dagobas* were painted with scenes from the Buddha's life.

Painting moved, along with the kings, to Polonnaruwa. Its Northern Temple has a wealth of wall frescoes. They depict stories from the life of the Buddha. But, like architecture and sculpture, classical painting diminished after the fall of Polonnaruwa along with the glorious civilizations built by the ancient Sinhalese.

Even people who have never heard of Sri Lanka are familiar with Ceylon tea. And with good reason. On this mango-shaped island of just over 25,000 square miles, more tea is produced than in any other country on earth, with the understandable exception of massive India. Tea is Sri Lanka's economic mainstay, its pride and profitable joy. Statistics bear out the importance of the leafy bush. In 1990, Sri Lankan growers produced 233 million kilograms (512 million pounds) of tea, the highest level ever recorded. That same year, Sri Lanka also became the world's largest exporter of tea (exporting 93 percent of total produce), beating its traditional competition, India, into second place. Foreign exchange earnings from tea exports grossed over US$495 million in 1990.

Exit Coffee, Hello Tea: The story of tea in Sri Lanka began in the year 1849. A Scotsman named James Taylor cleared 19 acres of forest in the district of Hewaheta Lower to plant his first seedlings in what is now known as the No. 7 field of the Loolecondera Estate.

By the mid 1870s, Loolecondera Estate had grown to almost 100 acres, while a few more tea estates had been established in different districts. Except for one or two 100-acre estates, most were very small, with less than 25 acres of cultivated land. But even at that time, it appeared that tea had come to Ceylon to stay.

Only a few years earlier, the first rumblings had been heard of the decline of coffee as the island's major export crop. The very active leaf fungus, *hemeleia vastatrix* (commonly called the coffee blight), had appeared in island plantations, resulting in the defoliation of coffee trees and consequently in meager crops. Adding to the ravages of *hemeleia*, the final blow for this crop came in the early 1930s with a slump in coffee prices.

Tea in Sri Lanka has come a long way since the days when James Taylor brewed his first cup on the veranda of his bungalow. Today, tea is grown in three elevational districts of the island. Low grown is found from sea level to 2,000 feet; mid-grown from 2,000 to 4,000

feet; and high grown over 4,000 feet. Low-grown tea districts include Balangoda, Ratnapura, the Kelani Valley and Galle. The medium and high-grown varieties are sub-classified as "Westerns" and "Easterns," in keeping with the geographical location of the estates. Most Westerns are grown in areas such as Dimbula, Dikoya, Maskeliya and Bogowanthalawa, while the Easterns – also known as Uva or Uda Pussellawa tea – are from areas such as Haputale, Bandarawela and Badulla. Two other tea-growing areas that are catego-

rized among the medium and high growns are Kandy and Nuwara Eliya, the latter renowned for teas of delicate flavor and aroma.

Teas manufactured in the different districts have their own distinctive characteristics. The low-grown teas are manufactured mainly for leaf appearance, but lack the liquor characteristics – the *sine qua non* – of the medium and high-grown teas. The low-grown teas are usually made to cater to the Middle East market.

The liquor characteristics of Western teas are color and thickness with flavor, while the Eastern varieties, not as colorful, have an accentuated flavor known to tea tasters as "pungent."

Tea manufacture really begins in the tea

Preceding pages: Tamil tea pluckers pursue the perfect cup of tea – two leaves and a bud. **Left,** a plucker holds onto her full basket and carries it to the factory for weigh-in, **right**.

fields during plucking. There are two types of plucking. Fine plucking is essential for the manufacture of teas with sound liquors and good leaf appearance; it involves the plucking of tea leaves and a bud, the classic rule of tea plucking. In coarse plucking, more than two leaves are picked in a sprig; this results in poorly made tea. At the factory, good healthy leaves plucked in the correct way will be manufactured into good tea, while badly plucked leaves would produce tea of inferior quality.

The processing of tea leaves into tea comprises five main phases: withering, rolling, fermentation, firing and sifting or grading.

Withering is usually done by spreading the green leaves that have just arrived from the round table equipped with battens (curved wooden slats) radiating from its center where an inverted cone is situated. A metal housing called the jacket rotates over the table crushing the leaves against the battens and the cone. The primary object of this operation is to get the sap out of the leaves by rupturing the cells. Only then can the necessary oxidation of the substances responsible for flavor take place.

This is followed by roll-breaking, a process to break up leaves that caked into balls during rolling, as well as to aerate and cool the hot leaves. The roll-breaker is a long mechanized sieve which vibrates while pushing the leaves over the mesh from one end to the other. The leaves that go through the mesh are taken away

field on hessian or nylon netting shelves called "tats." The leaves are kept like this for 18 hours, a process known as natural wither. Nowadays, this time-consuming process is usually replaced by artificial wither, during which the leaves are spread on nylon netting stretched over a fairly deep trough with warm air being forced through from below. This new method cuts withering time by almost two-thirds. One frequently used method for checking whether the leaf has been optimumly withered is to fold it in two (bringing the apex of the leaf and the stem together) without snapping the mid-rib.

After withering, the leaves are sent for rolling. This is done in a tea-roller, which has a

for the next stage of manufacture, while those that come over the top are taken for further rolling. This process is repeated twice.

Fermentation, the next stage, is done in a cool, airy and humid room in the factory. While one cannot underestimate the importance of every stage in the manufacture of tea, fermentation is undoubtedly the most crucial. Tea is fermented by oxidizing, through enzymic action, the tannin in the leaves. This is usually done by spreading the rolled leaves thinly and evenly on the floor. Fermentation time depends on the type and condition of the leaves, but usually takes 1½ to two hours.

It is during fermentation that tea acquires all

its good qualities, such as flavor, and perhaps its bad qualities too. With fermentation, the rawness and bitterness mellow down to more desirable characteristics. An under-fermented tea is harsh and bitter. A tea taster calls this "green." "Fruity and soft" tea is over-fermented; it tends to be sweetish and too mellow. Perfectly fermented tea makes "the cup that cheers."

Firing and Sifting: Firing follows fermentation. This is done in a machine called the drier. It consists of a stove for heating air to about 88°C (190°F), a fan to draw the hot air from the stove, and a chamber where a series of perforated trays move the tea into increasingly hotter temperatures prior to discharge. Firing arrests fermentation and dries the leaves to about two

ing. The mid-ribs and the veins of the leaves turn into stalks and fibers during manufacture, and these stick out like many sore thumbs against the black of the leaves. These are hand-picked by female factory workers or removed by special apparatus known as stalk extractors.

Sifting separates the processed tea leaves into different grades. The primary grade in most factories is called Broken Orange Pekoe (BOP). Other common grades are BOP Fannings, Broken Pekoe and Dust.

Some factories manufacture "fancy grades" like Flowery Fannings and Orange Pekoe, both of which sell well in the Middle East market. The buds in the tea leaves, under certain conditions of manufacture, turn a bright silver or

percent moisture content from about 65 percent moisture in the fermented leaves. Firing takes about 20 to 25 minutes. Even at this stage of manufacture, a close watch is required. An under-fired tea would still be moist and would get moldy within a few weeks of packing, while an over-fired tea would be burnt and most undesirable to the tongue.

The final stage before packing and marketing processed tea is sorting, sifting and grad-

Green leaves are spread on withering tats, far left; after rolling, fermentation and firing, they are graded, left. Above, a handful of the final product: black tea.

gold color and are known as "tips." Any grade that contains a large number (a "show") of tips is prefixed by the word "flowery." Orange Pekoe is characterized by the long wiry twisted appearance of the processed leaves. The percentage of turnout of these grades in a factory is very small, and as such they fetch premium prices at the tea auctions. The record price for a "flowery" grade in Sri Lanka is Rs 3000 (US$414) per kilogram.

Tea Marketing: The marketing of tea in Sri Lanka is highly organized. The tea trade comes under the Tea Board, Ministry of Trade and Commerce. Under the jurisdiction of this board are two high-ranking government officers: the

Commissioner of Tea Exports and the Tea Controller. The former looks into all aspects related to tea exports while the latter handles all matters pertaining to tea estates and their production. The tea trade involves the sellers (that is, the agency houses or proprietors of estates), the brokers and the buyers.

Since the 1975 land reform in Sri Lanka, most foreign agency houses have ceased to exist and only a handful of proprietory estates still functions. The largest seller of tea in the country today is the state. A large sector of these government estates is looked after by two organizations: the Sri Lanka State Plantations Corporation and the Janatha Estates Development Board. Both are organized in a similar vein to the old agency houses. The other state organizations that administer a few estates each are the Tea Small Holders Development Authority, Estate Management Services Land Reform Commission, and local cooperatives.

By law, all teas produced in factories must be sold through a broker at the Colombo auctions. But with permission of the Tea Board, a producer could send his produce to the London auctions at Mincing Lane through a London broker. The Colombo auctions are held at the Ceylon Chamber of Commerce every Monday and Tuesday. Three weeks prior to the auctions, brokers furnish buyers with copies of their catalogs of tea on offer, together with samples. the bidding at the auctions is brisk: about three lots are "knocked down" by the auctioneer every minute. There are provisions for brokers to sell certain teas of very high quality on a private-sale basis. This is done with the assistance of a second broker who has to certify the valuation given by the appointed broker before the tea can be sold to an exporter. This exercise is permitted so that an exporter can get the tea in the shortest possible time after manufacture. The auction system usually takes about four weeks from factory to buyer.

Tea Tasting and Exporting: In tea tasting, about three grams of processed tea are measured into a quarter-pint pot. This is filled with just-boiled water and left for six minutes. The tea liquor is then poured out into a cup of the same capacity and the infused leaves are turned out into the cap of the pot for examination. The tea taster takes into account the black leaves, the infused leaves and the liquor.

Tea tasting is done by all three parties of the trade. The producer tastes his tea purely for information as to the quality of his product.

Some of the bigger organizations have tasters to advise their estates on certain aspects of manufacture. The most important tasting is done by the broker. He is always in contact with both seller and buyer. After tasting samples received from the estates he is handling, he is able to advise buyers as to what quality teas will be available to them during the coming weeks or months, and also advise the producers as to buyers' requirements during a certain period, so that they may adjust their manufacture to meet the demand.

A taster with a well-trained palate can immediately determine any error in the tea-manufacture process, and may even be able to pinpoint the precise point of error.

The broker also tastes his tea for proper pricing at the auctions. Valuations are based on the previous week's prices and current market trends. Tasting done by the buyer is for valuing the broker's samples before purchasing and for blending teas for packing and export.

Sri Lankan teas reach many parts of the globe. Some of her biggest buyers are England, the United States, the Soviet Union, Canada, South Africa, Iraq, Egypt, Pakistan, Japan, Australia, Iran and Libya. Sri Lanka exports her teas both in bulk form and in packets, and in recent years in tea bags. Bulk tea is shipped either blended or in "straight lines" (un-blended), but packeted teas are always blended.

Tea, being a highly hydroscopic product that absorbs moisture very quickly, must be carefully stored. It must be kept in a cool, dry place, in a bottle with the cap tightly screwed on. When the bottle is opened, the cap must be replaced at the earliest possible moment. If these few rules are observed, the tea will keep well and provide you with many a cheerful cup.

It was the cheerful cup that made tea practically synonymous with Ceylon soon after James Taylor introduced it to the island. Before the end of the 19th Century, people had begun to sing its praises. America's Mark Twain cruised into Ceylon in 1896 to find that tea had turned into big business. As Twain noted in his journal *Following the Equator: A Journey Around the World:* "Tea-planting is the great business in Ceylon, now. A passenger says it often pays 40 percent on the investment. Says there is a boom."

The manager of a tea estate near Watagoda thoughtfully savors samples of his product to determine quality and sellability.

A TASTE OF RICE AND CURRY

When in Sri Lanka, you eat what the Sri Lankans eat: rice and curry. Although Western influence has crept into the palate of the people in Colombo and the island's other large towns, villagers in the more remote areas still continue to eat the traditional three plates of rice a day – said to give them health, strength and energy. It is a popular belief that if you forego any of your daily portion, you will become weak and lethargic!

On the whole, the food here, like that of so many other Southeast Asian countries, has absorbed much from its traders and conquerors. The island's rich heritage of indigenous dishes has been enhanced by the Dutch, Portuguese, British, Malays, Arabs and South Indians, who passed through this beautiful country leaving behind their own recipes, spices, herbs and methods of cooking.

Some old Dutch and Portuguese foods like *bolo fiado* (laminated cake), *broeder*, (Dutch Christmas cake) and *boroa* (semolina biscuits) are now very much a part of the Sri Lankan cuisine.

Other ethnic groups have made their own special contributions like the Muslim *buriyani* (special rice cooked in meat stock) and *wattalapam* (coconut milk pudding), and the Tamil *thosai* (pancakes) and *vade* (spicy doughnuts).

Rice and Curry, Curry and Rice: Rice and curry, however, still comprises the main meal in almost every Sri Lankan household. A complete meal of rice and curry consists generally of a plate full of rice with spoonfuls of various curries and *sambol* heaped upon it.

Curries come in a variety of colors and flavors. As all Sri Lankan meats, fish, vegetables and even eggs are curried, they are named after their seasonings rather than their main ingredients.

Curries are cooked in coconut milk. The white kernel of the coconut is grated with a *hiramane* (a serated metal disc fixed on a wooden bench), mixed with a little water, then squeezed, yielding a first squeezing called the *mitikiri* (thick milk) and two subsequent

A single ripe red chili nestles in a sea of green. Chilies are one of the prime ingredients in the spicy Sri Lankan curries.

squeezings of *diyakiri* (thin milk). The quantities of thick and thin milk to be used during preparation differ according to whether you want your curry to be mild, creamy, thick, thin or dry. There are creamy white curries (non-spicy), brown curries (using raw curry powder), bright red curries (fiery hot with plenty of pounded dried red chilies), and black curries which appeal more to the taste buds than the vision.

Most Sri Lankan housewives make their own curry powder, as the ready-mixed ones in the markets are often adulterated. Curry powder is a roasted and ground mix of fennel seed, coriander, cumin, turmeric, black and red pepper, mustard, cardamom, cloves, curry and bay leaves, cinnamon, fenugreek and a little raw rice.

Traditionally, food was cooked in a clay (*chutty*) over a glowing wood fire. This method gives curries a rich, subtle, earthy flavor. Metal pans, however, are fast replacing the *chutty* today.

With the curries comes *mallung*, a mild and nutritive addition to the diet. It is made of finely shredded green vegetables and (in some areas) dried shrimps, mixed with grated coconut and spices.

Spicy Sambols: *Sambol* is a very popular dish among locals, though foreigners may find the dish too hot and spicy for their tongues. This dish is commonly known as "rice puller," as it whets the appetite of those used to spicy foods. *Pol sambol* (coconut *sambol*), one of the most popular of *sambols*, is a simple preparation of grated coconut and plenty of red pepper, onions, lime, salt and slivers of Maldive fish. Maldive fish is a hard, fermented, sun-dried fillet of tuna that enhances the flavor of the *pol sambol*. As this has over the years become an expensive ingredient, it is not always used nowadays.

Papadams (crispy fried wafers), pickles and chutneys are also popular in a normal meal of rice and curry. Mango and amberella chutney, and date and lime pickle, are other all-time favorites.

Sri Lanka is the home of over 15 varieties of rice, each differing in shape, taste and color. There are short-grained rice, the long-grained and fat-grained varieties, and tiny round pearl-like grains. The color of rice varies from shades of white to burgundy. The most common way of preparing rice is by boiling.

On special occasions, one is treated to yellow rice - cooked in coconut milk and delicately flavored with spices. Turmeric is added to make the rice a bright yellow; it is served garnished with cashews, raisins and hard-boiled eggs.

Lamprais, a name derived from the Dutch word *lomprijst*, is another special dish commonly served at parties. The rice is cooked in stock. Curries, *sambols*, cutlets, a special prawn paste and eggplant curry are placed around the rice, which is wrapped in a banana leaf and baked. *Lamprais* has a unique flavor and an appetizing aroma.

and sweeter varieties like *vandupappa* and *paniappa*.

Another popular breakfast dish is a rice preparation known as *indiappa* or string hoppers. These are small strings of rice-flour dough squeezed through a sieve onto a small woven tray. The strands are placed on trays and steamed one-atop-the-other over a low fire. It is easy to eat at least 10 string hoppers at a meal.

Pittu is another local preparation. Rice flour, coconut and water are mixed into small dry lumps, packed into a bamboo mold and steamed. These tubes of *pittu* are served warm with coconut milk and curry.

Roti is a substitute for rice. These flat breads are made of a dough prepared from flour,

The Sri lankan cuisine offers a wide choice of breakfast dishes, too. Most popular are the *appa* (hoppers). These thin cup-shaped pancakes are made from fermented batter of rice flour, coconut milk and a dash of palm toddy.

The hopper pan is a deep iron dish with two handles, like a small Chinese *wok*. A coconut-shell spoonful of the batter is poured into the hot pan, which is rotated over the fire making sure that a thin coat of batter covers the upper half of the pan. The pan is then covered and the hopper baked for a couple of minutes.

A hopper, crispy on the outside, soft and spongy in the center, is best eaten with curries and *bithara* (egg) hoppers, *kiri* (milk) hoppers,

coconut, water and a dash of salt, cooked in dry pan and eaten with curry.

A simple preparation of rice cooked in coconut milk called *kiribath* (milk rice) is one of the traditions of the Sinhalese. On New Year's Day and the first day of each month, *kiribath* is a "must" for breakfast.

It is usually eaten with a hot *sambol*, but some prefer it with *pani pol* – a sweet made with grated jaggery (an unrefined brown sugar made from palm sap), coconut and a touch of vanilla flavoring.

Sri Lankan food is best eaten with your fingers using rice, string hoppers, *pittu*, hoppers and *roti* to mop up the different curries.

Fruits and Sweets: Desserts in Sri Lanka usually comprise fresh fruits. Sri Lanka is the home of a variety of tropical fruits. Succulent pineapples and papayas are among the most commonly eaten fruits, along with a numerous variety of bananas.

Seasonal fruits like the furry rambutans, sapodillas, mangosteens and infamous durians are abundant throughout the land. Avocados, ripe *jak* and all kinds of mangoes have more than one season a year. The sweetest mangoes and ripe *jak* come from Jaffna, where the hot dry weather does something special to them. Other indigenous fruits include oranges, grapefruits, limes, tangerines, guavas, jambus, passion fruits and woodapples.

Sri Lanka boasts a large assortment of *rasakevilis* (sweetmeats) which are served on special occasions. Most of them are very sticky and rich.

Made with batters of rice flour, coconut milk or jaggery, preparation of these sweetmeats takes a lot of time, energy and expertise. Some are prepared in special molds while others are shaped at the time of frying.

A very popular sweet is the *thalaguli* (sesame

Left, eight separate dishes traditionally accompany rice in a curry meal – which is almost always eaten with the fingers. Above, making proper hoppers is an art of fine cookery.

ball), of which the tastiest are perhaps, made at Jinadasa's. This small shop in Warakapola, halfway between Colombo and Kandy, is easily recognised by its smoking chimneys and the long line of vehicles that stop to patronize it.

Other sweetmeats include *halapes*, a mixture of coconut, jaggery and *kurakkan* flour; *dadols* and *aluwas*, fudge-like sweets; and *puhul dosi*, pumpkin preserves.

A wide variety of Indian sweets can be purchased at the numerous sweet shops lining the streets of Colombo and Kandy. These include *panivalalu* (honey bangles), *muscat* (oily sweet fudge), *gulab* jam and *rasagullas* (milk balls in sugar syrup).

Bibikan is a traditional Sinhalese cake made of rice flour, jaggery, coconut, cashews and dried fruit. *Wattalapam* is a rich pudding made of coconut milk, jaggery, cashew nuts, eggs, and various spices including cinnamon, cloves and nutmeg.

But the traditional favorite dessert is curd and treacle, said to be tastiest in the Weligama region, where open-air curd stalls line the highway. Thick buffalo curd (yogurt) is topped with the syrup of the *kitul* or coconut palm and savored.

Satisfying a Thirst: The most refreshing of local drinks is the *thambili*, or King Coconut. This bright orange coconut is full of sweet water. It can be taken plain, or sweetened with sugar, lime and a pinch of salt.

The local alcoholic favorite is made from the coconut sap known as "toddy." Villagers often consume it in its undistilled form fermented with yeast. Before fermentation, it is a refreshing, non-alcoholic drink called *thelijja*. Distilled *arrack* is sold commercially in liquor shops, bars and other outlets.

Local beers are of excellent quality. Mostly brewed in Nuwara Eliya, they were developed under the direction of Europeans during the British colonial period. Foreign liquors are also available in most restaurants.

Water is served with meals, although tea is of course the most popular drink. In combination with ginger or jaggery, it is unique and delicious. Herb teas, including coriander, fenugreek and garlic, are drunk for different illnesses.

In Sri Lanka, as in most countries, the most traditional food is cooked in the villages. Getting recipes is impossible, as no two women cook exactly alike, and no one measures ingredients. On this small island, the variety of foods available make eating a true pleasure.

The waters of Sri Lanka – saltwater, brackish and fresh – are as rich and varied in undersea life as any in the world. Equipped with only a face mask, a person can dive in bracing clear green rivers in wet forests. He can explore tidal lagoons where the crystal sea of the East Coast flows up estuaries and reveals a new world of mangroves, oyster-covered rocks and large edible crabs.

But it is the blue waters of the Indian Ocean that are Sri Lanka's premier diving attraction. Coral reefs and offshore ship-wrecks harbor a

the closest town to the International Airport, we will travel counter clockwise along the coast, exploring diving spots en route.

Negombo, from November till March, offers surprisingly good diving. Do not expect continuous clear water every day of the five months. The strong currents, heavy rainfall, and the nearby presence of a lagoon rich in silt and plankton, cause periodic turbidity. But this contributes to the fact that Negombo offers the finest seafood in the country. The young and energetic often spear barracudas, queenfish,

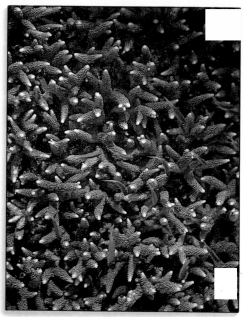

new world of breathtaking clarity. There are sensational fish and sand-stone formations in the Great and Little Basses reefs. And a foray off Negombo will bring about close encounters with sizeable and exciting game fishes.

It is important to know the best times of the year to visit these spots, as clarity of surrounding waters changes periodically according to monsoon seasons and other prevailing weather conditions. A rewarding diving expedition to Sri Lanka needs careful timing, patience and understanding. But the end result, whether you are photographing, collecting, fishing or just experiencing, is well worth it.

A Tour of the Island: Starting from Negombo,

caranx or hefty estuary perch without breathing gear. Lobster-grabbing can be done by night with a flashlight and strong gloves. For the camera, seek waters further out if the reefs are not clear enough. But if the preference is for close-ups, there are a few hundred subjects to click on the reef itself.

A few miles down the coast near Kapungoda (about two hours away by speedboat), there are two shallow shipwrecks which are treasure troves of invertebrates, lobsters and snappers. You may troll a line for that occasional hungry barracuda, too small (in this region) to be dangerous to human beings. A 25-pounder is considered a very big fish and he will hit a bait quite obligingly, especially in the evening.

Colombo was the very first dive site when face masks, snorkels and flippers came to Sri Lanka's shores in the pre-World War Two days. It is quite changed now, in every way. Good diving is now out at sea where the strong currents bring in clear water. Excellent spots for diving and hunting are a reef off south Colombo, where migrant schools of queenfish, caranx, barracuda and Spanish mackerel swim; and another reef more than a mile offshore, where some exciting (and perfectly harmless)

For a dive that is different, have yourself taken inland to a place called Badureliva, then to Atweltota where you can explore a lovely jungle rock pool with clear green waters, sunken long rocks, aquatic plants and some lovely little tropical freshwater fishes. Not to mention the fine rainforest around you, gentle friendly people, and an atmosphere far removed from that of a beach hotel.

Back on the coast, further south is Ambalangoda. At most times of the year, it is not absolutely clear because of a creek mouth

gray sharks show up occasionally.

A dive off the famous Mount Lavinia beach (only on the calmest days, though) will bring you face-to-face with a variety of photogenic fishes, the loveliest and commonest being the blue ring angels.

Further south is Beruwala. The rocky island off the Bentota hotel complex is quite an interesting dive spot with large parrot fish, snappers and other reef dwellers.

Preceding pages: a shoal of silver sardinella. Left to right, the colorful world of coral – Dendrophyllia, Staghorn Acropora, Goniopora and Cabbage Coral.

close by. But there are some really good calm days in January and February. You will pass a headland with fringing coral reef and sea breakers about a half-mile or so seawards at Akurala, which offers splendid rock and reef diving, two shipwrecks and an abundance of fishes.

Hikkaduwa, the famous diving center of the southwest coast, has unfortunately been "overdived." The fishes are nervous and confused. Using Hikkaduwa as a base, instead dive Dodanduwa further south and the marvelous rocky reefs off Gintota, Medagala and Ralagala, perhaps the greatest diving on the west coast. Medagala is not easily found, though, as the highest point does not break in calm weather.

Although much can be seen and enjoyed with a snorkel, tank-diving to the *Malabar* shipwreck, 60 to 80 feet deep on a rock reef, is a welcome adventure to those who are keen underwater photographers.

Galle Harbour is the perfect take-off point to enjoy some fine diving north at Alugala, which provides a new wreck to explore. Diving off the Koggala coast is not recommended unless you are a strong swimmer. But Weligama and its surroundings can be excellent. There are several rock and coral reefs to explore, especially off Mirissa with its teeming fishermen and boats.

Matara, a few miles from the southern-most tip of Sri Lanka at Dondra, provides diving only in February and March when drought can make the nearby Niwala River less turbid, enabling you to see some fine fish over the reef. Tangalla, which is beautifully located, has fine diving; but too often the sea gets over-lively. One of the better spots is Kupatha, a small rocky islet visible from the Tangalla rest house, haunted by huge schools of parrot fish, sweetlip and snappers.

The Incredible Basses Reefs: For the greatest diving in all Sri Lanka, check your map for the Great and Little Basses reefs off the Ruhuna National Park at Yala. Each of the rocky outcrops has a lighthouse on it and the reefs surrounding them are sandstone, carved into incredible formations by prehistoric seismic action and the more recent force of the waves and currents. At least four shipwrecks litter these reefs, one of them just a few years old, and another over 300.

But it is the fish you must see, hundreds and thousands of them, in almost constant gin-clear water. The larger creatures range from porpoises, sharks (harmless ones), dog-toothed tunas, groupers, huge carnax and snappers. But there are also thousands of small grunts, angelfish, sweetlips, skates and rays.

The one constraint is that it is so often rough and the currents so compelling that fewer than 50 days per year are available for diving in comfort. These fall around early March to mid-April; perhaps you also have fortnight in October when the monsoons change.

Arugam Bay could be your next stop. From here, rather breathless diving can be arranged. But it is better to move north now, along the East Coast till you reach a spot called Tirrukovil. Here you can be taken out to a wreck on the reef. All the reefs from here to Batticaloa make good diving, but it is hard to reach them if you are land-based with limited gear.

No major hotels are permitted south of Kalkudah so that accommodation is a problem on shore that there is a total lack of diving gear for rent. Nonetheless, Batticaloa has fishing boats and small fiberglass outboards for rent; they will take you through the mouth of the lagoon to some wonderful reefs and wrecks.

The Hermes Wreck: On the East Coast is Passekudah, just off Kalkudah, where there are several hotels and accommodation of all forms to suit all purses. Fabulous spots for diving include the wrecks just around the bay, nice coral islands up north, and the unparalleled

dive to the wreck of the British carrier *Hermes* in 180 feet of water.

Nowhere else within just five miles of land can you visit a wreck of this size with a fish population to boggle the mind. This dive is for the most experienced and best-trained divers; it is dangerously exciting but the dive of a lifetime. Some of the *Hermes* explorers include great divers like Peter Gimbel, Stan Waterman, Ron and Valerie Taylor, and Reg Vallintine.

It is not always easy to negotiate the several ferries on the road north to Trincomalee along the coast. A surer way is to be driven inland, first to Habarana and then to Trincomalee, a very large diving resort indeed. Dozens of bays, rocky islands and coral reefs mingle with spectacular rocky cliffs underwater and above.

There are rock inscriptions underwater off Fort Frederick, some fine drop-off dives near Rocky Point, the remains of a Portuguese galleon off Elephant Island, great shelling on the sand and rocks, corals at almost every spot you dive, and some beautiful tropical fish in the more current-swept rocky outcrops like Chapel Rocks.

Trincomalee is good from mid-March till September, except for a poor spell of green water, jellyfish and some chilly currents in June to July. April is by far the best month for the entire East Coast.

small fishing camps. In late January until the end of March, *beche de mer* and chank (conch) divers gather here.

The Bar Reef: To dive off Kalpitiya, which lies south on a peninsula, you must drive up from Negombo and organize a boat from Kalpitiya town to take you north and then west through a small gap into the open sea. Here is the beautiful Bar Reef, a coral wonderland and the closest thing to the Maldivian formations you will get in this country.

If you go to the teeming fishing village of Kandakuliya, just south of Kalpitiya, the small hotel there is a nice take-off spot to dive two fine reefs north and west. Do this only in October and February; at other times, these

Along the road south from Giant's Tank is Silavaturai. A few miles due west are the famed Pearl Banks. If you can find professional divers as guides, these still are worth a visit to see pearl oysters as well as a number of quite large crayfish.

At the end of the road is Marichchukadi, the site of the former colonial Pearl Fishery. An old British circuit bungalow still stands on the acacia-studded dunes – down by the beach are

Colorful reef fishes flourish in the waters surrounding Sri Lanka. This butterfly fish, left and wrasse, right were photographed in the rocky reefs off the South Coast near Hikkaduwa.

waters are affected by both monsoons and tend to get turbid.

From here south are sandstone reefs, not always clear but known to fishermen. At least one airplane wreck is reported off Katuneriya and perhaps a small ship or two.

Moving further south, you will encounter Negombo reef again off the mouth of the Maha Oya return river. We thus return to where we started this diving trip.

In this volume's "Travel Tips" section is a list of diving suggestions and the names of a few reputable underwater outfits through whom equipment can be rented and excursions arranged.

... Ordering by the beat of drum that no animals should be killed within a radius of seven gau from the city, he gave security to animals. He also gave security to the fish in the 12 great tanks, and bestowing on (the region's people) gold and cloth and whatever other kind of wealth they wished, he commanded them not to catch birds and so gave security to birds ...

This inscription, engraved in an upright stone slab at Anuradhapura's great *dagoba* of

her rich and varied wildlife and her equally rich and varied jungles. One-tenth of the island's entire land area comes under the jurisdiction of the Department of Wild Life Conservation, which administrates and serves as the primary authority on all matters concerning wilderness areas and their fauna.

All wilderness in Sri Lanka is called "jungle." It includes the semi-arid thorn-brush country and mangroves of coastal areas; the deeply forested dry zone of the North Central Province; the marshy mosquito-infested glades

Ruwanweli, is a transcript of a decree issued in the late 12th Century by King Kirthi Nissanka Malla of Polonnaruwa. It is testimony to the long-standing concern of Sri Lanka's people with the conservation of their rich wildlife.

Similarly, scattered through the pages of the *Mahavamsa*, the ancient chronicle of the Sinhalese people, are other records of royal protection for all forms of animal life. Perhaps the religious fervor which gripped the ancient Buddhist kings who ruled the land was to account for this concern. Whatever the reason, the theme of preservation has carried through to the present day.

Indeed, two of Sri Lanka's "purest gems" are

of the Mahaweli basin; the dry hills of Kantalai; and the fern-filled, dripping rainforests of the Hill Country. Within these varied landscapes are many unique species of animals and plants.

The National Parks: Most of the wildlife of the island is concentrated in national parks, the two primary ones being Ruhuna and Wilpattu. The former, more popularly known as Yala, is tucked away in the southeastern corner of the map. It is mainly thorny scrub forest, reminiscent of the African bush, and provides the visitor's best bet for seeing elephants. Some time ago, spotting a leopard or bear at Yala was only a remote possibility; but in recent years these animals have increased in the park and are now frequently sighted.

The best time for a visit is between December and May. There are scattered rain showers early in the year, but also large herds of elephants with calves during this period. A special entertainment at this time is the splendid mating dance of the beautiful peacock – a sight worth going a long way to witness.

Wilpattu National Park lies on the West Coast and is mainly thick secondary forest. One of the unique features of the topography of the park is the concentration of *villus*, basin-like natural tanks, where large flocks of water birds and herds of wild animals come to quench their thirst. These *villus* are also the home of crocodiles.

Unlike semi-arid Yala, the scenery here is more lush, and wide changes of vegetation can be experienced in different sections of the park. But the roads are fairly rough and the visitor is well advised to take a four-wheel drive vehicle if he wishes to see the better part of it.

Wilpattu is famous for its leopards and bears, but the visitor can consider himself very fortunate if he sees any elephants. During the last few years, however, sightings have increased. The big pachyderms seem to have found their way in numbers to this protected area, as surrounding forests have been opened out in large extent for cultivation. Herds of deer, and *sambhur* (elk) in groups of twos and threes, can easily be seen in the park. The best time to visit is between February and October.

Wilpattu is closed for the entire month of September, while Ruhuna shuts its gates from the first of August until mid-October.

Life in a Bungalow: Both Ruhuna and Wilpattu have many little bungalows where visitors can stay overnight. Most of these are reserved for Sri Lankan residents, however. Only two bungalows in each park are given out to tourists. In Yala, these are the Patanangala bungalow by the beach and the Heenwewa bungalow close to a jungle tank. In Wilpattu, they are the Panikkar Villu and the Mana villu bungalows, both by the sides of *villus* and both in prime

Preceding pages: a leopard yawns at Wilpattu; cross-tusked elephant charges near Yala; and a venomous cobra spreads its hood. Left, a close encounter in Ruhuna National Park.

game areas. Reservations can be made at the Department of Wild Life Conservation within three months of the date of occupation.

Life in these bungalows is a blend of rustic living with a few modern comforts. Basic facilities like linen, cutlery and crockery are provided; but visitors must take their own food, to be prepared by the bungalow keeper and his assistant. They are usually expert cooks, especially of tasty Sri Lankan curries prepared in the traditional village style.

None of these bungalows has electricity. Illumination is by kerosene lamps and lanterns. These definitely add to the jungle atmosphere, which undoubtedly would have been marred by electric lights. The bungalow visitor can stay up late into the evening listening to the sound of the jungle and its denizens – a fascinating experience difficult to describe. Sometimes large herds of deer, wild boar and even elephants wander very close. Occasionally, at Wilpattu, even a leopard or bear may be seen from the wildlife bungalow.

Visitors to the parks are always accompanied by a guide commonly called a "tracker." Most trackers have a fairly good knowledge of the jungle and its ways, and turn out to be very interesting companions.

Day visitors have the choice of seeing the parks either by morning or evening. Two buses leave the offices at the entrances to the parks, one at 6 a.m. and the other at 3:30 p.m. daily. A 2½ hour bus ride in either park can turn out to be a memorable experience, especially if a wild elephant or leopard is seen.

Where Elephants Come to Dine: Three other national parks in the island are Gal Oya, Uda Walawe and Lahugala. Gal Oya, inland from the East Coast near Amparai, mainly offers boating in the vast Senanayake Samudra tank where large herds of elephants come to drink and bathe during the evening hours. With some luck, one might even seen the great beasts swimming across the deep water to islands where they feed on lush grass.

Uda Walawe is the most recent national park. It is situated around a reservoir of the same name in the south central area of the island. Game, however, is still timid and wary of visitors – and is not easily seen.

Lahugala is a large tank situated 14 miles

inland of Pottuvil in the southeast coastal region. It lies in the centre of a jungle elephant passage that connects the Gal Oya range to the Southern (Yala) range. Occupying almost the entire tank is a tall reed-like grass known as *beru* or elephant grass, a favorite taste treat of its namesakes. There is hardly a day in the year that one fails to see elephants at Lahugala. However, the Department of Wild Life does not encourage visitors to stay over at Lahugala, as this would mean disturbing the animals at a crucial point on the narrow passage between the two ranges.

In addition to national parks, there are strict natural reserves, where only scientific expeditions are permitted; and game sanctuaries and

game reserves, where all animal life is protected but pre-existing human habitations are permitted – so long as present boundaries are not expanded and new living abodes are not constructed.

Tuskers and leopards: The elephant found in Sri Lanka is the same sub-species found in all of Asia. It is widely distributed throughout the island. A sub-variety called the marsh elephant is much larger than its cousin, but is confined to the floodplain of the Mahweli river. A herd of marsh elephants on the march is one of Sri Lanka's grandest sights.

The American crusader who trumpeted the resurgence of Buddhism in Ceylon during the last century, Henry Steel Olcott, recorded his delight at encountering elephants in his *Old Diary Leaves* of 1878:

"As I strolled down the road that passes through the town I met a string of tamed elephants with their mahouts, and stopped to pay them some agreeable civilities. I fed them with coconuts bought at a neighbouring stall, and patted their trunks and spoke friendly to them after the fashion of the wise."

Even at the turn of the 20th Century, Sri Lanka still had a fair number of tuskers among its wild elephants. However, due to heavy hunting for ivory, the tusker today is a very rare sight. In the 1960s, the elephant was an endangered species in the country. Strict laws and better wildlife management have enabled it to make a few steps toward recovery.

The magnificent spotted leopard is widely distributed around the island, but is not easily seen due to its nocturnal proclivities and its preference to keep away from human habitation. This, however, does not prevent it from occasionally prowling the perimeter of a jungle village hoping to get hold of a dog – believed to be its favorite change in diet. The best bet on seeing a leopard is in Wilpattu between February and May. Here, these felines have become used to cars, and may give the visitor a treat by rolling in the sand and playing. Special fare would be a leopardess with a cub or two.

Two man-eating leopards have been officially recorded in Sir Lanka. The most famous was known as the Man-eater of Punani, after a little hamlet on the Polonnaruwa-Valachchenai (Batticaloa) road. She was shot in 1923 with 20 recorded human kills; her mounted carcass can still be seen at the National Museum in Colombo. Another killer; the Kataragam Man-eater, preyed on pilgrims earlier in the 20th Century.

But the animal most dreaded by jungle village folk is the sloth bear – the only species of bear found here – because of its unpredictability. It is a big black shaggy creature with long coarse hair and a light-colored bony snout, with which it sucks up termites from their holes like a vacuum cleaner. Normally a vegetarian, it will readily consume carrion if easily come by. Bees' honey, however, is its favorite diet. A peaceful and gentle creature by nature, it will attack with savage ferocity if provoked, surprised or defending young cubs. A casual visitor to the island would be very fortunate to see a bear in its natural surroundings; but it can be found in the national parks, particularly at Wilpattu, between the months of June and August when the *palu* and *weera* fruits are in season.

Other Jungle Denizens: Four species of deer can be seen in the island: the *sambhur* (elk), spotted deer, barking deer and mouse deer. The *sambhur*, a dark brown animal standing around five feet at the shoulder, is the largest and handsomest. The spotted deer is smaller and lighter in color and is by far the most common in the jungle. Right throughout the year it can be seen in large herds, especially in the national parks. The other two varieties are very rarely seen due to the shy natures. However, if one is patient enough to spend some time quietly at a

to the large flaps of loose skin between its fore and hind feet which enable it to sail from one tree to another.

Two widespread species of monkey very easily seen in the jungle areas are the gray langur and the macaque or red monkey. The big langur is usually shy and docile. Gray with a jet-black face, it lives in large groups among the trees, often coming down to feed. The macaque is a brownish ape with a pink face; it is far more aggressive then the langur. There have been instances where the quick-tempered macaque has attacked humans, so visitors are well advised not to annoy these creatures.

Confined to the hills is a very smart ape known as the bear monkey or purple-faced leaf

water hole, there is a chance of seeing one of them very warily coming down to drink.

Among the other game are the wild boar and the wild buffalo. They are both strong animals and are held in deep respect by man as well as by other wild beasts. Even a great predator like the leopard would rarely, if ever, take on a full-grown boar or buffalo. Among the smaller game are the jungle cat, fishing cat, jackal, hare and three varieties of giant or rock squirrel. There is also the flying squirrel, so called due

Left, a black-faced grey langur sits atop a Tissamaharama fencepost. **Right,** a spotted deer stag begins his getaway in Wilpattu.

monkey. Its face is exactly the color, with a large white beard on its chin and cheeks. A visitor is indeed very lucky to see one of them, but during certain times of the year fairly large groups may be seen at World's End in the Horton Plains area.

The crocodile is the largest of Sri Lankan reptiles. It is found in almost all the jungle tanks and waterways. Most crocodiles are extremely shy and cause very little bother to humans, but the occasional man-eater is found. At the moment, one such creature is operating in a tributary of the Mahaweli River in Verugal, off the East Coast. Two other Sir Lankan reptiles are the water monitor, found in the foothills near Kandy and the riverine areas of the dry zone; and the widespread iguana, a tree-climbing insect eater.

Only a few of the large variety of snakes found in the island are poisonous. These include the cobra, the drait, the russel's viper and a little pinkish fellow known as *boiga forsteni*. All four are very aggressive and the first three are deadly. Poisonous or otherwise, snakes are hardly every seen in the jungles, for they choose to stay well-hidden in the bush, preferring the cool of the undergrowth to the heat of the open. The largest snake in the island is the python, a non-poisonous constrictor. It is fairly common in Wilpattu National Park.

Though the occasional snake bite is reported from remote jungle villages, the visitor should

with its loud raucous cawing. The little house sparrow is found in most homes, nesting among the roof tiles or in little pots kept especially for this purpose by residents who consider it lucky. The chocolate-colored mynah, an intelligent and aggressive bird, and the black-and-white magpie robin, a beautiful songster, also seem to prefer the clamor or town and village to the quiet of the forest.

Birds that are equally at home amidst humans or in the lonely jungles are the koel, coucal or crow pheasant, broad-billed roller, black-headed and golden orioles, barbet, many types of parrots, parakeets and lorikeets, and (if one has a large pond) the kingfisher, red-wattled lapwing and pond heron.

not worry about serpents, especially if he keeps to the beaten track. However, if the more bold and adventurous person should decide to take a walk around the forest, he should keep an eye open for piles of dried leaves and clumps of tall dried grass which are best avoided.

Bird Watchers' Paradise: It takes the visitor only a few miles of travel, or perhaps only a short walk in town or country, to be convinced that Sir Lanka is a paradise for the bird watcher. There are more than 400 species found here, indigenous varieties as well as migrants.

Among the birds inhabiting the more urban and populated areas is the stockily built crow, inevitably the first bird to greet new arrivals

The vast majority of birds, and also the prettiest, prefer the wooded regions. Most of them are widely distributed, spreading from the lowlands to the foothills and on to the mountains.

The beautiful peacock and the flashy jungle fowl, short-flighted primary birds, are both confined to the low country and foothills. A few birds found in this region are the haunting whistler, the elusive yellow-green Ceylon iora, the wedge-tailed drongo, the paddy bird, and that classic songbird, the orange and black long-tailed shama. Among the birds of prey are the Brahiminy kite, the serpent eagle and the majestic white-bellied sea eagle.

Some varieties are confined only to the hills. These include the pretty little bush chat, the dusky-blue flycather and the azure flycatcher. The mountain hawk eagle, Sri Lanka's finest bird of prey, is also confined to the hills.

The best time to watch birds in the island is between the months of September and April, when thousands upon thousands of migrants arrive. A large number of migrants are water birds; among then are the flamingo, whimbrel, godwit, plovers and sandpipers of many varieties, duck, teal, and some herons. Land birds include the chestnut-headed bee-eater, the beautiful paradise flycatcher, the pitta, the eastern peregrine and the shabin falcon.

For a detailed survey of all the birds of Sri Lanka, the reader should consult G.M. Henry's *Guide to the Birds of Ceylon.*

The Battle Against Poachers: Stringent game laws not only forbid the shooting of all types of game (except wild boar), but also outlaw the transportation of carcasses and the possession of skins and other "trophies" without a permit. But an alarming amount of poaching still goes on. Recently the sale of game meat and skins has taken on a big commercial trend; this and the illicit felling of timber on a massive scale have taken a toll on Sri Lanka's forests and their inhabitants.

The animal that has suffered most is the leopard. In some parts of the country, this splendid but unfortunate cat is baited with poisoned meat in order that its pelt may be claimed unmarked.

The Department of Wild Life is plagued by poor facilities and a lack of adequate vehicles to effectively patrol the vast stretches of land that come under its jurisdiction. Enthusiasm and loyalty, however, are two things not lacking in field officials. In recent years, a number of game guards have lost their lives, and others have been seriously injured, while trying to arrest poachers on the borders of national parks.

The government has set in motion urgent measures to counter the various threats to wildlife and forests. More areas have been singled out to be proclaimed national parks, which can be more easily patrolled and looked after than open forest. Elephant drives have been carried out in an attempt to drive these

large beasts to protected areas. The theme of wildlife conservation in Sri Lanka was given an added impetus by the visit in early 1982 of the president of the World Wildlife Fund, H.R.H. Prince Philip, the Duke of Edinburgh. During his stay, he inaugurated the "Save the Elephant Fund," a permanent tax-free charity which is open to contributions from all over the world.

Many private bird clubs and nature conservation organizations have sprung up in recent times in Sri Lanka, and all have contributed to the cause. Schools, too, have taken up the theme. The oldest and most active organization, the Wild Life and Nature Protection Society of Ceylon, has given a real push to conserving

wildlife and the environment.

The feather in the society's cap is the successful setting-up of turtle hatcheries in several coastal areas. The society's hatchery at Kosgoda on the south coast has, in a short time, showed amazing results. Tens of thousands of tiny turtles have been helped to cross the little strip of sun-baked sand to the comparative safety of the open sea.

Sri Lankan wildlife still faces an uphill battle for survival, in the face of poaching, development schemes, and other signals of "progress." But the widespread awareness of the importance of preserving the jungle and its denizens gives true hope for the future.

Left, a large crocodile gapes at a trespasser in a jungle pool at Wilpattu. Right, pond flies are among the fastest reproducing of Sri Lanka's many creatures, large and small.

Gull Billed Tern ▲   ▼ Green Bee Eater

Common Sandpiper ▼   ▲ Little Minivet

Serpent Eagle ▲

Malabar Pied Hornbill ▲   ▼ *Spoonbill*

Bar Tailed Godwit ▲   ▼ *Red Wattled Lapwing*

TRAVEL TIPS

GETTING THERE

BY AIR

Most visitors arrive by air at Colombo International Airport. Also known as Katunayake International Airport, it is located near the town of Katunayake, 34 kilometers (21 miles) north of Colombo city. There is no other major international airport on the island.

Air Lanka (UL), the national carrier, provides service to and from Europe (Amsterdam, Frankfurt, London, Paris, Rome, Vienna, Zurich), the Middle East (Abu Dhabi, Bahrain, Beirut, Dhahran, Doha, Dubai, Muscat, Kuwait, Riyadh), India (Bombay, Madras, Tiruchirappalli, Trivandrum) Pakistan (Karachi) and East Asia (Bangkok, Hong Kong, Singapore, Kuala Lampur, Fukuoka, Tokyo). There are also daily flights to the Maldives (Male) and weekly flights to Australia (Sydney, Melbourne).

Other carriers serving Sri Lanka are Condor Airways (DF), for cargo and charters only; Gulf Air (GF); Indian Airlines (IC); KLM Royal Dutch Airlines (KL); Kuwait Airways (KU); Balair (BB); Emirate Airways (EK) LTU (LT); Pakistan International Airline (PK); Singapore Airlines (SQ); Aeroflot (SU); Thai International (TG); and UTA (UT). See Useful Addresses for the addresses of these airline companies.

BY SEA

Cruise ships are no longer the main means of transportation to Sri Lanka, but a number of cruise lines still call at her ports. Each cruise line sets its own schedule according to customer demands which vary from year to year. If you are interested in cruising to Sri Lanka, contact several travel agents and make arrangements through the one which has schedules and itineraries most appealing to you. Several liners stop on round-the-world cruises (such as P & O Lines and the Queen Elizabeth II), while others (such as CTC) offer regional cruises.

Some freighters offer limited passenger space. Check directly with the shipping lines for this option.

TRAVEL ESSENTIALS

VISAS & PASSPORTS

Nationals of the following countries coming to Sri Lanka as tourists do not require entry visas for a period of 30 days (a valid passport, however, has to be presented): Australia, Austria, Britian, and its colonies, Bangladesh, Belgium, Bahrain, Canada, Denmark, Eire, Federal Republic of Germany, Finland, France, Indonesia, Israel, Italy, Japan, South Korea, Kuwait, Luxembourg, Malaysia, Maldives, Netherlands, New Zealand, Norway, Oman, Pakistan, Philippines, Qatar, Singapore, Sweden, Switzerland, Saudi Arabia, Spain, Thailand, the United States, United Arab Emirates and Yugoslavia.

Visas should be obtained through a Sri Lankan Consular Office, or through a British Consular Office if there are no Sri Lankan offices. If you need to extend your stay in Sri Lanka, you must apply for a visa extension in Colombo. Go to the Department of Immigration and Emigration, Unit 6, Galle Buck Road, Colombo 1, Tel: 29851, 21509. Conditions for extensions are a return or onward ticket and sufficient money for maintenance in the island at US$15 per day.

MONEY MATTER

CURRENCY RESTRICTIONS

Upon arrival in Sri Lanka, visitors are required to declare the amount of all foreign currency in their possession on the official Exchange Control Form D which is attached to the landing card. Keep this card with you as it is required to exchange foreign currency

The Bank Who Cares for your business.

BANK DAGANG NEGARA
(STATE COMMERCIAL BANK)

HEAD OFFICE : Jl. M.H. Thamrin No. 5, Jakarta   Phone : 321707, 3800800,
P.O. Box : 338/JKT Jakarta 10002, INDONESIA
Telex : 61628 BDNULN IA, 61649 BDNULN IA, 61621 BDNLN JKT, 61640 BDN F X IA.

OVERSEAS OFFICES :

NEW YORK (AGENCY) &
CAYMAN ISLANDS (BRANCH)
45 Broadway Atrium 30th floor
New York, N.Y. 10006,
U S A
Telex :   226698 BDN NYUR
          226690 BDN NYUR

LOS ANGELES (AGENCY)
3457 Wilshire Boulevard
Los Angeles, C.A. 90010
U S A
Telex :   3716724 BDN LA USAG
          3716705 BDN LA USAG

HONG KONG (REPRESENTATIVE) &
STACO INTERNATIONAL FINANCE LTD
6/F Admiralty Centre Tower II
Queensway, Victoria
Hong Kong
Telex :   60322 BDN – HX
          60323 BDN FX – HX

SINGAPORE (REPRESENTATIVE)
50 Raffles Place 13-05
Shell Tower, Singapore 0104
Telex : DAGANG RS 24939

Explore the World with

Whether you are relax
in Australia, exploring
cities in Europe, or dis
attractions in Asia, Ro
you a wonderful select
at very reasonable cost

Created more than
Holidays and Refreshe
bothersome details, inc
dation, air travel and s

The success of Roy
combined with long-es
connections, enable us
discounts, which we p

To enjoy your plac
sun, or wherever your
desires, contact your
local Thai office.

Thai
Smooth as silk.

Royal Orchid Holidays

a palm fringed beach
ch heritage of ancient
ng the diversity of
chid Holidays offer
travel opportunities

rs ago, Royal Orchid
care of all those
g hotel accommo-
eing tours.
hid Holidays,
hed hotel and tour
tain the best possible
to you.
e

MNCH / THA 2119

to Sri Lankan *rupees* (Rs). Each time money is exchanged, it should either be recorded on the form or you should get a receipt. Do NOT lose either the form or your receipts! Rupees cannot be taken out of the country and without your form, it is impossible (except in extreme circumstances) to re-exchange any unspent rupees. This form is surrendered to emigration officials when you leave the country.

Importing currency from India or Pakistan is not allowed. Also, import of any Sri Lankan currency in excess of Rs 250 is not allowed. Such currency will be held by customs and returned when you leave the country, provided you have the proper forms.

CURRENCY

The Sri Lankan rupee is divided into 100 cents. Coins are minted in 1, 2, 5, 10, 25 and 50-cent denominations as well as 1, 2, and 5 rupee coins. Notes come in Rs 2, 5, 10, 20, 50, 100, 500 and 1,000 denominations. The notes are brightly colored and vary in size depending on the denomination and the year in which they were printed. When held up to the light, the notes have the watermark of the Sinhala lion.

EXCHANGE RATES

The exchange rate fluctuates with the world market. New rates are printed daily in the press. In early 1991, the official exchange rates of the following currencies were: Rs 40.00 to one US dollar, Rs 78.50 to one sterling pound, Rs 8.00 to one French franc, Rs 27.00 to one German mark, and Rs 30.50 to 100 Japanese yen.

All commercial banks are authorized to exchange money, as are many hotels. Some major companies, including airlines, are also authorized to accept foreign currency for purchases. These always have a prominently displayed sign and a licensed number. It is illegal to exchange funds through any unlicensed dealer.

In Sri Lanka, traveler's checks enjoy a better rate of exchange than cash. Also, banks pay a higher rate of exchange than most hotels and/or other authorized dealers.

CREDIT CARDS

Most major credit cards are accepted at major hotels. In addition, many shops and restaurants readily accept credit cards. While it is not legal, some shops will try to add a surcharge to your credit card purchases. Insist that they remove the charge, then contact the card company so corrective action can be taken.

HEALTH

Health officials no longer require certificates of immunization *unless* you have passed through an infected area within 14 days of your arrival.

Immunization against cholera, however, is recommended for your personal safety. Anti-malarial medications (prescribed by your doctor), such as chloroquine, should be started at least one week prior to arrival and should be continued for two weeks after your departure.

Sri Lanka is renowned for its sunny climate, which can cause severe sunburns. The intense tropical sun is much stronger and more direct than in northern climes. It is best to avoid the midday sun. If you must go out, carry an umbrella or wear a large hat. However, for sun-worshippers, a good suntan lotion with sun-block agent is recommended. These are hard to find in Sri Lanka and very expensive, so it is best to bring it from home. With common sense and precaution you'll enjoy yourself much more.

The climate of Sri Lanka is much hotter and more humid than many people are accustomed to. The human body fights this heat by perspiring profusely, causing a great deal of fluid loss as well as salt depletion. Drink plenty of liquids. If you find yourself perspiring unceasingly and feel weak and dizzy, get away from the sun, sit down, eat some salt – either in tablet form or mixed in a soft drink or tea.

Never drink tap water!! Water should not be drunk unless you know that it has been boiled and filtered. Though all waterways and lakes in the island are safe for bathing, water should always be boiled before drinking. Water purification tablets, such as Puritabs, could also be used.

Most of the bigger hotels take particular care with their water. If in doubt, it is best to stick to bottled water (soda) or soft drinks. A good thirst quencher that is available almost anywhere is the King Coconut water (thambili), often drunk straight from the shell. A word of caution: most fruit juices are diluted with water, so be careful.

All fruits should be carefully peeled before being eaten and raw vegetables should be avoided unless cleaned in boiled water. Unboiled water carries organisms that can lead to amoebic dysentery and other problems.

What is sometimes refered to as "Delhi Belly", North Americans will call "Montezuma's Revenge". Whatever it is called, many Westerners traveling in Sri Lanka come down with diarrhea. This can be quite uncomfortable and inconvenient, but there are remedies. A good solution is to carry Lomotil tablets – have your doctor prescribe them. Some people also find Pepto-Bismol very effective. Whatever you take, stock up before you leave home.

WHAT TO WEAR

In Sri Lanka's heat, light cotton clothing is the most comfortable and practical. For women, shorts are *not* considered. When visiting temples or place of worship, a skirt (with a T-shirt or Blouse) or trousers would be appropriate. A light cotton dress is also recommended, but leave your nylon stockings at home – they are too hot, and nobody wears them anyway. For men, it is best to wear shorts or cotton trousers and a cool comfortable shirt. It is best to wear light slacks and a cool comfortable shirt. You'll need a tie if you go to the Hill Club in Nuwara Eliya, otherwise, there is little need for them.

If you are planning a trip to the hill country, especially Nuwara Eliya, you should dress for an English spring. The area is famous for scenic trails, so a good pair of walking shoes is recommended. At night, the temperature can be quite nippy, so a good wool sweater is a necessity.

Sandals or slippers are much more comfortable than shoes and much easier to remove when visiting temples and shrines. If you are really squeamish about going barefoot, most temples will allow you to wear socks. Sunglasses are also a necessity; it is hard to get good ones here, so bring them from home.

CUSTOMS

Upon arrival, visitors must declare all currency on the official exchange form. Any gems of Sri Lankan origin, set or unset, must also be recorded on this form.

Visitors are allowed to bring in the following articles duty-free:
– 200 cigarettes or 50 cigars or 200 grams tobacco or any combination thereof provided the total weight does not exceed 200 grams.
– 1.5 liters of hard spirits and two liters of wine and a small amount of perfume
– a reasonable amount of personal sports equipment
– personal photographic equipment, radios, cassette recorders and typewriters; and
– a reasonable supply of film for personal use only.

Sri Lanka prohibits the import of narcotics, pornography (literature, films, photos, etc.), firearms and ammunition.

ON DEPARTURE

When leaving Sri Lanka, baggage will be checked by security and customs on departure. You may take up to three kilo's tea duty free. A duty of Rs 5.00 will be levied on each additional kilo. You can buy more duty free goods once you enter the departure lounge.

Gems may be exported provided they were purchased with funds declared on the foreign exchange card. You will need to show your receipts for both purchases and money exchanges. To export gems received as gifts, permits from the Controller of Exchange, Central Bank, Colombo, and the Controller of Imports and Exports, National Mutual Building, Chatham Street, Colombo 1 are required.

The export of antiques (articles more than 50 years old) is banned. So is the export of wild animals, birds and reptiles or parts thereof, unless accompanied with proper documentation and licenses.

Any unspent repees should be reconverted to foreign currency at a commercial bank or at the exchange counter at the lobby of the airport.

An embarkation tax is levied when departing from Sri Lanka: Katunayake Airport – Rs 400. Passenger Jetty (Colombo) – US$2.00. After clearing customs and checking in at the airport, passengers await departure in the transit/departure lounge. Here, there are several shops selling duty-free goods such as tea, handicrafts and books.

All purchases are to be made in foreign currency only. There is also a restaurant here for those who prefer to eat and relax instead of shopping.

GETTING ACQUAINTED

GOVERNMENT & ECONOMY

Sri Lanka Janarajaya, or the Democratic Socialist Republic of Sri Lanka, is the official name of the former British colony of Ceylon.

Sri Lankan government is regulated by a constitution modeled upon that of France's Fifth Republic. The President, Mr Ranasinghe Premadasa represents the United National Party. He was elected to office in 1989. The prime minister is Mr D.B. Wijetunge.

The population of approximately 17 million is largely rural, with about one million in the capital city of Colombo and its surrounding metropolitan area.

Tea is by far the major export crop. In 1988, it earned about US$500 million in foreign exchange – about 43 percent of the country's export income. The second largest foreign-exchange earner was "inward remittances" from Sri Lankans working in the Middle East. Chief crops after tea are rubber, coconuts and spices (especially cinnamon). Gems, particularly sapphires and gement exports are also of great importance to the economy. The gross national product is US $7.31 billion (1990); per capita income is US$428 (1990).

GEOGRAPHY & POPULATION

Sri Lanka lies in the Indian Ocean between the northern latitudes 5°55' and 9°55' and the eastern longitudes 79°42' and 81°52'. Its maximum north-south length is 270 miles (435 km) and it measures 140 miles (225 km) in maximum east-west width.

TIME ZONES

Sri Lanka standard time is 5 hours 30 minutes ahead of Greenwich Mean time. When it is 12 noon in Sri Lanka, it is...

6.30 a.m. in London
7.30 a.m. in Paris, Rome, Madrid and Bonn
9.30 a.m. in Athens, Cairo and Johannesburg
10.30 a.m. in Moscow
noon in Bombay
1.30 p.m. in Bangkok and Jakarta
2.30 p.m. in Singapore
3.30 p.m. in Tokyo
4.30 p.m. in Sydney
8.30 p.m. (previous day) in Hawaii
10.30 p.m. (previous day) in San Francisco and Vancouver
1.30 a.m. in New York and Montreal

CLIMATE

For a relatively small country, Sri Lanka's climate is remarkably varied. From dry desert-like areas to verdant rainforests, from sunny ocean beaches to misty mountain tops, Sri Lanka has it all. And since Sri Lanka is definitely in the monsoonal tropics, it has a "dry" and a "wet" season which take place simultaneously on the opposite sides of the island.

This pearl-shaped island of 25,332 sq miles (65,608 sq km) is subject to two monsoons, the northeast and the southwest. The northeast monsoon, usually in November to February, brings rain to the dry northern and eastern parts of the island. The central hill region and the southern and western coasts receive most of their rain with the arrival of the southwest monsoon in May, usually lasting through September. Even during the monsoon season, most days are sunny with rain generally falling in the afternoon and evening.

Located off the southeast tip of India, approximately 400 miles (644 km) north of the equator, temperatures are high throughout the year. The low-lying coastal regions are the warmest; but the mercury falls as you climb into the hills.

In Colombo, the average annual temperature is 27°C (80°F). In Kandy, at an altitude of 1,000 feet (305 meters), the temperature falls to an average of 20°C (68°F). At Nuwara Eliya, nestled high in the hills at 6,200 feet (1,890 meters), the temperature averages 16°C (61°F) and can become quite chilly in the night. On rare occasions, there have been frosts.

The highest temperatures are usually reached between March and June, while November to January are considered to be the coolest months. In Sri Lanka, the difference between the "hot" and "cold" season is only a matter of a few degrees. However, the ocean remains a constant 27°C (80°F) all year long.

During October and November, there is an "inter-monsoon" season when rain and thunder-storms can appear anywhere. But don't let this talk of rain keep you away: Sri Lankan rains are usually delightful. One moment it is hot and stuffy, then all of a sudden the sky opens up and drops buckets of cool, refreshing rain. The plants release the most aromatic perfumes, the roads are filled with a myriad of miniature lakes, and best of all, the ever-present mosquitoes disappear. Then just as suddenly as it started, the rains stop and the sun is shining once again.

CULTURE & CUSTOMS

Common courtesy is as important in Sri Lanka as it is worldwide. There are a few general points and customs that should be especially mentioned.

Sri Lanka has a long history and is home to four of the world's main religions – Buddhism, Hinduism, Christianity and Islam. In many instances, superstition, religion and tradition have merged to create important customs.

When entering temples and highly venerated holy areas, shoes and hats must be removed. Remember, in Sri Lanka, "once a temple always a temple"; even if it has been reduced to rubble, it is still sacred and calls for respect.

When you encounter Buddhist monks and wish to show respect, raise both hands in a prayer fashion to just below your chin. Do not shake hands – a monk shouldn't be touched. If you wish to present a gift to a monk, it should be offered with both hands,

showing that it was given freely and without obligation. However, a monk is not allowed to touch money. When giving money, it should be placed in the temple offering box and never handed to anyone.

Buddhists wear white for religious observances. White is also considered the color of death. When a funeral is taking place, the road or drive is lined with white flags and strings of knotted palm fronds (*gokkola*) are hung across the street. *Gokkola* are also used in other processions and ceremonies.

In many parts of the world, shaking the head from side to side implies "no", while nodding the head up and down means "yes". Sri Lankans have another head movement as well, the "wobble" or "waggle", which is sort of a cross between a nod and a shake. While amusing and confusing to foreigners, it indicates agreement or approval or a simple "yes".

Throughout South Asia, people have traditionally (and most still do) use water and their left hands to clean themselves after a bowel movement. Therefore, the left hand is considered unclean and should never be used for eating – even if you always use toilet paper and wash your hands with soap. Since most Sri Lankans eat with the fingers of their right hands only, this custom is to be strictly observed even when using cutlery. Also, when handing objects to another person, it should never be done with the left hand. Use of both hands or the right hand alone is proper. If you are left-handed, it might be wise to practice eating with your right hand for awhile and think of it as a cultural experience.

One of the most awkward situations for foreigners to handle is when they are approached by beggars. Begging has always been a part of life in Asia. Buddhist monks must denounce all possessions. Lay people "earn merit" by providing for the monks as well as by giving to the needy.

It has also become an unholy profession, one of the most irksome aspects that hassle foreigners in Sri Lanka. Professional beggars haunt places of interest, busy streets and favorite tourist stops. Hoards of children chant "rupee, school pen, bon-bon (candy).

The government provides a variety of social services (free medical care, schooling etc.) and begging is discouraged except near temples. But as long as people continue to give away money, candy and pens, the problem grows. It may seem harsh, but it is recommended that you do not give to beggars. You can certainly refuse with a clear conscience because you are indirectly already giving money to the beggars: the government charges foreigners high admissions to zoos, gardens, archaeological sites and such, as well as a hotel tax (3 percent in 1991) to help pay for social services.

WEIGHTS & MEASURES

Sri Lanka officially converted from the English Standard system to the metric system in late 1981. The government is busy converting everything to metric measure but it will be some time before the conversion is complete. Sri Lanka has an elaborate road marker system with distances either chiseled into or painted onto stone. In late 1982, most of the major roads were marked in kilometers, while the secondary roads were often marked in miles, or a combination of both. To further complicate matters, some cars measure kilometers, others miles, and most people still think in English Standard (ounces, pounds, inches, miles, etc.)

One measure that you are likely to hear is a *lakh*. One *lakh* equals 100,000 of whatever you are talking about (e.g. money, bricks, etc.)

ELECTRICITY

Sri Lanka uses 230-240 volts, 50 cycles, alternating current. Most outlets are three-pronged.

Most hotels provide candles in the room as a matter of course. We suggest you bring along a good flashlight as well.

BUSINESS HOURS

In Sri Lanka, most businesses and government offices will say they are open from 8.30 a.m. to 4.30 p.m., Monday through Friday. But it is best to call ahead as these hours are somewhat flexible and often businesses close for lunch. Some businesses are open Saturday mornings as well. Banks have their own set hours (see below).

Most businesses close on holidays. Sri Lanka celebrates many Buddhist, Hindu and Christian holidays. *Poya* days – full moon

days – are also considered holidays when most businesses close. Observed as Buddhist religious days, no liquor is sold and all places of entertainment are closed. Some hotels make special arrangements for their guests.

Many holidays are based on the lunar calendar, so they vary from year to year. Most tourist services are open daily including holidays.

BANKING

Banking hours are usually from 9 a.m. to 1 p.m. on Mondays and until 1.30 p.m. on other weekdays. Banks are closed on Saturday, Sunday and public holidays. In 1991, there were 27 public and bank holidays.

SPECIAL EXCHANGE COUNTERS

BANK OF CREDIT & COMMERCE INTERNATIONAL
Airport Katunayake

BANK OF CEYLON
Ground Floor, York Street, Colombo 1. Tel: 28521. Open from 9 a.m. to 6 p.m. Weekdays and 9 a.m. to 4 p.m. holidays.
Foreign, Drafts Encashment Division
Cargills Building, Premises No. 34, Sir Baron Jayatilake Mawatha, Fort. Open on weekdays during normal banking hours and on Saturdays from 9 a.m. to 1 p.m.
Bureau de Change
Bank of Ceylon, 5th City Branch, York Street, Colombo 1. Open from 8 a.m. to 4 p.m. except on weekends and holidays.

PEOPLE'S BANK
Foreign Branch
27, M.I.C.H. Building, Bristol Street, Colombo 1. Tel: 26427, 546409. On Mondays open from 9 a.m. to 1 p.m. Tuesdays to Fridays from 9 a.m. to 1.30 p.m. Closed on weekends and holidays.
Night Service Unit
People's Bank, (H'Quarters Branch) Sir Chittampalam A. Gardiner Mawatha, Colombo 2. Tel: 27841/9. From Mondays to Fridays, open from 3.30 p.m. hrs to 7 p.m. on Saturdays 9 a.m. to 1.30 p.m. Closed on Sundays and Mondays.

Public, Bank, Full Moon Poya and Mercantile Holidays 1991

January 14	Tamil Thai Pongal Day
January 29	Duruthu Full Moon Poya Day•
February 4	National Day
February 12	Maha Sivarathri Day*
February 28	Navam Full Moon Poya Day•
March 29	Medin Full Moon Poya Day•
	Good Friday*
April 13	Day prior to Sinhala &
	Tamil New Year's Day
April 14	Sinhala & Tamil
	New Year's Day
April 17	Id-Ul-Fitr (Ramazan
	Festival Day)*
April 28	Bak Full Moon Poya Day•
May 1	May Day
May 22	National Heroes' Day
May 27	Wesak Full Moon Poya Day•
May 28	Day following Wesak Full
	Moon Poya Day
June 23	Id-Ul-Alha (Haj
	Festival Day)*
June 26	Poson Full Moon Poya Day•
June 30	Special Bank Holiday
July 26	Esala Full Moon Poya Day•
August 24	Nikini Full Moon Poya Day•
September 22	Milan-Un-Nabi
	(Holy Prophet's Birthday)
September 23	Binara Full Moon Poya Day•
October 22	Wap Full Moon Poya Day•
November 5	Deepavali Day*
November 21	II Full Moon Poya Day•
December 20	Unduwap Full
	Moon Poya Day•
December 25	Christmas Day
December 31	Special Bank Holiday

• Full Moon Poya Days
The days marked with * are not Mercantile Holidays but Public & Bank Holidays.
Bank Holidays: All Public Holidays and June 30, December 31.

BUDDHIST

Asokarama Temple
Thimbirigasyaya Road, Colombo 5.

Gangarama Temple
61 Jinaratana Road, Colombo 2.

Hatbodiya Temple
Off Hospital Road, Dehiwala.

Isipathanarama Temple
Isipathana Road, Colombo 5.

Kelani Raja Maha Viharaya
Kelaniya.

Vajiramaya Temple
Vajira Road, Colombo 5.

For more information on Buddhism and Buddhist meditation, contact the following:

All Ceylon Buddhist Congress
380 Bauddhaloka Mawatha, Colombo 7.
Tel: 691695.

The Buddhist Information Center
50 Ananda Coomaraswamy Mawatha, Colombo 7
Tel: 23079.

Buddhist Publication Society
54 Sangharaja Mawatha, Kandy
Tel: 08-23679.

Museum on Buddhism
At Gangaramaya Bhikku Training Centre, 61 Sri Jinaratana Road, Colombo 2
Tel: 27084, 435169.

CHRISTIAN

• Anglican

Cathedral of Christ the Living Saviour
Bauddhaloka Mawatha, Colombo 7
Tel: 696363.

Christ Church
Galle Face, Colombo 3
Tel: 25166.

Church of Ceylon
St. Paul's Milagiriya, Colombo 4
Tel: 588712.

St. Luke's Church
Colombo 8 (Borella)
Tel: 691543.

INSIGHT GUIDES

COLORSET NUMBERS

You'll find the colorset number on the spine of each Insight Guide.

Ask for it every day, everywhere you go.

Wherever you're going in the world, a copy of the International Herald Tribune is waiting for you. Circulated in 164 countries, on 70 airlines and in hundreds of quality hotels worldwide, the IHT brings you a view of the world that is concise, balanced and distinctly multinational in flavor. And you can get it six days a week, even when you're traveling.

INTERNATIONAL Herald Tribune
Published With The New York Times and The Washington Post

7th Floor, Malaysia Bldg, 50 Gloucester Road, Hong Kong
Tel.: (852) 861 0616. Fax: (852) 861 3073. Telex: 61170

INSIGHT *pocket* GUIDES

EXISTING & FORTHCOMING TITLES:

● ●

United States: **Houghton Mifflin Company, Boston MA 02108**
Tel: (800) 2253362 Fax: (800) 4589501

Canada: **Thomas Allen & Son, 390 Steelcase Road East**
Markham, Ontario L3R 1G2
Tel: (416) 4759126 Fax: (416) 4756747

Great Britain: **GeoCenter UK, Hampshire RG22 4BJ**
Tel: (256) 817987 Fax: (256) 817988

Worldwide: **Höfer Communications Singapore 2262**
Tel: (65) 8612755 Fax: (65) 8616438

" I was first drawn to the Insight Guides by the excellent "Nepal" volume. I can think of no book which so effectively captures the essence of a country. Out of these pages leaped the Nepal I know – the captivating charm of a people and their culture. I've since discovered and enjoyed the entire Insight Guide Series. Each volume deals with a country or city in the same sensitive depth, which is nowhere more evident than in the superb photography. **"**

Sir Edmund Hillary

St. Michael's and All Angels
St. Michael's Road, Colombo 3
Tel: 23660.

St. Peter's Church (Mission to Seamen),
26, Church Street, Colombo 1.
Tel: 422510.

• Baptist

Baptist Church
331 Grandpass Road, Colombo 14.

Baptist Manse (Cinnamon Gardens)
120 Dharmapala Mawatha, Colombo 7
Tel: 695153.

• Dutch Reformed

Bambalapitiya Dutch Reformed Church
Galle Road, Colombo 4
Tel: 580854.

• Presbyterian

St. Andrew's Church
Galle Road, Colombo 3
Tel: 23765.

• Methodist

Methodist Church
6, Station Road, Colombo 3.
Tel: 23033.

• Mormon

Church of Jesus Christ of Latter Day Saints
102A Horton Place, Colombo 7
Tel: 693794.

• Roman Catholic

All Saints' Church
Campbell Place, Colombo 8
Tel: 693051.

Holy Rosary Church
De Soysa Circus, Colombo 2
Tel: 20158.

St. Lucia's Cathedral
Kotahena, Colombo 13
Tel: 432080.

St. Mary's Church
Lauries Road, Colombo 4
Tel: 88745.

St. Philip Neri's Church
157, Olcott Mawatha, Colombo 11.
Tel: 421367.

St. Theresa's Church
364 Thimbirigasyaya Road, Colombo 5
Tel: 583425.

St. Lawrence's Church
Galle Road, Colombo 6.
Tel: 581549.

• Salvation Army

Salvation Army
2 Union Place, Colombo 2
Tel: 24660.

• Seventh Day Adventist

Seventh Day Adventist
7 Alfred House Gardens, Colombo 3
Tel: 585851.

HINDU

New Kathiresan Temple
Galle Road, Colombo 4 (Bambalapitiya).

Old Kathiresan Temple
Galle Road, Colombo 4.

Sri Bala-selva Vinayagam Kovil
Colombo 10.

Sri Manikka Vinayagam Temple
Colombo 11.

Sri Muthuvinayagam Swami Kovil
221 Sea Street, Colombo 11
Tel: 435154.

Sri Samankodu Kadirvekanda Swami Kovil
Main Street, Colombo 11.

ISLAM

Bambalapitiya Mosque
Buller's Road, Colombo 4.

Jami-ul-Alfar Mosque
2nd Cross Street, Colombo 11 (Pettah).

Kollupitiya Mosque
Colombo 3.

COMMUNICATIONS

MEDIA

THE PRESS

National daily newspapers are published in English, Sinhalese and Tamil language editions. The *Daily News* and the *Observer* are government sponsored papers with the *Daily News* appearing in the morning and the *Observer* in the afternoon. *The Island* is a private paper that enjoys large circulations.

Both *The International Herald Tribune* and *The Daily Telegraph* (British) arrive one day late but can be found at major hotels. Also available are *Newsweek, Time, The Far East Economic Review, Asiaweek* and several French and German publications.

TELEVISION

Television is in its 11th year in Sri Lanka. At the moment, there are only two TV channels – ITN and Rupavahini (the Sinhalese word for TV).

ITN starts broadcasting at 6.30 p.m. with a children's program, followed by a variety of programs till 9.30 p.m. when "News Magazine" is broadcast in English. This is followed by one or two programs, usually in English, before sign off at 11 p.m.

Rupavahini starts transmitting at 5.30 p.m. with their daily children's program. Rupavahini broadcasts "News Magazine" in Tamil at 7 p.m., in Sinhalese at 8.15 p.m., and in English at 9.30 p.m. Sinhalese films are broadcast one night each week. Rupavahini ends its transmissions at 11 p.m.

RADIO

In Sri Lanka, The Sri Lankan Broadcasting Corporation broadcasts in Sinhalese, Tamil and English between 5.30 a.m. and 11 p.m. It also beams programs to Europe, Southeast Asia and South Asia, adding the languages of Hindi, Urdu and Arabic. There are a variety of commercial broadcasts in Sinhalese, Tamil and English.

POSTAL SERVICES

The General Post Office (Janadhipathi Mawatha, Colombo Fort) is open 24 hours a day for the sale of stamps and for phone service (see "Telephone & Telex" notes). A "Tourist Only" counter is often open to provide postal rates and sell stamps to foreigners. It is usually much faster and less crowded than the other counters. An "Inquiries" counter is usually open and the Poste Restante (Tel: 26203) is located here.

Airmail rates vary with destinations; it costs Rs 8 to Europe and Rs 9 to America per half-ounce. Aerograms to any country cost Rs 10. Inland postage is Rs 1 for a normal letter.

When sending stamped airmail letters, it is a good idea to have them franked (cancelled) while you watch. There is a special counter for this purpose.

All important letters should be registered. If sending packages out of the country, a green customs label stating contents and value of the package must be attached. Never send money through the mail.

Post offices are located throughout the island with operating hours usually the same as those of other government offices. Some post offices have extended hours.

The easiest way to send letters is, of course, through your hotel.

TELEPHONE & TELEX

Local phone calls in Colombo cost one rupee. Calls to other areas of the island cost a flat rate of Rs 8 for trunk calls (through the operator). Direct dialing charges are Rs 7 for the first two minutes and Rs 2 or each additional minute.

International calls can be made from hotels and private phones with direct dialing facilities. Calls can also be booked by calling from a number that has opened an account with the authority to make overseas calls, or by booking and paying in advance at the post office.

International calls can also be made at one of the telecommunications (telephone, telex and cable) offices. The Central Telegraph Office (CTO) counter on Duke Street, Colombo Fort, is open 24 hours (Tel: 24340, 25799, 27167, 27187). The General Post Office also houses the Overseas Telecommunications Exchange which provides for direct dialing to a number of countries. The major hotels usually have businessmen's centers which provide telecommunications as well as secretarial services. There are also a number of private companies in Colombo which offer these services.

EMERGENCIES

SECURITY & CRIME

Like many parts of the world, Sri Lanka has its own share of crime. Fortunately for the tourists, most of the major crime is the result of domestic disputes and private vendettas. However, there is a problem of petty theft and pilferages of personal effects. You should never leave valuables unprotected even in a locked hotel room. Hotels provide safe deposit boxes and it is advisable to use these.

In case of a problem, a special unit called the "Tourist Police" is available to all visitors. Your hotel can contact them for you. The main office is located on the ground floor of the New Secretariat Building, Colombo Fort (Tel: 26941 or 421111, ext. 219). There are also branches at Mt. Lavinia, Bentota, Negombo and Hikkaduwa. The Central Liaison office shares the building with the Tourist Information Center at 76-78, Steuart Place, Colombo 3.

MEDICAL SERVICES

In the event that you must see a doctor, most hotels have doctors on call or for referral. Also, foreign missions usually keep a referral list and are happy to help you if necessary. Medical treatment can also be obtained from the state-owned **Colombo General Hospital**, Regent Street, Colombo 8 (Tel: 691111). The most advanced cardiology unit (Tel: 693039) in the country is located here. Medical service is still free for Sri Lankans, but the government now charges foreigners for certain services. Many foreigners prefer care at one of the privately owned and operated hospitals (see below).

Homeopathy and herbal medicine, called "ayurvedic", are also available. **The Government Ayurvedic Hospital** is located at Cotta Road, Borella, Colombo 8 (Tel: 695855).

Emergency service is rather limited outside Colombo. Emergency room service, called "Accident Centers", are only found in major towns such as Kandy and Jaffna.

Rabies and snakes bites take hundreds of human lives each year in Sri Lanka. Leave all unknown animals alone, even cute friendly ones. In the unlikely event of getting bitten, return at once to Colombo for rabies treatment: the serum is more likely to be fresh and refrigerated in the capital than the provinces. The same is true of anti-venom serum in the case of snake bites.

Most chemists and drug stores dispense drugs and act as pharmacists. **Osu Sala**, pharmacy of the State Pharmaceutical Corporation of Sri Lanka, maintains several shops in Colombo and throughout the island. The Osu Sala located at Hospital Junction near the General Hospital in Colombo is open 24 hours (Tel: 694716). Many other pharmacies are open until 10 p.m.

Generic and local drugs are inexpensive. Imported articles are more expensive, so it is a good idea to bring an adequate supply of your favorite remedies with you (e.g. aspirin, vitamins, allergy pills, etc.).

AMBULANCE SERVICE

General Hospital	691111
A.F. Raymond & Co.	693737
Red Cross Society	691905

HOSPITALS

• **Hospitals With Emergency Service (Accident Service)**

Asiri Hospital
181 Kirula Road, Colombo 5
Tel: 588267, 500608.

General Hospital
Srimath Baron Jayatilleke Mawatha, Colombo 8
Tel: 691111.

Nawaloka Hospital
23 Sri Saugathodaya Mawatha
Tel: 544444.

• **Other Hospitals**

Ayurvedic Centre and College of Indigenous Medicine
136 Cotta Road, Colombo 8
Tel: 695855.

Cancer Hospital
Maharagama
Tel: 0792-253.

Castle Street Maternity Hospital
Castle Street, Colombo 8
Tel: 691111.

Central Consultation Office
70 Kynsey Road, Colombo 8
Tel: 691111.

Central Hospital
37 Horton Place, Colombo 7
Tel: 696411.

Children's Hospital (Lady Ridgeway)
Danister de Silva Mawatha, Colombo 8
Tel: 693711.

Dental Clinic
Ward Place, Colombo 7
Tel: 693106.

De Soysa Lying-in Home
Kynsey Road, Colombo 8
Tel: 696224.

Durdans Hospital
3 Alfred Place, Colombo 3
Tel: 431361.

Eye Clinic
Deans Road, Colombo 10
Tel: 693911.

Grandpass Maternity and Nursing Home
36 Grandpass Road, Colombo 14
Tel: 435954, 422184.

Kandy Nursing Home
Kandy
Tel: (08) 3111.

MacCarthy Private Hospital
22 Wijerama Mawatha, Colombo 7
Tel: 693953.

Nawaloka Pvt Hospital
23 Saugathodaya Mawatha, Colombo 2
Tel: 546258.

Ratnam's Hospital
Union Place, Colombo 2
Tel: 27788.

St Michael's Nursing Home
4 Alfred House Gardens, Colombo 3
Tel: 585256.

Sri Lanka Nursing Home
High Street, Wellawatte
Tel: 585478.

Wycherley Nursing Home
2 Coniston Place, Colombo 7
Tel: 581407.

GETTING AROUND

FROM THE AIRPORT

There are three modes of transportation between the airport and Colombo – train, bus and taxi.

BY RAIL

The Katunayake train station is next to the airport. The train leaves the airport at 7.40 a.m., 8.40 a.m., and 4.56 p.m. and takes 1¼ hours to reach Colombo. Departures from Colombo to the airport are at 5.10 a.m., 5.26 a.m., and 3.10 p.m. This schedule is unsuitable for most travelers arriving or departing from Sri Lanka. Fares range between Rs 16.00 to Rs 7.25 for third, second and first-class carriage. Train tickets must be purchased at the airport for the ride to Colombo.

BY BUS

Sri Lanka Transport Board (SLTB) operates a public bus from the airport approximately every hour. The fare is Rs 7.00. The ride is slow, crowded and not recommended if you have much luggage. It is cheap, but you need to be very careful about your property – pickpockets have been known to ride this route.

Mini-buses are private buses that are much smaller than the SLTB buses and are also much faster, sometimes *too* fast. They run when they are full. Fare is somewhat negotiable for foreigners as it always starts off higher than the fare quoted for locals. The fare should be about Rs 7.00 for the trip to Colombo and for that to Kandy, which takes 3 hours, Rs 25. The mini-buses can be boarded near the Airport Terminal or at the Airport-Negombo road junction. They return to the Colombo Railway Station near Fort. Again these buses are not suitable if you have much luggage.

BY TAXI

Taxi is the most expensive (about Rs 600), but the easiest and fastest way to make the 34-kilometer (21-mile) trip to town. There is a taxi stand at the airport and a taxi from here will take you direct to your destination. It is still a slow (but interesting) ride into town, especially during the day when it seems that everyone is on the move in cars, bullock carts, bicycles, trucks and on foot.

The beach resort and fishing village of Negombo is located just 8 miles (13 km) from the airport and is often used as a starting or departing point in Sri Lanka. Taxi fare from the airport is about Rs 275. There are also frequent bus services and some of the Negombo hotels arrange airport transfers for their guests.

DOMESTIC TRAVEL

BY AIR

Air services within Sri Lanka is fairly limited due to the geographical layout of the country and the population centers. Upali Aviation (Pte) Ltd offers a charter service from Ratmalana Domestic Airport (about 18 kilometers south of Colombo Fort). Upali operates fixed wing Cessna aircraft and Helicopters that fly all over the island with charges based on the flying hour, as welll as a flexible charter service. For further information, contact Upali Aviation, 34 Galle Road, Colombo 3. Tel: 20465, 29399, or 28826.

Air Taxi Ltd. operates a charter service that flies Cessna aircraft that can accommodate five passengers. Their main office is at Ratmalana airport. Air Taxi charges by the flying hour and has landing facilities at Batticaloa, Hingurakgoda (near Polonnaruwa), Vavuniya, Anuradhapura, Kankesanturai, Koggala (near Galle) and Trincomalee. There are also services to Yala and Kataragama that are operated from Wirawila. For further information, contact Air Taxis Ltd at the Ratmalana Airport Tel. 717216. The Sri Lankan Air Force also operates air charters. The Air Force's air charters operates a variety of helicopters and planes that can seat anywhere from 1 to 44 people. All aircrafts are hired by the flying hour and can be retained over one night without charge. For further information, contact "Helitours", Sir Lankan Air Force Headquarters, Sir Chittampalam Gardiner Mawatha, Colombo, Tel: 31584 or 33184.

BY RAIL

In 1845 the British formed the first rail company in Ceylon and in 1867 train service commenced between Colombo and Kandy. During the British colonial period, the railroad reached its heyday and linked the country together. Later, due to the lack of riders and general economics, many lines were abandoned and subsequently fell into ruin.

Although no longer the extensive rail system of the past, Sri Lankan trains do serve a number of prime locations and offer an alternative mode of travel. On many services, only second and third class are offered. First class always means an air-conditioned coach, observation saloon, or sleeper berth. There are extra charges for first-class amenities, but most Westerners find them worthwhile. First class is offered on overnight trains, and on the service between Colombo and Nanu Oya/Badulla.

The main train station is located in Colombo Fort with trains leaving on a regular basis to important destinations.

Colombo-Kandy-Nanu Oya (near Nuwara Eliya)-Badulla line provides a picturesque journey into and through the spectacular Hill Country. There is daily service with the first train leaving Colombo at 5.55 a.m. for the 3-hour run to Kandy. The train stops in Kandy, then climbs into the hills, arriving in Nanu Oya at 1.21 p.m. and in Badulla at 5.00 p.m. The 9.45 a.m. train bypasses Kandy and goes straight to Nanu Oya, arriving at 3.33 p.m., then 3½ hours later reaches Badulla. There is also an overnight train that leaves Colombo at 8.15 p.m. and arrives in Badulla in time for breakfast. Three other runs leave Colombo and end in Kandy. Return services start about the same times.

A new intercity daily express service has been opened between Colombo and Kandy for only Rs 60. The express leaves Colombo at 7 a.m. and arrives in Kandy 2½ hours later after a short stop at Peradeniya Junction. Seats are sold according to *box plan seating* which guarantees a specific seat. Standing is not allowed. The train also has a restaurant with piped-in music. This run is so popular

that you must reserve well in advance. Also for Rs 53.75 is an express service between Colombo and Galle with short stops in Ambalangoda and Hikkaduwa.

There are numerous trains that ply the Colombo-Bentota-Hikkaduwa-Galle-Matara route daily. Galle is about a 3-hour train ride down the scenic southwest coast from Colombo. Matara is another hour beyond Galle.

For further information, contact **Ceylon Government Railway**, Tourist Information Office, Colombo Fort Railway Station, Tel: 35838. The *Sri Lanka Tourist Information* brochure available free from the Tourist Information Center (see section on "Tourist Information" for its location) includes a railway train schedule and current price structure.

PUBLIC TRANSPORT

BUSES

Traveling on the buses of the Sri Lanka Transport Board (SLTB) is not very pleasant. The buses are crowded and stuffy. They stop frequently, then lunge forward again abruptly, only to stop suddenly once more. However, they are probably the cheapest form of public transportation in the world and they go everywhere on the island.

For short distances they are tolerable, but if you have much luggage or plan to go very far, you may find it preferable to choose another form of transport. SLTB does offer some express services. Contact Central Bus Stand, Colombo (Tel: 28081) for further information.

There are a number of private companies that run Japanese mini-buses to most places on the island. These buses are much faster and more comfortable than the SLTB. They are more expensive than the SLTB but are extremely cheap by Western standards. (Colombo to Galle costs about Rs 25). In Colombo the mini-buses congregate at the rail station and leave when nearly full. They can also be flagged down along the road. If in doubt, just ask someone where to catch them.

Some companies maintain air-conditioned coaches. Prices vary according to the company; schedules and destinations are always changing. A local travel agent or the Tourist

Information Center can advise you on suitable transportation.

TAXIS

In the major cities (Colombo, Galle, Kandy and Jaffna), taxi service is available. Taxis are generally recognized by yellow tops. There should be a meter box and when you have boarded, the flag should be dropped. Taxis are more expensive than buses with a minimum rate of but most meters seem to run fast. Cost is Rs 14.00 per kilometer. "Autoshaws", the three-wheel scooters that run around Colombo and Galle, are supposed to charge Rs 12.00 a kilometer. However, their meters seem to have the same problem as the taxis.

In Colombo, Ace Radio Cab offer radio controlled cabs from a central point and offers customers a standard computerised rate of Rs 14.00 per kilometer. Tel: 501502, 3, 4. Radio controlled cabs have meters. Do not pay any sum at variance with the meter. Before your journey commences, ensure that the meter reading is at Rs 28.00 and the "flag" of the meter is down.

PRIVATE TRANSPORT

BY CAR

One of the peculiar but advantageous things about renting a car in Sri Lanka is that it is cheaper to hire a chauffeur-driven car than a self-drive. The major companies are very particular about having safe drivers, as cars are an expensive (and hard-to-get) investment that must be protected.

Driving in Sri Lanka can be described as a "death-defying sport" to the uninitiated. It is best to be driven by someone who knows the roads and the general driving habits of others. The roads are often narrow, winding, filled with children, cattle, bicycles, careening lorries (trucks), and speeding or stopped buses. For your own safety and peace of mind, leave the driving to an expert. The drivers also act as guides and speak English.

Hiring rates for cars vary between Rs 9 and Rs 12 per mile for non air-conditioned cars and between Rs 10 and Rs 15 per mile for air-conditioned cars depending on make, model, etc. Mini-buses and coaches can also be hired for larger groups. If you are out of Colombo for the night, the driver gets a allowance of between Rs 50 and Rs 100 per night. Hotels and guest houses always provide drivers' quarters at no extra charge.

Traveling by hired chauffeur-driven car is probably the easiest and most enjoyable way to see Sri Lanka. Local travel agents can make arrangements for vehicles and can help with an itinerary if you do not already have one.

If you are daring enough to want a self-drive car, arrangements can be made through a travel agent or a rental agency. (See below for listing of rental companies.)

The Automobile Association of Ceylon, 40 Sir Macan Marker Mawatha, Galle Face, Colombo (Tel: 421528), will help visitors with information on roads, regulations and driving licenses.

CAR RENTAL COMPANIES

Elbert Silva Touring Co. Ltd
(representing Toyota Rent-a-car)
P. O. Box 11, Dehiwala
Tel: 713356.

Mack Transport Ltd.
(representing Avis Rent-a-car)
Mackinnons Building, 11A York Street, Colombo 1
Tel: 29888.

Mercantile Tours (Ceylon) Ltd.
(representing Dollar Rent-a-car and Inter-rent)
23 York Arcade, Colombo 1
Tel: 500578/9, 502144.

Quickshaws Ltd.
(representing Hertz Inter-rent and American International Rent-a-car)
Kalinga Place, Colombo 5
Tel: 83133.

Travel Time Rent-a-car
10 Galle Face Court, Colombo 3
Tel: 20779.

BY MOTORCYCLE

Motorcycles can also be rented for the more adventurous. Rates vary greatly as do the quality of the bikes. Also, in most areas of the country, bicycles can be rented – from hotels, guest houses and small merchants. All you need to do is ask. However, a word of warning: bicycle maintenance is not exactly up to Western standards. Some bikes have no brakes and others have tires that continually leak. Check out the bike carefully before parting with your cash and trusting your safety to a mechanical mess.

WHERE TO STAY

Sri Lanka has a wide variety of accommodations available to travelers, from international-class luxury hotels to modest guest houses, dormitories and rooms in private homes. Not every town has a luxury or first-class hotel, but most communities can provide a pleasant place to stay.

Prices vary greatly throughout the country. Some inexpensive hotels or guest houses might actually be nicer than other more expensive lodgings. Generally, prices reflect the type of accommodation, number of amenities, location and demand for rooms. In some heavily touristed areas, there are different prices for the same lodging depending on the time of year, with rates sometimes as much as doubled for the "season". By contrast, certain hotels offer special all-inclusive off-season weekend rates as an attraction to Sri Lankan residents when the numbers of visitors have waned.

Outside of Colombo and a few beach resorts, air-conditioning is not always available. Most places provide ceiling fans which are quite adequate. In areas with mosquito problems, your room will also be furnished with a mosquito net. We recommend that you use it. Many hotels also spray their rooms every evening to help control mosquitoes and ensure their guests' comfort.

Hot water is another item that is a definite luxury in Sri Lanka. Most homes are not equipped with water heaters, but leading hotels now provide this amenity for their guests. In some areas of the island, hot water is just not available; but since the "cold" water isn't really cold, it shouldn't be a problem. Think of it as refreshing.

A note of interest: many small coffee, tea and snack shops call themselves "hotels" when there is absolutely no lodging at all.

Please see below for a listing of accommodations. We have classified hotels strictly by location and price range. In Colombo and some of the major resorts you can expect to pay US$60 and up per night for a double room in an expensive hotel. Moderate hotels run between US$20 and US$50 (Rs 800-Rs 2000). Prices are as low as US$12.50 (Rs 500) in an inexpensive hotel. Outside of heavily touristed areas, most hotels are considered inexpensive.

Guest houses are often homes that have been converted to small hostelries. They vary greatly in comfort from the sublime to definitely rustic. Prices vary as well, but costs are usually between Rs 125 and Rs 450 for a double room. Sometimes this price even includes breakfast.

For listings of really low-budget lodging preferred by backpackers and shoestring travelers, consult Tony Wheeler's book, *Sri Lanka: A Travel Survival Kit.*

HOTELS

EXPENSIVE

• **Ahungalla**

Triton Hotel
Ahungalla
Tel: 09-54041/4.

• **Bentota**

Bentota Beach Hotel
Bentota
Tel: 034-75176/9.

Hotel Ceysands
Bentota
Tel: 034-75073/4.

Robinson Club
Bentota
Tel: 034-75167, 75171.

• Beruwela

Neptune Hotel
Beruwela
Tel: 034-75218/9, 75301.

Riverina Hotel
Beruwela
Tel: 034-75377/9.

• Colombo

Hilton International Colombo
Lotus Road, Echelon Square, Colombo 1.
Tel: 544644 (30 Lines).

Holiday Inn Colombo
30 Sir Mohamed Macan Marker Mawatha,
Colombo 3
Tel: 422001/9, 449675.

Hotel Ceylon Inter-Continental
48 Janadhipathi Mawatha, Colombo 1
Tel: 421221.

Galadari Meridien
64 Lotus Road, Echelon Square, Colombo 1
Tel: 544544.

Pegasus Reef
P.O. Box 2, Wattala
Tel: 530205/8.

Ramada Renaissance
115 Sir Chittampalam A Gardiner Mawatha,
Colombo 2
Tel: 544200/9.

Taj Samudra Hotel
25 Galle Face Centre Road, Colombo 3
Tel: 546622.

The Lanka Oberoi
77 Steuart Place, Colombo 3
Tel: 20001, 421171.

• Habarana

The Lodge
Habarana
Tel: 20862, 421101/15 (Colombo).

• Hikkaduwa

Coral Gardens Hotel
Hikkaduwa
Tel: 09-22189, 23023.

• Kalutara

Tangerine Beach Hotel
Kalutara
Tel: 034-22295, 22640, 22794.

• Kandy

The Citadel
124 Srimath Kuda Ratwatta Mawatha, Kandy
Tel: 08-25314.

• Katunayake

Airport Garden Hotel
234 Negombo Road, Seeduwa
Tel: 030-3771-9

• Mount Lavinia

Mt. Lavinia Hotel
Hotel Road, Mt. Lavinia
Tel: 715221/9

• Negombo

Browns Beach Hotel
175 Lewis Place, Negombo
Tel: 031-2031/2, 2076/7

Royal Oceanic Hotel
Ethukala, Negombo
Tel: 031-2377, 2642, 3098/9

MODERATE

• Bentota

Hotel Serendib
Bentota
Tel: 034-75253, 75313.

Hotel Warahena Walauwa
Bentota.
Tel: 034-75372/4.

Lihiniya Surf Hotel
Bentota
Tel: 034-75126/7, 75486/7.

The Villa
Bentota.
Tel: 034-75312.

• Beruwela

Barberyn Reef Hotel
Beruwela
Tel: 034-75582, 75220

Beach Hotel Bayroo
Beruwela.
Tel: 034-75297

Confifi Beach Hotel
Moragalla, Beruwela
Tel: 034-75217, 75317.

Hotel Swanee
Moragalla, Beruwela
Tel: 034-75208/9

Pearl Beach Hotel
Beruwela
Tel: 034-75117/8

Palm Garden Hotel
Moragalla, Beruwela
Tel: 034-75263, 75273.

Riviera Beach Hotel
Beruwela
Tel: 034-75245

Wornels Reef Hotel
Beruwela
Tel: 034-75430/1

• Colombo

Ceylinco Hotels Limited
Ceylinco House,
69, Janadhipathi Mawatha, Colombo 1.
Tel: 20431/2

Cinnamon Gardens Inn
91, Wijerama Mawatha, Colombo 7.
Tel: 92987, 595218

Galle Face Hotel
2 Kollupitiya Road, Colombo 3.
Tel: 541010/6 (7 Lines)

Hotel Ranmuthu
112 Galle Road, Colombo 3.
Tel: 433986/9

Hotel Taprobane
York Street, Colombo 1.
Tel: 20391/3, 448734/5

Renuka Hotel
Galle Road, Colombo 3.
Tel: 573598, 573602

• Giritale

Giritale Hotel
National Holiday Resort, Giritale
Tel: 027-6311.

Royal Lotus Hotel
Giritale
Tel: 027-6316.

• Habarana

The Village
Habarana
Tel: 066-8316; Contact Tel: 20862, 421101/
15 (Colombo).

• Hambantota

Hotel Peacock
Hambantota
Tel: 047-20377.

• Hikkaduwa

Reefcomber Hotel
Hikkaduwa
Tel: 09-23374.

• Jaffna

Hotel Ashok
3 Cock Tower Road, Jaffna
Tel: 021-24246, 24336; Contact Tel: 25959,
29445 (Colombo).

• Kalutara

Sindbad Hotel
Kalutara
Tel: 034-22537/8.

Villa Ocean View
Wadduwa
Tel: 034-32463.

• Kandy

Hotel Hill Top
200/21 Bahiawakanda, Peradeniya Road,
Kandy
Tel: 08-24162.

Hotel Suisse
30 Sangarajah Mawatha, Kandy
Tel: 08-22637, 22672.

Hotel Thilanka
3 Sangamitta Mawatha, Kandy
Tel: 08-22060, 25497.

Hotel Topaz & Hotel Tourmaline
Anniewatte, Kandy
Tel: 08-24150, 23062.

Hunas Falls Hotel
Elkaduwa, Kandy
Contact Tel: 08-76402/3.

Mahaweli Beach Hotel
35 Siyambalagastenne Road, Kandy
Tel: 08-32062/3.

Queens Hotel
Dalada Veediya, Kandy
Tel: 08-22121/2, 32079.

• Katunayake

Hotel Goodwood Plaza
Canada Friendship Road, Katunayake
Tel: 45-2561/3.

Orient Pearl Hotel
Canada Friendship Road, Katunayake
Tel: 45-2356, 2268.

• Koggala

Hotel Horizon
Koggala, Habaraduwa
Tel: 09-53297.

Koggala Beach Hotel
Koggala, Habaraduwa
Tel: 09-53260, 53244.

• Mount Lavinia

Mount Royal Beach Hotel
36 College Avenue, Mt. Lavinia
Tel: 714001/3.

• Negombo

Blue Lagoon Tourist Holiday Resort
Talahena, Negombo
Tel: 031-2380.

Blue Oceanic Beach Hotel
Ethukala, Negombo
Tel: 031-2377, 2642, 3098/9.

Catamaran Beach Hotel
89 Lewia Place, Negombo
Tel: 031-2342, 2206.

Dolphin Hotel
Waikkal, Negombo
Tel: 031-3129.

Golden Star Beach Hotel
163 Lewis Place, Negombo
Tel: 031-3564/5.

Goldi Sands Hotel
161 Ethukala, Negombo
Tel: 031-2021, 2348.

Ranweli Holiday Village
Waikkal, Kochchikade
Tel: 031-2136.

Seashells Hotel
Palangaturai, Kochchikade
Tel: 031-2062, 3368.

Sunflower Beach Hotel
143 Lewis Place, Negombo
Tel: 031-2042.

• Nuwara Eliya

St. Andrews Hotel
Nuwara Eliya
Tel: 052-2445.

Grand Hotel
Nuwara Eliya
Tel: 052-2881, 2264/5.

Hotel Windsor
Nuwera Eliya
Tel: 052-2554.

The Hill Club
Nuwara Eliya
Tel: 0522-231.

• Sigiriya

Hotel Sigiriya
Sigiriya
Tel: 432895, 433268/9.

Sigiriya Village
Sigiriya
Tel: 698818, 699226.

• Tangalla

Tangalla Bay Hotel
Pallikkudawa, Tangalla
Tel: 047-40346, 449548.

• Trincomalee

Club Oceanic
Uppuveli, Trincomalee
Tel: 026-2307; Contact Tel: 20388, 20494.

Nilaveli Beach Hotel
Nilaveli, Trincomalee
Tel: 95, 96, Nilaveli; Contact Tel: 22518/9.

• Weligama

Dikwella Village Resort
Batheegama Dickwella
Tel: 041-2691.

INEXPENSIVE

• Anuradhapura

Ashok Hotels
Rowing Club Road, Anuradhapura
Tel: 025-2753

Miridiya
Rowing Club Road, Anuradhapura
Tel: 025-2112, 2519.

Nuwarawewa Rest House
New Town Anuradhapura
Tel: 025-2565; Contact Tel: 583133/5

Rajarata Hotel
Rowing Club Road, Anuradhapura
Tel: 025-2578.

Tissawewa Rest House
Old Town Anuradhapura
Tel: 025-2299; Contact Tel: 583133 (Colombo).

Helainn Tourist Hotel
Ratnayakepura, New Town, Anuradhapura
Tel: 025-2642

Hotel Monara
Freeman Mawatha, Anuradhapura
Tel: 025-2110.

Shanthi
891 Mailagas Junction, Anuradhapura
Tel: 025-2515.

• Bandarawela

Bandarawela Hotel
Bandarawela
Tel: 447161, 26767 (Colombo).

Orient Hotel
10 Dharmapala Mawatha, Bandarawela
Tel: 057-2407, 2377; Contact Tel: 27959, 545948 (Colombo)

• Beruwela

Berliner Bear Hotel
Beruwela
Tel: 034-75525.

Ypsylon Hotel
Beruwela
Tel: 034-75132.

• Colombo

Hotel Ceylon Inns
501, Galle Road, Colombo 6.
Tel: 583337, 587991, 580474/6

Hotel Duro
429, Galle Road, Colombo 3.
Tel: 581772

Hotel Empress
383 R. A. de Mel Mawatha, Colombo 3
Tel: 574930/1

Hotel Golden Topaz
502/1 Galle Road, Colombo 3
Tel: 547605.

Hotel Janaki
43 Fife Road, Colombo 5
Tel: 581524, 585336, 502169

Hotel Sapphire
371 Galle Road, Colombo 6
Tel: 583306/8, 589680, 585455

Hotel Galaxy
388, Union Place, Colombo 2.
Tel: 696372/3.

Sea View Hotel
15 Sea View Avenue, Colombo 3
Tel: 26516.

• **Galle**

Closenburg Hotel
Closenburg Road, Galle
Tel: 09-23073.

New Oriental Hotel
10 Church Street, Fort, Galle
Tel: 09-2059.

Unawatuna Beach Resort
Parangiya-watta, Unawatuna, Galle
Tel: 09-22147.

• **Giritale**

Hotel Hemalee
Polonnaruwa Road, Giritale
Tel: 027-6257.

• **Hikkaduwa**

Blue Corals
332 Galler Road, Hikkaduwa
Tel: 09-22679.

Coral Reef Beach Hotel
Hikkaduwa
Tel: 09-22197.

Coral Rock Hotel
Hikkaduwa
Tel: 09-22021.

Coral Sands Hotel
326 Galle Road, Hikkaduwa
Tel: 09-22436.

Hotel Lanka Supercorals
390 Galle Road, Hikkaduwa
Tel: 09-22897, 23387.

Sunils Beach Hotel
Narigama, Hikkaduwa
Tel: 09-32187.

Sun Island Village
Galle Road, Kahawa
Tel: 09-27274.

• **Jaffna**

Subhas Tourist Hotel
15 Victoria Road, Jaffna
Tel: 021-23228.

• **Kandy**

Chalet Hotel
32 Gregory's Road, Kandy
Tel: 08-24353.

Hotel Casamara
12 Kotugodella Vidiya, Kandy
Tel: 08-24052/3.

Janaki Hotel
40 Devani Rajasinghe Mawatha, Kandy
Tel: 08-24261.

Riverdale Hotel
32 Anniewatte Road, Kandy
Tel: 08-23020.

• **Katunayake**

Sirimedura Tourist Hotel
Ambalanmulla, Seeduwa
Tel: 030-2346/7.

• **Koggala**

Beach Haven Hotel
Talpe, Koggala
Tel: 09-52663.

Hotel Club Lanka
Ahangama, Koggala.

• Matara

Polhena Reef Gardens
30 Beach Road, Polhena
Tel: 041-2478; Contact Tel: 436268 (Colombo).

• Mount Lavinia

Hotel Riviras
50/2 De Saram Road, Mt. Lavinia
Tel: 717786, 717731.

Palm Beach Hotel
52 De Saram Road, Mt. Lavinia
Tel: 712713.

• Negombo

Aquarius Beach Hotel
Negombo
Tel: 031-2448, 2120.

Ceylonica Beach Hotel
47 Lewis Place, Negombo
Tel: 031-2976.

Interline Beach Hotel
5 Carron Place, Off Lewis Place, Negombo.

Topaz Beach Hotel
Ethukala, Negombo.

Palm Beach Hotel
159/161 Lewis Place, Negombo
Tel: 031-2631.

• Nuwara Eliya

Grosvenor Nuwara Eliya
Tel: 0522-307.

• Polonnaruwa

Amaliyan Nivas
National Holiday Resort, New Town, Polonnaruwa
Tel: 027-2405; Contact Tel: 448457/8.

Hotel Seruwa
National Holiday Resort, New Town, Polonnaruwa
Tel: 027-2411/2; Contact Tel: 23501/4.

• Ratnapura

Hotel Kalawathie
"Polhengoda Village", Outer Circular Road, Ratnapura
Tel: 045-2465.

Ratnaloka Tour Inns
Kosgala, Kahangama, Ratnapura
Tel: 045-2455.

• Weligama

Bay Beach
Kapparatota, Weligama
Contact Tel: 0415-201.

• Yala

Browns Safari Beach Hotel
Yala, Amaduwa
Tel: 047-20326, 433145, 28842 (Colombo).

Yala Safari Beach Hotel
Amaduwa, Yala
Tel: 698818 (Colombo).

GUEST HOUSES

• Ambalangoda

Ambalangoda Rest House
Ambalangoda
Tel: 09-27299
Contact Tel: 20862 (Colombo).

Blue Horizon Tour Inn
129 Devale Road, Ambalangoda
Tel: 09-27475

Randomba Inn
738, 740 Galle Road, Ambalangoda
Tel: 09-27406.

Sangrela Beach Inn
Sea Beach Road, Ambalangoda
Tel: 09-27342.

• Badulla

Dunhinda Falls Inn
35/11 Bandaranayake Mawatha, Badulla
Tel: 055-2406.

• Bandarawela

Alpine Inn
Ellatota, Bandarawela
Tel: 057-2567

Ideal Resort
Wlimada Road, Bandarawela
Tel: 057-2476

Kirchhayan (Tea Estate) Bungalow
Aislaby Estate, Bandarawela
Contact Tel: 20862, 548016 (Colombo).

Vye Estate (Tea Estate) Bungalow
Bandarawela.

• Belihul Oya

Belihul Oya Rest House
Belihul Oya
Tel: 045-7200, Contact Tel: 23501, 23504(Colombo).

• Bentota

Dilmini Tourist Guest House
304 Welipanne Road, Bentota
Tel: 048-5052.

Ripples Tourist Inn
Induruwa.

Susanta Guest House
Bentota.

Thewalauwa Guest House
Bentota.

• Bibile

Bibimo Motel
54 Badulla Road, Bibile
Tel: 898.

• Colombo

Chanuka
29 Francis Road, Colombo 6
Tel: 585883, 502983.

Colombo Guest House
26 Charles Place, Colombo 3
Tel: 574900/1.

Flamingo Inns
710 Galle Road, Colombo 3
Tel: 589688.

Halwa Tourist Inn
50/3 Sir Marcus Fernando, Mawatha, Colombo
Tel: 692265.

Hill Top Holiday Inn
51 High Level Road, Homagama
Tel: 436862.

Kuru Chesme
236 Havelock Road, Colombo 5
Tel: 84698.

Lanka Inns
239 Galle Road, Colombo 4
Tel: 584220.

Lake Lodge
20 Alwis Terrace, Colombo 3
Tel: 26443.

Omar Khayyam
442 Galle Road, Colombo 3
Tel: 435762.

Omega Inn
324 Galle Road, Colombo 6
Tel: 582277, 585604, 587820.

Orchid Inn
571/6 Galle Road, Colombo 6
Tel: 583916.

Ottery Inn
29 Melbourne Avenue, Colombo 4
Tel: 583727.

St. Georges
43 Peterson Lane, Colombo 6
Tel: 588545.

Wayfarers Inn
77 Rosmead Place, Colombo 7
Tel: 693936.

Y.W.C.A. International Guest House
393 Union Place, Colombo 2
Tel: 24694, 422196.

- **Dikoya**

Upper Glencairn
Dikoya
Tel: 0512-348.

Ottery Tourist Bungalow
Ottery Estate, Dikoya
Tel: 0512-837.

- **Ella**

Ella Rest House
Ella
Tel: 057-2636.

- **Galle**

Harbor Inn Rest House
Buona Vista, Unawatuna, Galle
Tel: 09-2822; Contact Tel: 23501 (Colombo).

Lucky Cottage
86 S.H. Dahanayake Mawatha, Galle.

Orchard Holiday Home
61 Light House Street, Fort, Galle
Tel: 09-2370.

Hotel Beach Haven
Galle-Matara Road, Talpe
Tel: Res. 536321.

- **Habarana**

Habarana Rest House
Habarana
Tel: 066-8355.

- **Hikkaduwa**

Coral Front Inn
279 Main Road, Hikkaduwa.
Tel: 09-23303.

Coral Seas Beach Resort
346 Colombo Road, Hikkaduwa
Tel: 09-23248.

Hansa Surf Guest House
Narigama, Hikkaduwa
Tel: 09-22651.

Seaside Inn
Patuwata, Dodanduwa
Contact Tel: 09-23413, 27337.

Sun Lagune Inn
Sri Saranjothi Mawatha, Dodanduwa,
Hikkaduwa

- **Horana**

Wasana Tourist Inn
Hegalla Estate, Horana
Tel: 209 Horana.

- **Horton Plains**

Farr Inn
Horton Plains, Ohiya
Tel: 027-2411, Contact Tel: 23501, 20194

- **Kandy**

Castle Hill
22 Rajapihilla Mawatha, Kandy
Tel: 08-24376.

Elmhurst Tourist Lodge
26/5 Sangaraja Mawatha, Kandy
Tel: 08-23190.

Sandy River Inn
Getembe, Kandy
Tel: 08-22585.

The Dawn Tourist Inn
124 Mapanawathura Road, Kandy
Tel: 08-23020.

- **Kegalle**

Kegalle Guest House
Concept Randeniya, Kegalle
Tel: 295 Rambukkana.

- **Kitulgala**

Kitulgala Rest House
Kitulgala
Tel: 28 Kitulgala, Contact Tel: 23501, 23504.

- **Matale**

Matale Tourist Guest House
145 Moisey Crescent Road, Matale
Tel: 0662-2259.

• Matara

Maheeka Tourist Inn
363 Meddawatha, Matara
Tel: 041-2131.

Matara Rest House
Matara
Tel: 041-2299.

• Mount Lavinia

Blue Horizon
2/0 Lady de Soysa Drive, Moratuwa.

Concord
139 Galle Road, Dehiwela
Tel: 717727.

Estorial Tourist Lodge
5/2 Lilian Avenue, Mt. Lavinia
Tel: 715494.

Mount Inn
17/4 De Saram Road, Mt. Lavinia
Tel: 716413.

Mt. Lavinia Holiday Inn
17 De Saram Road, Mt. Lavinia
Tel: 717187.

Ocean View Tour Inn
34/4 De Saram road, Mt. Lavinia
Tel: 717200.

Ranveli Beach Resort
56/9 De Saram Road, Mt. Lavinia
Tel: 717385.

Sea Breeze Tour Inn
22/5a De Saram Road, Mt. Lavinia
Tel: 714017.

Sea Spray Beach Resort
45 Vihara Road, Mt. Lavinia
Tel: 716304.

Starr Inns
73/22 Sri Saranankara Road, Dehiwela
Tel: 717583; Contact Tel: 82359.

• Negombo

De-Phani Beach Guest House
189/15 Lewis Place, Negombo
Tel: 031-3225.

Golden Haven
Kimbulapitiya, Negombo
Tel: 031-2324.

Hotel Sea Gardens
Ethukala, Negombo
Tel: 031-2150.

Rainbow
3 Carron Place, Negombo
Tel: 031-2082.

Sea Drift
2 Carron Place, Negombo
Tel: 031-2601.

Silva's Beach Guest House
5 Porutota Road, Ethukala, Negombo
Tel: 031-3408.

Star Beach
83/3 Lewis Place, Negombo
Tel: 031-2606.

• Nuwara Eliya

Oatlands
St. Andrews Drive, Nuwara Eliya
Tel: 0522-572.

Princess Guest House
12 Wedderburn Road, Nuwara Eliya
Tel: 052-2462; Contact Tel: 431398.

Wattles Inn
13 Srimath Jayatilake Mawatha, Nuwara Eliya
Tel: 052-2804.

• Polonnaruwa

Polonnaruwa Rest House
Polonnaruwa
Tel. 027-2299; Contact Tel: 23501/4.

Ranketha Rest
Batticaloa Road, Polonnaruwa
Tel: 027-2080.

Sri Lanka Inns
2nd Channel road, New Town, Polonnaruwa
Tel: 027-2403.

• **Sigiriya**

Sigiriya Rest House
Sigiriya
Tel: 066-8324, Contact Tel. 23501/4.

• **Tangalla**

Palm Paradise Cabanas
Goyambokke, Tangalla
Tel: 553228.

• **Tissamaharama**

Priyankara Guest House
Kataragama Road, Tissamaharama

Tissamaharama Rest House
Tissamaharama
Contact Tel: 23501/4.

• **Weligama**

Bay Inn Rest House
Weligama
Tel: 0415-299, Contact Tel: 23501/4.

YOUTH HOSTELS

• **Colombo**

Boy Scouts Hostel
65/9, Sir Chittampalam A
Gardiner Mawatha,
Colombo 2.
Tel: 433131.

Girl Guides Hostel (women only)
10 Sir Marcus Fernando Mawatha, Colombo 7
Tel: 697720.

Horton Youth Hostel
35/1 Horton Place, Colombo 7.

Youth Council Hostel
50 Haig Road, Colombo 4.

WITHIN THE WILDLIFE SANCTUARIES

Gal Oya National Park
(1 bungalow), Ekgal Oya (outside the park, electricity available).
Inginiyagala Safari Inn, Inginiyagala
Tel: 063-2499; Contact Tel: 26611-9 (Colombo).

Horton Plains Nature Reserve
(1 bungalow), Ginihiriya Lodge
Contact Tel: 432698, 434040.

Ruhunu National Park
(6 bungalows), Palatupana, Buttuwa, Yala, Talgasmankade, Heen Wewa and Patangala.

Wilpattu National Park
(7 bungalows) Maradanmaduwa, Manikpola Uttu, Kalli Villu, Kokmottai, Talawila Penike-vila and Manavila.

Yala East National Park
(2 bungalows), Tunmulla and Okanda.

Bungalows within the wildlife sanctuaries are in great demand and booking have to be made in advance. For bookings, contact: Department of Wild Life Conservation, 82 Rajamalwatta Road, Battaramulla. Tel: 433012, 433787. Occupation charges are about Rs 125 per person for a minimum of 5 persons.

Bungalows are also maintained by the Wild Life and Nature Protection Society outside the Parks at Yala and Wilpattu. For advance reservations, contact Headquarters at Chaitya Road, Marine Drive Fort, Colombo 1 (Tel: 25248). These cost about Rs 50 per day.

FOOD DIGEST

WHERE TO EAT

Colombo is a growing metropolis with a wide variety of restaurants and styles of food. The restaurant scene is continually expanding, changing and improving in quality. Generally the best restaurants are located in hotels but now a number of fine restaurants have established themselves in other areas of Colombo such as along Galle Road, Havelock Road, Duplication Road, and in Cinnamon Gardens.

Outside Colombo, you are largely restricted to hotels or rest houses. Some hotels serve reasonable selections, but all too often it is pseudo-European. They also have a tendency to make their curries too bland as they believe foreigners can't handle "local" style. For breakfast, it's always eggs, eggs and more eggs, unless you order an Eastern breakfast the night before. If you order in advance such wonderful treats as hoppers (see food feature), you will receive the real home-cooked item.

RESTAURANTS

Chinese

Chinese Dragon Cafe
232 Galle Road, Colombo 4
Tel: 588144.

Chinese Golden Gate Hotel
25 Galle Road, Colombo (Wellawatte)
Tel: 582510.

Chinese Lotus Hotel
265 Galle Road, Colombo 3
Tel: 26843.

Chinese Park View Lodge
70 Park Street, Colombo 2
Tel: 26255.

Flower Drum
26 Thurstan Road, Colombo 3
Tel: 574216.

Hong Kong
19/1 Daisy Villa, Duplication Road, Colombo 4
Tel: 501606.

Hotel Nippon
123 Kumaran Ratnam Road, Colombo 2
Tel: 431887.

Jade Garden
126 Havelock Road, Colombo 5
Tel: 584174, 580678.

Long Feng
Ramada Hotel
Tel: 544200 ext. 1949.

Mandarin Palace
Longden Place, Colombo 7
Tel: 587740.

Nanking Restaurant
33 Chatham Street, Colombo 1
Tel: 27888.

Park View Lodge
70 Park Street, Colombo 2
Tel: 26255.

Ran Malu
Oberoi Hotel
Tel: 20001, 421171, 437437.

French

La Palme D'Or
Meridien Hotel
Tel: 544544.

Rendezvous
Taj Hotel
Tel: 546622.

German

Alt Heidelburg
11 Galle Face Court, Colombo 3
Tel: 421577.

Indian & Moghul

Alhambra
Holiday Inn, Mohammed Macan Markar
Mawatha, Colombo 3
Tel: 422001.

Greenlands Hotel
3/A Shrubbery Gardens, Colombo 4
Tel: 81986.

Iban Batuta
Ramada Hotel
Tel: 544200, ext. 1948.

Navaratne
Taj Hotel
Tel: 546622.

Ran Malu
Hotel Lanka Oberoi, Colombo 3
Tel: 20001.

Saras Indian Restaurant
450E R.A. de Mel Mawatha, Colombo 3
Tel: 575226.

Shanti Vihare
Havelock Road at Bauddhaloka Mawatha
(Vegetarian restaurant.)

Italian

Pizzeria/Tharanga Terrace
Hotel Ceylon Intercontinental
Tel: 421221.

Ristorant Italiano "Da Guido"
Havelock Road, Colombo 5
Tel: 587110.

Japanese

Ginza Hohsen
Colombo Hilton
Tel: 544644, ext. 2123.

Hakata
110 Havelock Road, Colombo 5
Tel: 501397.

Japan Doll
32B Sir Mohammed Macan Markar
Mawatha, Colombo 3.
Tel: 546589.

Kyoto Restaurant
19 De Vos Avenue (off Duplication Road),
Colombo 4
Tel: 83194.

Sakura
14 Rheinland Place, Colombo 3
Tel: 573877.

Uwoden Restaurant
28 Thurstan Road, Colombo 3
Tel: 573430.

Sri Lankan

Akasa Kade
Ceylinco Building
69 Janadhipathi Mawatha, Colombo 1
Tel: 20431.

Curry Corner
24 Deal Place, Colombo 3
Tel: 570157.

Ginza Aralinya
286 Galle Road, Colombo 3
Tel: 575906.

Iban Batuta Restaurant
Hotel Ramada, 115 Sir Chittampalam
Gardiner, Mawatha, Colombo 2
Tel: 544200-9.

Green Cabin Cafe
453 Galle Road, Colombo 3
Tel: 88-811.

Pagoda Tea Room
De Mel Bldg., Chatham Street, Colombo 3
Tel: 23086.

Palmyrah Restaurant
Hotel Renuka, 328 Galle Road, Colombo 3
Tel: 26901.

Ran Malu
Hotel Lanka Oberoi, Colombo 3
Tel: 20001.

Walauwa Restaurant
278 Union Place, Colombo 2
Tel: 28658/9.

Seafood

Beach Wadiya
2 Station Road, Colombo 6
Tel: 88568.

Pearl Seafood Restaurant
Hotel Ceylon Inter-Continental, 48
Janadhipathi Mawatha, Colombo 1
Tel: 21221.

Sea Fish
15 Chittampalam Gardiner Mawatha, Colombo 2
Tel: 26915.

Seaspray
Galle Face Hotel, Colombo 3
Tel: 28211.

The Fish
Meridien Hotel
Tel: 544544.

Western

Akasa Kade
Ceylinco Building, 69 Janadhipathi
Mawatha, Colombo 1
Tel: 20431.

Emerald Tea Coffee Shop
Hotel Ceylon Inter-Continental
Tel: 21221.

Gables
Colombo Hilton
Tel: 544644.

Gardenia
Holiday Inn, Colombo
Tel: 22001.

La Palme D'Or
Meridien Hotel
Tel: 544544.

London Grill
Hotel Lanka Oberoi, Colombo 3
Tel: 20001.

Moonstone Barbeque Terrace
Hotel Ceylon Inter-Continental, Colombo 1
Tel: 21221.

Mt. Lavinia Hotel
Hotel Road, Mt. Lavinia
Tel: 071221.

Noblesse Restaurant and Bar
Hotel Ramada, 115 Sir Chittampalam
Gardiner, Mawatha, Colombo 2
Tel: 544200-9.

Palms Roof Top Restaurant
Hotel Ceylon Inter-Continental, Colombo 1
Tel: 21221.

Semiramis Restaurant
Hotel Sapphire, 371 Galle Road, Colombo 6
Tel: 83306.

Supper Club
Hotel Lanka Oberoi, Colombo 3
Tel: 421171.

Verandah Restaurant
Galle Face Hotel, Colombo 3
Tel: 28211.

CULTURE PLUS

MUSEUMS

The most important museum in Sri Lanka is the **National Museum** on Sri Marcus Fernando Mawatha. Colombo 7 (Tel: 694767). It contains a large collection of antiques and objects d'art, from classical times to the modern day, as well as an interesting display of gifts of state. There are also exhibits of cultural and historical importance, as well as on natural history. The museum is open from 9 a.m. to 5 p.m. Sunday through Thursday.

The Cultural Triangle has also decided to have small museums on the archaeological sites themselves to exhibit findings. However, important finds will still be transferred to the National Museum. Other museums in Colombo are:

Bandaranaike Museum

In the Bandaranaike Memorial International Conference Hall (BMICH) on Bauddhalokha Mawatha, Colombo 7
Tel: 91131
Open 9 a.m. to 4 p.m. daily except Mondays and poya days.
It covers the life and times of the late Prime Minister S.W.R.D. Bandaranaike.

Dutch Period Museum

Prince Street, Colombo 11 (Pettah)
Open 9 a.m. to 5 p.m. Sunday through Thursday. The building has been completely restored with assistance from The Netherlands.
Opened in late 1982, it covers the period from 1658 to 1796.

Simamalaka Museum on Buddhism

Beira Lake, Sir James Pieris Mawatha, Colombo 2
Open daily 6 a.m. to 10.30 p.m.
A daily service at 6 p.m. is open to the public. Additional Buddhist items not on display here can be seen at the nearby **Gangaramaya Bhikkhu Training College**, 61 Sri Jinaratana Road, Colombo 2 (Tel: 27084 or 435169).

OUT-COUNTRY MUSEUMS

Anuradhapura Archaeological Museum

Open 8 a.m. to 5 p.m., closed Fridays.
Collections of antiquities from the northern and eastern provinces.

Anuradhapura Folk Museum

Open 9 a.m. to 5 p.m., closed Fridays.
Contains valuable objects pertaining to the study of anthropology in the Vanni district; agrarian items and handicrafts.

Jaffna Archaeological Museum

Open 8 a.m. to 5 p.m., closed Tuesdays.
Collection of folk-art objects, discoveries from the Kantharodai excavations, and Buddhist-Hindu sculptures found in the Jaffna Peninsula.

Kandy National Museum

Open 9 a.m. to 5 p.m., closed Fridays.
Collection of articles from the Kandyan kingdom, including a wide range of jewelry and household articles.

Polonnaruwa Archaeological Museum

Open 8 a.m. to 5 p.m., closed Tuesdays.
Collection of antiquities, stone sculptures and inscriptions found at Polonnaruwa.

Ratnapura Gem Bureau and Museum

Getangama
Interesting collection of gems, silver and gold art work, and some antiquities. Attached art and handicrafts gallery. Also has gems, silver and brass for sale.

Ratnapura Gemmological Museum

Houses a collection of gems and minerals, with thorough explanation of mineralogy. Also sells gems and batiks.

Ratnapura National Museum

Open 9 a.m. to 5 p.m., closed Fridays.
Collection of prehistoric artifacts and fossils of rhinoceroses, hippopotamuses and elephants found in gem pits.

Sigiriya Archaeological Museum

Open 8 a.m. to 5 p.m., closed Tuesdays.
Collection of objects found in archaeological excavations and nearby villages.

Archaeological museums are also located at Amparai, Dedigama, Panduvas Nuwara and Yapahuwa.

ART GALLERIES

When one thinks of Sri Lanka art, the classical periods first come to mind: the Sigiriya frescoes and the many ancient temple carvings. But the names of those who wielded the brushes or chisels have been lost to time.

Modern Sri Lanka, however, is gifted with several talented contemporary artists. Best known among them are two painters active from pre-World War Two right up into the 1980s. The late **L.T.P. Manjusri's** style conformed to that of the classical temple paintings, while the work of **George Keyt** is more abstract – containing a noticeable touch of Picasso.

Currently, the most famous name in Sri Lankan art is that of **Senaka Senanayake**. He made his entry into the art world as a young teenager and was called a "child prodigy". Now in his 30s, he has had many one-man exhibitions in the United States and Europe. His modern style has been highly acclaimed both in Sri Lanka and abroad. Two late, unsung heroes of Sri Lankan art are George **de Neise** and **David Paynter**. Both were outdoor men who converted to canvas with utter brilliance the glory of Sri Lanka's natural beauty. The work of these artists can be seen in numerous galleries in the Colombo area:

Art Gallery
106 Ananda Coomaraswamy Mawatha, Colombo 7
Tel: 693965
Open 8 a.m. to 5 p.m. daily except *poya* days. In addition to a permanent portrait exhibit, many special exhibits are given here.

Kalagaraya Art Gallery
54 Ward Place, Colombo 7
Tel: 694162
Open 9 a.m. to 1 p.m. and 5 to 7 p.m. Monday through Friday.
Located at the Alliance Francaise de Colombo. Contemporary art exhibition and sales.

Lionel Wendt Memorial Art Center
18 Guildford Crescent, Colombo 7
Tel: 695794.
No permanent exhibit; many special contemporary art exhibitions.

Manjusri Home
215, 2/E Block, Anderson Golf Links Flat, Park Road, Colombo 5
Tel: 582417.
By appointment only. Original Manjusri oils and watercolors; some items for sale.

Sapumal Foundation
32/4 Barnes Place, Colombo 7
Tel: 695731.
By appointment only with Mr. Harry Pieris, director. Private collection; some items for sale.

Serendib Gallery
100 Galle Road, Colombo 4.
Handicrafts, antiques, paintings and rare books for sale.

Vipula's Galleries, 12 Halgaswatte Lane, Collombo 6 (tel. 553422).

There are also permanent exhibitions in the **Hotel** and the **Colombo Hilton.**

THEATERS

Bandaranaike Memorial International Conference Hall (BMICH)
Bauddhaloka Mawatha, Colombo 7
Tel: 691131.

Cary College Hall
28 Kynsey Road, Colombo 8
Tel: 695603.

John de Silva Memorial Theatre
3 Ananda Coomaraswamy Mawatha, Colombo 7
Tel: 693965.

Ladies College Hall
Flower Road, Colombo 7
Tel: 421014.

Lionel Wendt Memorial Theatre
18 Guidford Crescent, Colombo 7
Tel: 695794.

Lumbini Theatre
Skelton Gardens, Colombo 5 (Havelock Town)
Tel: 582006.
Top Sinhala theatre.

Navarangahala Theatre
Racecourse Avenue, Colombo 7
Tel: 694988.

New Kathiresan Hall
339/10 Gale Road, Colombo 4.

Ramakrishna Mission Hall
40 Ramakrishna Road, Colombo 6 (Wellawatte)
Tel: 588253.

Royal College
Racecourse Avenue, Colombo 7
Tel: 691020.
Produces one college play a year.

St. Bridget's College Hall
85 Alexandra Place, Colombo 7
Tel: 693030.

Tower Hall
43 Panchikawatte Road, Colombo 10
Tel: 692945, 431878.
Traditional venue for Sinhala plays.

YMBA Hall
70 D.S. Senanayake Mawatha, Colombo 8
Tel: 695786.

YWCA Hall
7 Rotunda Gardens, Colombo 3
Tel: 23498.

MOVIES

The Sinhalese film industry is still in its infancy. By international standards, the acting tends to be overly dramatic and the films a bit too long. But strides are beginning to be made.

The first Sinhala film was screened in the 1940s. Titled "Broken Promise", it was done in black-and-white with sound. But financial and technological obstacles permitted only slow progress until the 1960s, when the first color movie in the Sinhala language was made. Since then, the film industry has accelerated its pace.

The country's best-known director is Lester James Peiris. His films, such as "Kurulubedde" and "Gamperaliya", have won international awards and overseas acclaim.

English-language films are the standard fare at several Colombo cinemas, including the following:

Liberty
38 Dharmapala Mawatha, Colombo 3
Tel: 25265.

Majestic
782 Galle Road, Colombo 4 (Bambalapitiya)
Tel: 581759.

New Olympia
95 T.B. Jayah Mawatha, Colombo 10
(Maradana)
Tel: 693141.

Regal
8 Sir Chittampalam Gardiner Mawatha, Colombo 2
Tel: 432936.

Savoy
12 Galle Road, Colombo 6 (Wellawatte)
Tel: 588621.

Other cinemas include:

Empir
Braybrooke Place, Colombo 2
Tel: 23250.

Central
151 Maradana Road, Colombo 10
Tel: 431133.

Cinema Concord
141 Galle Road, Dehiwala
Tel: 712759.

Gaiety
George R. de Silva Mawatha, Colombo 13
(Kotahena)
Tel: 25163.

Ruby
Jayantha Weerasekera Mawatha, Maligawatte, Colombo 10 (Maradana).

LIBRARIES

American Center
39 Sir Ernest de Silva Mawatha, Colombo 7
Tel: 691461.

British Council
49, Alfred House Gardens, Colombo 3.
Tel. 581171/2.

Colombo Public Library
Sir Marcus Fernando Mawatha, Colombo 7
Tel: 695156.

Gangaramaya Bhikkhu Training Center
61 Sri Jinaratana Mawatha, Colombo 2
Tel: 27084.

University of Colombo Library
Colombo 7
Tel: 586432.

SCIENCE

Meteorology Department and Observatory
383 Bauddhaloka Mawatha, Colombo 7
Tel: 94846
Open 8.30 a.m. to 4.15 p.m.
Apply in writing, various instruments on view.

Planetarium

University of Colombo, Reid Avenue, Colombo 7

Tel: 586499

Open 8 a.m. to 4.15 p.m. Tuesday through Saturday.

Public show usually on the last Saturday of each month, with a guest lecturer in English at 3.30 p.m.

NIGHTLIFE

Sri Lanka is not famous for its nightlife. Outside of Colombo, the activities are centred around the hotels which organise special programmes for its guests.

Eating at a restaurant is considered a night out by many Sri Lankans. The restaurants open between 7 and 7.30 p.m. For after-dinner entertainment, Colombo has several places which one could visit:

Bars: Bars are located in the hotels. Most of the bars have live music or recorded music.

Casinos: Colombo's casinos have an excellent reputation for its wide range of facilities and entertainment. Complimentary drinks and transport are offered. The Casinos are mainly located in the hotels – The Hotel Ceylon Intercontinental, Hotel Lanka Oberoi, Galadari Meridien Hotel, Colombo Hilton Ramada Rennaissance Hotel, Taj Samudra Hotel and the Holiday Inn.

Nightclubs & Discos: Supper Club: Hotel Lanka Oberoi

Chapter One: Hotel Lanka Oberoi
Blue Elephant: Colombo Hilton
Colombo 2000: Galadari Meridien
The Library: Ramada Rennaissance Hotel
My Kind of Place: Taj Samudra Hotel
Little Hut: Mt. Lavinia Hotel

Colombo also has several private gambling clubs. The **Hotel Golden Topaz** at 502/1 Galle Road, Colombo 3 (Tel: 547605), features **Gaylord's Casino**. Open from 8 p.m. to 1 a.m. to members only (with memberships available at the door), its games are roulette and blackjack.

Underground and unpublicized diversions exist as well. Your taxi driver will know.

SHOPPING

Gems may be exported provided they were purchased with funds declared on the foreign exchange card. You will need to show your receipts for both purchases and money exchanges. To export gems received as gifts, permits from the **Controller of Exchange** (Central Bank, Colombo) and the **Controller of Imports and Exports** (National Mutual Building, Chatham Street, Colombo 1) are required.

The export of antiques (articles more than 50 years old) is banned. So is the export of wild animals, birds or reptiles, or parts thereof, unless accompanied with proper documentation and licenses.

SPORTS

Sri Lankans are very sports-conscious people. The most popular games are cricket and rugby. The advent of television in 1979, however, has widened the arena of sports on the island. After seeing certain athletic pursuits for the first time, many up-country schools took up new sports. In all probability, this will lead to a broader base of talent from which international sports teams can be selected.

The federal government and large mercantile organizations are giving enthusiastic backing to all sports, providing expert foreign consultants as well as financial support.

Many of the sports clubs and associations in Sri Lanka accept foreign visitors as temporary members. In addition, most of the major hotels have swimming pools and tennis courts. The Hotel Ceylon Intercontinental, Hotel Lanka Oberoi, Taji Samudra Hotel and the Ramada Rennaissance Hotel also have squash courts.

CRICKET

The cricket season starts in September and ends in April with the championship of the Lackspray Trophy, an elite tournament between the large cricketing clubs played in rounds on a league basis. Matches invariably draw large and enthusiastic crowds.

In 1982, Sri Lanka became a full member of the International Cricket Conference, along with India, Pakistan, the West Indies, England, Australia and New Zealand, thereby achieving official status in international tournaments. The inaugural match was lost to England; however, Sri Lanka did win a one-day official game against that same team. In 1984, the cricket team played a Test Match in England which was drawn. In late 1985, India toured the island and Sri Lanka won the Test Series 1-0. The following listing indicates where cricket can be seen/or played.

Bloomfield Cricket and Athletic Club
Reid Avenue, Colombo 7
Tel: 91419.

Dikoya and Maskeliya Cricket Club
Dikoya
Tel: 0512-216.

Nondescripts Cricket Club
29 Maitland Place, Colombo 7
Tel: 95293.

Singhalese Sports Club
35 Maitland Place, Colombo 7.

Uva Club, Bailey Road
Badulla, Tel: Badulla 216.

BADMINTON & SQUASH

Badminton and squash have recently become very popular sports. Sri Lankans have participated in the Thomas Cup tournament since the early 1960s, during the course of which it has won occasional games against leading badminton powers. Squash is a late 1970s arrival; Sri Lankan teams have participated in many international competitions.

FISHING & HUNTING

Fishing: There are four main types of fishing available to enthusiasts in Sri Lanka: high streams and lakes (for trout), mid and low-country rivers and tanks, estuaries and surf, and deep-sea fishing.

For information on fishing in streams of the Horton Plains or in Lake Gregory at Nuwara Eliya (elevation 6,000 to 7,000 feet), contact the Director, **Department of Wildlife Conservation**,

82, Rajamalwatta Road, Battaramulla. Tel: 433012, 433787

You can also contact the **Game Range**, Department of Wildlife Conservation, Horton Plains, Ohiya; or the **Hill Club** (Tel: 052-2654) or **Grand Hotel** (Tel: 052-2881) in Nuwara Eliya.

The **Ceylon Anglers Club**, Chaitya Road, Colombo 1 (Tel: 421752), accepts temporary memberships and can help arrange fishing trips anywhere in the country. They can provide much useful information.

The **Sea Anglers Club**, China Bay, Trincomalee is currently inoperative due to the unrest in the area. It specialised in deep-sea fishing and had club facilities for fishing, swimming and limited lodging. It is expected to reopen no sooner normalcy returns to this troubled spot.

Sunstream Boat Services, National Holidays Resort, Bentota, can arrange deep-sea excursions.

Hunting: There is no sport hunting allowed in Sri Lanka.

FOOTBALL

Football is fast becoming a a popular National sport. Large crowds attend the matches and participation in Intermational tournaments is a regular feature, although this is mainly in the tournaments held in the regional countries.

GOLF

Golf was introduced to Sri Lanka by the British. It was such an exclusive colonial sport that outside of the elite, it never really caught on. Nonetheless, Sri Lanka has two well-maintained golf courses – one in Colombo, the **Royal Colombo Golf Club** which is a nine-hole course located on Model Farm Road, Colombo 8 (Tel: 695431); the other in Nuwara Eliya, the **Nuwara Eliya Golf Club**, an 18-hole course considered as one of the finest in Asia (Tel: 052-3833).

BOATING & ROWING

On Beira Lake, the **Colombo Rowing Club** on 51/1 Sir Chittampalam Gardiner Mawatha, Colombo 2 (Tel: 4337558)

RUGBY

Rugby season runs from April to August, and is climaxed by the Clifford Cup. Like the Sara Trophy, the Cup is fought for on a league basis, with matches well attended by fanatically enthusiastic and loyal crowds. Rugby in Sri Lanka, however, still has not achieved international standards.

SCUBA DIVING & SNORKELLING

The following advice comes courtesy of professional diver Rodney Jonklass:

Always bring your own mask, snorkel and flippers. If you are concerned about weight, you can perhaps buy your equipment in Colombo and sell it before you leave the country. Rent tanks and other equipment from the larger outfits, which are far more reliable than the opportunists who solicit diving trips on the beach or in hotels. There is the dangerous possibility that they might rent you faulty gear. There are no recompression chambers in the country suitable for visiting divers, so do not go on deep dives unless you are a pro! Avoid even repetitive dives, however much you may be tempted by your local guides.

Carry your own supply of anti-histamine pills in case of minor stings from jellyfish or fish spines. Also carry sunburn lotion and anti-seasickness pills in case your boat rides are bouncier than usual.

If you are planning photography, bring your own underwater camera. They are not easy to find in Sri Lanka, except perhaps at the Duty Free Shop in Colombo. You will almost always be late for lunch if you go out diving in the morning, so make advance arrangements with your hotel to keep a big meal waiting when you return. Better still, carry substantial sandwiches, fruits and lots of cool liquids; and consume most of it *after* your dive. Try to be generous and share some of it with your crew – but it's best to keep the beer and cigarettes out of their reach. Three days' consecutive diving is best enjoyed with a fourth day of land relaxation. The little scratches and bruises will have a chance to heal; the sunburn will soften; and you'll be doubly fit and raring to go on the fifth day.

The following firms are reliable examples of diving companies:

Underwater Safaris
25 Barnes Place, Colombo 7
Tel: 694012 and 694255;
also Coral Gardens Hotel, Hikkaduwa
Tel: 09-23023.
U.K. and U.S. qualified; pool instruction followed by two sea dives for certification. Underwater expeditions are conducted; all types of diving equipment can be supplied.

Poseidon Diving Station
Galle Road, Hikkaduwa
Tel: 09-23294.
A variety of diving equipment is available.

Aqua Tours Ltd.
108 Rosmead Place, Colombo 7
Tel: 695170.
Glass-bottomed boats; equipment rental;
excursions.

SWIMMING & LIFESAVING

Most hotels have swimming pools for guests.
When sea-bathing, visitors are warned to
check swimming conditions locally. Some
beaches are only safe during certain seasons
of the year. It is safer to use areas most
frequented by local residents. Lifesaving is
fairly rare (except as a sport), so extra caution is necessary.

Kinross Swimming & Lifesaving Club
10 Station Avenue, Colombo 6
Tel: 586461.
Sea bathing, skin diving, lifesaving.

Otter Aquatic Club
380/1 Bauddhaloka Mawatha, Colombo 7
Tel: 695070, 692308.
Pool swimming, tennis, badminton, billiards.

Sinhalese Sports Club
Maitland Place, Colombo 7.
Tel: 695362.

Surf Club of Mt. Lavinia
21/21 Sri Dharmapala Road, Mt. Lavinia.
Sea bathing.

TENNIS

Tennis is perhaps the next most popular
sport. The island has produced a few good
players in the last couple of decades, but has
failed to achieve international status. A team
is fielded, however, for the worldwide Davis
Cup tournament.
    The following are some places where ten-
nis may be played.

The Gymkhana Club
31 Maitland Crescent, Colombo 7
Tel: 691025.

Oberoi Tennis Courts
Hotel Lanka Oberoi, Colombo 3
Tel: 420001.
Reservations through pool reception. In-
structor available 4 to 8 p.m.

Orient Club
Racecourse Avenue, Colombo 7
Tel: 695068.

The Women's International Club
16 Guildford Crescent, Colombo 7
Tel: 695072.

Sri Lanka Tennis Association
45, Marcus Fernando Mawatha, Colombo 7
Tel: 686174.

Nondescripts Cricket Club
Maitland Place, Colombo 7.
Tel: 695293.

WATER SKIING & WIND SURFING

Water sport activities, including water ski-
ing and wind surfing are available from
many hotels. Where hotels do not have their
own facilities, arrangements can be made
from the hotel reception with the water sports
centres in the area.

Blue Oceanic Water Sports Ltd
Blue Oceanic Hotel, Negombo.
Tel: 031-2377, 031-2642.

Sun Stream Boat Services
National Holiday Resort, Bentota.

Club Nautique Boat House
Bentota Beach Hotel, Bentota.
Tel: 034-75176 ext. 370.

YACHTING & COASTAL CRUISING

If you are arriving in Sri Lanka aboard a
private yacht, agents in Sri Lanka should be
appointed to act on behalf of the vessel and
occupants prior to arrival in Sri Lanka's
territorial waters. You may contact the following for yachting or cruising activities.

Ceylon Motor Yacht Club
Indebedda Road, Bolgoda Lake, Moratuwa;
Mail address: P.O. Box 1268, Colombo.
Sailing, wind surfing, swimming.

Kelani Yacht Co.
1A Dharmaraja Mawatha, Colombo 3
Tel: 587507;
also 101 Kew Road, Colombo 2
Tel: 435710.

Coastal cruising.

Royal Colombo Yacht Club
Colombo Harbour, Colombo 1
Tel: 434926.
The club must be contacted in advance, as no one may enter the harbor area without prior permission.

YOGA

Justin Saparamadu
227D, Galle Road, Colpetty.
Tel: 26387, 714869.

His Eminence Mahaguru, Ashram
38, D.S. Senanayake Mawatha, Udugampola, Western Province.

PHOTOGRAPHY

Sri Lanka is virtually a photographer's delight – if you have brought enough film with you. Films are freely available and can be found at most shops and hotels. The exposed film can be processed locally where a 24 hour service is offered.

The x-ray machines at the Airport are film proof. So, you do not have to worry about sending your exposed films through the security x-ray machine.

Permits are required before you can take photographs at a number of interesting sites. If you are going to visit the Ancient Cities (Anuradhapura, Polonnaruwa and Sigiriya), you can save time and money by buying an all-round "Culture Triangle" ticket in Colombo which includes permits for photograph taking and admission to all archaeological sites, monuments, and museums, as well as entry for vehicles. The all-round ticket (Rs 600) is available from the Cultural Triangle Fund, 212 Bauddhaloka Mawatha, Colombo 7. Tel. 587912, 500733.

Single permits are usually available at the sites – Anuradhapura, Polonnaruwa and Sigiriya – and admission to each of them costs Rs 200. Admission to the national museums at Anuradhapura, Colombo and Kandy cost Rs 25 each, excluding photography permits.

At other religious sites, you must obtain permits from the temple offices. (Permits to Aukana, Dambulla cave temple and Kandy's Temple of the Tooth cost Rs 30 each; to Mihintale, Rs 25.)

All permits are issued with the provision that unless in a respectful posture, no human figure should be featured in your photographs. This means, simply, that posing is not allowed in front of holy monuments or paintings.

LANGUAGE

Most Sri Lankans involved in the visitor industry, as well as nearly all educated urbanites, speak English very fluently. In rural areas and with lower-caste persons, however, a few words in the vernacular can be very useful. The following list may help.

ENGLISH
SINHALESE
TAMIL

Hello (to a gentleman)
Mahatmaya
Aiya

Hello (to a lady)
Nona mahatmaya
Thirumadhi

Good morning
Suba Udasanak way va
–

Good night
Suba rathriyak way va
–

357

Greeting (general)
Ayubowan
Vanakkam
(In the vernacular, the people of Sri Lanka do not differentiate times. A general greeting while meeting and departing is the custom.)

Please
Karunakara
Thayavu sai du

Thank you
Es-thu-ti
Nandri

Thank you very much
Bohoma es-thu-ti
Miga nandri

Yes
Ov
Ahm

No
Na-tha (nay-hay)
Illai

Maybe
Venna puluvan
Sila way lai

How are you?
Kohomada sahpa sahneepa?
Ehppadi sugam?

I am fine
Sanee-pen innava
Nalla sugam

I am not well
Sanee-pa na-tha (nay-hay)
Sugamillai

Please call a doctor
Karunakara dosthara mahatmaye kuta enna kiyanna
Thayavu seidu darktarai kootti kondu varungal

My name is…
Mage name…
Ennudaya payar…

What is your name?
Obeh nameh monawada?
Ungal payar enna?

I'm please to meet you
Obeva muna gaseemata labeema loku sathutak.
Ungalai santhikka kidaiththadu miga sandosham.

Where do you live?
Oba vah-sa-ya karannay kohayda?
Neengal engay val gi reergal?

I come from…
Mama vasaya karannay…
Naan… ill val-gi rain.

How old are you?
Obeh vayase kee ya da?
Ungal vayasu eth-thanai?

I am…years old.
Magay vayasa avurudu…
En vayadu…

Are you married?
Oba we-va-ha ve-la-da?
Neengal kalyanam ana warah?

Do you have children?
Obata da-ru-vo in-navada?
Ungalukku piilai gal irukku rargalah?

Pardon me ...
Samavenna ...
Manniyungal ...

Excuse me (asking permission) ...
Avasarai ...
Thayavu seiyungal...

Do you speak English?
Obata ingreesee kata karanna puluvan da?
Ungalukku angilam pesa mudiyuma?

I'm sorry. I don't speak Sinhala (Tamil).
Kanagatui. Sinhalen kata karanna mama danne nehe.
Manniyungal. Thamilil pesa enak-ku thariyadu.

I don't understand
Mata thayrennay nehe.
Enakku vilangavillai.

Do you understand?
Obata thayrunada?
Ungalukku vilanginadah?

Who can speak English?
Katada ingreesee kata karanna puluwan?
Yarrukku angilam pesa mudiyum?

Where is the train station?
Dum riya stanaya koheda?
Puga irada nilayam engay?

When will the train leave?
Dum riya kee yata-da pitath venne?
Eth-thanai manikku puga iradam purappadum?

Which way is it to Colombo?
Kolambata yannay kohomada?
Kolumbukku povadu eppadi?

How far is it to (Kandy)?
(Maha Nuwara) ta hatakkma kee yada?
(Kandy) koku evvalavu thooram?

Please leave me alone.
Mawa paduven inna arinda.
Ennai summa irukka vidungal.

Why do you ask so many questions?
Aee och chara prashna ahannay?
Ei-n ath-thanai kaylvi ket kreergal?

May I have a menu please?
Kahmata monarada thiyennay?
Sappida enna erukkiradu?

I'd like rice and curry.
Bahth denna.
So ru tharungal.

Has this water been boiled?
May wathura unu karalada?
Idu kodikka vaith-tha neera?

Bring the bill, please.
Karunakara bila gaynna.
Bill kondu varungal.

How much does this cost?
May kay gana kee yada?
Ihdan vilai enna?

That's too much.
Ah vadi neda.
Kooda vilai thanay.

I'll pay... rupees.
Rupiyal... dennam.
...rubai tharugirain.

one (1)
eka
on dru (oru)

tow (2)
deka
irandu

three (3)
thuna
moondru

four (4)
hathara
naangu

five (5)
paha
eyendu

six (6)
haya
aaru

seven (7)
hatha
eilu

eight (8)
ata
ettu

nine (9)
namaya
onbadu

ten (10)
dahaya
patthu

one hundred (100)
siiya
—

one thousand (1,000)
daaha
—

FURTHER READING

BOOKSTORES

Asoka Trading Co.
Galle Road, Colombo 4
Tel: 435501.
Novels, used books, general reading.

Cargills Ltd.
York Street, Colombo 1
Tel: 29331.
Trade books, children's books, novels general reading.

H.W. Cave and Co.
Gaffor Building, Colombo 1
Tel: 422675.
Children's books, novels general reading.

C.L.S. Bookshop
60A Galle Road, Colombo 6 (Wellawette).
Christian literature and general reading.

K.V.G. de Silva and Sons (Colombo)
415 Galle Road, Colombo 4 (Bambalapitiya)
Tel: 584146;
and 5, Ground Floor, Liberty Plaza, Colombo 3.
Trade books, fiction, reference, children's books, general reading.

K.V.G. de Silva and Sons (Kandy)
YMBA Building, Colombo 1 (Fort)
Tel: 26831;
also 86 D.S. Senanayake Vidiya, Kandy
Tel: 08-23254.
Maps, fiction, reference, children's books.

Lake House Bookshop
100 Sir Chittampalam A. Gardiner Mawatha, Colombo 2
Tel: 432104.
General reading, reference, paperbacks, craft books.

McCallum Book Depot
Olcott Mawatha, Colombo 1
Tel: 20611.
Magazines, general reading.

J.L. Morrison, Son and Jones
Aluthmavata Road, Colombo 13
Tel: 431441.
General reading, reference.

Pragna Bookstore
204 Galle Road, Colombo 4 (Bambalapitiya)
Tel: 581691.
Christian books and tapes.

Serendib Gallery
100 Galle Road, Colombo 4.
Old and rare books, travel books.

GENERAL

American Women's Association. *Colombo Handbook*. Third edition. Colombo: AWA, 1981.

Bandaranayake, Senake and Christian Zuber. *Sri Lanka: Island Civilisation*. Colombo: Lake House Investment, 1978. Pictorial survey.

Beny, Roloff. *Island: Ceylon*. London: Thames & Hudson, 1971. Pictorial essay with extracts from early writers.

Brohier, R.L. *Seeing Ceylon and Discovering Ceylon*. Colombo: Lake House Investments, 1965, 1981. Fascinating series of travel essays.

Cave, Henry W. *Golden Tips*. London: Cassell & Co., 1900. Interesting account of the tea industry and turn-of-the-century Ceylon.

Clarke, Arthur C. *The View From Serendip*. New York: Random House, 1977. A personal account of the sci-fi writer's life in Sri Lanka.

Darnton, Iris. *Jungle Journeys in Ceylon*. Galaxy Books, 1975.

De Silva, K.M. (ed.) *Sri Lanka: A Survey*. Honolulu: The University Press of Hawaii, 1977. Concise essays by several erudite authors.

Goonetileke, H.A.I. *A Bibliography of Ceylon*. 5 vols. Zug, Switzerland: Inter Documentation Company, 1970 (I and II), 1976 (III), 1982 (IV and V). The only definitive bibliography.

Handbook for the Ceylon Traveller. Colombo: Studio Times, revised 1983. Detailed guide to all possible visitor destinations.

Hulugalle, H.A. *Ceylon Yesterday, Sri Lanka Today.* Colombo: M.D. Gunasena, 1976.

Ondaatje, Michael. *Running in the Family.* New York: Norton, 1983. A Canadian writer's search for his "roots" in Sri Lanka.

Page, Tim. *Sri Lanka.* 1984.

Raffel, Douglas. *In Ruhuna Jungles.* Colombo: K.V.G. de Silva & Sons, 1959.

Raven-Hart, Roland. *Ceylon: History in Stone.* Colombo: the Associated Newspapers of Ceylon, 1964. A fascinating, anecdotal travelogue. Must reading.

Utoff, Hans Rudolf. *Sri Lanka Ceylon.* 1983.

Vijaya-Tunga, J. *Grass for My Feet.* London: Edwin Arnold, 1935. Nostalgic recollections of a childhood near Galle.

Wheeler, Tony. *Sri Lanka: A Travel Survival Kit.* South Yarra, Australia: Lonely Planet, 1982 edition. A budget traveler's best reference.

Woolf, Leonard. *Village in the Jungle.*

HISTORY

Alles, A.C. *Insurgency 1971* Colombo: Colombo Apothecaries, 1976. Account of insurrection.

Arasaratnam, Sinnapah. *Dutch Power in Ceylon.* Amsterdam: Djambatan, 1958. Scholarly.

Baldaeus, Phillipus. *Ceylon.* Colombo: Ceylon Historical Journal, Vol. VIII. Translated by Pieter Brohier. Authoritative and readable Dutch account from the 18th Century.

Baker, Samuel. *Eight Years in Ceylon.* London: Longman, Brown, Green & Longmans, 1855. By the founder of Nuwara Eliya.

Baker, Samuel. *The Rifle and Hound in Ceylon.* London: London, Brown, Green and Longmans, 1954. Classic of the Victorian school of big-game hunting.

Brohier, R.L. *Links Between Sri Lanka and the Netherlands: A Book of Dutch Ceylon.* Colombo: Netherlands Alumni Association of Sri Lanka, 1978.

Cleghorn, Hugh. *The Cleghorn Papers.* London: A. & C. Black, 1927. Edited by William Neil. About the fall of the Dutch.

Codrington, H.W. *A Short History of Ceylon.* London: Macmillan, 1926. First venture beyond the authority of the *Mahavamsa.*

Cordiner, James. *A Description of Ceylon.* 2 vols. Aberdeen: A. Brown; and London: Longman, Hurst, Rees & Orme, 1807.

Daniell, Samuel. *A Picturesque Illustration of Ceylon.* London: T. Bensley, 1808. Twelve fine aquatints and descriptive text.

Davy, John. *An Account of the Interior of Ceylon.* London: Longman, Hurst, Rees, Orme & Brown, 1821. Important British account.

De Lanerolle, Nalini. *A Reign of Ten Kings.* Ceylon Tourist Board.

De Queyroz, Fernado. *Conquest of Ceylon.* Colombo: Government Printer, 1930. Most complete Portugues history. Translated by S.G. Perera.

De Silva, Colvin R. *Ceylon Under the British Occupation 1795-1833.* Colombo: Colombo Apothecaries, 1942. Well documented.

De Silva, K.M. *A History of Sri Lanka.* Delhi: Oxford University Press, 1981. A thorough and analytical but controversial modern account.

Deraniyagala, P.E.P. *The Pleistocene of Ceylon.* Colombo: National Museum, 1955. Palaeontologist's account of prehistoric Ceylon.

Dhammakitti, Buddharakkhita, et al. *The Culavamsa.* 2 vols. Colombo: Ceylon Government Information Department, 1953. Translated by Wilhelm Geiger.

Geiger, Wilhelm. *Culture of Ceylon in Mediaeval Times.* Wiesbaden: Otto Harrassowitz, 1960. Edited by Heinz Bechert. By the great Indologist.

Goonetileke, H.A.I. (ed.) *Images of Sri Lanka Through American Eyes: Travellers in Ceylon in the 19th and 20th Centuries.* Washington, D.C.: International Communication Agency (U.S.A.), 1976. Compendium of 35 essays from Mark Twain to Thomas Merton.

Goonewardena, K.W. *The Foundation of Dutch Power in Ceylon.* Amsterdam: Djambatan, 1958. Scholarly.

Jupp, James. *Sri Lanka: Third World Democracy.* London: Frank Cass, 1978.

Knox, Robert. *An Historical Relation of Ceylon.* London: Royal Society, 1681. Reprinted by Dehiwala: Tisara Prakasakayo,

1958. One of the most important books ever written on Ceylon; believed to be the basis of Daniel Defoe's *Robinson Crusoe.*

Law, B.C. (ed.) *The Dipavamsa.* Colombo: Ceylon Historical Journal, Vol. VII.

Liyanagamage, A. *The Decline of Polonnaruwa and the Rise of Dambadeniya (Circa 1180-1270 A.D.).* Colombo: Department of Cultural Affairs, 1968.

Ludowyk, E.F.C. *The Modern History of Ceylon.* London: Weidenfeld & NBicholson, 1966. Fine survey.

Ludowyk, E.F.C. *The Story of Ceylon.* 2nd edition. London: Faber, 1967.

The Mahavamsa. Colombo: Ceylon Government Information Department, 1950. Translated by Wilhelm Geiger.

Marshall, Henry. *Ceylon.* London: William H. Allen, 1846. Essential account of the last days of the Kandyan kingdom.

Mendis, G.C. *The Early History of Ceylon.* Calcutta: YMCA Publishing House, 1932. The first critical history.

Mendis, V.L.B. *The Advent of the British to Ceylon, 1762-1803.* Dehiwala: Tisara Prakasakayo, 1971.

Mendis, Vernon. *Foreign Relations of Sri Lanka, From Earliest Times to 1965.* Colombo: Tisara Prakasakayo, 1983.

Paranavitana, Senerat. *Sinhalayo.* Colombo: Lake House Investments, 1967. Informative and entertaining, especially through 14th Century.

Perera, G.F. *The Ceylon Railway.* Colombo: Ceylon Observer, 1925. Good reading for train buffs.

Pieris, P.E. *Sinhale and the Patriots.* Colombo: Colombo Apothecaries, 1950. Story of the "Great Rebellion" that ended the Kandyan kingdom.

Pieris, Ralph. *Singhalese Social Organisation: The Kandyan Period.* Peradeniya: Ceylon University press Board, 1956.

Rasanayagam, C. *Mudaliyar: Ancient Jaffna, Being a Research into the History of Jaffna from Very Early Times to the Portuguese Period.* Madras: Everymans Publishers, 1926. Only English account.

Ribeiro, Joao. *The Historic Tragedy of Ceilao.* Galle: Albion Press, 1907. First detailed European account of Ceylon. Translated by P.E. Peiris.

Seneviratne, H.L. *Rituals of the Kandyan State.* London: Cambridge University Press, 1978.

Skinner, Thomas. *Fifty Years in Ceylon.* London: W.H. Allen, 1891. Edited by Annie Skinner. Autobiography of the great surveyor.

Suckling, Horatio John. *A General Description of the Island...Ceylon.* London: Chapman & Hall, 1876. Important account, written under the name: "An Officer, Late of the Ceylon Rifles."

Tennant, James Emerson. *Ceylon.* 2 vols. London: Longman, Green, Longman and Roberts, 1859. The best documented book of the time. Essential reading on mid-19th Century Ceylon.

Tomlinson, Michael. *The Most Dangerous Moment.* London: William Kimber, 1976. Account of Ceylon's role in World War II.

Toussaint, J.R. *Annals of the Ceylon Civil Service.* Colombo Apothecaries, 1935. Anecdotal and highly readable.

Wilson, N.J. *The Gaullist System in Asia: The Constitution of Sri Lanka (1978).* London: Macmillan, 1980.

Winius, G.D. *The Fatal History of Portuguese Ceylon: Transition to Dutch Rule.* Cambridge, Mass: Harvard University Press, 1971.

Wriggins, W. Howard. *Ceylon: Dilemmas of a New Nation.* Princeton, J.J.: Princeton University Press, 1960. Authoritative work on post-independence politics.

RELIGION & SOCIETY

Arumugam, S. *Ancient Hindu Temples of Sri Lanka.* Colombo: 1982.

Bapat, B.P. (ed.) *2,500 Years of Buddhism.* Delhi: Government of India Publications Division, 1956. Useful collection of essays.

Chaudhuri, Nirad C. *Hinduism.* Oxford, England: Oxford University Press, 1979. Compact survey, easy to understand.

Coomaraswamy, Ananda, and Sister Nivedita. *Myths of the Hindus and Buddhists.* London: Dover, 1913.

De Silva, C.L.A. *The Four Essential Doctrines of Buddhism.* Colombo: Associated Newspapers of Ceylon, 1948.

De Silva, Lynn. *Buddhism: Beliefs and Practices in Sri Lanka.* Colombo: Ecumenical Institute, 1974, 1980. Good concise survey of local Buddhism.

De Silva Gooneratna, Dandris. *On De-*

monology and Witchcraft in Ceylon. Colombo: Royal Asiatic Society, Ceylon Branch. Concise and reliable.

Gombrich, Richard. *Precept. and Practice: Traditional Buddhism in the Rural Highlands of Ceylon.* London: Oxford University Press, 1971.

Houtart, F. *Religion and Ideology in Sri Lanka.* Colombo: Hansaa Publishers, 1974.

Leach, E.R. *Pul Eliya.* London: Cambridge University Press, 1961. Interesting sociological study of the bearing of kinship on land tenure.

Ludowyk, E.F.C. *The Footprint of the Buddha.* London: Allen & Unwin, 1958. Influence of Buddhism on the arts.

Malalasekera, G.P. *The Buddha and His Teachings.* Colombo: Lanka Bauddha Mandalaya, 1957.

Paranavitana, Senerat. *The God of Adams Peak.* Ascona, Switzerland: Artibus Asiae Publishers, 1958.

Parker, H. *Ancient Ceylon.* London: Luzac, 1909. Study of traditional Sinhalese villages in early 20th Century Ceylon.

Perera, H.R. *Buddhism in Ceylon: Its Past and Its Present.* Kandy: Buddhist Publication Society, 1966.

Raghavan, M.D. *Handsome Beggars: The Rodiyas of Ceylon.* Colombo: Colombo Book Centre, 1957. Only book-length study of gypsies.

Raghavan, M.D. *The Karava of Ceylon.* Colombo: K.V.G. de Silva and Sons, 1961. Only serious study of a Sinhalese caste.

Raghavan, M.D. *Tamil Culture in Ceylon: A General Introduction.* Colombo: Kalai Nilayam, 1971.

Rahula, Walpola. *The Heritage of the Bhikku.* New York: Random House, 1974.

Rahula, Walpola. *History of Buddhism in Ceylon.* Colombo: M.D. Gunasena, 1966.

Rahula, Walpola. *What the Buddha Taught.* New York: Random House, 1977.

Ryan, Bryce. *Caste in Modern Ceylon.* New Brunswick, N.J.: Rutgers University Press, 1953.

Ryan, Bryce. *Sinhalese Village.* Coral Gables, Fla.: University of Miami Press, 1958. Life in a low-country society.

Sangharakshita, Bhikshu. *Anagarika Dharmapala: A Biographical Sketch.* Kandy: Buddhist Publication society, 1964.

Seligmann, C.G. and B.Z. *The Veddas.* London: Cambridge University Press, 1911.

The classic on this race.

Spittel, R.L. *Far-Off Things.* Colombo: Colombo Apothecaries, 1933. Also: *Savage Sanctuary* (London: Rich and Cowan, 1941), *Vanished Trails* (Bombay: Oxford University Press, 1950), *Wild Ceylon* (Colombo: Colombo Apothecaries, 1924) – books about the Veddhas by a surgeon who made a study of these people his life's avocation.

Wirz, Paul. *Exorcism and the Art of Healing in Ceylon.* Leiden, Netherlands: Brill, 1954. Detailed study of the tradition of devil dancing.

Wirz, Paul. *Kataragama: The Holiest Place in Ceylon.* Colombo: Lake House Investments, 1966.

ARTS & CULTURE

Archaeological Department. Series of monographs on traditional arts with the following titles: *Embekke Devale Carvings; Panavitiya Ambalama Carvings; Medawala Vihara Frescoes; Murals at Tivanka Pilimage; Polonnaruwa Bronzes; Buddha States; Guard Stones; Moonstones; Sinhalese Doorways; Terracotta Heads; Terracotta Decorative Tiles; and Sinhalese Dance and Music.* Various authors, published 1970 to 1982.

Archer, W.G., and Senart Paranavitana. *Ceylon: Paintings from Temple, Shrine and Rock.* Paris: New York Graphic Society, 1958. Fine reproductions. Part of the UNESCO World Art Series.

Brohier, R.L. *Ancient Irrigation Works in Ceylon.* 3 vols. Colombo: Ceylon Government Press, 1934, 1935. Fascinating survey with illustrations.

Brohier, R.L. *Furniture of the Dutch Period in Ceylon.* Colombo: National Museum, 1969.

Cave, Henry W. *Picturesque Ceylon.* 4 vols. London: Sampson, Low, Marston, 1893, 1897. Landscape photography.

Coomaraswamy, Ananda K. *Mediaeval Sinhalese Art.* Broad Campden, England: Essex House, 1908. Reprinted New York: Pantheon, 1956. Monumental study.

De S. Kulatillake, C., and Ranjan Abeysinghe. *A Background to Sinhala Traditional Music of Sri Lanka.* Colombo: Department of Cultural Affairs (monograph), 1962.

De Silva, R.K. *Early prints of Ceylon (Sri*

363

Lanka) *1800-1900.* Serendip Publications Ltd.

Devendra, D.T. *The Buddha Image and Ceylon.* Colombo: K.V.G. de Silva and Sons, 1957.

Devendra, D.T. *Classical Sinhalese Sculpture, 300 B.C. to A.D. 1000.* London: Alex Tiranti, 1958.

Disanayaka, J.B. *National Languages of Sri Lanka I – Sinhala.* Colombo: Department of Cultural Affairs (monograph), 1976.

Godakumbure, C.E. *Architecture of Sri Lanka.* Colombo: Department of Cultural Affairs (monograph), 1963.

Godakumbure, C.E. *Literature of Sri Lanka.* Colombo: Department of Cultural Affairs (monograph), 1962.

Goonatilleka, M.H. *Masks of Sri Lanka.* Colombo: Department of Cultural Affairs (monograph), 1976.

Goonatilleka, M.H. *Masks and Masks Systems of Sri Lanka.* Colombo. Tamarind Books, 1978.

Goonatilleka, M.H. *The Rural Theatre and Social Satire of Sri Lanka.* Colombo: Ceylon Tourist Board, no date.

Goontilleka, M.H. *Sokari of Sri Lanka.* Colombo: Department of Cultural Affairs (mongraph), 1976.

Gunawardana, A.J. *Theatre in Sri Lanka.* Colombo: Department of Cultural Affairs (monograph), 1976.

Hocart, A.M., and Senarat Paranavitana. *The Temple of the Tooth in Kandy.* Colombo: Government of Ceylon, 1931.

Hopfner, Gerd. *Masken Aus Ceylon.* Berlin: Museum of Folk Art, 1969. German. Superb collection of plates.

Kailasapathy, K., and A. Sanmugadas. *National Languages of Sri Lanka II – Tamil.* Colombo: Department of Cultural Affairs (monograph), 1976.

Keyt, George. *A Felicitation Volume.* Colombo: The George Keyt Felicitation Committee, 1977.

Makulloluwa, W.B. *Dances of Sri Lanka.* Colombo: Department of Cultural Affairs (monograph), 1976.

Manjusri, L.T.P. *Design Elements from Sri Lankan Temple Paintings.* Colombo: Archaeological Society of Sri Lanka, 1977.

Mitton, G.E. *The Lost Cities of Ceylon.* London: John Murray, 1916. Archaeologist's report.

Obeyesekere, Ranjini, and Chitra Fernando (eds.). *An Anthology of Modern Writing from Sri Lanka.* Tucson, Ariz.: University of Arizona Press, 1981.

O'Brien, C. *Views in Ceylon.* London: Day & Son, 1864. Fifteen aquatints.

Paranavitana, Senarat. *Art and Architecture of Ceylon: Polonnaruwa Period.* Colombo: Arts Council of Ceylon, 1954.

Paranavitana, Senarat. *Glimpses of Ceylon's Past.* Colombo: Lake House Investments, 1972. Personal chronicle of excavations by former archaeological commissioner.

Paranavitana, Senarat. *The Stupa in Ceylon.* Colombo: Ceylon Government Press, 1946. Study of the stupa's local significance and evolution.

Parker, H. *Village Folk Tales of Ceylon.* 3 vols. London: Luzac, 1910, 1914.

Russel, Martin. *George Keyt.* Bombay: Marg Publications, 1950. The work of the internationally acclaimed artist in 101 plates.

Sarachchandra, E.R. *The Sinhalese Fold Play.* Colombo: Daily News Press, 1953. Valuable pioneer survey.

Smither, J.G., *Architectural Remains, Anuradhapura, Ceylon.* Colombo: Ceylon Government Press, 1894. Folio album of first architectural drawings.

Tilakasiri, J. *Puppetry in Sri Lanka.* Colombo: Department of Cultural Affairs (monograph), 1961.

Wendt, Lionel. *Lionel Wendt's Ceylon.* London: Lincolns-Prager, 1950. A memorial to Ceylon's internationally famous photographer; 120 reproductions.

Wickramasinghe, Martin. *Sinhala Language and Culture.* Dehiwala: Tisara Prakasakayo, 1975.

Wijesekera, Nandadeva. *Ancient Paints and Sculpture in Sri Lanka.* Colombo: Department of Cultural Affairs (monograph), 1962.

Wijesekera, Nandadeva. *Early Sinhalese Painting.* Maharagama: Saman Press, 1959. Covers murals and iconography up to the 12th Century.

Wijesekera, Nandadeva. *Early Sinhalese Sculpture.* Colombo: M.D. Gunasena, 1962. Up to the 12th Century.

NATURAL HISTORY

Bond, Thomas. *Wild Flowers of the Ceylon Hills*. Madras: Oxford University Press, 1953.

De Zylva, Dr. T.S.U. *Birds of Sri Lanka*. Trumpet Publishers.

Deraniyagala, P.E.P. *A Coloured Atlas of Some Vertebrates from Ceylon*. 3 vols. Colombo: National Museum, 1952, 1955. Fish and reptiles covered in detail.

Fernando, Dorothy. *Wild Flowers of Ceylon*. Mitcham, England: West Brothers, 1954. Identifies 173 species.

Henry, G.M. *A Guide to the Birds of Ceylon*. London: Oxford University Press, 1955. Recently reprinted. Good notes, accurate plates; extremely useful. Accompanied by *Coloured Plates of the Birds of Ceylon* (London: Ceylon Government, 1927, 1935), 4 vols.

Legge, W. Vincent. *A History of the Birds of Ceylon*. London: The Author, 1878, 1880. 3 vols. The first systematic study of Ceylon birds. Reprinted in 1984. Colombo: Tisara Prakasakayo.

Mendis, A.S., and C.H. Fernando *A Guide to the Freshwater Fauna of Ceylon*. Colombo: Fisheries Research Station, 1962.

Munro, Ian, *The Marine and Fresh Water Fishes of Ceylon*. Canberra: Department of External Affairs, 1955.

Philips, W.W.A. *Manual of the Mammals of Ceylon*. Colombo: The Director, Colombo Museum, 1935.

Roberts, Emmanuel. *Vegetable Materia Medica of India and Ceylon*. Colombo: Plate Limited, 1931. Ayurvedic remedies.

Trimen, Henry. *A Handbook to the Flora of Ceylon*. London: Dulau, 1893, 1900. 5 vols. With complementary Atlas of Plates, 4 vols. Invaluable standard reference.

Wall, Frank. *Snakes of Ceylon*. Colombo: Government Printer, 1921. Fullest work on subject.

Wijesekera, Dr. N. *Heritage of Sri Lanka*. 1984.

Woodhouse, L.G.O. *The Butterfly Fauna of Ceylon*. Colombo: Government Press, 1942. Remarkable work.

Worthington, T.B. *Ceylon Trees*. Colombo: Colombo Apothecaries, 1959. Identifies 429 species.

MISCELLANEOUS

Clarke, Arthur C. *The Fountains of Paradise*. New York: Random House, 1979. Sci-fi about an elevator to the moon from an island suspiciously like Sri Lanka.

Clarke, Arthur C. *The Reefs of Taprobane*. New York: Harper & Brothers, 1957. An account of skin divers' opportunities.

Clarke, Arthur C. *The Treasure of the Great Reef*. London: Arthur Barker, 1964. Thrilling account of exploration of sunken treasure ships.

Codrington, H.W. *Ceylon Coins and Currency*. Colombo: Memoirs of the Colombo Museum, 1924. The only major work on the subject.

DeSilva, P.H.D.H. *Snakes of Sri Lanka*. 1980.

DeSilva, Colin. *The Winds of Sinhala*. Garden City, N.Y.: Doubleday, 1982. Historical novel about Sri Lanka in the 1st Century B.C.

Dissanayake, Chandra. *Ceylon Cookery*. Colombo: Metro Printers, 1968. Authentic recipes.

Jayawardena, S.A.S. *Gems of Ceylon*. Colombo: Government Press, 1966. Sketchy but available.

Kautzch, Eberhard. *Waterfalls of Sri Lanka*. Colombo: Tisara Prakasakayo, 1983.

USEFUL ADDRESSES

TOURIST INFORMATION

Operated by the government's Ceylon Tourist Board, the Tourist Information Center (TIC) advises visitors on local customs, culture and history as well as answers all travel questions. In addition, it provides information on special events, tour itineraries, and schedules of trains and domestic aircraft; and arranges tour guides for visitors who request them. The TIC also distributes travel literature, including the quarterly *Sri Lanka Accommodation* and the biannual *Sri Lanka Tourist Information*. All the services, except for those of the tour guides, are offered free of charge.

The main office of the TIC is at 78, Steuart Place, Colombo 3. Tel: 437059, 437060. It also has information counters in the lobby of the Colombo Airport, Katunayake (tel: 452411) and at the passenger jetty, Port of Colombo. The TIC in Kandy is located at "Headmans Lodge', 3, Deva Veediya, Kandy.

Tourist information and literature may also be obtained from Sri Lanka's foreign missions, the Ceylon Tourist Board and its overseas representative offices. (See below for listing.)

OVERSEAS OFFICES OF THE CEYLON TOURIST BOARD

Australia
Tourist Board Representative: F P Leonard Advertising Pte Ltd., 241 Abercrombie Sttreet, Chippendale, NSW Australia 2008 Tel: 698-5266.
Ceylon Tourist Board: Western Australia Office, 439 Albany Highway, Victoria Park, West Australia 6100 Tel: (09) 362-4579.

Denmark
Tourist Board Representative: Ceylon Touristrad, Sollerodgardavej 38, DK 2840 Holte.

France
Mr O.L.M. Nawaz, Assistant Director 19 rue du 4 Septembre, 75002 Paris Tel: 42604999.

Federal Republic of Germany
Ceylon (Sri Lanka) Tourist Board Allerheiligentor 2-4 D-6000 Frankfurt/Main 1 Tel: (069) 287734/288216.

Japan
Director, Ceylon Tourist Board Dawa Building 7-2-22 Ginza, Chuo-Ko, Tokyo Tel: (03) 289-0771/2.

Thailand
Ceylon (Sri Lanka) Tourist Board: Thailand Office, 1/18 Soi 10, Sukhumvit Road, Bangkok Tel: 251-8062.

United Kingdom
Director, Ceylon Tourist Board 53-54 Haymarket, London SW1Y UK Tel: (071) 925-0177, (081) 321-0034

United States of America
Embassy of the Democratic Socialist Republic of Sri Lanka 2148 Wyoming Avenue NW, Washington DC 20008 Tel: (202) 483-4025/9.

AIRLINES

Air Lanka
14, Sir Baron Jayatilleke Mawatha, Colombo 1
Tel: 21291; Telex: 21401; Cable: Air Lanka Reservations: 421161; Ticket Office: 421291; Flight Information: 030/2281.

Aeroflot Soviet Airlines
79/81, Hemas Building, York Street, Colombo 1
Tel: 25580, 433062, 29192.

Balkan Bulgarian Airline
6 York Street, Colombo 1
Tel: 24431.

British Airways
General Sales Agent: Ceylon Hotels Corporation, 63, Janadhipathi Mawatha, Colombo 1
Tel: 20231-4
Flight Inquiries: 20236-7 or 030-2303/2.

Garuda Indonesian Airlines
c/o Carson Cumberbatch & Co. Ltd., Janadhipathi Mawatha, Colombo 1
Tel: 25984.

Gulf Air
11 B/C York Street, Colombo 1
Tel: 26633.

Maldives International Airlines
General Sales Agent: Indian Airlines, 95, Sir Baron Jayatilleka Mawatha, Colombo 1
Tel: 23136.

Indian Airlines
95, Sir Baron Jayatilleka Mawatha, Colombo 1
Tel: 23136, 29838, 23987.

Korean Airlines
47, Galle Face Court, Colombo 3
Tel: 26144, 23977, 22921; Telex: 21271 A/b "Finco" Colombo.

Kuwait Airways
South Asian Travels Ltd., Ceylinco House, Colombo 1
Tel: 545531/3.

K. L. M. Royal Dutch Airlines
c/o Carson Cumberbatch & Co. Ltd., 61, Janadhipathi Mawatha, Colombo 1
Tel: 26359, 25984/5/6.

Pakistan International Airlines
45, Janadhipathi Mawatha, Colombo 1
Tel: 573475, 574445.

Royal Nepal Airlines
434, Galle Road, Colombo 3
Tel: 24045.

Singapore Airlines
General Sales Agent: ASET Airways Ltd., 15A, Sir Baron Jayatilleka Mawatha, Colombo 1
Tel: 22711.

Swissair
General Sales Agent: A. Baur & Co. Ltd., 5, Upper Chatham Street, Colombo 1
Tel: 435403/4/5.

Thai Airways International Ltd.
Browns Tours Ltd., 16, Janadhipathi Mawatha, Colombo 1
Tel: 436201/5.

UTA French Airlines
5, York Street, Colombo 1
Tel: 27605/6.

BUSINESS ADDRESSES

Ceylon Chamber of Commerce
P O Box 274, 50 Nawam Mawatha, Colombo 2
Tel: 421745/7.

Foreign Investment Advisory Committee
(non-Free Trade Zone projects) International Economic Corporation Division, Ministry of Finance and Planning, 3rd Floor, Galler Face Secretariat, Colombo 1
Tel: 547478, 26286.

Greater Colombo Economic Commission
(Authority for Free Trade Zone projects) 14 Sir Baron Jayatilleke Mawatha, Colombo 1
Tel: 548880.

Sri Lanka Chamber of Small Industries
12 Rotunda Gardens, Colombo 3
Tel: 549692.

Sri Lanka Export Development Board
Sir Chittampalam Gardiner Mawatha, Colombo 2
Tel: 573004.

EMBASSIES & CONSULATES

Most Asian and large Western nations maintain consulates and embassies in Colombo. They are able to assist nationals of their countries in the case of emergency or common requests. In addition, several of them –

including the American, British, French and German embassies – have libraries and various cultural activities available to visitors and residents alike. See below for a full listing.

Arab Republic Of Egypt
39 Dickmans Road, Colombo 5
Tel: 583621.

Australian High Commission
3, Cambridge Place. Colombo 7
Tel: 596464/5/6.

Austria Consulate
1, Park Drive, Off Park Road, Colombo 5
Tel: 691613.

Bangladesh High Commission (People's Republic of)
207/1, Dharmapala Mawatha, Colombo 7
Tel: 595963, 93565.

Belgium Consulate
22 Palm Grove, Colombo 3
Tel: 574453.

Brazil Consulate (Honorary)
143, Fife road, Colombo 5
Tel: 84585.

Bulgaria Embassy (People's Republic of)
29/2, Jayasingha Road, Colombo 6
Tel: 553173.

Burma Embassy (Socialist Republic of the Union of)
17 Skelton Gardens, Colombo 5
Tel: 587607/8.

Canada High Commission
6 Gregory's Road, Colombo 7
Tel: 695841/2/3.

China Embassy (People's Republic of)
191, Dharmapala Mawatha, Colombo 7
Tel: 696459.

Cuba Embassy
18 Pedris Road, Colombo 3
Tel: 573041/2.

Cyprus Consulate
25, Layard's Road, Colombo 5
Tel: 588098.

Czechoslovakia Embassy
47, 47A, Horton Place, Colombo 7
Tel: 94766.

Denmark, The Royal Danish Consulate-General
264, Grandpass Road, Colombo 14
Tel: 447806.

Dominican Republic Consulate-General
108, Barnes Place, Colombo 7
Tel: 697602, 547213.

France Embassy
89, Rosmead Place, Colombo 7
Tel: 698815, 699750.

Finland Embassy
No. 35/2, Guildford Crescent, Colombo 7
Tel: 698819/20.

Finland Cosulate-General
81 Barnes Place, Colombo 7
Tel: 547806.

German Embassy (Federal Republic of)
16 Barnes Place, Colombo 7
Tel: 595814, 595815/6/7.

Greece Consulate
25, Layard's Road, Colombo 5
Tel: 588098.

Holy See, Apostolic Nunciature
1, Gower Street, Colombo 5
Tel: 82554.

Hungary Embassy of the Hungarian People's Republic and Commercial Section
79/2, Horton Place, Colombo 7
Tel: 91966.

India High Commission
36-38 Galle Road, Colombo 3
Tel: 421604/5.

Indonesia Embassy (Republic of)
1 Police Park Terrace, Colombo 5
Tel: 580113, 580194.

Iran Embassy (of the Islamic Republic)
226 Bauddhaloka Mawatha, Colombo 7
Tel: 584547, 501137.

Iraq Embassy (Republic of)
19, Barnes Place, Colombo 7
Tel: 696600.

Italy Embassy
55 Jawatte, Colombo 5
Tel: 588622, 588388.

Japan Embassy
20 Gregory's Road, Colombo 7
Tel: 693831/4.

Korea Embassy (Republic of)
98, Dharmapala Mawatha. Colombo 7
Tel: 699036/8.

Liberia Consulate
62œ, Park Street, Colombo 2
Tel: 431181.

Libya Embassy (Socialist People's Libyan
Arab Jamahiriya)
30, Horton Place, Colombo 7
Tel: 694874, 695671.

Malaysian High Commission
87 Horton Place, Colombo 7
Tel: 694837, 696591.

Maldive Embassy
25, Melbourne Avenue. Colombo 5
Tel: 586762, 500943.

Mexico Consulate
760-762 Baseline Road, Colombo 9
Tel: 698292/6.

Norway Consulate-General
Royal Embassy, 34 Ward Place, Colombo 7
Tel: 698936, 692263.

Netherlands Embassy
25, Torrington Avenue, Colombo 7
Tel: 589626/8.

Pakistan Embassy
211 De Saram Place, Colombo 11
Tel: 696301/2.

Polish Embassy (People's Republic of)
120, Park Road, Colombo 5
Tel: 581903.

Philippines Embassy
10 Gregory's Road, Colombo 7
Tel: 696861/3.

Royal Nepalese Consulate-General
5th Floor Vision House, 52 Galle Road,
Colombo 4
Tel. 583536, 502139.

Romania Embassy
15, Clifford Avenue, Colombo 3
Tel: 34217.

Spain Vice-Consulate
36 Dr. Wijewardene Mawatha, Colombo 10
Tel: 434446.

Swedish Embassy
315, Vauxhall Street, Colombo 2
Tel: 435870, 28822.

Swedish Consulate-General
264, Grandpass Road, Colombo 14
Tel: 447806, 27707.

Switzerland Embassy
Baur's Building, 1st Floor, 7-1/1, Upper
Chatham Street, Colombo 1
Tel: 447157, 447663.

Thailand Embassy
43 Dr. CWW Kannangara Mawatha,
Colombo 7
Tel: 697406.

Togo (Republic of)
Honorary Consul, 415, Galle Road,
Colombo 3
Tel: 575200, 573218.

Turkey Consulate
c/o Leechman & Co. Ltd., Vauxhall Lane,
Colombo 2
Tel: 434311, 29573.

**United Kingdom of Great Britain &
Northern Ireland High Commission**
Galle Road, Colombo 3
Tel: 437336/9.

United States of America Embassy
210, Galle Road, Colombo 3
Tel: 421271-80.

Union of Soviet Socialist Republic Embassy
62, Sir Ernest de Silva Mawatha, Colombo 7
Tel: 573555, 573657.

Vietnam Embassy (Socialist Republic of)
5, Dudley Senanayake Place, Colombo 8
Tel: 595188.

Yugoslavia Embassy (Socialist Federal Republic of)
32, Cambridge Place, Colombo 7
Tel: 699082/3.

Art/Photo Credits

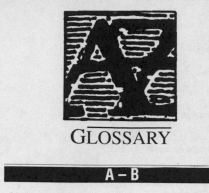

GLOSSARY

A – B

abhaya mudra – bestowing of protection: hand raised from elbow, fingers together, palm outward. A Buddhist posture.

adauwas – certain movements in a "devil dance".

Aiyannar – Hindu deity who safeguards agriculture.

akasha – ether.

aluwa – a kind of sweet meat.

amalaka – a stupa shape similar to the "bell".

amba – mango.

ambalama – a traveler's rest.

appa – hoppers, a sour dough made of rice flour, a pancake-like food.

arama – monastery.

Arjuna – warrior of the *Bhagavad-Gita*.

arrack – distilled alcohol from *toddy* (coconut sap).

aru – Tamil word for stream.

Avalokitesvara – a Mahayana Buddhist *bodhisattva*.

avasa – monk's quarters in a monastery.

avatar – incarnation.

ayurvedic – traditional island medicine stressing herbal remedies and naturophathic healing.

BY AIR

bali – sacrificial ritual.

banamaduwa – preaching pavilion at a monastery.

bata – split bamboo.

beru – elephant grass, a tall reed-like grass.

bhavana – meditation.

Bhagavad-Gita – poetic Hindu scripture with Krishna as central figure.

Bharata Natyam – a form of classical Indian dance.

bihikkus – Buddhist monks.

bibikan – a traditional cake.

biraluvada – "spoolwork", a technique of decorating lacquerware.

bisokotuwa – valve pit, prototype of sluices.

bithara – egg.

bo tree – *ficus religiosa*, the ficus (pipal) or a descendant of the tree under which the Buddha (Siddhartha Gautama) achieved enlightenment.

bodhi-ghara – housing for cuttings from the original *bo* tree.

bodhi-maluwa – raised terrace for sacred *bo* tree.

bodhisattva – "Buddha-to-be".

boiga forsteni – a small pinkish poisonous snake.

bolo fiado – laminated cake.

boroa – semolina biscuits (cookies).

Brahma – the god of creation in Hindu mythology.

brahmans – the highest Hindu caste, originally that of priests.

brahmin – a Hindu priest.

Brahminism – an ancient polytheistic religion with a god-creator. Precursor of Buddhism and Hinduism.

broeder – Dutch Christmas cake.

brinjal – long elephant.

Buddha – the "Englightened One".

bumisparasa mudra – gesture of hands where fingers of right-hand touch ground, calling witness to Mother Earth. A posture of the Buddha.

Burghers – the descendents of the Dutch.

buriyani – rice cooked in meat or chicken stock and served with garnishes.

C

cadjan fences – barriers or fences made out palmyra palm leaves.

chakra – a war quoit (ring of metal) identified with gods.

chena – slash-and-burn agriculture, and the fields created by this method.

Chera – an ancient South Indian kingdom.

Chola – an ancient South Indian kingdom.

chutty – a cooking pot made of clay.

Culavamsa – the literary sequel to the *Mahavamsa*.

D – E

dagoba – a stupa or Buddhist reliquary.

Dalada Maligawa – the temple where the Sacred Tooth Relic is kept.

dana – alms giving.

dansela – an alms hall, where food is given out, especially during Wesak.

deva – god.

devala – a temple or shrine with a residing deity used for worship by Buddhists as well as Hindus.

deviyo – resident god.

dhal – lentils.

Dharma – the Buddhist doctrine.

dhiyani mudra – gesture where the hands are lightly cupped and resting on the center of the lap. A posture of the Buddha.

digge – a room for chanting at a *devala*.

diyakiri – thin coconut milk.

Diyawadana Nilame – the chief trustee of the Dalada Maligawa and the highest lay official in the land.

dodols – a type of sweet meat.

dorje – thunderbolt symbol common to Tibetan Tantrism.

Draupadi – a goddess: the joint consort of five Pandyan princes of the *Mahabharata* tale.

ellé – a game similar to baseball, also called rounder.

G – H

gana-denu – "give and-take", the first transaction of the new year, traditionally with someone personally close.

Ganesha – the elephant-headed god, son of Shiva and Parvati.

Ganeswara – another name for Ganesha or Ganesh.

ganga – river.

garbhagrha – the inner sanctum, part of a Hindu temple containing the main image.

gata bere – Kandyan drum.

gedige – an image house in the form of a brick arched vault.

gopuram – a multi-tiered ornamental structure depicting various deities found over the entrance to a Hindu temple.

gourami – a large lake fish introduced from Japan.

Garuda – a mythical eagle that is half human. The vehicle of Vishnu.

gurula – Garuda, mythical eagle.

gurunnase – teacher.

H

halape – a type of sweet meat.

Hanuman – mythical monkey general of the *Ramayana*.

hiramane – a serated metal disk for grating coconut.

horana – a double reed musical instrument similar to an oboe.

howdah – a structure carried on the back of an elephant.

I – J

illam – course water-borne gravel buried beneath a layer of alluvial clay, often gem bearing.

indiappa – string hoppers, steamed rice flour, vermicelli-like food.

isvaram – the divine residence for the supreme Hindu god.

itli – a small round rice flour cake favored by Tamils.

jaggery – an unrefined brown sugar made from palm sap, palm sugar.

jak – a large tropical fruit that is eaten cooked or raw when ripe.

Jataka – a story of the Buddha's previous lives.

K

kachchan – a hot dry wind.

Kachcheri – a government secretariat.

kalapuwa – brackish lagoons.

Kali – Shiva's consort in her most terrifying form.

kapurala – a priest or one who officiates in a *devala*; also a priest (Shamanist) or benevolent gods.

karanduwa – a *dagoba*-shaped replica or the casket enshrining the Tooth Relic.

karava – fisherfolk claiming to be descendents of a North Indian warrior caste.

karma – cause-and-effect chain of actions, good and bad, from one life to the next.

Kataragama – the Hindu war god also called Skanda.

Kathakali – a form of classical Indian dance.

Kathiresan – an aspect of Skanda.

kattadiya – a priest of demons.

kavadi – a decorated arched framework carried by Hindu devotees as penance or to satisfy vows.

Kavi Nadagm – a rare form of folk drama.

kaymans – Dutch word for crocodiles.

kiri – milk.

kiribath – milk rice, rice cooked in coconut milk.

Kohomba – a god, particularly important to Kandyan dancers.

kolam – masked drama with dance and a certain

amount of ritual.

kotkarella – the spire of a *dagoba*.

kovil – Hindu temple.

Krishna – the eighth incarnation of Vishnu, a Hindu deity.

kurakkan – a red, heavy grain used in flour, especially for sweets.

Kuveni – a Yaksa enchantress who helped subdue Lanka for Vijaya and bore him two children.

L – M

Lakshmi – the goddess of wealth and consort of Vishnu.

lamprais – a packet of rice and curried meats wrapped and cooked in a banana leaf.

lasya – a graceful, feminine dance form.

lingum a symbolic male phallus, generally associated with Shiva.

maha – the main rice season or crop.

maha baba – a giant effigy with two faces.

Maha Nuwara – "the great city", another name for Kandy.

Mahabharata – an important Hindu epic.

maharab – Muslim prayer hall.

Mahavamsa – ancient chronicle of Sinhalese kings written in the 6th Century A.D.

mahout – elephant trainer.

mahseer – a large river fish related to carp, excellent game fish.

Maitreya – the future Buddha.

makara – dragon.

malliya – brother.

mallung – mixture of shredded green vegetables, dried shrimp, grated coconut and spices.

massina – cousin.

minnihalanga – the seat of power.

mitikiri – thick coconut milk.

Moors – descendents of the early Arab (Muslim) traders.

mudra – a gesture of hands and related posture of a Buddha image.

muezzin – one who calls devout Muslims to prayer.

Murugan – another name for Skanda.

muscat – oily fudge-like sweet.

N

Nadagm – a rare form of folk drama; a mixture of puppetry and live theater combining straight prose dialogue with a stylized song-drama.

naga – a cobra snake.

Nagas – one of the indigenous tribes of Lanka.

nagaraj – cobra snake king.

Nandi – a bull, Shiva's vehicle and a symbol of fecundity.

Natha – a Mahayana deity; according to tradition he is the *bodhisattva* Maitreya.

natya – drama.

netra mangalya – the eye festival at a religious site during which the eyes of the Buddha image are painted.

nibbana – the state of "neither existence nor non existence" for which every Buddhist strives.

niyakas – sects of Buddhiast monks.

niyapotuvada – "nailwork" technique of decorating

lacquerware.

nona gathe – the neutral period between the old year and the new one, according to Sinhalese astrology.

nritta – pure dance form.

nritya – expressive dance form.

nuwara – city.

O – P

ola – dried and prepared palm leaf which is written upon with a stylus.

oruva – a dugout outrigger canoe.

oya – stream or small river.

paddy – unhusked rice; rice plant.

padhanaghara – meditation center.

padma – lotus flower.

padrao (Port) – a large inscribed or carved boulder.

Pallava – an ancient South Indian kingdom.

palmyra – a species of palm often found in dry areas.

palu – a type of wild fruits.

panchama – fruit salad containing five kinds of fruits.

pandal – a bamboo framework on which are mounted various paintings and lights in Buddhist festivals.

Pandya – an ancient South Indian kingdom.

paniappa – a sweet type of hoppers.

panipol – a type of sweat meat.

panivalalu – honey bangles, a type of sweet meat.

pansala – a Buddhist temple.

papadam – a crispy fried bread that is wafer thin.

parinibbana – the Buddha's physical death and transcendence to *nibbana*.

Parvati – Shiva's consort, mother of Ganesha and Skanda, also called Uma.

pasa – a lasso identified with Vishnu.

patimaghara – image house.

Pattini – Hindu goddess of chastity and health.

pel kavi – musical form originating in the *chena* fields, literally "songs of the huts".

perahera – a procession, normally festive and grandiose.

pesavalulu – concentric masoned rings around the dome of a dagoba.

Pillaiyav – another name for Ganesha or Ganeswara.

pin-kate – a till or offering box.

pirit – chanting of protective *suttas*.

pirivena – monastery.

pittu – a steamed mixture of rice flour, coconut and water.

pohuna – ornamental stone bath.

pol sambol – coconut *sambol*, mixture of grated coconut, chilies, onions, lime, salt and Maldive fish (fermented dried tuna).

pol-thel pahana – a coconut oil lamp.

pongaal – a spiced sweetened rice consumed at sacremental feasts.

potgul – library.

poya – a lunar phase.

poyage – a hall for religious ceremonies.

puhul dosi – pumpkin preserves.

puja – religious offering.

punya karma – merit-making.

R

raj – king.

Rama – Prince hero of the Ramayana.

Ramayana – classical Asian literary epic.

ran masu – goldfish.

randoli – the golden palenquin(s) bearing the consorts of the deities in a *perahera*.

rasakevili – a type of sweet meat.

rasam – a mixture of spices, garlic, chilies, tamarind juice and coconut oil.

rasgullas – milk balls in syrup.

Rawana – the anti-hero (demon king) of the *Ramayana*.

roti – an unleavened bread.

S

Sakra – king of the gods.

samadhi – state of deep meditation.

Saman – guardian deity who lives atop Sri Pada (Adam's Peak).

samanalayo – small yellow butterflies that converge on Adams Peak.

samanera – novice monk.

sambhur – a large elk-like deer.

sambol – mixture often containing coconut, chilies, onions and lime.

samsara – cycle of rebirth.

samudra – inland sea or large tank.

Sangha – the brotherhood of Buddhist monks.

sankha – conch shell.

sanni vidiya – an offering altar to the demons

sanni yakuna – ceremony for dealing with demons of disease.

sarama – sarong worn by men.

Shiva – the most awesome of Hindu gods. He destroys all things, good as well as evil, allowing new creations to take shape.

sikhara – a beehive-like crown atop a temple.

sil – meditating, reading religious books and listening to scriptures.

sila – morality.

silpasastras – codified Buddhist texts.

sinha – lion.

Sita – wife of Rama who was kidnapped by Rawana in the *Ramayana* epic.

Skanda – the Hindu god of war and son of Shiva and Parvati, also called Kataragama.

sokari – a folk dance to assure fertile rice crops.

sthapana mandapam – the part of a Hindu temple where offerings are made.

suriputra – canon of measurements and proportions used when constructing Buddha images.

suttas – discourses of the Buddha.

T

tandava – dance form characterized by vigorous, masculine movements.

tellapia – a small lake fish introduced from Japan.

thalagali – sesame ball sweet meat.

thali – a gold necklace with a medallion showing the symbols of the Hindu trinity – a conch, a trident and a ring. The wedding necklace.

thambili – king coconut.

thera – Buddhist sage.

thosai – rice flour cake fried in a flat pan, also called *dosai*.

tikka – "divine eye", a colorful vermilion powder applied by Hindus to the forehead, between the eyes, as a symbol of the presence of the divine.

Tipitaka – the sacred Buddhist scriptures.

tivanha – "thrice-bent" posture of an image, flexed at hips and neck.

toddy – undistilled fermented coconut sap.

torana – gateway or lintel.

trisula – trident of gods.

U – V

ulama – Islamic teacher.

upasampada – ordination ceremony of Buddhists monks.

Upulvan – another name for Vishnu in his aspect as protector of Buddhism in Sri Lanka.

vadai – balls of mashed *dhal* that are fried.

vade – spicy doughnuts.

vadis – temporary fishing camps.

vahalkada – a screen at one of the cardinal points of a *dagoba*, before which an altar for flower offerings stands.

valavva – manor house of Sinhala landed gentry.

vali-kangana – a parapet with four gateways surrounding a dagoba.

vanduappa – a sweet type of hoppers.

vannama – secular dance entertainment often portraying (superficially) a bird or animal.

vatadage – a circular pillared building that protected and housed a *dagoba*.

Vedas – any of four canonical collections of the earliest Brahministic religious verses, dating from the second millennium B.C., They define a polytheistic faith.

Veddhas – a primitve, aboriginal tribe of Sri Lanka.

vel – the trident of Skanda, god of war.

vellala – farming caste of Tamils.

Vesamuni – chief of the demons, demon king.

vevel – split cane.

Vibeheshana – one of the four guardian deities of Sri Lanka, brother of Rawana.

vihara – image house.

villus – natural basin like ponds or lakes.

Vishnu – one of the Hindu trinity, a god who preserves life and the world itself. Also called Upulvan.

vitarka mudra – hand gesture indicating discourse, fingers raised. A Buddhist posture.

Vuvera – god of wealth.

W – Y

wattalapam – a coconut and *jaggery* (palm sugar) pudding or custard.

weera – a type of wild fruit.

Wesak – the day commemorating the birth, the enlightenment and the death of the Buddha.

wewa – irrigation tanks, man-made lakes.

yakadura – a lower caste demon priest.

yak bere – a demon drum.

yakdessa – shaman or priest.

Yaksas – tribe of indigenous inhabitants of Sri Lanka.

yala – a supplementary rice season or crop.

yoni – female phallic symbol associated with Tantrism or Shiva worship.

INDEX

C

D

N

O

P